BEYOND BONDAGE

THE NEW BLACK STUDIES

Series Editors
Darlene Clark Hine, *Northwestern University*
Dwight A. McBride, *Northwestern University*

BEYOND BONDAGE

Free Women of Color in the Americas

Edited by DAVID BARRY GASPAR
AND DARLENE CLARK HINE

UNIVERSITY OF ILLINOIS PRESS
URBANA AND CHICAGO

© 2004 by the Board of Trustees
of the University of Illinois
All rights reserved
Manufactured in the United States of America
1 2 3 4 5 C P 5 4 3 2 1

∞ This book is printed on acid-free paper.

Library of Congress Cataloging-in-Publication Data
Beyond bondage : free women of color in the Americas /
edited by David Barry Gaspar and Darlene Clark Hine.
p.   cm.
Includes bibliographical references and index.
ISBN 0-252-02939-9 (cl. : alk. paper)
ISBN 0-252-07194-8 (pbk. : alk. paper)
1. Women, Black—America—History.
2. Free blacks—America—History.
3. America—Social conditions.
4. America—Race relations. 5. Slavery—America—History.
I. Hine, Darlene Clark.
II. McBride, Dwight A.
E29.N3B49   2004
305.48'896073'09—dc22   2004002533

To the memory of our valued colleague
Kimberly S. Hanger

and to

Fannie Venerable Thompson,
Lucy, Ena, and Amy Headley,
and Andrea Long

CONTENTS

PREFACE

The chapters in this volume explore collectively a number of issues related to the lives and experiences of women of color who were not, strictly speaking, held in full legal bondage, or who did not consider themselves to be so bound, in the slave societies of the Americas. The emphasis of discussion here is thematic. The sample of societies covered, however, is wide enough to illuminate slave societies of the Americas more generally in ways that invite comparative analysis of these societies and the place of free women of color within them. Each chapter makes its contribution to the multilayered texture of the thematic focus of the volume through treatment of the free women of color of a particular society or set of societies, illustrating that the book's main title, *Beyond Bondage*, is meant to convey as much a statement of fact regarding legal status as an implicit question about the actual lives of free women of color.

If these women of mixed blood or of unmixed African ancestry were free, how far beyond bondage were they in reality? How far were their lives as free persons still shaped by the development of slavery? What forms did their marginality take, how effective were these forms, and how did free women of color cope with them in their struggle to survive in the shadow of slavery and at the same time achieve some progress or even limited success? How was their freedom actualized? Each chapter in this volume is constructed around careful consideration of such questions, drawing on a wide range of rich source materials that permit probing inquiry into the many meanings of freedom in slave societies for people of African descent who somehow escaped bondage and some of its devastating effects. Ultimately, in all slave societies of the Americas, free women and men of color were well aware that they and their children who were free could not completely escape the ravages of slavery and its dominating influence over slave society.

In keeping with the volume's overall thematic approach, the chapters are organized into two sections. The first, "Achieving and Preserving Freedom," consists of six chapters that explore several interrelated issues and establish a foundation for the inquiries pursued in the volume's second section, "Making a Life in Freedom," which consists of eight chapters. The significance of race, class, and gender is explored in some depth in each of the volume's fourteen chapters, which are concerned with at least eight societies or groups of societies within the United States, the Caribbean, and South America. Although by no means exhaustive, such coverage across the Americas is nonetheless valuable in drawing attention to many possibilities for further research in a wide field in which considerable variations and similarities can be found from one society to another, including those not covered in this volume.

The chapters clustered in the first section cover the slave societies of colonial Spanish America, Cuba, Martinique, Guadeloupe, Antigua, Jamaica, and the U.S. South and draw attention to the range of conditions under which women of color achieved freedom, legally or not, and the strategies, maneuvers, or means they deployed, particularly those whose freedom was precarious, to preserve their free status. Women of color might achieve freedom through avenues other than the polar extremities of flight or escape and legal manumission supported by official or other acceptable documentation. The pursuit of freedom through all available means is clear evidence that freedom, however precarious and challenging, was preferable to slavery. However they may have achieved freedom, free women of color were motivated by a desire to place themselves beyond slavery, and that desire might be the beginning of a long-range plan to assist family members or friends and relatives in doing the same. The actual process of becoming free could involve much calculation and patient resilience, but every opportunity for freedom was worth seizing.

For free women of color, to be no longer enslaved in the full sense of that status represented only an intermediate objective along the route from slavery to freedom that they could recognize as such. Beyond the circumstances and moment of becoming free stretched a challenging road of making freedom work to their advantage, of extending its positive possibilities as much as possible within limitations imposed by slave society and making a life in freedom that might provide resources for survival. Free women of color tried to meet these challenges in a variety of resourceful ways, some of which, it is not surprising, were more successful than others. But even among those for whom freedom meant mighty struggles and frustrations, simply being free in a wide sea of the oppressed enslaved could be a matter of much pride and satisfaction.

The chapters in the second section address these and related issues about lives shaped by and in freedom within slave society. They focus on how free women of color in the slave societies of the United States, Suriname, Brazil, Puerto Rico, colonial and antebellum New Orleans, and Peru faced up to the challenges of freedom, from economic and occupational resourcefulness to household and family organization and the pursuit of religious lives, in an impressive range of initiative. But the successes of these women of color should also remind us that slave society was not organized to facilitate the success of free people of color.

Most of these people lived truly marginalized lives struggling against poverty and want. Female slaves in all of the slave societies of the Americas were more often beneficiaries of opportunities for freedom than male slaves. Having become free, however, the women faced major challenges in giving meaning to their freedom in societies that continued to be deeply influenced by the laws and practices associated with slavery, race, class, color, and gender.

This volume would not have been possible without the generous cooperation and patience of the scholars who contributed chapters based on their careful research. We owe them much and are happy that now readers will be able to appreciate the results of their labor for this project. We also wish to thank Joan Catapano at the University of Illinois Press for her gentle encouragement at every stage in the preparation of the manuscript. She believed it was possible to finish the project when we were inclined to falter under the weight of this and other pressing assignments. Finally, we thank Jenna Golnik, Andrea Long, and particularly Judith Martin for their word-processing expertise which provided considerable inspiration to bring the project to completion satisfactorily.

PART I

Achieving and Preserving Freedom

Maroon Women in Colonial Spanish America: Case Studies in the Circum-Caribbean from the Sixteenth through the Eighteenth Centuries

Jane Landers

With rare exceptions, women have remained largely invisible in the literature about maroons.[1] The generalized maroon experience—a daring and dangerous escape from closely supervised plantations, followed by a harrowing chase by slave catchers and dogs through rough forests and swamps inhabited by dangerous creatures—is most often depicted as a male endeavor, as in the case of war. Marronage became so threatening and disruptive in many colonies of the circum-Caribbean region that officials engaged in what they termed "maroon wars." Their reports described military leaders and rebel tactics in some detail, but because these reports were basically battlefield accounts they rarely dealt with women. To be identified in such reports women had to be almost mythical or supernatural figures such as Nanny, for whom Nanny Town in the Blue Mountains of eastern Jamaica was named. The few graphic images we have of maroons such as Cudjoe and his warriors in the Jamaican Maroon Wars reinforce this masculine association.[2] Muscled young men race through exotic landscapes, muskets in hand and large knives or hatchets at their belts.[3] The virtual absence of women in either the written or iconographic record is due in part to the traditional male bias in history and in part to the lack of sources for women's history in general, particularly in more remote times.

The historical neglect of maroon women is, however, also due in great part to the real sexual imbalance of maroon communities. More men than women became runaways. As other scholars have noted, women were often restrained from flight by maternal or family obligations.[4] When women did flee from slavery, however, they faced the same dangers encountered by their male counterparts. They had to evade surveillance systems and pursuers, cope with unknown terrain, and brave animals and sometimes hostile Indian groups to find safe refuge in areas remote from European control.[5]

Despite these terrors and challenges, many slave women fled, and at least some of them survived to establish new and free lives in the hinterland. Some escaped with family members or friends; others were rescued by husbands or lovers already established in wilderness hideouts. Although maroons sometimes raided Indian villages for women, that action entailed additional danger and engendered resentment among indigenous communities with which they needed to maintain defensive and commercial alliances. To raid in order to seize women brought almost certain retaliation and was therefore not the best solution to the maroons' demographic imperative. Women of African descent were clearly critical to the success and longevity of any maroon settlement for both their reproductive and productive abilities. Their children became the next generation, and they helped their mothers with the agricultural labor that sustained the larger community.

This essay examines the experiences of women of African descent who successfully escaped slavery and participated in the establishment of maroon communities in colonial Spanish America from the sixteenth to the eighteenth centuries, using case studies of Hispaniola (the modern-day Dominican Republic), Ecuador, Mexico, Colombia, and Spanish Florida. The fragmentary information about such women is recorded in archaic Spanish in widely dispersed archives in Spain and Latin America. Scholars have examined some of these records, but few of them have employed gender analysis or focused on the women mentioned there. Some of the richest sources for the history of female maroons are the accounts generated by churchmen and military officials who were either sent to "reduce" maroon settlements peacefully or extirpate them.

When Spanish authorities succeeded in capturing maroons they interrogated and tried both men and women and thereby created criminal records that are also valuable sources of information.[6] The authorities often complained that maroons enticed or stole away other slaves (often women) and carried on contraband trade with corsairs and Spain's enemies. Their fugitive communities also challenged Spanish notions of civilized living as well as the desired racial and social order. For all these reasons, Spanish officials expended considerable resources and energy attacking maroon camps, and they produced a significant "paper trail" in the process.

Repeated military efforts to eradicate the fugitives' settlements were more often than not unsuccessful. Maroons built remote strongholds that were protected by wooden palisades and camouflaged pits that concealed sharpened stakes. They created false trails to deceive the enemy and established sentry systems to patrol the settlements. When discovered, maroons habitually melted into the jungle, mountains, and swamps, only to regroup and form new encampments. If left in peace, many of these became stable communities based on agriculture rather than, as the Spaniards alleged, theft.[7]

Spanish records are somewhat limited in providing information about life in *palenques, manieles, mocambos,* and *cumbes,* as maroon communities were variously called. Contemporary observers did not always appreciate or record what they saw there, but the accounts of priests who were sent among the maroons, and even those of military opponents, can offer useful clues about the physical layout, demographics, ethnicity, and civil, religious, and military leadership of the communities. They also provide scattered information about subsistence patterns and trade networks with Europeans, Indians, and other Africans, free and enslaved. Through these records it is possible to trace the names, approximate ages, ethnic backgrounds, and family relationships of female maroons. Some information can also be found about the women's enslaved lives and occupations and their roles in maroon camps.[8]

The earliest Spanish record about maroons in the Americas appears in Governor Nicolás de Ovando's complaint in 1503 to the Spanish crown that runaway slaves could not be recovered from Indian hideouts in the mountains of Hispaniola.[9] Black runaways fiercely resisted reenslavement, and in the 1540s the Spaniards considered maroons such a threat that they referred to their expeditions against them as a "war."[10] By the mid-sixteenth century an estimated seven thousand maroons inhabited settlements scattered across the island. At the close of the century the free population of the island, including Europeans, free mestizos, and mulattos, numbered only two thousand, whereas the enslaved population stood at around twenty thousand. A similar demographic profile characterized other sixteenth-century Spanish settlements.[11]

More than a century later the maroons of Hispaniola still occupied the high regions of the southern mountains of Baoruco, and Spanish priests were still attempting to talk them down. In 1662, after repeated military campaigns against them failed, the archbishop of Santo Domingo (the capital city of Hispaniola) attempted to persuade six hundred maroon families that were still gathered into four palenques along the mountainous southern coast to be "reduced." The Baoruco maroons had already ignored a previous offer, and they rejected this overture as well because they did not believe the word of the Spanish authorities. The maroons were self-sufficient and apparently felt no pressure to compromise. According to the archbishop's report, they produced corn in abundance and a variety of other crops and were also raising livestock. The women panned for gold in the rivers. The maroon economy supported purchases of clothing, drink, and other items in the capital of Santo Domingo. From iron and steel thus acquired maroon men made arrows and short, broad swords.[12]

The Spanish authorities launched a series of aggressive attacks against the Baoruco settlements four years later, but scattered maroon communities persisted well into the eighteenth century. Archaeological work at José Leta, an early-eighteenth-century maroon settlement in eastern Hispaniola, confirms some of the archbishop's observations about such camps. Researchers have found numerous bones that indicate that the inhabitants subsisted largely on wild pigs, although it is presumed that they also grew garden crops and gathered wild honey. The site has also yielded seventeen copper bracelets, metal arrowtips, incised clay pipes, and a variety of iron objects, including tongs and lance points. Iron slag deposits are evidence that the runaways manufactured the objects on this site, as the archbishop said they did at Baoruco.[13]

A 1785 census of Neyba, a maroon community in the same region, indicates that the maroons of Baoruco had fallen on hard times. The Neyba settlement was composed of fifty-seven households, or 133 persons. The population had once been larger, but epidemics of measles and dysentery killed many residents, including two aged males "who were much venerated" and who must have organized the maroon community sometime earlier in the century. By the time a Spanish envoy contacted them in 1777, the maroon population was much reduced. There were forty-three adult males, thirty-seven adult females (twenty of whom had been born onsite), and fifty-two children. The ages of these people must have been estimated. The oldest women, like Catalina and María, both born at Neyba, were said to be about sixty. The youngest female who headed her own household was a single mother named Rosa, age fourteen, who had also been born in the settlement. She had a four-month-old daughter, Barbara. The number of children indicates that the population was once again growing, despite having experienced epidemic stress.[14] Some of the population increase may have also been connected with the escalating exploitation of African labor on the sugar plantations across the French border in Saint Domingue (modern-day Haiti). Eleven women and thirty-one men had once been the slaves of French masters. Some refugees bore French names and spoke some French and, occasionally, some Spanish. Others, however, still bore African names such as Quamina, Macuba, and Musunga.[15]

The maroons at the Neyba settlement lived in simple, palm-thatched huts. They had no church or elaborate fortifications or defense systems such as those noted at some earlier maroon settlements. In their isolation these maroons lived much like any poor Spanish peasant on the island might have. They cultivated rice, corn, plantains, sugar cane, and assorted other food crops for their own consumption. Plots of land may have been assigned on the basis of need as well as ability to make use of them. Each plot measured a thousand *varas* (a Spanish linear measurement of .84 meters), and nuclear families of a man, a woman, and several children usually worked two plots; childless couples and single males or females usually had only a single plot of land. It is also possible that age and seniority warranted additional land. The elderly couples María and Roro, and Catalina and Andrés, all of whom were said to be about sixty, each worked two plots. María and Roro had two grown sons at the settlement who may have helped them, and perhaps Catalina and Andrés's son-in-law did the same. Surprisingly, the young single mother, Rosa, also had two plots of land, and it is possible that her father or father-in-law helped her work them.[16]

While the maroons of Hispaniola were engaged in their sixteenth-century protracted "war" with the Spaniards, a ship carrying "Guinea" slaves from Panama to Peru was wrecked on the coast of Ecuador.[17] Led by a black man named Anton, seventeen men and six women escaped to the dense inland forests where they allied themselves with the Pidi Indians in 1553. The men served as warriors for the Pidi, but they also apparently made unwelcome demands on the native population's resources and women. When six of the black men were killed in an enemy encounter, the Pidi attempted to rid themselves of the rest. Anton retaliated "with such cruelty that he sowed terror throughout the province." Thereafter, Anton ruled unchallenged, but when he died some years later a civil war broke out among the black men contending for leadership. Only seven black men and three black women survived that conflict. These Africans intermarried with Indians of the coast and formed a new *zambo* (person of mixed Indian and African heritage) culture in a settlement called Esmeraldas.[18] The early Esmeraldas, although ruled by Africans and their descendants, was thus a multiracial settlement to which many cultural-linguistic groups contributed.

This information comes from one of the first Spaniards who actually made contact with the maroons, Fray Miguel de Cabello Balboa. In 1577 the leader at Esmeraldas, Alonso Illescas, his Indian wife, their children and spouses, and a sizable entourage of gold-bedecked Indians and mulattos met the priest and his companions on the beach, listened to prayers, and deposited golden ornaments on the crude altar the churchmen erected there. Before the *zambos* left they promised to bring other villagers to receive religious instruction. When the maroons failed to reappear, Cabello Balboa canoed up the Esmeraldas River to look for them. Two leagues up-river, the priest found a site where the maroons had destroyed more than a hundred canoes. Further upstream one of his companions found many fruit trees that were also destroyed. In this way we know that the maroons were engaged in timbering and shipbuilding, agriculture, and metallurgy, among other occupations. Later accounts document that they also grew plantains, corn, yucca or cassava, cacao, tobacco, cotton, rice, and sugar cane in their fields along the river Esmeraldas. They also raised pigs and chickens for their own consumption and for sale to nearby Indian villages. The women of the settlement probably performed much of the labor associated with agriculture and small animal husbandry while the men also occupied themselves in hunting and fishing.[19]

In New Spain (modern-day Mexico) Africans also pursued freedom through marronage. In the 1570s Yanga (or Ñanga), an African of the Bran nation (and reputedly of royal lineage), escaped from slavery and formed a long-lived palenque at Cofre de Perote in the Orizaba region near Vera Cruz. Yanga's maroons frequently plundered the cargoes of goods transported along the Camino Real from Vera Cruz to Mexico City, and they were also reputed to have kidnapped Indian men and women and even some Spaniards. Yanga's community withstood retaliatory attacks for more than thirty years until, in 1609, Viceroy Luis de Velasco commissioned a wealthy landowner from Puebla to lead a major expedition against the settlement.[20] After a long and arduous series of battles, and just when the Spaniards were almost upon them, Yanga led the women and children of Cofre to the safety of another nearby palisaded fort.[21]

The following morning the Spaniards reconnoitered, and they later reported on the emptied but apparently prospering settlement Yanga had abandoned. Although the maroons had only been at the site for nine months they had assigned half the population to agriculture. It was probably the women who planted fields of cotton, sweet potatoes, chiles, tobacco, squashes, corn, beans, sugar cane, and other vegetables. The maroons left behind chickens, cattle, and horses, and it is probable that men herded the larger animals and women raised the fowl. While women worked at growing food crops and tending households, men of the camp built impressive fortifications and sixty houses. In these homes the Spaniards found a wide variety of clothing, swords, hatchets, a few arquebuses, some salt, corn, and money. The last find suggests that the maroons were probably involved in some commercial transactions as well as their reputed banditry.[22]

Maroon encampments like Yanga's also sprouted in the densely forested jungle landscapes surrounding South America's main slave port of Cartagena in Colombia. In 1693 Spanish forces were finally able to destroy one Colombian palenque called Matudere. The governor himself led the spectacular and devastating night raid, calling on Santiago, patron saint of Spain, who allegedly helped the Christians defeat Muslim and Indian enemies. A lightning bolt that hit the house where maroons had stored their arms and munitions caused a great explosion.[23] By the light of the flames the Spaniards tracked down the scattered maroons, some of whom resisted recapture and were killed. Others managed to slip away, but their plan to regroup at the nearby palenque of María proved impossible for many because "the mountains were covered with soldiers."[24] After three days of tracking, the governor and his troops captured Matudere's leader, Domingo Padilla. When he was finally taken, Padilla had no knowledge of his wife's whereabouts. Other families must also have been scattered by the surprise attack. The governor offered a reward of forty pesos for the capture and delivery of any escapees, and in the following days Spaniards and blacks alike claimed payment for prisoners delivered to the jail in Cartagena. Among the recaptured maroons were some women.[25] The interrogations that followed generated valuable information about life in a Spanish palenque.[26]

Domingo Padilla and his wife, Juana, claimed to have founded Matudere in 1681. Padilla recounted that, twelve years earlier, he and Juana and their three sons had fled slavery and spent the first six months of freedom living in the jungle in a rude shelter made of branches. After some time the family moved to a second spot where they built two *bohios* (huts), but they found the land there unaccommodating. Finally, they moved to the place called Matudere, where some fifty-four men and forty women were already living as a community.[27] Domingo called himself the Captain of Matudere, but Juana adopted a Spanish title, *virreina* (vicequeen). That choice of rank may have carried political significance; only Mexico (New Spain) and Peru at that time rated viceroys, and the highest Spanish official of Colombia (New Granada) was only a governor. The presumption of the title led interrogators to ask husband and wife separately why Juana was called *virreina*, and they each answered that it was because she was a founder (*fundadora*) of the place.[28]

Matudere's success is evident in its rapid growth. When the Spaniards destroyed the settlement in 1693 it was home to 250 people, including forty women and forty-nine children. The community was obviously reproducing itself, and families had also adopted three orphans. Some of the increase appears to have been the result of a deliberate policy to reunite family members. One Spanish raiding party led by Captain Francisco Arará returned with the wife and four children of Francisco Popo, who had earlier escaped from the hacienda of Pedro Pérez.

Evidence from Matudere suggests that the common complaint of Spanish officials that maroons stole women from Spanish haciendas and Indian towns was sometimes true. When Francisco Arará, a war captain, led the Matudere maroons in a raid against the enemy Indian town of Piojon, they killed ten men and carried off nine Indian women and a young girl. An attack against the Indian town of Bifagua added three more women and seven boys to the Matudere population. Domingo Padilla later told Spanish officials that Matudere's African shaman, Antonio, had ordered the capture of the nineteen Christian (Spanish) women who were recovered from the settlement. Like the Indian women, the Spanish women were meant to be wives for the unmarried men at Matudere.[29]

More than a hundred of the black captives who survived the Spanish attack on Matudere were either African-born or born to African-born parents. Among the Africans identified by nation were twenty-eight Minas, nineteen Ararás, ten Congos, nine Luangos, five Angolas, three Popos, three Yolofes, two Caravalíes, one Bran, one Goyo, and at least one Biafara. Those designated as *criollos* (persons born in the Americas rather than in Africa) were divided into two groups: *criollos de la montaña,* to identify those born free in the palenque, and *criollos escapados,* to designate Creole runaways from Spanish cities (persons described in other contexts as *ladinos,* meaning acculturated, Spanish-speaking Catholics).[30] Forty of the captives were women, twenty of whom were designated as criollas. The African-born women included six Minas, six Ararás, four Congos, one from Angola, and another from Luanda. One Arará, María, was listed as "muy vieja" (very old) and must have been older than sixty, the age of Matudere's virreina, Juana, who was not so described.[31]

María and other African elders were valuable resources for the community. They provided direct knowledge about a wide range of sociotechnical skills that helped sustain the maroons in the backcountry, among the most important being related to architecture, agriculture, healing, and warfare. Respected elders also helped the maroons retain language, belief, identity, and other cultural practices.

A Catholic priest who visited Matudere shortly before its destruction reported disapprovingly that the Minas of the community celebrated his arrival with their "customary dances," but he did not specify whether women and/or men danced. Although the residents of Matudere continued to observe African traditions, the priest was pleasantly surprised to find that at least some maroons "lived in Christianity, knew the prayers, sustained the church, and prayed the rosary." The practicing Christians had built an "adequate" Catholic church that they decorated with "paper images" (presumably Christian ones to which he did not object). The priest asked for and received a demonstration of one of their church services. He said the maroons recited the rosary as a chorus "with devotion" and knew and seemed to understand the proper responses.[32] Although the officials of Matudere's Catholic church were all males, it is possible that some women were involved in ceremonial aspects of the church, as they may have been before they came to Matudere.

It is probable that women were also largely responsible for food production at Matudere, as they had been in Africa, in Spanish communities, and in Indian towns. Women cultivated a variety of crops at Matudere; each household planted its own corn, rice, black beans, potatoes, plantains, and other foodstuffs.[33] Women, of course, also cared for the children, and it may be safely assumed that some served as midwives and nurses.[34] The war parties of Matudere frequently brought back prizes of clothing, but surely the women also made some of their own.[35]

Once the governor and his counselors had concluded their interrogations of the captured maroons of Matudere and found them guilty, they hanged and quartered thirteen, including Domingo Padilla, and posted their mutilated body parts along country roadsides "as an example and terror to others of this class." The virreina, Juana, who was then approximately sixty, received two hundred lashes and exile, as did many others. The sick, very old, or very young captives received one hundred lashes each before their owners were allowed to post bond and recover them.[36] Before he was finished with Juana, Governor Martin de Cevallos brought an artist to the jail to paint the virreina's portrait "for the novelty," but he later remarked caustically that the artist had favored her by making her appear more clean and tidy that she really was.[37]

* * *

Although many historians have alleged that there was less slave resistance in the United States than in any of the other major slave societies of the Americas, Herbert Aptheker's early work documented the existence of at least fifty maroon communities in the U.S. South, dating from the late seventeenth century up to the Civil War.[38] Because Aptheker's important study relied solely on English-language sources, even that number of communities seriously underestimates the phenomenon. It is possible to identify, for example, many more incidents of marronage in the Spanish records for Florida that date back to the sixteenth century.

The examples of marronage already discussed involved slaves who escaped to interior hideouts within Spanish territory, but early runaways from the English colony of Carolina parlayed geopolitical conflicts between Spain and England into a free and legitimate frontier town of their own in Spanish Florida. In 1687 Spanish authorities reported that eight men, two women, and a three-year-old nursing baby girl had arrived at St. Augustine from Carolina in a "stolen" boat. The names of these women are not known, but the wife and child of one of the men, Mingo, survived a harrowing escape during which Mingo allegedly killed one of the men who attempted to capture and reenslave them.[39] The runaways claimed they were seeking religious conversion, and after lengthy deliberations the Spanish king decided to free them in 1693, "granting liberty to all . . . the men as well as the women . . . so that by their example and by my liberality . . . others will do the same."[40] During the following decades more runaways from Carolina sought asylum in Florida and were frequently aided by Indians. Although Carolinians set up a patrol system and placed several scout boats along the water routes to St. Augustine, they were unable to completely staunch the southward flow of runaways.

Male runaways outnumbered females, but despite the grave dangers involved, women continued to try for freedom. Runaway slave notices from colonial South Carolina newspapers described some of them. In the summer of 1732, Delia, who spoke very little English, took her "sucking child" and fled with Clarinda, whose English was good. The two women succeeded in escaping in their owner's cypress canoe. That same year Amoretta and Sarah, "very clever Negroes," joined three men in their own successful escape by canoe. Similar accounts about female runaways can be found in colonial newspapers for Georgia.[41]

By 1738 a sizeable community of Carolina fugitives lived in St. Augustine and, as the likelihood of war between England and Spain increased, a new governor, Manuel de Montiano, granted the freedmen and women lands to homestead and a town of their own called Gracia Real de Santa Teresa de Mose, about two miles north of St. Augustine.[42] They built homes, churches, and fortifications there and planted fields of maize and vegetables. It is probable that the women at Mose worked these fields and also tended garden plots following practices in Africa and Carolina. Kathleen Deagan of the Florida Museum of Natural History headed an interdisciplinary team in 1988 and 1989 that excavated the moated fort of Mose and its interior buildings. Many of the recovered artifacts were of a military nature, but others pointed to the role of women. Bone buttons in manufacture, needles, and a thimble give some idea about domestic activities. Food preparation and child care would also have occupied Mose's women. It is also possible that they wore the beads and rosaries that the archaeologists uncovered.[43]

At the end of the Seven Years' War in 1763, when Spain was forced to cede Florida to Great Britain, runaway slaves could no longer claim religious sanctuary at Mose. Instead, they sought refuge in other maroon communities or in newly emerging Seminole towns on the Alachua Savannah (near present-day Gainesville). When the Spanish returned to Florida in 1784, however, fugitive slaves resumed their southward flight from British territory, and planters there complained that their very livelihood was threatened.[44]

Once again enslaved women risked their lives to liberate themselves by fleeing to Florida, usually in the company of males. This may have improved their chances of success, but in some cases it led to added danger. When Sara joined three men in an escape from South Carolina in 1789, one of the men with whom she fled, Thomas, demanded that she enter a sexual relationship with him in return for his protection. Sara reluctantly agreed to Thomas's demands, on the condition that the arrangement would cease when they got to Florida. Thomas reneged on the agreement in Florida, and when Sara attempted to leave him he tied her to a tree and beat her unconscious. Spanish officials arrested him. During his interrogation Thomas told the court that "he found himself with rights and dominion over the said woman, because he had helped her flight and she had agreed to be his woman."[45] Sara's case may be entirely anomalous, but it might also indicate the hidden and additional dangers women faced when they became involved in marronage.

In 1790 the Spanish finally yielded to the strong persuasions of Thomas Jefferson, the secretary of state for the new government of the United States, and abrogated the religious sanctuary policy that had been in place in Florida since 1693 and had helped to liberate hundreds of runaways.[46] Thereafter, runaways were forced to find refuge in more interior and remote reaches of the Spanish Floridas. During the War of 1812 the British established a large number of fugitive slaves from Georgia, Mobile, Pensacola, and St. Augustine, along with Indians allied to the British, at a small fort at Prospect Bluff on the Apalachicola River, about twenty-five miles north of the Gulf of Mexico. An estimated force of 1,100 warriors, including several hundred blacks, garrisoned the fort and protected the maroon village built behind it. Unknown numbers of women and children lived in the village, but the population must have been considerable because the residents planted corn fields that were said to stretch along the river for more than forty-five miles.[47]

Not far from Prospect Bluff, Georgians were also establishing settlements, and General Andrew Jackson demanded the "immediate and prompt interference of the Spanish authority to destroy or remove from our frontier this banditti," a term that encompassed escaped slaves and Indians as well as assorted whites who were their allies.[48] Although the Spanish governor demurred, he sent Captain Vicente Sebastián Pintado to investigate and attempt to retrieve from Prospect Bluff the slaves who belonged to Spanish owners in East and West Florida. Pensacola slave-owners gave Pintado the names of 136 slaves who had escaped to the fort, including seventy-eight men, twenty-three women, eight boys, four girls, and twenty-three whose gender was not specified.

Pintado's reports offer other evidence about the Apalachicola maroons, including their age, color (black or mulatto), family status, occupations, specified value, and, in some cases, the circumstances by which they arrived at Prospect Bluff. Garçon, the black man identified as the commander at the fort, had fled with four other men and three women from the plantations of Don Antonio Montero. Among the slaves who fled from the mercantile firm of John Forbes and Company in Pensacola were Ben, a twenty-nine-year-old baker valued at 700 pesos; his wife, María, a "good domestic servant" valued at an equal sum; Ambrosio, a shoemaker valued at 900 pesos; and Harry, a caulker and navigator who knew how to read and write and was valued at 2000 pesos. Whole families escaped to the fort together. The thirty-four-year-old Billy escaped with his thirty-two-year-old wife, Lally, and their five children—Cressy, age ten, Flora, age nine, Beck, age eight, Cynthia, age seven, and Nero, age six. The runaways included sailors, master carpenters, bakers, servants, laundresses, cooks, sawyers, masons, cartwrights, and field hands. If this group is representative, and there is no reason that it should not be, the blacks who lived at Prospect Bluff were certainly equipped to be self-sufficient. Although they may not have been "black Robin Hoods" as Aptheker called them, neither were they the parasitical "villains" described by the Americans at the time.[49]

When Pintado finally arrived at Prospect Bluff, the British officer in charge would not allow the maroons to be forcibly removed, but he agreed that they could return with Pintado if they so chose. Only twenty-eight of the 128 fugitive slaves whom Pintado interviewed agreed to return to their owners, and overnight several of those ran away or changed their minds. Pintado was able to convince only ten interviewees to accompany him voluntarily. All of them were women.[50]

Meanwhile General Jackson had already ordered the destruction of the fort, which encouraged the "stealing and enticing away our negroes" and had "been established by some villain for the purpose of murder, rapine, and plunder." When U.S. naval forces launched an attack on the fort on July 27, 1816, the blacks inside hurled insults as well as cannon shots at the Americans. They made it clear that they would fight to the death. Indeed, that was their fate. The first American shot hit their powder magazine and blew up the fort. Only forty maroons survived the explosion, and few of those lived long.[51]

Two years later General Andrew Jackson and more than three thousand troops launched a three-week military campaign in Florida in what came to be called the First Seminole War. The doomed trader Alexander Arbuthnot, whom Jackson would later execute, in a last letter to his son, alleged that "the main drift of the Americans is to destroy the black population of Suwany."[52] On April 16, 1818, Jackson's troops burned almost four hundred black and Seminole homes at Bowlegs Town on the Suwannee River, destroyed large quantities of food supplies, and spirited away herds of cattle and horses.[53] Blacks and Seminoles, whom Arbuthnot had forewarned, put up a desperate fight. Three hundred black warriors held back a greatly superior force at the Suwannee River to give women and children time to cross over to safety. The Seminole's northern settlements and associated maroon villages were ruined. In 1821 Florida became a territory of the United States, and the Seminoles and their black allies lost their Spanish support. The new U.S. government prosecuted two more long and costly wars against the Seminoles and blacks, and in the end most were "removed" to the western territories as Andrew Jackson and other policymakers had recommended.[54] These political shifts and forced removals dramatically reduced opportunities for marronage in the southeastern United States, where incoming planters quickly instituted more typical and repressive antebellum systems of slave control.[55]

This study is only a preliminary step toward placing women squarely in the maroon landscape. It argues that at great risk these little-known or recognized women participated in more than three hundred years of ongoing resistance to slavery. They also made possible and sustained the long-term maroon settlements that existed on the remote frontiers of the Spanish Americas. The Spanish documentary and legal tradition offers a way to study particular maroon communities over a broad temporal and geographic range that includes wide regions of what is today the United States. From the rich Spanish records it is possible to begin to tease out details about the variety of the enslaved experiences of specific women, about their forms of resistance, and how they helped reconstruct African and African American families and networks free of slavery. Their histories will contribute toward a reexamination of the role of maroon women in cultural adaptation and the process of creolization and in the formation of an African American culture. Further archaeological inquiry into the lives of maroon women is also necessary, for material deposits, unlike documentary records, are not notably biased toward men. The artifactual record can help scholars reconstruct more fully the daily life of women who lived in maroon settlements and know more about their handicrafts, the food they grew or raised, how they prepared them, and possibly even details of their socioreligious life.[56]

By combining these different kinds of evidence it is possible to recover significant portions of the history of a group of people who for too long have been thought not to have one. These women and their families can be seen as real historical actors. Their inclusion in larger histories will certainly enrich and improve understanding of American colonial societies.

Notes

1. The essays included in Richard Price's classic collection contain only scattered references to the women who lived in maroon settlements. See *Maroon Societies: Rebel Slave Communities in the Americas,* ed. Richard Price (Baltimore: Johns Hopkins University Press, 1979). Two subsequent works by Barbara Bush and Hilary Beckles discuss maroon women in the British Caribbean but are limited by the nature of their sources or area of study. Bush argues that "most slaves were individual runaways and did not aspire to join maroon communities" but tried to pass for free in

nearby towns (*Slave Women in Caribbean Society, 1650–1838* [Kingston: Heinman Publishers, 1990], 63–65). Hilary McD. Beckles considers this strategy of urban marronage, but he had no real frontier experience to discuss for Barbados. See *Natural Rebels: A Social History of Enslaved Black Women in Barbados* (New Brunswick: Rutgers University Press, 1989), 164–70.

2. For images of Cudjoe and the Jamaican maroons see R. C. Dallas, *The History of the Maroons* (London: T. N. Longman and O. Rees, 1803).

3. Classic examples appear in John Gabriel Stedman, *Narrative of a Five-years' Expedition, against the Revolted Negroes of Suriname . . . from the Year 1772 to 1777* (London: J. Johnson and J. Edwards, 1796).

4. Stedman, *Narrative*.

5. Ethnohistorians and archaeologists have begun to explore the important role of Indian women as cultural mediators on the frontier, but few have yet recognized that African and African American women played similar roles. Clara Sue Kidwell, "Indian Women as Cultural Mediators," *Ethnohistory* 39 (Spring 1992): 97–107; Kathryn E. Holland Braund, "Guardians of Tradition and Handmaidens to Change: Women's Roles in Creek Economic and Social Life during the Eighteenth Century," *American Indian Quarterly* (Summer 1990): 239–57; Bonnie E. McEwan, "The Archaeology of Women in the Spanish New World," *Historical Archaeology* 25 (1991): 33–41.

6. Spanish concepts of *buen gobierno* (just government) extended access to groups, including women and slaves, that were often excluded by other systems. Charles Cutter, *The Legal Culture of Northern New Spain, 1700–1810* (Albuquerque: University of New Mexico Press, 1995). For examples of Africans' use of Spanish law, see Jane G. Landers, *Black Society in Spanish Florida* (Urbana: University of Illinois Press, 1999), and Kimberly S. Hanger, *Bounded Lives, Bounded Places: Free Black Society in Colonial New Orleans, 1769–1803* (Durham: Duke University Press, 1997). Spanish records are full of first-person dialogue and idiomatic usages generated by Spanish-speaking persons of African descent. If the person could not speak Spanish, court officials were required to employ translators for them, just as they did for non-Spanish-speaking witnesses of other ethnicities. That may have added new layers of linguistic filters, but it was, nonetheless, an effort to understand and record the voice of Africans and African Americans.

7. Price, ed., *Maroon Societies*, 33–103.

8. Records generated by other European powers about "notorious" African maroons or rebels occasionally add to the historical record of Africans in areas of Spanish settlement. Jane Landers, "Gracia Real de Santa Teresa de Mose: A Free Black Town in Spanish Florida," *American Historical Review*, 95 (Feb. 1990): 9–30.

9. Royal Cédula Replying to Governor Nicolás de Ovando, March 29, 1503, Indiferente General, Archivo General de Indias, Seville, Spain (hereafter AGI); Slave Codes, Santo Domingo (hereafter SD), Jan. 6, 1522, Patronato 295, AGI.

10. Carlos Estéban Deive, *Los guerrilleros negros: Esclavos fugitivos y cimarrones en Santo Domingo* (Santo Domingo: Fundación Cultural Dominicana, 1989), 31–54; Roberto Marte, ed., *Santo Domingo en los Manuscritos de Juan Bautista Muñoz* (Santo Domingo: Ediciones Fundación García Arévalo, 1981), 359–60, 412–15.

11. In 1553 Viceroy Luís de Velasco estimated New Spain's black population at more than twenty thousand. Despite Velasco's recommendation to limit slave imports, blacks were estimated to number ten times the white population by the early seventeenth century. See David M. Davidson, "Negro Slave Control and Resistance in Colonial Mexico, 1519–1650," *Hispanic American Historical Review* 46 (1966): 235–53. Gonzalo Aguirre Beltrán also noted the preponderance of blacks over whites. See *La población negra de México, 1519–1810* (Mexico: D. F. Ediciones Fuente cultural, 1946), 208–13.

12. Carlos Larrazábal Blanco, *Los negros y la esclavitud en Santo Domingo* (Santo Domingo: Editorial Postigo, 1975), 151–53.

13. In nearby caves explorers have also found metal daggers, clay water jugs, and triton shell trumpets that they identify to be the work of African runaways. José Juan Arrom and Manuel A.

García Arévalo, *Cimarrón* (Santo Domingo, Dominican Republic: Fundación García-Arévalo, 1986), 48–55.

14. Luis de Chávez y Mendoza, "Lista de los negros ques se contienen en el Maniel de Neyba," April 12, 1785, SD 1102, AGI.

15. de Chávez y Mendoza, "Lista de los negros."

16. Ibid.

17. Relación de Miguel Cabello Balboa, 1578, Audiencia de Quito (hereafter AQ) 22/4, AGI, on microfilm at the Banco Central de Quito; P. Rafael Savoia, "El negro Alonso de Illescas y sus descendientes (entre 1553–1867)," in *Actas del primer congreso de historia del negro en el Ecuador y el sur de Colombia*, ed. P. Rafael Savoia (Quito: Centro Cultural Afro-ecuatoriano, 1988), 29–61.

18. Ibid.

19. Relación de Miguel Cabello Balboa, 1578, Audiencia de Quito 22/4, AGI; Joel Monroy, *Los religiosos de la Merced en el Antiguo Reino de Quito* (Quito: Editorial Labor, 1943), 2: 98–123, cited in Savoia, "El negro Alonso de Illescas," 28–29.

20. Davidson, "Negro Slave Control," 235–53; Colin A. Palmer, *Slaves of the White God: Blacks in Mexico, 1570–1650* (Cambridge: Harvard University Press, 1976), 126–30.

21. Andrés Pérez de Ribas, "Relación de la misión á que fué enviado el P. Juan Laurencio, acompañando a una esquadra de soldados que salía á la reducción de negros foragidos y salteadores," in *Corónica y historia religiosa de la Provincia de la Compañia de Jesus de México en Nueva España*, 2 vols. (Mexico: Impr. del Sagrado Corazon de Jesús, 1896), 282–94.

22. Pérez de Ribas, "Relación de la misión."

23. Report of Martín de Cevallos, May 29, 1693, Santa Fe 213, AGI. For a more detailed discussion of Matudere, see Jane Landers, "African Ethnicity and Culture in the Americas: The Historical and Archaeological Records," in *Identifying Enslaved Africans: The "Nigerian" Hinterland and the African Diaspora*, ed. Paul Lovejoy (London: Continuum, 2000), 30–54; see also María del Carmen Borrego Pla, *Palenques de negros en Cartagena de Indias a fines del siglo XVII* (Seville: Escuela de Estudios Hispano-Americanos de Sevilla, 1973).

24. One of the settlement's war captains, Pedro Mina, escaped capture and ruled the Matudere survivors for two more years, but in 1695 Mina, too, was apprehended at the palenque of Norossi. Report of Sancho Ximeno, Sept. 22, 1695, Santa Fe 212, AGI.

25. Report of Sancho Ximeno, Sept. 22, 1695, Santa Fe 212, AGI. María Francisca's unnamed black captor received his forty pesos and the mayordomo of the estate of Don Juan de Mier; five of the estate slaves received eighty pesos for bringing in one female and one male captive.

26. Report of Sancho Ximeno, Sept. 22, 1695, Santa Fe 212, AGI.

27. Although Padilla and Juana claimed to be Matudere's founders, in fact they only organized a preexisting settlement. By what means they did this, and how they garnered the support necessary to claim leadership, are unknown. Report of Martín de Cevallos, May 29, 1693, Santa Fe 213, AGI.

28. Report of Martín de Cevallos, May 29, 1693, Santa Fe 213, AGI.

29. Report of Martín de Cevallos, May 29, 1693, Santa Fe 213, AGI. The party also brought back two other women and three children from the Pérez hacienda whose relationship to the Matudere maroons (if there was one) was not stated. Surprisingly, the Spaniards asked no questions about (nor did Padilla volunteer any details) when or where the maroons captured the Spanish women.

30. Report of Martín de Cevallos, May 29, 1693, Santa Fe 213, AGI.

31. Report of Martín de Cevallos, May 29, 1693, Santa Fe 213, AGI.

32. Father Fernando Zapata to Governor Martín de Cevallos, April 21, 1693, Santa Fe 213, AGI.

33. Claire C. Robertson and Martin A. Klein, "Women's Importance in African Slave Systems," in *Women and Slavery in Africa*, ed. Claire C. Robertson and Martin A. Klein (Madison: University of Wisconsin Press, 1984), 3–25.

34. Report of Martín de Cevallos, May 29, 1693, Santa Fe 213, AGI.

35. Maroons in other camps were known to harvest cotton from the silk-cotton (*ceiba*) tree,

which they used in textile production. The ceiba also has strong religious connotations for Afro-Hispanics, and to this day in Cuba it is considered unlucky to cut one down.

36. Report of Martín de Cevallos, May 29, 1693, Santa Fe 213, AGI.

37. Cevallos said that he hung the portrait in the governor's mansion. Report of Martín de Cevallos to Antonio Ortíz de Talora, May 29, 1693, Santa Fe 213, AGI.

38. Herbert Aptheker, "Maroons within the Present Limits of the United States," *Journal of Negro History* 24 (1939): 167–84.

39. "William Dunlop's Mission to St. Augustine in 1688," *South Carolina Historical and Genealogical Magazine* 34 (Jan. 1933): 1–30; Royal officials to the king, March 3, 1689, cited in Irene Wright, "Dispatches of Spanish Officials Bearing on the Free Negro Settlement of Gracia Real de Santa Teresa de Mose," *Journal of Negro History* 9 (1924): 144–93; Landers, "Gracia Real."

40. Royal Edict, Nov. 7, 1693, SD 58–1–26, John B. Stetson Collection, P. K. Yonge Library of Florida History, University of Florida, Gainesville (hereafter PKY).

41. Windley A. Lathan, comp., *Runaway Slave Advertisements: A Documentary History from the 1730s to 1790*, vol. 3: *South Carolina* (Westport: Greenwood Press, 1983), 2, 3 (quotations); Windley A. Lathan, comp., *Runaway Slave Advertisements: A Documentary History from the 1730s to 1790*, vol. 4: *Georgia* (Westport: Greenwood Press, 1983). See also Daniel E. Meaders, "South Carolina Fugitives as Viewed through Local Colonial Newspapers with Emphasis on Runaway Notices, 1732–1801," *Journal of Negro History* 60 (April 1975): 288–317; and Philip D. Morgan, "Colonial South Carolina Runaways: Their Significance for Slave Culture," *Slavery and Abolition* 6 (Dec. 1985): 57–78.

42. Landers, "Gracia Real."

43. Faunal analysis by Elizabeth Reitz, historical reports on Gracia Real de Santa Teresa de Mose by Jane Landers, and archaeological reports by John Marron, all on file at the Florida Museum of Natural History, University of Florida, Gainesville; also see Kathleen A. Deagan and Jane Landers, "Excavating Fort Mose: A Free Black Town in Spanish Florida," in *I, Too, Am American: Studies in African American Archaeology*, ed. Theresa A. Singleton (Charlottesville: University of Virginia Press, 1999), 261–82; and Kathleen Deagan and Darcie MacMahon, *Fort Mose: Colonial America's Black Fortress of Freedom* (Gainesville: University Press of Florida, 1995).

44. Daniel Schafer, "'Yellow Silk Ferret Tied Round Their Wrists': African Americans in British East Florida, 1763–1784," in *The African American Heritage of Florida*, ed. David R. Colburn and Jane L. Landers (Gainesville: University Press of Florida, 1995), 71–103; Landers, *Black Society.*

45. Sara, Thomas, and Juan escaped from the plantation of Isaac Wied and were joined by Diego, who escaped from an unnamed owner. All the runaways left spouses behind. Criminal Case against Thomas, 1789, East Florida Papers, microfilm reel 122, PKY.

46. Royal decree in letter from Luís de las Casas to Governor Zéspedes, July 21, 1790, Letters from the Captain General, 1784–1821, reel 1, East Florida Papers, PKY; see also Landers, *Black Society.*

47. James W. Covington, "The Negro Fort," *Gulf Coast Historical Review* 5 (Spring 1990): 72–91; John D. Milligan, "Slave Rebelliousness and the Florida Maroon," *Prologue: The Journal of the National Archives* 6 (Spring 1974): 5–18.

48. Milligan, "Slave Rebelliousness."

49. List of the blacks belonging to owners in Pensacola, May 4, 1815, SD 2580, AGI; Jane Landers, "Slave Resistance on the Southern Frontier: Fugitives, Maroons, and Banditti in the Age of Revolutions," *El Escribano* (1995): 12–24.

50. Vicente Sebastián Pintado to José de Soto, April 29, 1815, and May 6, 1815, both in SD, AGI; Owner's declarations, May 8, 1815, SD, AGI.

51. Milligan, "Slave Rebelliousness," 10–17; Landers, *Black Society;* Landers, "Slave Resistance."

52. Alexander Arbuthnot to John Arbuthnot, April 2, 1818, cited in *Narrative of a Voyage to the Spanish Main on the Ship* Two Friends, facsimile reproduction of the 1819 edition with introduction and index by John W. Griffin (Gainesville: University Presses of Florida, 1978), 216–18.

53. J. Leitch Wright, Jr., "A Note on the First Seminole War as Seen by the Indians, Negroes, and Their British Advisors," *Journal of Southern History* 34 (Nov. 1968): 565–75; William S. Coker and

Thomas D. Watson, *Indian Traders of the Southeastern Spanish Borderlands: Panton Leslie and Company and John Forbes and Company, 1783–1847* (Pensacola: University of West Florida Press, 1986), ch. 15.

54. Canter Brown, Jr., *Florida's Peace River Frontier* (Orlando: University of Central Florida Press, 1991), 9–10; Landers, *Black Society;* George Klos, "Blacks and the Seminole Removal Debate, 1821–1835," in *The African American Heritage of Florida,* ed. David R. Colburn and Jane L. Landers (Gainesville: University of Florida Press, 1996), 128–56; John K. Mahon, *History of the Second Seminole War* (Gainesville: University of Florida Press, 1967); Kevin Mulroy, *Freedom on the Border: The Seminole Maroons in Florida, the Indian Territory, Coahuila, and Texas* (Lubbock: Texas Tech University Press, 1993); Kenneth W. Porter, *The Black Seminoles: History of a Freedom-Seeking People,* rev. and ed. by Alcione M. Amos and Thomas P. Senter (Gainesville: University Press of Florida, 1996).

55. Daniel L. Schafer, "'A Class of People Neither Freemen nor Slave': From Spanish to American Race Relations in Florida, 1821–1861," *Journal of Social History* 26 (Spring 1993): 587–609.

56. For examples of recoverable evidence, see E. Kofi Agorsah, "Archaeology of Maroon Settlements in Jamaica," in *Maroon Heritage: Archaeological Ethnographic and Historical Perspectives,* ed. E. Kofi Agorsah (Barbados: Canoe Press, 1994), and Leland Ferguson, *Uncommon Ground: Archaeology and Early African America, 1650–1800* (Washington, D.C.: Smithsonian Institution Press, 1992).

CHAPTER 2

Of Life and Freedom at the (Tropical) Hearth: El Cobre, Cuba, 1709–73

María Elena Díaz

> . . . the natives of El Cobre were all treated and known as free people for they knew no other owner than the King . . . [and that Rafaela Sanchez] enjoyed freedom without subjection to any other person but to her referred mother.
>
> —Jose Basilio Maestre, 1793

> . . . everyone lived in his house serving their parents, without any other known master than the King.
>
> —Francisco Xavier de Quiala, 1793

The inhabitants of El Cobre, an Afro-Cuban village on Cuba's eastern frontier region, were slaves of the king of Spain during the late seventeenth and eighteenth centuries. In this corner of the Caribbean, royal slavery became an ambiguous and gendered status that blurred boundaries between freedom and bondage in many spheres of life. The court testimonies of Jose Basilio Maestre and Francisco Xavier de Quiala suggest ways in which the blurring of status occurred, or was perceived to occur, among these enslaved villagers.[1]

Having houses of their own, living with their own families and relatives, heading their own households, and having *potestad* (authority over their own children) were, according to Maestre and Quiala, distinctive practices of the *cobreros* (natives of El Cobre) as free subjects, despite their subjection to the king. If, as some scholars have stated, slavery entailed the natal alienation of a person and his or her "social death," then any tie to family and kin—or any entitlement over them, even if acquired by customary right—could presumably be regarded as a manifestation of personal freedom.[2] That seems to be the main proposition implicit in the declarations of Maestre and Quiala. Lack of a private master whose property or quasi-absolute rights over a slave could directly interfere with those prerogatives further blurred boundaries between freedom and slavery in the case of the royal slaves of El Cobre.

Not to be overlooked in Maestre's and Quiala's statements either is the reference to the possibility of female domestic authority and a mother's potestad over her child, in this case a daughter. As elsewhere in the early modern world, the pervasive (and hegemonic) discourse of hierarchy is used to depict the proper relation between parents and children or elders and juniors in the domestic sphere. Yet there is no rigid patriarchal language here because the maternal figure is also invoked as a possible symbol of power and authority. As I argue elsewhere, the royal slaves of El Cobre also claimed natal ties to local territory and homeland, but those broader communal ties that further blurred lines between freedom and slavery in a slave society will not be a direct concern in this chapter.[3]

The village of El Cobre is mostly known today as the abode of a "miraculous" image of the Virgin of Charity (patroness of the Cuban nation) and, since colonial days, as an important copper-mining center. The unusual history of the village as Cuba's only Afro-Cuban pueblo is less known, however. Neither a maroon community on the periphery of Spanish colonial society nor a mere slave community in the plantation world, El Cobre constituted a peasant mining village of royal slaves and free people of color and was in many ways similar to an Indian corporate community. In 1670 the Spanish crown confiscated the copper mines of El Cobre after decades of declining mine production and neglect in the hands of a private contractor. At that point, 271 private mining slaves became the king's slaves, a category whose ambiguous meaning would be negotiated in subsequent years.

By the end of the seventeenth century the former mining settlement had been transformed into a pueblo. The establishment of a pueblo of royal slaves and free people of color with a corporate land grant, limited self-government, and local militia companies that had their own officers strikes historians as unusual. Legally, slaves, as "outsiders" in the body politic, were not allowed to form such a polity. Even pueblos constituted largely or exclusively by free people of color were uncommon in the Spanish Americas. The transformation of El Cobre into a pueblo, and its acquisition of land, meant that royal slaves had increasing autonomy in provisioning themselves and their families. The family-based, peasant mining economy that resulted had far-reaching repercussions in regard to social identity and status.

After the crown confiscated the mines of El Cobre, the export productive role of the enslaved community underwent some major changes. Given the frontier location of the village on Cuba's eastern coast, the crown's newly acquired community of royal slaves became incorporated into the Spanish state's larger Caribbean defense scheme as a source of forced labor in the construction and repair of royal fortifications, soldiers in the militias, and, more generally, as a buffer settlement to protect and defend the nearby capital of Santiago de Cuba from enemy attack. During the late seventeenth and eighteenth centuries the church also took a growing interest in El Cobre as popular devotion to a local Marian image began to expand. By the mid-eighteenth century the bishop of Cuba reported that "the sanctuary of El Cobre is the richest, most frequented, and most devout in the Island, and the Lady of Charity the most miraculous statue of all those venerated."[4] Both church and state developed their own stakes in the preservation of this black village, sometimes at odds with each other.

This chapter examines the domestic household sphere as a site for the practical construction of personal freedom—or forms of freedom—in a black community in a nonplantation region of colonial Cuba. Geographically located in a Caribbean frontier zone, the black community of El Cobre also existed in a metaphorical (and mercurial) social frontier between slavery and freedom. Freedom in colonial slave societies was not merely constituted and fixed by juridical status. It was also imagined, performed, and contested at the interstices of social life and the multiple practices, arrangements, and micro events that constituted the texture of everyday life. One of the most noteworthy aspects of the community of El Cobre is that spaces of de facto freedom were opened and exploited in multiple ways within the confines of frontier slave society.[5]

Also important are the ways in which a locally or territorially based identity as cobreros was developed above and beyond juridical distinctions between villagers' slave or free status. Such distinctions were particularly blurred in the case of females in El Cobre, as illustrated by the relative homogeneity of many aspects of social life in the domestic sphere of women in this community. I will examine the significance of the domestic or social reproductive sphere of females in the production of de facto forms of personal freedom in El Cobre through issues concerning household composition, residential pattens, and reproductive and sexual practices in the female population's life-cycle. My aim is to link issues and methods in the field of "family history" to issues related to the gendered construction of freedom and slavery in colonial slave societies.

The case of El Cobre provides a rich array of local censuses that allows historians to map several sexual, familial, and residential patterns of the community. Studies of black families in freedom and slavery have been fairly common for the Caribbean and elsewhere in the Americas. Yet little exists so far on colonial Cuba. Beyond issues of how freedom and bondage were linked to the female domestic and reproductive sphere in El Cobre, I will also examine several aspects of the life-cycle of local females and the shape of familial and residential life. Although this study for the most part focuses on the life-cycle patterns of El Cobre's females as a group, it also interrogates whether internal distinctions existed between the formally free and the royally enslaved.

One of the most remarkable aspects of social life in the community of El Cobre is the absence of major distinctions in practices related to the domestic sphere among females. It reflects some of the de facto ways in which the boundaries between slavery and freedom were blurred along gendered lines. When possible, I will set these local formations against the broader comparative background of white and black, as well as free and slave women, in Cuba and elsewhere in the Americas.[6]

Two village hearth listings, one drawn up in 1709 and the other in 1773, provide the empirical base of this study and offer glimpses of two moments in the history of El Cobre.[7] The local family census of 1709 portrays the community four decades after the crown confiscated the mining settlement, when it had already become a small but full-fledged village organized into autonomous households. The 1773 hearth listing represents the community a century after the confiscation, once it had become a sizable pueblo.

More than an opportunity to explore a diachronic axis, however, the two local censuses can be used to evaluate persistent trends and patterns. Scholars are by now well aware of the limitations of hearth listings as sources. Although they have often been made to reflect too many kinds of social formations and support too many generalizations regarding the "family," these sources can nonetheless provide a valuable window (often the only window) into many aspects of familial and domestic life or at least contribute to the possibility of informed speculation about them.

Free Status and Gender in El Cobre: An Unusual Profile

Throughout the century (1670–1780) during which El Cobre existed as a pueblo of royal slaves and free people of color under crown jurisdiction, its population flourished and became, literally and in some ways metaphorically, more "free." In 1670, when the crown confiscated the mines, there were 271 slaves. By 1709 the number of royal slaves had grown to 495, and the village as a whole had 604 inhabitants. At this time, 82 percent of the pueblo's population were royal slaves. An additional 2 percent were private slaves, and the rest (16 percent) were *libres* (free people of color). By 1773 El Cobre had grown into a sizable village of 1,320 inhabitants, of which about 836 (64 percent) were royal slaves and about 2 percent were private slaves. Most of the libres (34 percent) were manumitted descendants of royal slaves or free people of color who had married into the community.

Free people of color and royal slaves in El Cobre therefore tended to be kin and compatriots, not masters and slaves of each other. The population of libres grew in absolute and proportional terms throughout the century. Distinct from the royal slaves was a small number of private slaves, most of whom were African. Both libres and royal slaves were owners and masters of these few personal slaves. The parish priest and the famous Marian sanctuary of El Cobre also owned some private slaves.

As elsewhere in the Americas, gender strongly influenced and shaped the legally free and slave populations of El Cobre. The gender profile of these local populations, however, was actually very different from that of their counterparts elsewhere in Cuba and the Americas.[8] Females consistently made up a higher proportion of the free population of color in Cuba and, more generally, through-out the slave societies in the New World. In the city of Santiago de Cuba, for example, 54 percent of the free population of color in 1778 were females; in Havana the corresponding proportion of females was 58 percent. In fact, females in Cuba predominated only among this sector of the population.[9] In El Cobre, males, and not females, predominated among the population of libres.

The first surviving local family census of 1709 shows that males in El Cobre constituted 55 percent of the free population of color and only 47 percent of the royal slaves. By 1773, when the overall proportion of the free population in the community had roughly doubled, males constituted 59 percent of libres and only 44 percent of royal slaves. At both times the sex ratios in the total population of the village were balanced. During the early part of the eighteenth century that particular gendered pattern was probably most influenced by the migration of free men into the community, where they often married native royal slave women and perhaps obtained family land in the village. Manumission patterns during the first four decades of the eighteenth century show that annual *coartaciones* (manumissions through self-purchase) were few, but males manu-mitted themselves as often as females.[10]

Toward the middle of the century, however, manumission trends probably became more significant in shaping the gender profile of libres. After the 1740s there was not only a dramatic increase in the local annual self-manumission rates but also a significant gender shift in the pattern. Self-manumissions in-creased from barely 1 to an average 4.2 each year. Males represented 79 percent of all the self-manumissions during this period, and females made up 21 per-cent of them.[11]

Reasons for the change in manumission patterns cannot be easily ascertained, but they may have been due to greater access to freedom through military ser-vice, better possibilities to save for self-purchase, and—perhaps—greater will-ingness (or perceived need) to invest in the individual coartacion of males, par-ticularly adult males, to free them from forced labor requisitions to the state. Paradoxically, the prominent role of females in the material and social reproduc-tion of the family may have obstructed possibilities for earning and saving money for their own coartacion or that of their children, particularly if it meant leav-ing the village to find employment. It is still difficult to determine the gendered factors that shaped the different sex profile of the libre population in El Cobre when compared to that found in other areas of Cuba and the Americas.

The king's slaves of El Cobre were incorporated into the crown's defense sys-tem. The regime of forced labor to which royal slaves were subjected, however, was strongly gendered. All royal slave males between the ages of sixteen and sixty were subject to labor obligations in the state's fortification projects on a two-week rotating basis, for a total of three to four months a year. Married women and females under the age of sixteen were in principle relieved from those obligations. Unmarried young women, however, were obligated to work on a rotational basis "in occupations proper to their sex" in the royal hospital in the city of Santiago de Cuba or sometimes in personal service to royal officials in that city. Female labor requirements to the Spanish crown, however, were more sporadic and less structured than the corvée labor system imposed on males.[12]

Thus, male royal slaves undoubtedly carried the major burden of forced labor—and bondage. One may even say that despite their juridical slave status, females in El Cobre were in practice more "free" than their male counterparts. Thus, if enslaved females in El Cobre were for the most part free of forced labor requisitions to the state, would the possibility of individual legal manumission not have greater immediate impact on the lives of enslaved males, who would thereby be freed from service to the state? Freedom from forced labor requisitions would also allow manumitted males to dedicate more time to self- and family-provisioning activities in the village.

While male royal slaves in El Cobre went back and forth to labor in the crown's defense projects and served alongside fellow free cobreros in the militia, most married women stayed behind in the village, overseeing the survival of their own autonomous households and families. From the calculating point of view of the state, the main role of royal female slaves may have been reproduction of the state's slave labor force. From a local native perspective, however, that reproductive role could be seen instead as women's contribution to the natural, social, and cultural reproduction of family, lineage, and community. The reproductive role of most women in this unusual pueblo can also be understood from below, therefore, as materially and symbolically reproducing the autonomous natal ties of family and community that could be regarded as practical manifestations of freedom in a slave society. These material, social, and cultural reproductive practices also took their own particular shapes.

Life-Cycle-Related Sexual Practices and Residential Patterns

Most women in El Cobre were likely to embrace marriage and motherhood at some time in their lives, usually during their twenties. In 1709, for instance, 54 percent of cobrera women over twenty were married, and 70 percent of all women in the village over that age had "ever been married" (a broader category that includes married and widowed women).[13] In 1773, 54 percent of adult women over twenty were married, while 73 percent of adult women had "ever married." At either of these two times, more than two-thirds of local women who were more than twenty had been married, and many young women in their early twenties would be married within a few years. Although this proportion may not at first seem impressive, it is by no means low if placed in a wider context. In many parts of the colonial Americas marriage was not a likely outcome in the lives of many people—even free people.[14]

In the context of Cuba, the marriage trend among free or enslaved women in El Cobre was similar to that of women in Santa María del Rosario, a mostly white, ethnic town in the island's western region. In fact, the proportions of married and ever-married adult cobrera women were closer to those among the white, ethnic female population of Santa María del Rosario than to those of the same town's enslaved or free population of color. In Santa María del Rosario, married women constituted at least 54 percent of white females over twenty, and ever-married women constituted 73 percent of the white adult female population. Among the small (10 percent) free population of color in that town, however, married women formed 36 percent of the female population over twenty; ever-married women formed only 47 percent of that population. Among the slave population, 12 percent of women over twenty were married, and only 13 percent had "ever been married." Against this general comparative background, marriage rates among juridically enslaved or free women in El Cobre seem very high.

Internal marriage trends among free and enslaved women in El Cobre had varied earlier in the century but were very similar in 1773. In 1709, 51 percent of royal *slave* women over twenty were married, and 68 percent had "ever been married." The proportion of married and ever-married women among *libres,* however, was higher (67 percent and 81 percent, respectively). It is still unclear how significant these differences may have been given the small size of the free female population at the time. By 1773, however, the gap (if it had ever been significant) no longer held. By then, 52 percent of royal slave women over twenty were married, and 73 percent had once been married. Similarly, 57 percent of free cobreras over twenty were married, and 70 percent had been married at some point in their lives.

Single women and unwed mothers were not absent from the community. The local clergy made sure that the status of these women was distinctly registered in various village censuses. In the hearth listing of 1709, unwed mothers were inscribed simply as *solteras* (single), and a listing of their children followed their names. In 1773 the "unchaste" status of these women was registered even more explicitly. The status of unmarried women was recorded either as *soltera,* with the usual listing of children following in the case of unwed mothers, or as *doncella* (maiden) in the case of presumed virgins. It is not clear how important these distinctions actually were in the social life of El Cobre, particularly in regard to matters of female honor.

In 1709 9 percent of females over the age of twenty in El Cobre were single mothers; in 1773 that proportion was 13 percent. To be sure, single mothers could be found among all age groups and statuses in the village. At least by 1773, however, the ages of most of them suggest a strong pattern of premarital pregnancies. Premarital sexual practices and pregnancies took place among cobrera young women regardless of their free or royal slave juridical status. That many such pregnancies constituted a transitional "stage" in the female life-cycle pattern can be inferred from an analysis of aggregate trends in the female population of El Cobre (table 2.1). Single mothers registered in the local family census of 1773 clustered around the age groups of twenty to twenty-four. Among the fifteen-to-nineteen-year-old age group, an overwhelming majority (90 percent) were registered as doncellas. Only four of fifty in that age group had become unwed mothers, and only one had married. In that sense it is possible that sexual activity among females in the community may have not begun until quite late in adolescence or young adulthood.

The critical years of transition in the female life-cycle seemed to lie between the ages of twenty and twenty-four. Although there were sixteen "maidens" in that age group, as many as seventeen women registered as "unwed mothers" (*solteras*), and thirteen were inscribed as "married." Thus, the twenty-to-twenty-four-year female cohort was composed of roughly similar proportions of maidens, single mothers, and married women. Half a decade to a decade later in the life-cycle of cobrera women (the age cohorts of twenty-five to twenty-nine and thirty to thirty-four), most were already registered as "married," although one-fourth to one-third in those age groups were still unmarried. A few married women had already become widows by their late twenties. Among subsequent age groups in the local female population, the proportion of unwed mothers and maidens decreased further in relation to married women (*casadas*). The proportion of widows (*viudas*), however, became increasingly significant, particularly among women over fifty. Unwed mothers and maidens, however, did not altogether disappear, even after the advanced age of forty.

Premarital pregnancies among cobrera women, then, appear to have ended in marriage more often than not. The local church, or its clergy, may have been quite vigilant regarding the sexual and marital status of women in El Cobre, as shown by their record-taking practices. It may have been difficult, however, to convince young women of the absolute necessity of preserving themselves as pure maidens until marriage, even though they may not have engaged in pre-

Table 2.1. Female Marital Status by Age, 1773

Age (Years)	Maidens	Single Mothers	Married	Widows	All
Unknown or under 5	86	12	25	6	129
5–14	89	1	1	0	91
15–19	45	4	1	0	50
20–24	16	17	13	0	46
25–29	4	4	18	1	27
30–34	2	3	16	1	22
35–39	0	0	10	4	14
40–44	1	1	19	6	27
45–49	0	1	10	3	14
50–54	1	0	11	8	20
55–59	2	0	2	3	7
Over 60	2	0	8	10	20

Source: Family census of El Cobre, 1773 (SD-1628, AGI).

marital sexual activities until about their twenties. Premarital sexual practices leading to pregnancies may have taken place during the period when the young royal slave women were subject to labor requisitions in Santiago de Cuba. Yet premarital pregnancies also occurred as often among free women not subject to labor requisitions away from their families and village, so unregulated sexual practices may have been due to altogether different factors. Perhaps they were part of an experimental period of sexual activity in the female life-cycle. Or perhaps premarital sexual relations may have been customarily accepted as part of a more drawn-out process of courtship, betrothal, and marriage whereby the male partner eventually moved into his girlfriend's (and later wife's) parental house and one day became an independent household head himself.

Most unwed mothers in El Cobre, particularly younger ones, continued living in their parental house with their "illegitimate" children. In 1709, 67 percent of single mothers lived with their parents or mothers; in 1773, the proportion was as high as 81 percent. Single mothers and their children may thus be said to have been incorporated into the bosom of the parental family, where they often resided alongside married and "legitimately" born kin.[15]

The prevalence and openness of out-of-wedlock pregnancies, and other fragments of evidence, suggest that although premarital sexual relations were not altogether sanctioned, neither were they taboo. Thus, although most cobrera women did not spurn marriage itself, many young women rejected the dominant colonial Christian precept of female virginity before marriage. Premarital sexual practices and pregnancies, even when they ended in marriage, represented young women's control of their sexuality despite church dicta or possible parental regulation. The study of single mothers as a group and/or as a transitional stage in the lives of women remains an important but complex subject whose multiple ramifications cannot be pursued further here.

Although unwed mothers tended to reside in the parental household, marriage did not entail immediate residential independence. Perhaps one of the most remarkable traditions in El Cobre was the widespread custom of young husbands moving into their brides' parental houses during the early years of marriage. Local custom in this regard tended to override church doctrine that supported a neolocal type of residential arrangement for newly married couples. For the church, marriage represented a step into adulthood often symbolized by a young married couple's immediate establishment of a new independent household. Although this neolocal custom also had force in El Cobre, cases of uxorilocal (wife-centered) residence were more widespread, at least during the initial years of a marriage.

The uxorilocal residential arrangements found in El Cobre were common both among free and royal slaves. In fact, these marital residential arrangements seemed to be so anchored in local tradition and so widespread that even a young white man who married into the community in the 1730s saw fit to reside for at least four years in his cobrera wife's family house. Despite the fact that a neolocal

residential custom seems to have been normative among the white ethnic Spanish population in Cuba, the young white groom adapted to local custom and
to his bride's family tradition. The force of local custom in overriding church
precept on these residential matters is made particularly clear by the fact that
the young white groom was the brother of the local parish priest. The parish
priest, Don Juan Jacintho Silva, himself may have been responsible for register-
ing the young couple's marital and residential story in the local hearth listings
of the 1730s.

In any case, cobrera women did not necessarily become mistresses of their
own houses when they married, nor did their husbands (or brothers or sons)
become masters. Men had to reside in the family houses of their brides, even
though they may have worked on the farms and land of their own families of
origin.[16] Indeed, most young people in El Cobre lived in the extended parental
house far beyond the legal age of majority (twenty-five years in Spanish law)
and beyond marriage. The presence of a large proportion of complex and extended family households in the village (41 percent of all households in 1773),
and the strong uxorilocal stress of those residential arrangements, represent a
clear and distinct pattern not found elsewhere in Cuba.[17] Ironically, the strong
presence of the church in El Cobre did not seem to "reform" these residential
arrangements, which were maintained among the best local families as well as
more modest ones in the village.

Paradoxically, if royal slaves in El Cobre were less subjected to a master than
regular private slaves they may have been more subjected to familial control than
even their cohorts among the free elsewhere in colonial society. That is, if
neolocal living arrangements are taken to be an indication of familial emancipation, young people in El Cobre may have found it harder to free themselves
of parental oversight than other young men and women in Spanish colonial
society. But here we are moving dangerously close to informed speculation, for
we do not know how these inscriptions of household headship and dependence
translated into real-life practices. Overall, it is difficult to determine the internal dynamics of power in these uxorilocal households or larger blocs of kin-
related households. What shape did *patria potestad* (the rule or authority of the
father)—or for that matter *matria potestad*—take effectively in extended households and familial spaces? And what was the relation between elder and junior
couples? One may speculate that, for women, these uxorilocal arrangements may
have meant greater subjection to their father's or mother's authority than to
their husband's authority, or, conversely, that they may have been empowered
or even cushioned from excesses in the conjugal tie by their own blood relatives.
Unfortunately, these and other related questions remain beyond the purview
of this study.

The uxorilocal or wife-centered arrangements found in El Cobre seem to be
related to more encompassing matrifocal trends.[18] When uxorilocal residential
arrangements among cobreros are examined within a longer time frame or from

a multigenerational perspective, they can be shown to reflect matrilocal dwelling practices. The wife's family house into which a groom moved, for example, tended to be the bride's mother's house. Indeed, it was the same space into which the mother's husband had moved when the elder couple married a generation before, and so on back the generational chain. Matrifocal trends, therefore, were not only manifested in the female-headed households with which they are usually associated (and which were also present in El Cobre) but also in two-parent households in the village.

The case of El Cobre points to the existence of matrifocal trends among black families in Cuba as far back as the eighteenth century. The extended debate over the matrifocal character of the black family, particularly in the Caribbean region, is a complex one that has long occupied anthropologists, sociologists, and also some social historians.[19] This is not the place to extend that debate, but it is worth pointing to some possibilities in the shaping of the character of family and domestic life in El Cobre. The matrifocal stress evinced in the residential arrangements and traditions in the village may have been related to the domestic networks on which women relied to support the household while male royal slaves left the village to work for the state or perform militia service throughout the year. Matrifocal tendencies may thus reflect the preeminent role of women in the social reproduction of natal ties and in the activation of familial identities in the community.

Moreover, matrifocal trends in the residential patterns of El Cobre may have been reinforced by the tendency toward gender-segregated spaces and the sexual division of labor underlying them. In the village's internal local economy, males were generally engaged in agricultural activities, and they controlled land and farms on the periphery of the village. Women controlled house plots in the spatial core of the village and worked on female occupational activities such as surface-copper mining, sewing, and weaving, all of which were carried out in the central area or in the family houses.[20]

The matrifocal stress evident in the residential practices of the community could have also reflected a type of kinship system in which blood ties were privileged over conjugal ties. Or they could have been related to Afrocentric precepts that were reinvented and creolized in the village's domestic situations. Even the experience of New World slavery—and its juridical mother- or "womb"-based transmission norms—could have presumably affected a mother line–centered stress found in residential practices. In short, no single factor can be shown at this point to have determined the matrifocal tendencies found in the village.

Despite the strong matrifocal current in the cobreros' residential arrangements, the overwhelming majority (between two-thirds and three-fourths) of household heads in El Cobre were male. Thus, as elsewhere in the Spanish empire, household headship was still a predominantly male-related practice, presumably reflecting patriarchal principles.[21] Yet, as elsewhere in the Americas, too, women in El Cobre did head a high proportion of households themselves. In 1709, 33 percent of the eighty-five households in the village were headed by women, and women headed 26 percent of the 157 households recorded in 1773.[22]

The proportion, however, was higher because many married women would have actually headed the households when their royal slave spouses were away working on fortification projects or on military duty. As in other aspects of their life-cycle, cobrera women's experience of household headship was for the most part not differentiated according to juridical status. Free women in El Cobre were no less prone to heading their own households than were royal slave women.[23] But who were the female cobreras who actually did so?

Although single women and unwed mothers headed some households, most female household heads in El Cobre were widows. High mortality rates in the early modern world made widowhood a common marital status everywhere. In 1709 widows constituted 16 percent of the adult female population over twenty in El Cobre, and by 1773 the proportion was slightly higher at 18.2 percent.[24] Widows, after age fifty, became a particularly large percentage of the female population, whether it was because females lived longer or were by choice or force of circumstances more likely than males to remain unmarried (table 2.1).

Once she became a widow, a woman was very likely to head her own household. In 1709 and 1773 females constituted 86 percent of the local widowed population of El Cobre, and most of these widows were the heads of their own households; 79 percent of them headed their own households in 1709, and 70 percent did so in 1773. Thus, if and when cobrera women reached maturity they were likely to end their lives as widows and heads of their own households. And yet it is also at this advanced age, generally speaking, that women may have been most dependent on older children and relatives for their own sustenance and that of their households.

It is significant, however, that when adult male children, even married children and their spouses, resided in a household, the widowed older woman was registered as the household's head. Perhaps it was as widowed household heads that women became—at least symbolically—independent, not only of private masters but also of husbands and, particularly in El Cobre, parental control. Was it at this point in life that women in El Cobre experienced their greatest moment of freedom, authority, and power? Were their adult children really subject to them, or were elderly cobrera widows more than ever dependent on their children? Questions about the internal dynamics of domestic relations of the past are difficult to research and answer.

Final Reflections

For about a hundred years in colonial eastern Cuba, to be a cobrero or a cobrera meant to be born, grow up, play, work, grow old, and die among family, kin, and kindred in an unusual corporate community of royal slaves and free people of color. Royal slavery in El Cobre became an ambiguous social category that blurred distinctions between freedom and bondage in many spheres of every-day life. Although enslavement to the king entailed part-time forced labor to the state, it also came to mean, if only by customary entitlement, the possibility of living with one's kin in that material, social, and symbolic space that was a house of one's own.

Control over (or, paradoxically, dependence on) the family, the affirmation of autonomous familial and/or kinship identities, and the material and social reproduction of those bonds should be regarded as one of several ways in which "freedom" was enacted in colonial slave societies. That is, such practices con-stituted significant manifestations of personal and social if not yet civic free-dom in societies where they did not constitute fundamental entitlements, or for that matter "human rights," to be taken for granted by all. Despite the "social death" that (in principle) slavery entailed, royal slaves in El Cobre established natal ties to family, land, and community and activated these autonomous ties in multiple ways in everyday social life, including residential practices.

Royal slavery in El Cobre was a strongly gendered status. Its critical link to the Spanish crown's military defense system, a masculine sphere par excellence, made it an especially gendered labor system in which females played an oblique, marginally productive role. Female royal slaves, particularly adult married women, were for the most part free of forced labor requisitions to the state. They were more associated with the biological, material, and social reproductive sphere of life. While male royal slaves of the village went back and forth to work in the defense system and serve alongside fellow free cobreros in the militias, most married women stayed behind in the village, taking care of—or reproduc-ing—their autonomous family households. Moreover, they did so in a predomi-nantly matrifocal family framework.

And yet, paradoxically, the preeminent social reproductive role of women in the community may have obstructed their individual access to manumission through self-purchase. Although royal slave women in El Cobre enjoyed de facto freedom in multiple ways, and through their reproductive labor they produced subjects with autonomous familial identities and de facto freedoms, they were more likely than men to remain in juridical bondage. Royal slave women who reared families in El Cobre may not have had the mobility, access to resources or employment, and savings to invest in self-manumission. They remained unable to transmit juridical freedom to their progeny automatically through the womb and were only able to transmit de facto forms of freedom through so-cial reproductive labor.

Although the social labor entailed in the reproduction of families and famil-ial identities among cobrera women may have been quite similar, the possibil-ity of embodying and transmitting legal freedom may have well constituted the main distinction between Cobera females who were juridically free and those who were enslaved.[25] To be sure, male cobrero spouses also engaged in social reproductive labor, but females did so in a more sustained way: solely by themselves when males were away laboring as slaves or soldiers for the state, and in complementary ways while males worked in the village.

The forgoing analysis of the social reproductive role of women in El Cobre has led to several further observations regarding life-cycle sexual practices and familial residential patterns in the community. Most cobrera women married at some time in their lives, usually by their mid-twenties. They were more likely to marry than slave or even free women of color elsewhere in the Americas and were as likely to do so as ethnic white women in other eighteenth-century Cuban towns. The strong presence of the church in El Cobre, particularly through its popular Marian sanctuary, may have influenced the high propensity of cobreras to marry. Cultural considerations regarding, for instance, issues of honor and respectability as related to legal marriage are more difficult to assess.

Another contributing factor for the high incidence of marriage was the incentive provided to married enslaved women to free themselves from labor requisitions for the state. It is not clear, however, if it was marriage or motherhood that in principle—if not always in practice—freed enslaved cobrera women from forced labor requisitions. Similarly, the possibility of transmitting familial inheritance rights (in access to land, houses, and in some cases personal slaves and other forms of property) may have also played a role in encouraging marriage.

In addition, the corporate and relatively closed character of this local Afro-Cuban community precluded the strong hierarchical class, race, and status relations that pervaded social life in other colonial settings. Although sexual relations were common among socially unequal subjects in Iberian colonial society, particularly among high-status males and low-status females, marriage was proscribed between them.[26] Thus, despite local differences in juridical free and slave status among cobreros, the relatively socially homogenous character of the population of El Cobre—indeed, their identity as cobreros—may have facilitated the "embrace" of marriage among social equals.

Finally, "marriage" constituted a way of "legalizing" the family in a legally and socially ambiguous frontier community. It was also a way of legitimizing the cobreros' claims to familial autonomy—and to some personal freedom—in colonial slave society. We know little, however, about how marriage was actually lived and what shapes it took in terms of duties and obligations.

In El Cobre, early pregnancy or even marriage for young women did not entail immediate separation from the parental home (more often than not the maternal family house) nor perhaps autonomy from parental authority. One salient feature of familial residential patterns in the community that did not seem to exist in other towns in Cuba at the time was the uxorilocal residential practice among young spouses. Uxorilocal custom called for young husbands to reside in the parental houses of their wives for some time, sometimes years, although it is not clear what other duties and obligations the arrangement entailed. A young couple would not have their own household until some years after their marriage, often not until they reached their thirties. The gender-related labor requisitions of royal slavery in El Cobre required that males be periodically absent from their households and village. It is thus not difficult to imagine that complex and extended family households would have been socially organized around the natal ties of the females who remained behind, working and raising families while husbands, father, brothers, and sons were away.

The uxorilocal custom may have been illustrative of a deeper matrifocal tendency found elsewhere among other Afro-American communities in the hemisphere. These matrifocal tendencies, in turn, may be linked to multivaried factors that need to be more carefully interrogated to determine their dynamics in Creole societies. In any case, local custom in El Cobre may have imposed itself over hegemonic Hispanic practices of neolocal and even patrilocal tendency despite church prescriptions.

Uxorilocal/matrifocal stress in residential practices, however, did not mean that patriarchal ideals and relations did not exist in El Cobre. Nor were the latter displaced by "matriarchal" systems. In El Cobre, matrifocal tendencies coexisted with patriarchal ones. The matrifocal residential inflection may have balanced domestic patriarchal prerogatives, but it did not obliterate them. Although most women acted as household heads when husbands were absent from the village, male household heads predominated, and males were the main household heads, even in the familial houses of their wives. Furthermore, male cobreros controlled most of the family farms and provisioning land surrounding the village as well as all the community's public offices. Females seemed to control a good share of the house plots at the core of the village.

Despite the strong predominance of male-headed households in El Cobre, there was still a high proportion of long-term, female-headed households. But as in other towns in Cuba, these female heads tended to be older widows. In any case, the matrifocal trends in the village may have reflected and symbolized women's (or mothers') prominent role in the social reproduction of family and community. That prominent role may well have been represented in the Virgin of Charity's symbolism as mother and patroness of the local community.

Overall, natives of El Cobre were likely to spend part of their childhoods and youths living with immediate family and alongside kin and kindred such as grandparents, uncles and aunts, cousins, and the families of those relatives. If the large bustling households of an imagined past existed and proliferated anywhere, it was not in early modern Western Europe or other places of the Americas—or, for that matter, elsewhere in Cuba.[27] These large households thrived more than anywhere else in this remote corner of the Caribbean. Compared to other places in Cuba or Brazil, non-nuclear households seemed to constitute an unusually large proportion of dwellings in El Cobre. Kinship duties among the cobreros seem to have included coresidence in large households. And familial and kinship coresidence in the context of a slave society took on particular connotations of personal and de facto freedom, particularly when accompanied by other autonomous familial practices such as self-provisioning.

Many aspects of family and domestic life in El Cobre still remain beyond reach. Further research must focus on the internal dynamics of domestic relations, which are more difficult to get at. Although the present study suggests, for instance, that residential family arrangements had a strong matrifocal inflection (or at least a wife- or female-centered one), it is more difficult to assess the significance of this pattern in terms of actual relations of power within the domestic sphere. Referring to one such setting, as Jose Basilio Maestre stated, Rafaela Sanchez "enjoyed freedom without subjection to any other person but to her referred mother." What kind of "subjection" did she and other daughters and sons in the community experience with respect to their mothers and fathers in the space of the hearth?

If, as suggested in this chapter, having a house of one's own and living among one's family could be construed in colonial slave societies as prerogatives of freedom, it is ironic that such manifestations could also entail internal forms of subjection and unfreedom. Studies of patriarchal familial relations and of relations between parents and children (minors) amply demonstrate such power relations and conflicts.[28] Thus, beyond the study of the role of women in the social reproduction of autonomous family hearths and in the production of de facto forms of freedom in El Cobre may be other intimate histories that are harder to reach. Such stories may eventually lead to the revelation of other forms of "freedom" and "unfreedom" within the bosom of the "free" family hearth.

Notes

1. The quotations in the epigraphs are taken from hearings regarding the individual freedom of the natives of El Cobre: Cuaderno 42/34, 1793, Santo Domingo (hereafter SD) 1628, Archivo General de Indias, Seville, Spain (hereafter AGI).

2. Orlando Patterson, *Slavery and Social Death: A Comparative Study*, (Cambridge: Harvard University Press, 1982); see also Claude Meillassoux, *The Anthropology of Slavery: The Womb of Iron and Gold* (Chicago: University of Chicago Press, 1991).

3. María Elena Díaz, *The Virgin, the King, and the Royal Slaves of El Cobre: Negotiating Freedom in Colonial Cuba, 1670–1780* (Stanford: Stanford University Press, 2000).

4. Pastoral visit of Bishop Don Pedro Agustin Morell de Santa Cruz, Santiago de Cuba, Dec. 8, 1756, AGI-SD 534.

5. Díaz, *The Virgin, the King, and the Royal Slaves*, particularly 10–14, 89–94, 285–313.

6. I will focus on the mostly white town of Santa María del Rosario in the western region of Cuba. Family census of Santa María del Rosario, 1800, Cuba 1689, AGI.

7. I will cite only once the complete references for the various village hearth listings that I have used in this study. Subsequent references to these sources are made by citing, in the text, the dates of the family census in question. Family census of 1709 (Escribanía 93A, AGI) and Family Census of 1773 (SD 1628, AGI); also cited in passing are the censuses of 1731 (SD 493, AGI), 1735 (SD 451, AGI) and 1739 (SD 385, AGI).

8. In Bahia, Brazil, Stuart Schwartz has found a constant 2:1 ratio of female-to-male freed slaves in both urban and rural sectors. Stuart Schwartz, "The Manumission of Slaves in Colonial Brazil: Bahia, 1684–1745," *Hispanic American Historical Review* 54 (Nov. 1974): 611. For an even broader survey see David W. Cohen and Jack P. Green, eds., *Neither Slave nor Free: The Freedmen of African Descent in the Slave Societies of the New World* (Baltimore: Johns Hopkins University Press, 1972).

9. The proportion of females in the general population was 43 percent (Census of Cuba, Dec. 31, 1778, Indiferente 1527, AGI). There were towns on the island, however, in which females constituted a smaller proportion even among the free people of color. Matanzas and Santa María del Rosario, two highly white areas in the island's western region, are cases in point. In these towns, the free population of color was very small and did not surpass 10 percent of the local population. Females in these towns did not predominate among any sector of the social order.

10. From 1689 to 1734 there were forty-two registered self-purchases of freedom, or an annual average of .91 self-manumissions. Of the forty-two, 45 percent (nineteen) were males and 55 percent (twenty-three) were females. Royal Treasury Entries 1689–1734, SD 451, AGI.

11. There were 152 registered *coartaciones* between 1740 and 1775—32 females and 120 males. Royal Treasury Entries, 1740–1742, SD 1628, AGI, and 1743–1775, SD 1627, AGI.

12. Díaz, *The Virgin, the King, and the Royal Slaves*, ch. 9.

13. Different hearth listings followed slightly different conventions. Overall, they all registered a male household head, if there was one, and identified their spouses as *su mujer* (his wife). Single mothers were inscribed as *solteras* (single), with their children labeled as *hijos*. In the family census of 1773, the local census taker went as far as to distinguish *solteras* from *doncellas* (maidens). Widows were also identified as such (*viudas*), although at times they may have been confused with mature single mothers. In some places of the Spanish Americas, however, these categories may have represented customary and not necessarily legal marital status. For a discussion related to the case of Mexico City, see Silvia Arrom, *The Women of Mexico City, 1790–1857* (Stanford: Stanford University Press, 1985).

14. In Vila Rica for 1838, ever-married women constituted only 26.8 percent of the female population and 35.4 percent of females over the age of twelve (the legal age for marriage). The percentage would be higher if calculated in terms of females over the actual—not legal—age of marriage, though. Donald Ramos, "Single and Married Women in Vila Rica, Brazil, 1754–1838," *Journal of Family History* 16 (1991): 264. Metcalf finds higher rates of slave marriage in Santana de Parnaíba but lower than among free persons. Alida Metcalf, *Family and Frontier in Colonial Brazil: Santana de Parnaíba, 1580–1822* (Berkeley: University of California Press, 1992), 163–69. More recently, Sandra Lauderdale Graham points out that between a quarter and a third of adult slaves married in Brazil (*Caetana Says No* [New York: Cambridge University Press, 2002], 30 and discussion on 26–44). For a particularly high incidence of slave marriages and families in a Jesuit fazenda confiscated by the Portugese crown, see Richard Graham, "Slave Families on a Rural Estate in Colonial Brazil," *Journal of Social History* 9 (Spring 1976): 382–402. A. J. R. Russell-Wood points to findings of a low incidence of church unions among slaves in his review of the more recent historiography in Russell-Wood, *Slavery and Freedom in Colonial Brazil* (New York: One World, 1992), xl–xliii.

15. It is difficult to determine the significance of "illegitimacy" in this community. What happened to illegitimate children, for example, after their mother married? There is some evidence that illegitimacy may not have played an important role in social life or even inheritance in this community.

16. Díaz, *The Virgin, the King, and the Royal Slaves*, 171–73.

17. At least not found in the towns of Santa María del Rosario in 1800 (Cuba 1689, AGI) or in Matanzas in 1765 (Cuba 1083, AGI). More studies of the family and of household residential arrangements need to be done for Cuba.

18. For a general discussion of the term *matrifocal*, see "The Matrifocal Family," in Raymond T. Smith, *The Matrifocal Family: Power, Pluralism, and Politics* (New York: Routledge, 1996), 39–57.

19. Smith, "The Matrifocal Family," 21–57.

20. Díaz, *The Virgin, the King, and the Royal Slaves*, chs. 6–8.

21. In fact, patriarchal principles were also reflected in the use of patronyms; children took on the father's surname. Thus, family lines were named after the father despite uxorilocal and/or matrifocal residential trends.

22. Yet in the mostly white town of Santa María del Rosario in Cuba, white women headed only

17 percent of all white households, whereas free women of color headed 30 percent of households among the small population of libres in the town, a proportion closer to that among cobreras.

23. If free women headed only 14 percent of the female-headed households in the village in 1709, they also constituted no more than 15 percent of the local female population. Similarly, if in 1773 free women headed a larger proportion of female-headed households (29 percent), their proportion among the local female population had also increased to 31 percent.

24. In Santa María del Rosario, widows constituted a slightly lower proportion among the white female population: 14 percent of white females over the age of twenty.

25. Another distinction in the life-cycle was the (unsystematic) labor requisitions to which enslaved cobreras were subject for several years in their lives, between adolescence and marriage. During childhood and after marriage the experience would have been otherwise quite similar. Women married to enslaved males in El Cobre would also be burdened with more labor in the material reproduction of their families, because their spouses would be less available in the village. But that burden in the reproduction of a family would vary with many other factors such as family size and the number, age, and gender of members among whom work could be distributed and rotated.

26. Verena Martínez Alier, *Marriage, Class and Colour in Nineteenth Century Cuba* (New York: Cambridge University Press, 1974).

27. The reference here is to Peter Laslett's *The World We Have Lost* (New York: Scribner, 1971), where the conception that large and bustling extended households were typical or even widespread in "traditional" societies of Western Europe's preindustrial past is debunked. There were exceptions in time and place, such as Southern France and Italy. In Eastern Europe, the existence of complex households seems to be associated with serfdom in the seventeenth and eighteenth centuries, and there may be significant analogies to El Cobre's case. Beatrice Gottlieb, *The Family in the Western World from the Black Death to the Industrial Age* (New York: Oxford University Press, 1993), 12–18.

28. Patricia Seed, *To Love, Honor and Obey in Colonial Mexico: Conflicts over Marriage Choice, 1574–1821* (Stanford: Stanford University Press, 1988); see also Asunción Lavrin, ed., *Sexuality and Marriage in Colonial Latin America* (Lincoln: University of Nebraska Press, 1989).

CHAPTER 3

In the Shadow of the Plantation:

Women of Color and the *Libres de fait* of

Martinique and Guadeloupe, 1685–1848

Bernard Moitt

Although it was always possible for slaves in the French Antilles to acquire freedom, not all who did so followed legal and official channels. From the very early development of slave society in these colonies there existed a group of people—*libres de savane,* also known as *libres de fait*—who lived in a state of quasi-freedom, having been manumitted by their owners without the authority of the state or the official documents of free status.

Libres de fait were male and female, black and of mixed race, African and Creole, urban and rural, and specialized and nonspecialized by profession or occupation. Most of them, however, were mixed-race and Creole women of color and their children. Throughout slavery the number of libres de fait remained small compared to the total population of free persons with clear titles, which was insignificant compared to the number of slaves in each French colony. During the 1830s and 1840s, when new legislation made normalization of their status more attainable, however, more libres de fait came out into the open, giving colonial authorities a stronger sense of the size of the group and abolitionists more ammunition to argue that the pace of liberation was too slow. At this time, when the amelioration of slavery came under greater scrutiny, French authorities paid more attention to libres de fait. These people, however, like others without clear titles, made no remarkable strides toward fully recognized freedom until the abolition of slavery in the French colonial empire in 1848.

This chapter examines the libre de fait phenomenon as a mode of manumission and its effects in Martinique and Guadeloupe. It shows that the status of libre de fait dates to the early days of plantation slavery in the seventeenth century and that this mode of manumission persisted until 1848. The libre de fait phenomenon endured largely because of restrictive metropolitan and colonial laws that circumscribed the freedom of people of color and made official manumission difficult to obtain. Even so, sincere and determined slave-owners willing to pay the required legal fees and support slaves who sought freedom could follow the process through to official manumission.

Most slave-owners circumvented the law and adopted a casual, and economical, approach to manumission. One advantage of this approach was that while slave-owners released slaves from the day-to-day drudgery of slavery they still retained some measure of control because the slaves were not entirely and officially (or legally) free. Indeed, in a pattern that suggests connivance, the labor of libres de fait was exploited by their owners, by people to whom their owners rented them, and by others to whom they contracted themselves. As a result, libres de fait were able to live in the shadows of plantations. In time they might even exit the slave system quietly if their owners died. Or—if they lived in a state of independence long enough—they could be regarded as free, even without official documentation. Contrary to Gabriel Debien's portrayal of libres de fait as carefree socialites, this chapter demonstrates that they were not a monolithic group.[1] They generally lived a precarious existence, almost as vulnerable as that of slaves, between slavery and freedom in the French colonies. Many, conscious of their vulnerability, tried to obtain outright freedom when legislation made it possible.

French scholars have largely ignored libres de fait in their work on colonial slave societies and have paid more attention to *gens de couleur libres* (free coloreds) because data on libres de fait, who remained hidden from official view, are fragmentary at best.[2] They were not counted in censuses. The lack of studies about manumission in French colonies also helps make scholarly exploration of libres de fait particularly challenging. Apart from works by Victor Schoelcher, Augustin Cochin, and Pierre Baude, there is little work that deals directly and substantially with the subject.[3] In her work about slave women, Arlette Gautier gave libres de fait scant treatment.[4] In one of the few detailed studies of manumission in the French Antilles, Léo Elisabeth made no mention of libres de fait at all. Rather, he subsumed them under the category of *soi-disant libres* (so-called free), a term that appears to have gained currency in the nineteenth century. According to Elisabeth, soi-disant libres people were "an intermediary class between freemen and slaves composed of people having been unable to obtain de jure liberty in the colonies [and who had to] obtain deeds of liberty abroad."[5] But few libres de fait had the resources or were able to exercise that option, which was usually at the slave-owner's sole discretion. Curiously, in later work Elisabeth gives the example of a black male, a probable libre de fait, who sought and received the consent of Adm. Jean Joseph Dupotet, governor of Martinique, to marry a mixed-race woman (apparently his freed slave) in 1736.[6] Josette Fallope has paid attention to the libres de fait but only for the colony of Guadeloupe.[7] A comprehensive treatment of the libres de fait is therefore lacking, and this chapter is an attempt to draw attention to this gap in French Caribbean historiography.[8]

Evolution of the Libres de Fait

The terms *libre de savane* and *libre de fait* encompassed different categories of unfree people. Both stand in opposition to *libre de droit* or *libre de plein droit*—terms that denoted complete freedom—an elusive status in that former slaves were still denied titles like "man" or "citizen" as Pierre Baude pointed out.[9] Baude confined the term *libre de fait* to three categories of slaves: those freed by owners through an unofficial act of renouncement of ownership; those freed through the expressed desire of slave-owners that this should happen upon their deaths but who made no real provisions for such freedom; and those freed through the want of heirs of persons who acted as their guarantors or sponsors but who died before the official process was complete.[10]

For Victor Schoelcher, the meaning of the term *libre de savane* can be explained by way of example. A slave-owner who wished to bypass administrative channels and free a slave simply said, "Go, you are free. I am relinquishing all my rights in you."[11] In such a case, the slave-owner permitted the slave to establish residence in the savanna or outlying area of the plantation, where manumitted persons, who constituted a virtual caste, had the pleasure of being free. As if to reinforce the legitimacy of this explanation, Schoelcher made reference to the insensitivity of a Monsieur Sébastiani, an official of the Ministry of Marine and Colonies during the 1840s, "who made a blunder in remarking naively . . . that these so-called freed slaves were really slaves dumped in the middle of the savanna like beasts of burden."[12]

The definitions of libre de fait and libre de savane have merit from the point of view of law and custom, but they are limited in that they do not take into account the full range of individuals who acquired this status from the earliest days of French colonization of Martinique and Guadeloupe, which started in 1635. Debien notes that slaves freed in the manner Schoelcher described were usually elderly and faithful domestics, women who had several children, and formerly elite slaves such as slave drivers, sugar boilers, and coach drivers. Before his involvement as a leader in the Saint-Domingue revolution that broke out in 1791, for example, Toussaint-Louverture lived as a libre de fait for several years on the Breda plantation in Haut-du-Cap, thanks to the *gérant* (administrator) there.[13]

There were, however, many libres de fait, including the ill and elderly, who acquired their status through simple abandonment by their owners.[14] Others acquired their status through wills and last testaments, when the wishes of the slave-owner were honored.[15] In cases where there was an absence of a precise will and last testament granting liberty, and there were no heirs, a slave could still be freed. "Unfortunately," Baude observes, "this *liberté de fait* was rare and precious because the slave, like furniture, animals or other instruments of exploitation, was owned by the estate and could, like them, be resold."[16] There were also other slaves who became libres de fait by virtue of being of mixed race at a time when laws that relegated them to slave status were lenient or ambiguous.

In some cases it was possible for libres de fait to obtain their status through the practice of *rachat* (redemption from slave-owners through purchase). In Martinique and Guadeloupe, however, rachat among libres de fait usually amounted to a monetary arrangement with the slave-owner that released the libres de fait temporarily from the confines and rule of the plantation. These people were mainly independent slaves (many of them artisans, petty traders, and domestics) who lived in urban centers and paid their owners an arranged sum of money weekly or monthly. Besides carpenters, blacksmiths, masons, bakers, cooks, valets, and watchmen, the group included midwives, nurses, and seamstresses. Fallope noted that they were usually children of domestic slaves whom slave-owners wanted to reward for loyalty, and they often did so by sending them to learn a trade, either in the colonies or in France.[17]

Those who went to France were lumped under the category *liberté de voyage* and considered free as long as they remained there, slavery being illegal in France. A new law of 1738, however, made it mandatory for slaves to return to the colonies when their owners so desired. Sue Peabody maintains that the legislation was not "registered by France's most powerful court, the Parlement of Paris." Moreover, "This put the law's status in a state of legal limbo for the high court's jurisdiction."[18] In any case, a royal ordinance of April 29, 1836, reinforced the 1738 law just when the number of libres de fait (women of color in particular) was expanding.[19]

Military service provided yet another means by which slaves could become libres de fait. While serving an eight-year term in a military or colonial battalion, male slaves were considered libres de fait even when their service was not continuous. Some slave-owners willfully disrupted the military service of such slaves, thus preventing them from gaining outright freedom sooner and profiting from their labor as much as possible.[20]

In light of the different ways in which slaves obtained the status of libre de fait, the evolution of this status is worth probing. Some sources suggest that the libre de fait phenomenon began during the seventeenth century with the emergence of mixed-race individuals well before the promulgation of the *Code noir* (Black Code) of 1685, a body of metropolitan codes concerned with slavery.[21] After 1685, mixed-race slaves constituted the largest number of libres de fait, but slaves, regardless of phenotype, could and did obtain this status.

In the period before the *Code noir*, French policy regarding mixed-race individuals was somewhat ambiguous. Colonial society appears to have circumvented the problem of status by seeking, however halfheartedly, to prevent miscegenation, particularly between white males and black females. At the same time, it was deemed appropriate to introduce ordinances that created strict boundaries between slave and free, white and colored. During the 1660s, Jean Baptiste (Père) Dutertre observed that to avoid suspicion white planters usually preferred married black women over spinsters as concubines. Dutertre regarded such men as "lost men" who were engaged in cohabitation with a different species; their progeny was an aberration.[22]

Because the stigma that mixed-race children bore was not their fault and was penalty enough without the additional burden of enslavement, colonial governors had pity on them and exempted them from automatically taking the status of their mothers. They were declared free in order to punish their fathers. They lived in limbo, belonging not to father, mother, or mother's owner. Under the prevailing laws, however, their fathers were responsible for them until age twelve.[23]

Was there a specific law that governed the determination of slave status in the French Antilles before 1685? Debbasch noted that Philippe Lonvilliers de Poincy, the *lieutenant général* of the French Antilles who arrived in the colonies in 1639, apparently declared that mixed-race individuals were to be considered slaves.[24] Debbasch, however, adopted Dutertre's position that subsequent governors were lenient with mixed-race individuals on the issue of status. Debbasch postulated that a retreat occurred after 1664 or thereabout when French colonies fell under the hegemony of metropolitan France and were no longer in the hands of proprietors. Mixed-race children were to be slaves of their mothers' owners until age twenty. It appears, however, that the law was not implemented and a natural father could immediately seek indemnity for his mixed-race child from its mother's owner, freeing the offspring by this act.

Debbasch argued that the *conseil souverain* (sovereign council) of Guadeloupe adopted Roman-Dutch law around 1680. Thereafter, colonial society developed along hierarchical lines based on race. Indeed, "After 1680, the frontier between natural liberty and servitude was determined by pure white and all those who possessed, however partially, the color black."[25] These principles, Debbasch writes, were soon formalized in the *Code noir* of 1685. There is no doubt that the code closed avenues to manumission, but the articles within it grew from the day-to-day situation in French colonies, where racism was reflected in colonial laws from as early as the 1660s. Institutionalized racism in French colonies existed before 1680.

The *Code noir* and Manumission

The *Code noir* established manumission in law, but in fact manumission, like libres de fait, already existed.[26] Before 1685, mixed-race individuals lived in a state of what Lucien Abénon has termed "ambiguity." Such people, Abénon noted, constituted a particular category in the Guadeloupe census of 1671, and most of the ninety-eight individuals listed were libres de fait.[27]

Under the *Code noir,* manumission could be obtained in several ways. An unmarried slave-owner who had a child or children by a slave concubine whom he owned was required by Article 9 to marry her in the Catholic church, freeing her and the child or children by this act.[28] Contravention of Article 47, which prohibited the breakup of a slave family in cases where the same person owned all its members and the children were minors (under fourteen), sometimes led to manumission of slaves as well.[29] And as long as slave-owners were twenty years of age they could free their slaves, according to Article 55.[30] In addition to these measures, marriage of free mixed-race males to slave women resulted in the liberation of the latter.[31] Moreover, the state freed slaves for meritorious actions such as defending the colonies against enemies.

In 1711, when Governor Raymond Balthazar Phélypeaux told the minister of marine and colonies that colonists were permitted to free their slaves when and how they pleased, he gave the impression that manumission could be obtained at will.[32] But that was not the case. Although the *Code noir* made manumission possible, amendments introduced after 1685 were restrictive and curbed the practice. These amendments, metropolitan and local, usually applied to all French colonies at one time or other. They were introduced largely out of fear of a growing free colored population whose numbers, although statistically small, were still seen as a threat to the established social and economic order.[33] In drafting legislation to limit manumission, therefore, French administrators used various pretexts, such as curbing abuse of the laws, reining in colonists who disrespected them, and ensuring that only those who met the requirements received manumission. This resulted in repeated attempts to renew and tighten legislation. From 1685 to around 1830, French authorities adopted a stringent attitude to manumission. A period of leniency followed but did not yield substantial results. Paradoxically, the effect of a tight policy of manumission was to increase the number of libres de fait as slave-owners turned increasingly to unofficial means of freeing slaves.

The earliest amendments to the *Code noir* were aimed at conjugal relations between white males and black and mixed-race women. In the late seventeenth century, a legislative document from Guadeloupe hinted at what was to come when it mentioned that for every one hundred slaves who were freed, only about five were freed for laudable motives. The others were favorite concubines and their children.[34] In 1777 instructions from the king of France to colonial administrators mentioned that concubinage was a primary means of acquiring manumission and that manumission should be limited and granted with discretion. The king believed that the advantages and disadvantages of the existence of a large number of free people in society should be considered.[35]

In a royal ordinance of 1713 that applied to the French colonies, Governor Phélypeaux of Martinique ruled that all slave-owners had to obtain written permission from the authorities whenever they wished to free slaves. He was concerned that slaves were paying their owners to set them free unofficially. In a comment aimed mostly at women a few years earlier, the governor mentioned that some slaves engaged in any activity, however infamous, to obtain manumission (a possible reference to prostitution):

> We must put a halt to this overly free method of manumitting slaves by introducing an ordinance that will henceforth prohibit any colonist from freeing a male or female slave . . . without the permission of the Governor General or the Intendant, who must first examine the reasons for manumission. If they determine that the reasons are justified, they will register the manumission with the [Superior] Council; if they find the reasons to be unacceptable, they will reject them, and the slave will not be granted freedom.[36]

The difficulty for slave-owners was that authorities would determine what constituted a legitimate demand.

A second amendment to the *Code noir* was a royal ordinance of 1736 for all the colonies. It reinforced the previous measure and carried the severe penalties of confiscation and sale of slaves, with proceeds going to the crown.[37] The clergy were also forbidden to baptize children of women of color as if they were free unless there was proof of free status.[38]

Renewal of these measures by an ordinance of 1768 in Martinique shows that they "had not had the desired effects." According to a report that described as "reprehensible" the action of persons who went before priests to baptize slave children as free, such action had "dangerous consequences." To remedy the situation the ordinance called for compliance with the ordinances of 1713 and 1736.[39] For baptisms to take place, the ordinance ruled, priests should verify that the mothers of black and mixed-race children who came before them had been baptized and had obtained freedom through administrative acts. Verification should be provided in writing from the governor or intendant and recorded in baptismal registers. The rule pertaining to verification also applied to notaries, who could not legitimize any act of liberty without abiding by it. Contravention of this particular measure carried a penalty of 1,000 *livres d'amende* and seizure of the notary's license for a year.[40] The 1768 ordinance also prohibited slaves from acquiring liberty somewhere outside the French colonies.[41]

By the late eighteenth century, administrative attention turned to verification of titles in Guadeloupe and Martinique and was aimed at people of color, most of them women. In Guadeloupe an ordinance, passed in 1761, was updated in 1774, and it carried virtually the same provisions as measures later adopted by Martinique in 1789.[42] In general, the measures sought to curb the libre de fait status, especially of independent slaves said to be disruptive of public order. These slaves apparently did not pay taxes, and neither did they donate money to the municipality, an undertaking to which all legitimately freed slaves were bound. The ordinance charged that these slaves, forced to satisfy their basic needs, became the source of various disorders that plagued society.[43]

During the first years of the nineteenth century the verification of titles remained an administrative preoccupation. It is as if the measures of the 1760s and later were never adopted. In 1803 authorities in Martinique set up tribunals and special commissions to assess titles that people of color were required to present to the courts within three months. Failure to comply within the prescribed period resulted in persons without proper papers being placed in the category *épaves* (derelicts), to be sold at auction for the benefit of the state.[44]

These measures were potentially disastrous for libres de fait, but it was the free people of color, mostly of mixed race, who acted first. Free for up to five generations, they were humiliated by the official emphasis on verification of titles.[45] They were now being lumped with people of servile status. The outrage they felt culminated in what became known as the "Bissette Affaire," which had important consequences for libres de fait.

For circulating a pamphlet entitled *De la situation des gens de couleur aux Antilles Françaises,* which denounced the disabilities and indignities that people of color in the French colonies endured, Cyrille Bissette and two other mixed-race males, Louis Fabien and Jean-Baptiste Volny, were condemned by the Royal Court of Martinique on January 12, 1824 to be branded in public with the letters *G.A.L.* and then sent to the galleys to serve life sentences with hard labor.[46] After a new hearing in 1827, however, Fabien and Volney were freed, but Bissette was banished for ten years.[47] The Bissette Affaire galvanized the mixed-race community. It drew attention to their plight and, to a lesser extent, to that of libres de fait.

At the time of the Bissette Affaire, unofficial manumission was still very common. A significant number of documented manumissions have been found in the notarial records of Guadeloupe for the period before 1830. One, dated July 1816, was outlined in the will of Monsieur le Pelletier de Liancourt, who indicated that he believed slaves were happier with partial liberty without administrative approval. He therefore granted the status of libre de fait to his former cook, Etienne, and to Etienne's wife, the slave Monique, who served as wet nurse to his children. He acknowledged that he had allowed them to live in a state of semifreedom for many years, which permitted them to tend their gardens beyond the ordinary. He also recommended that his successor should follow his example and only draw upon their services sparingly when in need.[48] He requested further that a similar status should be granted to the slaves Laurentine and Désirée when they reached age fifty as long as they continued to serve with zeal and loyalty. Because the male slave, Elie, continued to demonstrate enthusiasm in serving him, he, too, was to be granted the status. This method of granting liberty, he indicated, produced many excellent dependents without depriving him of services. Another unofficial manumission was that of Sophie and her daughter, Parfaite, of Basse-Terre. For their loyalty, the planter Moreau de Saint-Méry granted them their liberty on August 5, 1820.[49]

Amelioration of Slavery and Its Effects

During the last decades of slavery, amendments to slave laws made it possible for more libres de fait to gain outright freedom in the French colonies. The sociopolitical factors that led to changes in the law during this period are beyond the scope of this chapter, but two elements are worth attention. First, a new administration in France, the July Monarchy of 1830, was more willing to confront the problem of slavery, pushed, to some degree, by a stronger antislavery movement. Second, the plantation economies of the French Antilles became more integrated into the world market economy and declined as a result of increased competition.[50]

Colonial economies therefore experienced crisis during the 1830s, and the viability of the slave system was questioned. The result was an attempt at amelioration of slavery. Among the first new legislation introduced was a law of November 11, 1830, which abolished most discriminatory statutes to which gens de couleur had been subjected since the eighteenth century, including ones prohibiting the purchase of arms and the practice of specified professions such as medicine and surgery.

The French administration considered restoration of such rights a first step in gradually ameliorating slavery. That the amelioration of slavery should start with improving the condition of free coloreds rather than slaves may appear odd, but that strategy was probably the more expedient. The experience of Saint-Domingue, where shifting alliances among free coloreds proved detrimental to French efforts to win the war of liberation waged by slaves in the 1790s, was probably instructive.

Other measures of amelioration were directed at libres de fait in the French colonies. Under a royal ordinance of March 1, 1831, the fee for individual liberty patents, which cost as much as 3,000 French francs before 1831, was dropped. The measure facilitated freedom for slaves who had limited access to cash. A slave-owner, however, still had to assume responsibility for a slave's sustenance before an official patent could be issued. Victor Schoelcher has contended that this discouraged slave-owners from emancipating slaves.[51] The 1831 ordinance should also have made it easier for libres de fait to obtain clear titles, but Schoelcher's comment about the continuing influence of slave-owners can also be applied to them. The 1831 ordinance was followed by a royal decree of July 12, 1832 that permitted all categories of slaves not covered by previous legislation to bid for freedom through sponsorship by a patron, usually a slave-owner.[52]

The process of sponsorship appeared to offer quick and positive results, but there were hurdles. Indeed, the bureaucracy that colonial authorities established to carry out the legislation was cumbersome and lacked the power, if not the will, to deal with slave-owners who blocked or willfully delayed the process leading to emancipating their slaves. There is no doubt that slave-owners had the authority (and many of them used it) to manipulate the process to their advantage.

In Martinique and Guadeloupe, colonial authorities appointed a *directeur de patronage* (director of patronage) to administer the patronage system as a result of the 1832 legislation. This administrator acted as an intermediary between the authorities and the slaves. Regarded as the slaves' benefactor, he was assisted by a delegate or lieutenant in each parish or district. These assistants were required to keep registers of detailed information about slaves within their jurisdiction, including their age, gender, and profession. They were also charged with assessing the legitimacy of the slaves' claim to liberty. They submitted monthly reports to the directeur de patronage, who in turn sent detailed trimestrial reports to the governor of the colony. The governor reported to the minister of marine and colonies in Paris.

Depending on the nature of the slave's petition, the director of patronage also communicated and worked with other administrators, including the *procureur général* (attorney general), the chief legal officer in the colonies. The director of patronage sometimes corresponded with the *procureur du roi,* a legal representative of the crown, who assisted and was subordinate in rank to the attorney general. He thus acquired police reports from various towns and reports from mayors of rural communes. To ensure that the patronage system functioned as it should, the director of patronage was obliged to visit each district every six months, but it is unlikely that he did so.

A slave's bid for legally recognized freedom began in his or her respective district with a petition to the director of patronage, who could retain legal counsel or represent the slave before the judiciary. Proper documentation was required. For libres de fait, a major problem concerned a lack of proof of status, without which their names could not be inscribed legally in the provisional register open to public scrutiny. In 1832 a commission of inquiry raised concerns that any slave could claim to have the status of libre de fait, which could cause an exodus from plantations. To guard against that possibility, the commission recommended to the minister of marine and colonies that the status of libre de fait be conferred on all slaves presumed to have had the title—indeed, upon all who had irregular, nonfree status—and that they be required to present a certificate, signed by a justice of the peace in the presence of seven free property-holders, confirming their status. The commission also proposed that a three-month period of public announcements leading to liberation be established. Declarations confirming a slave's status and intention were to be posted in public places and printed at least three times in colonial newspapers. If there were no claims against the slave, or if such claims proved to be unfounded, the attorney general, who made the final decision, then authorized preparation of an *arrêté* (a decree that permitted the governor of the colony to inscribe the slave's name in the civil register).[53] Slave-owners opposed these new measures, as well as the additional powers granted to the attorney general, who would now play a greater role in determining free status. By their opposition, of course, slave-owners showed that they were still powerful and that the slaves were still vulnerable.[54]

Women of Color, Patronage, and the Growth of Libres de Fait

The decision to sponsor a slave did not spring from an obligation on the part of slave-owners. It was personal. Thus there were those libres de fait who had sponsorship and those who did not. The latter sometimes sponsored themselves, although it is unclear what that process involved. It is possible that self-sponsorship occurred when slaves had the means to sponsor themselves or were gainfully employed. Such was probably the case for two individuals from Guadeloupe in 1832, Etienne, forty-four, a black slave and proprietor in Habitans, and fifty-one-year-old Marguerite, who was employed at the vestry in Pointe-à-Pitre.[55]

Could slaves also sponsor themselves in cases of abandonment, or did they have to find a new sponsor? The sources offer no answers. However, when slave-owners who had sponsored slaves died before the process of liberation was complete, or if they left the colonies altogether, they put libres de fait in a vulnerable position, because if they ran afoul of the law and their owners could not be found they were considered derelict slaves whom the authorities could auction. Indeed, some slaves who were imprisoned in Martinique and Guadeloupe and whose owners could not be traced were likely libres de fait. In 1810 a black woman who had lived as a libre de fait for perhaps eight or nine years before the death of her mixed-race husband and former owner was arrested and put in the Pointe-à-Pitre prison as a derelict because she could not present freedom papers.[56] The resolution of her case involved, in essence, a reversion to slavery because such persons were subject to auction after two to three months in prison.

All categories of libre de fait sought emancipation under the 1832 measures. The demand for freedom papers, which can be gleaned from colonial newspapers, was high. The number of slaves granted freedom in Guadeloupe rose significantly after 1833 (table 3.1). From 1833 to 1837 the number of patents granted rose by a little more than 380 percent over the number for the period from 1830 to 1833. Of the 6,839 patents granted between 1833 and 1837, libres de fait accounted for 4,033, or 58.97 percent.[57] If Fallope's calculation of 7,576 (rather than Schoelcher's 8,637) is accepted as the number of slaves freed in Guadeloupe between 1833 and 1837, a difference of sixty-one slaves, the statistical picture does not change that much. All districts in Guadeloupe, however, experienced an increase in the number of slaves freed between 1833 and 1835, particularly the large urban communities of Pointe-à-Pitre and Basse-Terre.[58]

In general, most libres de fait who gained freedom were urban slaves. Also, the number of slaves freed, whether libres de fait or not, constituted only a small minority of the total slave population (table 3.2). The 3,190 slaves freed in Guadeloupe in 1833, the largest number by far for any year during the decade, represented only 3.2 percent of the total slave population. Abolitionists were quick to point out that the number of freed slaves was exaggerated and that slave-owners used the new legislation to get rid of or abandon old and disabled slaves who could scarcely make a living as free persons.[59]

Table 3.1. Number of Slaves Freed in Guadeloupe,
1830–37

Period	Number of Slaves
1830–33	1,798
1833–37	6,839
	8,637

Source: Victor Schoelcher, *Des colonies Françaises: Abolition
immédiate de l'esclavage* (1842, reprint Basse-Terre: Société
d'Histoire de la Guadeloupe, 1976), 308.

Table 3.2. Slave Populations of Martinique and
Guadeloupe, 1831–38

Year	Martinique	Guadeloupe
1831	86,300	97,300
1832	82,900	99,500
1833	79,800	99,000
1834	78,200	96,700
1835	78,100	96,300
1836	77,500	95,600
1837	76,000	94,600
1838	76,500	93,900

Source: Phillip Curtin, *The Atlantic Slave Trade: A Census*
(Madison: University of Wisconsin Press, 1969), 78.

Antislavery supporters did not always provide concrete evidence to back their allegations, but they were correct in asserting that the pace of liberation was too slow, particularly for field slaves. According to Jean-Baptiste Rouvellat de Cussac, a legal adviser attached to the Royal Court of Martinique and Guadeloupe from 1829 to the early 1840s, the ratio of freed slaves to slaves in Martinique was around 1:300 annually for 1837 and after, not including contraband slaves freed by the state.[60] Yet the response of the slaves to changes in the law should not be minimized. Indeed, an administrative report of 1835 pointed out that although there was confusion among slaves about the legal process of obtaining liberty papers, eight thousand demands had been received since the 1832 law was introduced.[61]

Claims for liberty among libres de fait cut across age groups, and women made the overwhelming number of requests. Does this mean that slave-owners were reluctant to sponsor male slaves? A significant number of sponsored slaves were mixed-race women and their children and, to a lesser degree, black women and their mixed-race children. To be sure, women of color and their children usually accounted for at least two-thirds of the individuals whose names were listed in the colonial newspapers. The patrons of these women of color were almost always white males. That cannot be coincidental. Most often, these males owned the women, and they were sometimes also the father of their children, whom they also owned, by virtue of a slave law under which children of slave women belonged to their mothers' owners. Sponsorship of women of color by white males who had power over them may have involved sexual exploitation that was common during slavery. Only a minority of male slaves received sponsorship from white women. Moreover, requests for liberty from male slaves seldom included children.

Slave women and children were sponsored directly or indirectly by white males. In 1834 Rosette, a washerwoman aged forty-eight, along with her mixed-race daughter Cécile, nineteen, were sponsored by Pierre Xavier Ruffi Belleville, a plantation overseer from St. Pierre, Martinique. That same year, François St. Catherine sponsored Archil-Victoire, a thirty-nine-year-old mixed-race washerwoman, and Joseph Albert of Basse-Pointe, Martinique, authorized his wife to sponsor a fourteen-month-old mixed-race child, Sebastien (Etor).[62] In 1837 Louis Numa of Fort-Royal, Martinique, sponsored the mixed-race slave La Pearl (Florine), a seamstress.[63] In 1844 the thirty-seven-year-old mixed-race seamstress Louise and her mixed-race son Celse-Léon, libres de fait, received their freedom through sponsorship by Alexandre Berne, a merchant in St. Pierre who owned them.[64] In Guadeloupe in 1832, Marcel (Cotreau) from Petit-Bourg sponsored Sophie, fifty-one and of mixed race, and her four children who ranged in age from thirteen to nineteen, as well as her two grandchildren, one four years old and the other eighteen months. That same year, Jacques Paricard of Pointe-à-Pitre sponsored Eloise, thirty-eight, who was of mixed race, and her children, Marie-Louise, nine, and Jean-Elie, five, as well as her four-month-old twins, Joseph and Marie-Joséphine.[65]

The number of elderly slaves, mainly women of color, who sought liberty patents under the 1832 law is noteworthy and shows that freedom was desirable at any age. In 1833 the slave Petrus, seventy-six, received sponsorship from Colette Grimchaud, a seamstress who owned him in Guadeloupe.[66] Sponsored by Ann, the Ibo slave Agathé, ninety-six, received her freedom in Martinique in 1834.[67] In 1836 the slave Charlotte, a nurse aged eighty-five, asked for her freedom from her women owners, Valéry Garrou and Carré from Mouillage in Saint-Pierre, Martinique.[68] In 1837 the mixed-race slave Victoire (Zoboyo), eighty-one, was granted her freedom in Martinique "under the provisions of the July 12, 1832 law, as she was one of the *libres de fait*."[69]

Down to the end of slavery in 1848, requests for liberty patents from libres de fait remained strong in spite of opposition from some colonists who sponsored slaves for freedom but did little to see the process through to a conclusion. In 1835 the privy council of Martinique threatened to impose a fine of 41 to 60 livres on slave-owners who, as of March 1, 1836, failed to show progress in such cases.[70] Thus, the difficulties of obtaining freedom through sponsorship by patrons notwithstanding, women of color in particular still took advantage of the opportunity provided by the 1832 law.

The case of Marie Louise, a slave of Martinique, demonstrates that libres de fait used ingenuity to gain outright freedom. In a will probated on October 23, 1831, Laïs, an abbot in the district of Lamentin, bequeathed that Marie Louise and her children (Creole male and female slaves) be granted the status of libre de fait. This he did in the belief that with hard work they would eventually free themselves from slavery through self-purchase. The abbot's request was not honored, however. With the authorization of a judge, the abbot's nephew sold the slave family. That the judiciary viewed Marie Louise and her children as heritable property reveals the vulnerability of libres de fait. The family benefited, however, from an 1833 ruling by the Royal Court of Martinique that made it more difficult for the bequests of testators to be ignored.

The family now lacked sponsorship, but that was provided by Toussaint, a former libre de fait who had been free for some time. With the help of appropriate civil servants, Toussaint succeeded in the civil registers of two different districts, Fort-Royal and Lamentin, when only one such inscription was required and permitted. The act of inscription meant that the process of liberation was complete. Was Toussaint fully aware of the process that sponsors who wanted to free slaves had to follow, a process outlined in the 1832 measures, or did he intentionally ignore it? It appears that the names of the slave family were inscribed in the registers, but they were not previously advertised in colonial newspapers as the 1832 regulations required. In any case, Toussaint's actions led to Marie Louise's freedom and that of two of her children, Fortuné, twelve, and Céraline (Bridgette), eight, on May 9, 1834.

Information that came to light after this freedom was granted revealed that Toussaint had profited from cracks in the system. Indeed, the procureur du roi only became aware of the dual inscription when Geneviève Félicité, Marie Louise's former owner, contested her manumission and sought his support. Because the procureur du roi did not know about the dual inscription and was embarrassed by its revelation, he did not inform the attorney general of Félicité's challenge. Caught off-guard, French authorities called the dual inscription theft and fraud, citing the many discrepancies in the two listings.[71]

The dual inscription became the object of administrative scrutiny. The inscriptions in the Fort-Royal and Lamentin records were not identical. There were differences in age and sex of some members of the family, including Marie-Louise herself, who appeared as fifty-eight in the Fort-Royal register and forty in the Lamentin register. Moreover, her daughter, Fortuné, was listed as a thirteen-year-old female at Fort-Royal and as a twelve-year-old male at Lamentin. As for her alleged son, Nicolas, thirty-three, he vanished from the Lamentin register altogether.

The embarrassed authorities blamed inexperienced civil servants for not being more vigilant and for failing to record discrepancies in the margins of the registers, a common administrative practice. But the chaotic state of plantation records would not have allowed these clerks to determine the age of Marie Louise and her children. Neither would the clerks have known the gender of Fortuné unless the slave family appeared before them in person, an unlikely prospect. In this case the question of civil rights appears to have played an important role in the decision to uphold Marie-Louise's freedom.

In the end, the main question was whether, having been freed in Lamentin, Marie-Louise and her children could be reenslaved in spite of the protection their new status afforded them under the civil code of Martinique. The authorities were aware also that her case was not an isolated one. After 1832 libres de fait who had unclear identity had their names inscribed in registers in different districts.[72]

It may well be that for libres de fait multiple inscriptions were a way to ensure that freedom would be achieved, if not in one district then in another. They probably profited from their unofficial status by adding the names of relatives or close acquaintances to registers if they could. Because requests for manumission appeared in colonial papers and were listed by district, it was possible for officials to cross-check listings although such work would have required additional personnel. Ultimately, the volume of requests for liberation overwhelmed the administration during the period when Marie-Louise's proceedings were taking place.

The children of libres de fait may have used their mothers' status to gain advantages. In 1820 the mixed-race male slave Jahan complained to Martinique authorities about the physical abuse he received from newly engaged staff on the plantation de Haumont, and he asked to be freed from bondage to escape it. This was not an unusual request. The authorities of Martinique and Guadeloupe sometimes deprived slave-owners of their slaves for being cruel to them. But Monsieur de Haumont, owner of the plantation, refused to grant Jahan's wish on the grounds that it would set a dangerous precedent and was also manipulative. De Haumont took this decision even though Jahan's mother, a libre de savane who behaved "as if she had her legal freedom," was his concubine.[73]

An investigation showed that Jahan's charges were legitimate, but the authorities sided with de Haumont, a recent proprietor, as was often the case when slaves challenged their owners. The authorities recommended, however, that de Haumont and Jahan's mother, both of whom were away from Martinique when the judgment was handed down, must remain out of the colony for six months so calm could be restored on the plantation. De Haumont was victorious, but the authorities advised him to consider making a conciliatory gesture to Jahan's mother even though he was not the father of her son. Thus, although Jahan was given no special consideration, the sentiments of the authorities suggested that women of color with the status *libre de fait* and who were the concubines of white males deserved some consolation.

Male libres de fait were probably as vulnerable as females, as in the following case. Félix Félicien, a libre de fait and fireman of St. Pierre, Martinique, since 1828, had a disagreement with a white male who reported him to the procureur du roi, who then had him arrested and imprisoned. Without a trial, and on the

orders of the procureur du doi, Félicien was placed in the *quatre piquets* position, face down on the ground with his hands and feet tied to four iron stakes,
and given twenty-nine lashes, the maximum number allowed. When the time
came for prison costs to be paid, an expense slave-owners normally bore, the
procureur du roi discovered that Félicien was a libre de fait who ought not to
have received such treatment. Consequently, he requested that the prison war-
den pay Félicien the equivalent of the cost of his whipping and incarceration.
The whipping cost 1 franc, 70 centimes; five days in prison as a slave at 85 centimes per day amounted to 4 francs, 25 centimes; and one day as a libre de fait,
the day the procureur du roi made the discovery, was valued at 1 franc, 25 centimes.[74] It seems odd that the procureur du roi did not know that Félicien was
at least a libre de fait, because it is unlikely that slaves held positions of firemen.
Also, Félix Félicien carried a first and last name, whereas the vast majority of
slaves possessed only first names. Could the procureur du roi have known of
Félicien's status and ignored it so as to teach him a lesson?

In regard to criminal justice, libres de fait appear to have received no special
consideration throughout the slave period. There are too many cases where such
persons committed the same crimes as free people but were more severely punished. In May 1832, Jean-Louis, a libre de fait, along with Bertrand, a free person, and Séraphin, a slave, were condemned by the Royal Court of Martinique
for stealing sugar cane at night. In citing Article 36 of the *Code noir,* which stated
that theft by slaves of items (including sugar cane) should be punished according to the nature of the theft, the judiciary applied slave law to both Seraphin,
and Jean-Louis.[75] The court sentenced Seraphin to a whipping of twenty-nine
lashes, to be administered in public by the prison director, and it imposed one-
third of the court costs on Bertrand. Jean-Louis was also forced to pay one-third
of the court costs, but he received a two-year prison term as well.[76]

The possibility of gaining liberation increased with the introduction of a new
law of June 11, 1839, but the effect was very limited. Under the new law, slaves
could be sponsored by free relations, including spouses and biological and adop-
tive parents. That arrangement, however, required approval of slave-owners who
often opposed it, particularly when slaves had committed "infamous" offenses
(those that required correctional punishment amounting to the maximum
number of lashes permitted by law).[77] It is also likely that slave-owners opposed
the law because of the potential loss of control over the process of liberation.

Yet freedom via sponsorship by relatives appears to have pre-dated 1839. Cases
of family sponsorship exist, but they are not numerous. In 1832, Zabeth, a spinster, sponsored her eight-month-old colored daughter, Annaise, a libre de fait.[78]
Zabeth's status was not revealed, but it is likely that she was a slave, given the
status of her infant daughter. Likewise, Jeanne, a thirty-six-year-old cleaning
woman who had four colored children, sponsored two of them, both artisans:
Jean Baptiste Ferdinand, sixteen, and Chérubin, eighteen. The case is striking
because Jeanne and her two other children, aged four and fourteen, were co-

sponsored by a white male, Danglebermes, and by Jeanne herself.[79] Because she and her children were libres de fait, she must have been a slave, and therefore she would not qualify, at least on her own, as a legitimate sponsor.

In general, the 1839 law had much less effect than the law of 1832. Indeed, the 1839 law would only have been effective had the population of free coloreds been large enough to provide a significant pool of individuals who could act as sponsors. Thus the following contemporary observation by Rouvellat de Cussac is apt: "No one has ever seen a free person contract marriage with a slave in the last fifty years or so. Neither has any one seen a slave legally adopted by his master or another free person. Common sense dictates that whoever wishes to adopt or marry a slave should first free that slave."[80]

Libres de Fait in Society

The effects of all the legal changes on libres de fait may be evident enough from 1832 onward, but little is known about their daily lives. The work they performed offers some insights, however. For the most part, libres de fait did the same work as free people of color. They were field-workers, both on plantations where they were once enslaved and on other plantations. As many cases of sponsorship showed, some libres de fait women were seamstresses, a popular occupation among women of color in slavery and in freedom. Libres de fait women were also domestics, general laborers, merchants, and tavern keepers. Libres de fait who remained on plantations were generally allotted larger garden plots than slaves to grow their own produce, and they were given more time (Saturdays and Sundays on some plantations) to tend them. Indeed, some of their garden plots resembled small farms. Debien argued that this gave some degree of economic autonomy to libres de fait who worked in agriculture and a different character to bondage that was more akin to serfdom than to slavery.[81]

It is likely that some libres de fait worked in agriculture away from the plantation where they were once enslaved. In a study dealing with labor in the French Antilles during the 1840s, Jacques Adélaïde-Merlande found that a significant number of people of color, both slave and free, worked for wages in the agricultural sector. A large number of slaves were rented out to proprietors by their owners. It is possible that some were libres de fait, because renting out libres de fait was very common among slave-owners. Among the free workers there may have been those who were former libres de fait. In the early 1840s, seven hundred slaves rented themselves out in Gros Morne, Martinique, and most of them were engaged in agricultural work. They earned 2 to 2½ francs per day and were left with 1 to 1½ francs after they paid their owners a share of their earnings. On a plantation owned by Monsieur Barada in French Guiana, a free woman of color made at least 200 francs per year doing task work in 1843.[82] Domestics, too, did task work. Many of them rented their own dwellings in the town of St. Pierre.[83]

Most libres de fait were quite mobile people whose life-styles, Debien reports, were highly sought after by those in bondage. For some libres de fait, however, life was tenuous. There were petty traders among them who went from plantation to plantation to sell knick-knacks and trinkets "indispensable to women's appearance." The assortment of goods they carried was chosen and paid for by the slave-owners, who either took a part of the profits or a fixed daily sum from the slave.[84] Among these commodities, which Moreau de Jonnès called *"objets de mode,"* was madras fabric, still an item of cultural significance in the French Antilles, which slaves sold at marked-up prices.[85] Debien made this form of trading sound easy, advantageous, and beneficial to all when he noted that "a smooth-talking, clever black male could do a brisk business. One [the slave] had his freedom; the other [the slave-owner] gained resources, and everyone was content except the administration which grumbled."[86]

Likewise, Moreau de Jonnès indicated that such commercial activities helped libres de fait purchase their freedom in little time. Could that really have been true, considering the vagaries of the market place, the limited access to cash of ordinary plantation slaves, and the relatively low number of libres de fait who acquired outright freedom? Petty traders may well have targeted specific groups on plantations and transacted business with them, but there was no guarantee of bright prospects on a daily basis. Whatever the case, the onus was on libres de fait to turn a profit. De Jonnès acknowledged that some who were domestics had difficulty settling accounts with their owners, but, he contended, the number of libres de fait was low because emancipation was approaching by the late 1840s, and many did not care to spend money on the process.[87] Manumission, however, remained popular among all age groups until the end of slavery in 1848.

It is difficult to determine what resources libres de fait had at their disposal, given the constraints that obligations to their owners placed upon them. Their owners, not they, were legally required to pay taxes that amounted to 18 francs 13 centimes (30 *livres coloniales*) per head by 1804.[88] But the obligations of libres de fait were probably heavier. They could not renege on obligations to owners, whereas owners could refuse to pay taxes. Rouvellat de Cussac knew several sixty-to-seventy-year-old female libres de fait of Fort-Royal (now Fort-de-France, Martinique) who were obligated to remit 15 to 20 francs per month to their owners. In March 1844 he encountered several elderly women of color in this age group who were doing task work at Fort-Bourbon. They earned 25 to 30 *sous* per day, carrying on their heads tubs of earth that were passed on to other women who also carried mortar and rocks.[89]

Other French sources paint a general picture of struggle for libres de fait. Administrative reports from Martinique are not that informative about those who rented boutiques and rooms, particularly in the town of St. Pierre where doing so was common, but they categorize most of the rooms as brothels and hideouts for maroons or fugitive slaves and petty criminals. In 1765 the Superior Council of Martinique, acting on a series of complaints regarding the rent-

ing out of slaves, prohibited slave-owners from permitting their slaves to wan-
der about on their own or to rent dwellings on the pretext of carrying on a
business or other activities. Those who disobeyed the law faced confiscation of
the slaves and the effects found on them, as well as other penalties. In addition,
the council prohibited all property owners from renting or subletting rooms and
boutiques to male and female slaves. A first conviction carried a penalty of 500
livres d'amende, half going to the informer and the other half to the public treasury. Although not specified, the penalty for a second conviction was to be much
stiffer. At the same time, the council made an exception for slaves who, by virtue of their profession, could not be supervised by their owners.[90] The renewal
of some of these provisions in 1803, when slave-owners were again forbidden
to allow slaves to keep dwellings under the pretext of carrying on commerce,
shows that the laws were not obeyed.[91]

The town of St. Pierre in Martinique also contained many bars and nightclubs, but it is not clear what role libres de fait played in such establishments. It
is possible that women of color ran them.[92] These places, however, which remained the target of administrative scrutiny down to the nineteenth century,
were forbidden to serve blacks. In 1794 Martinique authorities renewed an ordinance of 1763 that emphasized the need for proper licensing to serve liquor,
and they placed limits on the number of bars and nightclubs and their hours
of operation.[93] Some of these measures were renewed in 1804.[94]

Aside from participating in establishments geared to entertainment, urban
libres de fait formed slave associations that had their own flags, kings and
queens, and emblems (usually flowers). In the district of Moule in Guadeloupe
the associations were named Grenat, Corail, and Violette. In Martinique during the 1840s there were seventeen associations at Fort-Royal and seventeen at
St. Pierre. The associations were, in fact, mutual aid societies that held public
dances and fetes. Proceeds were used to assist members in times of trouble and
distress; for example, they were assured a decent funeral. During the 1840s,
authorities in Martinique feared the influence that libres de fait exercised in
these associations. Women of color were particularly dominant, and free
women of color who led some associations carried such titles as "woman of
honor." However, the "queen of one such association located in Petit-Bourg
in Guadeloupe around 1845 was a slave."[95]

Authorities feared subversion but dared not suppress associations.[96] In Guadeloupe, planters objected to an idea put forward by priests that associations
should become religious bodies headed by saints, but they refrained from attacking the associations because of their large membership.[97] Membership in
such associations can be taken to indicate a significant level of social and political consciousness among libres de fait nurtured by the sociological and political underpinnings of their condition.

From the promulgation of the *Code noir* in 1685 to the end of slavery in the
French colonial empire in 1848, most slaves who acquired libre de fait status in

Martinique and Guadeloupe were mixed-race Creole women of color along with their children. Although libre de fait status fell short of complete and legal manumission, statistics reveal a strong demand for this status, particularly after 1832 when legislation made sponsorship possible. Colored women of all ages profited from changes in legislation to obtain libre de fait status, but the overwhelming majority of them were young women who had close domestic associations with slave-owners. Thus it would be easy to highlight the exploitation of libres de fait to which this situation gave rise. These persons were certainly vulnerable, and they lived precarious lives on the margins of freedom. But libres de fait women in particular played an active economic role in urban sectors of Martinique and Guadeloupe as domestics, seamstresses, and petty traders. Most of all, the mutual aid societies they helped create, and in which they played active roles as leaders, entertainers, and fund-raisers, were instrumental in promoting social welfare among slaves and helping them acquire freedom. This level of social and political consciousness indicates that the men and women of color who had libre de fait status contributed far more to the development of society in Martinique and Guadeloupe than French sources have revealed thus far.

Notes

1. Gabriel Debien, "Les colons des Antilles et leur main d'oeuvre à la fin du XVIIIe siècle," *Annales Historiques de la Révolution Française* 27 (1955): 275.

2. See, for example, Emile Hyot, *Les gens de couleur libres du Fort-Royal, 1679–1823* (Paris: Société française d'histoire d'Outre-Mer, 1971); Auguste Lebeau, *De la condition des gens de couleur libres sous l'ancien régime* (Paris: Guillaumin, 1903); Jean Terrade, "Affranchis et gens de couleur libres à la fin du XVIIIe siècle d'après les minutes *notaires*," *Revue Française d'Histoire d'Outre-mer* 49, no. 1 (1974): 80–116; and David Geggus, "Esclaves et gens de couleur libres de la Martinique pendant l'époque révolutionnaire napoléonienne: trois instants de résistance," *Revue Historique* 295–96, no. 597 (1996): 105–32.

3. Victor Schoelcher, *Des colonies Françaises: Abolition immédiate de l'esclavage* (1842, reprint Basse-Terre: Société d'Histoire de la Guadeloupe, 1976); Augustin Cochin, *L'abolition de l'esclavage,* 2 vols. (Paris: J. LeCoffre, 1861); P. Baude, *L'affranchissement des esclaves aux Antilles Françaises, principalement en Martinique, du début de la colonisation à 1848* (Fort-de-France: n.p., 1948).

4. Arlette Gautier, *Les soeurs de solitude: La condition féminine dans l'esclavage aux Antilles du XVIIe au XIXe siècle* (Paris: Editions Caribéennes, 1985), 172–73; see also Gabriel Debien, *Les esclaves aux Antilles françaises XVIIe-XVIIIe siècles* (Basse-Terre: Société d'Histoire de la Guadeloupe, 1974), 148; and Nicole Vanany-Frisch, "Les esclaves de la Guadeloupe à la fin de l'ancien régime d'après les sources notariales (1770–1789)," *Bulletin de la Société d'Histoire de la Guadeloupe,* nos. 63–64 (1985): 87.

5. Léo Elisabeth, "The French Antilles," in *Neither Slave nor Free: The Freedmen of African Descent in the Slave Societies of the New World,* ed. David W. Cohen and Jack P. Greene (Baltimore: Johns Hopkins University Press, 1972), 145.

6. Léo Elisabeth, "La société Martiniquaise aux XVIIème et XVIIIème siècles, 1664–1789," 2 vols., Ph.D. diss., University of Paris, 1989, 2: 607.

7. Josette Fallope, "Les affranchissements d'esclaves à la Guadeloupe entre 1818 et 1848," *Annales de l'Université d'Abidjan,* ser. 1, vol. 6 (1978): 5–32.

8. For a detailed treatment of French Caribbean historiography with particular emphasis on

gender, see Bernard Moitt, *Women and Slavery in the French Antilles* (Bloomington: Indiana University Press, 2001), xiii–xviii.

9. Baude, *L'affranchissement des esclaves aux Antilles Françaises*, 41.

10. Ibid., 37.

11. Schoelcher, *Des colonies Françaises*, 306.

12. Ibid.

13. Debien, "Les colons des Antilles," 275.

14. Schoelcher, *Des colonies Françaises*, 10.

15. Fallope, "Les affranchissements d'esclaves à la Guadeloupe," 10.

16. Baude, *L'affranchissement des esclaves aux Antilles Françaises*, 20.

17. Fallope, "Les affranchissements d'esclaves à la Guadeloupe," 7; Debien, "Les colons des Antilles," 275.

18. Sue Peabody, *"There Are No Slaves in France": The Political Culture of Race and Slavery in the Ancien Régime* (New York: Oxford University Press, 1996), 6.

19. Fallope, "Les affranchissements d'esclaves à la Guadeloupe," 8.

20. Archives Nationales, Section d'Outre-Mer, Aix en Province, France (hereafter ANSOM), Fonds Généralités, carton 660, dossier 2843, July 24, 1832.

21. *Le code noir ou Receuil des règlements rendus jusqu'à présent* (1685, reprint Basse-Terre: Société d'Histoire de la Guadeloupe, 1980).

22. Jean Baptiste Dutertre, *Histoire générale des Antilles habitées par les Français*, 4 vols., (1667–1761, reprint Fort-de-France: Editions des Horizons Caraïbes, 1973), 2: 478.

23. Dutertre, *Histoire*, 2: 479.

24. Ivan Debbasch, *Couleur et liberté: Le jeu du critère ethnique dans un ordre juridique eslavagiste*, 2 vols. (Paris: Dalloz, 1967), 1: 22–23.

25. Debbasch, *Couleur et liberté*, 23–27.

26. Adrien Dessalles, *Les annales du Conseil Souverain de la Martinique*, 2 vols. (1786, reprint, Paris: L'Harmattan, 1995), 1: 374.

27. Lucien Abénon, *La Guadeloupe de 1671 à 1759: Étude politique, écomique et sociale*, 2 vols. (Paris: L'Harmattan, 1987), 1: 33, 1: 55.

28. *Code noir*, 33–34.

29. Ibid., 51.

30. Ibid., 55.

31. Fallope, "Les affranchissements d'esclaves à la Guadeloupe," 8.

32. Archives Nationales Colonies, Paris, France (hereafter ANC), 8A 18 F 18, June 3, 1711.

33. Adrien Dessalles, *Histoire générale des Antilles*, 5 vols. (Paris: Libraire-Editeur, 1847), 3: 418–19; Geggus, "Esclaves et gens de couleur," 105.

34. Cited in Baude, "L'affranchissement des esclaves aux Antilles Françaises," 19.

35. Cited in Dessalles, *Histoire générale des Antilles*, 3: 416; also cited in Baude, L'affranchissement des esclaves aux Antilles Françaises," 23.

36. ANC, 8A 18, F18, June 3, 1711.

37. ANSOM, Fonds Généralités, carton 666, dossier 2845, July 12, 1832.

38. Dessalles, *Les annales du Conseil Souverain*, 1: 374–75; Baude, L'affranchissement des esclaves aux Antilles Françaises," 22.

39. "Ordonnance de MM. les Général et Intendant concernant les soi-disant libres et les libertés non-registrées," Sept. 10, 1789, in M. Durand-Molard, *Code de la Martinique*, 5 vols. (St. Pierre: Impr. de J.-B. Thounens, fils, 1807–14), 4: 157.

40. The worth of currencies used in the French Antilles during slavery is hard to estimate because there was a lack of standardization in currency exchange before the law enacted on August 30, 1826, that made the French franc the predominant currency. In the eighteenth century, the colonial livre was worth about 20 sols; 1 sol was worth about 12 deniers (about 12 cents U.S.). The

expression *livre d'amende* was used when fines were imposed (hence "amende"). Moitt, *Women and Slavery*, 178n29.

41. "Ordonnance de M. les Général et Intendant," 2: 558–59.

42. Gérard Lafleur, *Saint-Claude: Histoire d'une commune de Guadeloupe* (Paris: Karthala, 1993), 80.

43. "Ordonnance de MM. les Général et Intendant concernant les soi-disant libres et les libertés non-registrées," Sept. 10, 1789, 157.

44. *Gazette de la Martinique*, March 26, 1803, 91–93; "Arrêté qui donne la vérification des titres dont se trouvent porteurs les gens de couleur libres," March 15, 1803, in M. Durand-Molard, *Code de la Martinique*, 5 vols. (St. Pierre: Impr. de J.-B. Thounens, fils, 1807–14), n.p.

45. Lafleur, *Saint-Claude*, 17.

46. Eric Mesnard, "Les mouvements de résistance dans les colonies Françaises: L'Affaire Bissette, 1823–1827," in *Les abolitions de l'esclavage de L.F. Sonthonax à V. Schoelcer*, ed. Marcel Dorigny (Paris: UNESCO, 1995), 295.

47. This pamphlet can be found in ANSOM, Fonds Généralités, Martinique, carton 51, dossier 420, Paris, 1823.

48. Fallope, "Les affranchissements d'esclaves à la Guadeloupe," 12.

49. Ibid., 12–13.

50. Josette Fallope, *Esclaves et citoyens: Les noirs à la Guadeloupe au XIXe siècle* (Basse-Terre: Société d'histoire de la Guadeloupe, 1992), 247–49, 286; Dale Tomich, *Slavery in the Circuit of Sugar: Martinique and the World Economy* (Baltimore: Johns Hopkins University Press, 1990), 53–75; Christian Schnakenbourg, *Histoire de l'industrie sucrière en Guadeloupe (XIX–XX siècles): La crise du système esclavagiste* (Paris: L'Harmattan, 1980), 124–36.

51. Schoelcher, *Des colonies Françaises*, 305.

52. Ibid., 304.

53. ANSOM, Fonds Généralités, carton 660, dossier 2843, July 24, 1832.

54. Fallope, *Esclaves et citoyens*, 288.

55. *Gazette Officielle de la Guadeloupe*, Jan. 5, 1832, 2.

56. *Gazette Officielle de la Guadeloupe*, Sept. 30, 1810, 2.

57. Schoelcher, *Des colonies Françaises*, 308.

58. Fallope, *Esclaves et citoyens*, 296.

59. Schoelcher, *Des colonies Françaises*, 308–9; Jean-Baptiste Rouvellat de Cussac, *Situation des esclaves dans les colonies Françaises* (Paris: Pagnerre, 1845), 135–36, 150–51.

60. Rouvellat de Cussac, *Situation des esclaves*, 151.

61. AMSOM, carton 666, dossier 2845, Fort Royal, Feb. 15, 1835.

62. *Journal Officiel de la Martinique*, April 19, 1834, 1.

63. *Journal Officiel de la Martinique*, March 11, 1837, 1.

64. *Journal Officiel de la Martinique*, March 2, 1844, 1.

65. *Gazette Officielle de la Guadeloupe*, Jan. 5, 1832, 3.

66. *Gazette Officielle de la Guadeloupe*, Jan. 5, 1833, 3.

67. *Journal Officiel de la Martinique*, July 16, 1834, 1.

68. *Journal Officiel de la Martinique*, Jan. 30, 1836, 1.

69. *Journal Officiel de la Martinique*, Jan. 4, 1837, 1.

70. ANSOM, Fonds Généralités, carton 666, dossier 2845, Extrait du Conseil Privé, Martinique, Dec. 1835.

71. AMSOM, Fonds Généralités, carton 666, dossier 2845, Fort-Royal, Aug. 26, 1833, March 6, 1834.

72. ANSOM, Fonds Généralités, carton 666, dossier 2845, Paris, May 29, 1835.

73. Archives Départmentales de la Martinique (hereafter ADM), 33, 281, July 21, 1820.

74. Victor Schoelcher, *De l'esclavage des noirs et de la législation coloniale* (Paris: Paulin, 1833), 24–25.

75. *Code noir,* 46.

76. Hearing of May 9, 1832, series U, Arrêts correctionnels (1832–33), Archives Départementales de la Martinique.

77. Fallope, *Esclaves et citoyens,* 290.

78. *Journal Officiel de la Martinique,* March 26, 1834, 1.

79. *Journal Officiel de la Martinique,* April 5, 1834, 1.

80. Rouvellat de Cussac, *Situation des esclaves,* 134.

81. Debien, "Les colons des Antilles," 275.

82. Jacques Adélaïde-Merlande, "Problématique d'une histoire de l'esclavage urbain: Guadeloupe, Guyane, Martinique (vers 1815–1848), *Bulletin de la Société d'Histoire de la Guadeloupe* 65–66 (1985): 3–23; "Travail libre et travail servile (Antilles et Guyane françaises, 1840–1848)," *Bulletin de la Société d'Histoire de la Guadeloupe* 75–78 (1988): 9.

83. Adélaïde-Merlande, "Problématique d'une histoire," 19.

84. Debien, "Les colons des Antilles," 275.

85. A. Moreau de Jonnès, *Recherches statistiques sur l'esclavage colonial et sur les moyens de le supprimer* (Paris: Bourgagne et Martinet, 1842), 127.

86. Debien, "Les colons des Antilles," 275.

87. Moreau de Jonnès, *Recherches statistiques,* 128.

88. *Gazette de la Martinique,* Oct. 22, 1804.

89. Rouvellat de Cussac, *Situation des esclaves,* 18.

90. ANC, Colonies, C 8A 67 F40, Aug. 11, 1765.

91. *Gazette de la Martinique,* March 16, 1803.

92. Moreau de Jonnès, *Recherches statistiques,* 128.

93. "Proclamation de son excellence le gouverneur général, concernant les cabarettiers," May 13, 1794, in M. Durand-Molard, *Code de la Martinique,* 5 vols. (St. Pierre: Impr. de J.-B. Thounens, fils, 1807–14), 4: 257.

94. *Gazette de la Martinique,* Oct. 22, 1804.

95. Bernard Moitt, "Slave Women and Resistance in the French Caribbean," in *More Than Chattel: Black Women and Slavery in the Americas,* ed. David Barry Gaspar and Darlene Clark Hine (Bloomington: Indiana University Press, 1996), 254; Moitt, *Women and Slavery,* 125–50.

96. Adélaïde-Merlande, "Problématique d'une histoire," 20.

97. M. L'abbé Dugoujon, *Lettre sur l'esclavage* (Paris: 1845), 94–95.

CHAPTER 4

"To Be Free Is Very Sweet":
The Manumission of Female Slaves
in Antigua, 1817–26

David Barry Gaspar

By 1823 the antislavery campaign in Britain reached a significant milestone when Parliament supported a new attempt to ameliorate slavery by legislation in the colonies. An earlier attempt at amelioration had been launched during the 1780s and 1790s. It was aimed at achieving sufficient improvement in the conditions of slavery through several measures, including some of a pronatalist variety, to reduce, if not to eliminate, reliance on the slave trade. The amelioration strategies followed in the colonies generally strengthened slavery. The colonial plantocracy was therefore able to survive many of the effects of the abolition of the slave trade in 1808. That valuable trade may have been lost, but slavery continued to flourish, and by the 1820s antislavery interests in Britain began an organized effort that would lead gradually to the abolition of slavery itself.[1]

On May 15, 1823, the House of Commons adopted several resolutions in support of measures to prepare slaves for freedom through "a determined and persevering, but judicious and temperate enforcement." One resolution was related to the manumission of slaves. On July 9, 1823, the secretary of state, Lord Bathurst addressed a circular despatch to the governors of the Caribbean colonies where there were representative legislatures in which he detailed the importance of the parliamentary resolutions. In regard to manumission, Bathurst indicated that the legislatures should take steps to remove "every unnecessary obstacle." The governor and legislature of Antigua (the leading colony within the group known as the British Leeward Islands) received such instructions, and in subsequent years the colony organized its own particular response.[2]

The main concern of this study is to explore the character of the manumission of slaves in Antigua, mainly for the period from 1817 to 1826. The manumission lists and other data for these years will be analyzed with special reference to female slaves, and an attempt will be made to uncover how manumitted females fared in their new lives as free persons.

When imperial authorities began to exert pressure on the Antigua legislature to reform the colony's system of slavery, this colonial body, supported by many leading pro-slavery planters and other whites, pointed out that several of the suggested reform measures had already been anticipated in the legislation and common practice of the enlightened colony. The most important source of reform was the Leeward Islands Slavery Amelioration Act of 1798, which the General Council and Assembly of the islands brought into existence during a special series of meetings at the island of St. Christopher. Under this act a wide variety of ameliorative measures was adopted that were "best calculated to obviate the Causes which hitherto may have impeded the natural Increase of Negroes already in these Islands . . . to diminish the Necessity of the Slave Trade, and ultimately to lead to its final termination." At the same time, though, legislators were careful that amelioration should not subvert "that good Order, Discipline, and Obedience, which it is absolutely necessary to preserve and maintain." The act, in stressing the wisdom of humane treatment of the slaves, was actually meant to strengthen slavery by getting rid of its worst abuses, one of which was related to the treatment of slave women, whose plight received much attention in the act and formed the cornerstone of pronatalist amelioration. A close reading of the act reveals that it was true that several of the amelioration proposals of 1823 had been anticipated, but it was also true that close attention to reforms in the system of manumission was conspicuously absent from the act.[3]

In Antigua other ameliorative legislation had been passed earlier during the 1790s and was aimed at giving slaves greater protection from cruel treatment and allowing them trial by jury. Manumission, however, was not addressed. Even when an article in the Leeward Islands Slavery Amelioration Act of 1798 mentioned that topic, the relevant legislation was framed to deal with what amounted to cruelty to slaves: "No person shall set free any slave disabled from procuring his own maintenance, unless he deposit in the hands of the island treasurer, three hundred pounds as a provision for such slave's maintenance." The rationale, clearly stated in the act, was "to avoid the Inconveniences that do sometimes arise from persons manumitting and setting free their Slaves when they are rendered incapable of service by Age, Infirmity, Accident, or Calamity, to avoid the Expence of providing a proper Subsistence for such Slave."[4]

Mention of the special context of inhumane manumission did not, in fact, represent any step forward in attitudes to amelioration; nearly fifty years earlier, in a colonial act of 1757, similar legislation was included.[5] It appears that for the entire period of slavery in Antigua, even after strong persuasion from the imperial authorities in 1823 and later to promote and regulate manumission legislatively, the colonial legislature did not pass laws that systematically dealt with it. No such statutory apparatus emerged, but that is not to say that the legislature did not try to pass laws during the 1820s. The attempts failed in the face of opposition that was largely from within the legislature.[6]

Nonetheless, slaves were manumitted at Antigua in sizable numbers by general custom, particularly during the late slave period of the nineteenth century before general emancipation (without apprenticeship) came in 1834.[7] An official report about recent amelioration laws enacted in the British Caribbean colonies printed in 1831 stated, "It would not appear that there has ever existed in Antigua the slightest restraint on fair and bona fide manumission of slaves, nor has any duty or tax ever been laid on such manumissions." That succinct statement summarized Antigua's record, but some other colonies had passed laws that were identified in the report.[8]

The manumission of slaves in Antigua started on a very small scale during the early years of slavery in the seventeenth century and increased gradually in later years. The process contributed to the growth of the population of free persons of African descent, whether of mixed (colored) or unmixed (black) racial ancestry. The number of these free people of color (coloreds and blacks) rose from 18 in 1707 (12,892 slaves, 2,892 whites) to 1,230 in 1787 (36,000 slaves) and 3,895 (31,064 slaves) in 1821 when the last census was taken in Antigua before general emancipation. It is estimated that the rate of manumission (per 1,000 slaves per year) was 2.5 in 1808, 1.7 in 1820, and 2.9 in 1834.[9]

Slaves in Antigua and other British Caribbean colonies could be freed in several ways during the long period of slavery, but certainly by the 1820s these were mostly by deed, purchase, or will. "Manumission by deed could be granted directly by a slave-owner as a favor or 'gift' in recognition of special services or relationships," but slaves could also purchase themselves from their owners, paying only an agreed amount for the deed to be executed. That sum could be considerably less than the actual market value of the slaves. Many were also purchased by white or nonwhite free benefactors or by friends who then freed them. It is possible that in some cases the slaves themselves may have contributed to the purchase price with money they had earned or saved. Several owners of slaves freed them in their wills or by bequest. Whatever the route to manumission "the ultimate power to grant or withhold freedom lay in the hands of the slaveowner."[10] Lists of manumissions therefore, however detailed and illuminating they may be, mask much of the complex reality that shaped slaves' experiences on their road to freedom. In any case, by the 1820s in Antigua and the rest of Britain's Caribbean slave colonies, the role of slave-owners in originating processes of manumission was superseded by that of the slaves themselves or other free persons who acted on their behalf.[11]

This study bases its analysis of manumission in Antigua largely on the manumission lists that were issued by the colony's Office of the Registrar of Deeds.[12] These are supplemented by other sources but not by the slave registration records that have been investigated so thoroughly and fruitfully by Barry W.

Higman.[13] Two detailed manumission lists from the Antigua registrar of deeds are of particular value here. The first list covers the period from 1821 to 1825. It is organized to provide the date of manumission; the name, sex, and age of the person being manumitted; the price paid; "At those Expense effected"; the tax or fine; and the registration fee. The second list covers the period from 1821 to 1826 but does not record the names of the slaves who were freed.

The two lists, which record manumissions by "Purchase, Bequest, or otherwise," can therefore be combined for the period from 1821 to 1826. Additional data about manumissions for 1820 to 1826 can be obtained from a report of 1827 that tracked the prospects of several former slaves. Our concern in exploring these records is mainly with the female slaves who were freed. The total number of manumissions granted annually for 1821 to 1826 was incorporated in a list from the registrar of deeds for the longer period from 1817 to 1830, which, in recording the manumissions by year, also showed whether they were "Gratuitous, or for a nominal consideration only" or were paid for (table 4.1).

The number of manumissions (except those by will) for 1821 to 1826 does not correspond exactly to the number that can be extracted from the lists for 1821 to 1825 and 1821 to 1826, although the three compilations originated in the Office of the Registrar of Deeds. Some data from the combined lists for the 1821 to 1826 period are summarized in table 4.2, so the two tables can be compared. Table 4.2, however, shows the number of female and male slaves manumitted in that

Table 4.1. Antigua Manumissions, 1817–30

| Year | Type of Manumission | | |
	Gratuitous or for Nominal Amount	Paid For	Total
1817	146	54	200
1818	55	44	99
1819	104	43	147
1820	50	39	89
1821	85	47	132
1822	80	27	107
1823	136	36	172
1824	102	53	155
1825	103	46	149
1826	66	67	133
1827	101	44	145
1828	79	64	143
1829	127	60	187
1830	156	46	202
	1,390	670	2,060

Source: Gov. Patrick Ross to Sec. of State Goderich, Oct. 16, 1832, no. 61, enclosure, *Colonial Office 7/34,* Public Record Office, Kew, Surrey, England.

Note: This list does not include manumissions by will.

Table 4.2. Antigua Manumissions, 1821–26

Year	Not by Will			By Will			Total Manumissions
	Females	Males	Total	Females	Males	Total	
1821	87	67	154	9	5	14	168
1822	79	49	128	7	7	14	142
1823	108	78	186	1	0	1	187
1824	89	70	159	3	6	9	168
1825	81	70	151	3	2	5	156
1826	82	50	132	0	0	0	132
							953

Sources: Gov. Patrick Ross to Sec. of State Bathurst, June 6, 1826, no. 17, enclosure, *Colonial Record Office 7/14,* Public Record Office, Kew, Surrey, England; and Ross to Sec. of State Goderich, July 12, 1827, no. 36, enclosure, *Colonial Record Office 7/20,* Public Record Office, Kew, Surrey, England.

period, including those freed by will. Of the total number of 910 slaves freed other than by will, 526 (57.8 percent) were females compared with 384 (42.2 percent) males. Of the 43 slaves freed by will, 23 (53.5 percent) were females, and 20 (46.5 percent) were males. Of the 953 slaves freed by whatever methods, 549 (57.6 percent) were females, and 404 (42.4 percent) were males.

The general tendency in Antigua, therefore, although not overwhelmingly so, was for more female than male slaves to be manumitted. According to Higman, who examined manumission data for the British Caribbean colonies as a whole, "Females were roughly twice as likely to be manumitted as males in the period before 1820, but this difference was narrowed significantly in many colonies as emancipation approached."[14] In Antigua from 1821 to 1826, female slaves were, like male slaves, more likely to attain manumission by gift or "for a nominal consideration" than by other means. In the deeds of manumission by gift the rationale frequently cited was for "divers good causes, and valuable considerations." The gender significance of that description is far from clear. Nonetheless, many female slaves were able to benefit from circumstances related to their gender at a time when several ideas about ameliorating slavery focused on relieving the burden of slave women. One important measure, for example, that imperial authorities promoted was that women should not be punished by whipping.[15] Freedom, however problematic, for most slave women in Antigua was the ultimate measure of amelioration.

More than one hundred slaves, female and male, were freed annually between 1821 and 1826 (table 4.3), and females outnumbered males every year, the widest margins being in 1823 (109 females, 78 males) and 1826 (82 females, 50 males). In 1823, 187 slaves were manumitted, the largest number for the period; 58.3 percent of them were females, and 41.7 percent were males. Over the period color or racial descent played a role in the incidence of manumissions in general, but a little more than 60 percent of the females freed were of mixed ancestry or colored. The rest were designated as "black."[16]

Table 4.3. Gender Distribution of Antigua
Manumissions, 1821–26

Year	Females	Males	Total
1821	96	72	168
1822	86	56	142
1823	109	78	187
1824	92	76	168
1825	84	72	156
1826	82	50	132
	549	404	953

Sources: Gov. Patrick Ross to Sec. of State Bathurst, June 6, 1826, no. 17, enclosure, *Colonial Record Office 7/14,* Public Record Office, Kew, Surrey, England; and Ross to Sec. of State Goderich, July 12, 1827, no. 36, enclosure, *Colonial Record Office 7/20,* Public Record Office, Kew, Surrey, England.

In 1823, sixty-eight females were recorded as being of mixed blood ancestry; at least thirty-seven other females were in the "black" category. The overall number of manumissions for 1823 may have been related to political and humanitarian forces activated in Antigua by parliamentary debates about the amelioration of slavery, which resulted in the new proposals of that year. Most Antigua slave-owners, however, were not inclined to free their slaves at this time. They held on to their property in persons, believing that should the terrible day come when they might be forced to free them by imperial command, then they should receive monetary compensation.[17] In any case, given the enormous size of the slave population—cited at 31,064 in 1821—only a fractional number of manumissions occurred from 1821 to 1826.[18]

Who then were inclined to free their slaves at Antigua and from what motives did they act? Manumission lists do not answer these questions, although the names of some persons who facilitated manumission in some conspicuous form appear several times. The simple designation of them and others in the documents as having borne the expenses of each case of manumission makes it difficult to identify their connection with the slave set free; other kinds of records are needed to establish those relationships. Among the more conspicuous names, however, is that of Randall Righton, who bore the expense for freeing seventeen slaves (twelve females and five males) in February and March 1823. All were freed by gift, and, with the exception of Alexandrine, all were of mixed blood or colored. The ages of the slaves, which ranged from five to fifty, are recorded in every case, although in general the age at manumission was "seldom noticed" in the deeds of Antigua.[19]

If Righton was the owner of these slaves, he must have taken some care to have the manumissions fully recorded. Among the twelve females freed were Marie Rose, Josephine, Marie Emilie, Fabien, Silvain, Eloise, Marie Antoinette, Marie Roselie, Lézette, Angelle, Marie Luce, and Alexandrine. Fabien, five, was the youngest, and Marie Luce, fifty, was the eldest. Silvain was six. Marie Rose (nineteen) and Josephine (seventeen) were in their teens. In their twenties were Marie Antoinette (twenty-one), Marie Roselie (twenty-seven), and Lézette (twenty-eight). In their thirties were Eloise (thirty-five), Angelle (thirty), and Alexandrine (thirty-three). Marie Emilie was forty. Whether family ties existed among the females and males cannot be established from the manumission lists, but the slave registration returns recorded at triennial intervals for Antigua from 1817 should prove useful here and in other cases.[20]

A striking feature of the list of slaves Randall Righton was instrumental in setting free is the frequency of French names. Every name except that of Paul (who was fifteen) fell into this category, and even he carried the alias "Rose-main."[21] Antigua was one of Britain's old sugar colonies in the Caribbean, stretching back to the seventeenth century, but French names abound in the list of slaves manumitted there from 1821 to 1826. Several persons who paid expenses for manumissions also bore French names. In 1821 Mondesir Lélé freed by gift Remy and Elisee, two male slaves of mixed blood. Marie Clotilde Léandre freed by gift in 1823 five female and three male slaves ranging in age from eleven to forty-six. Among the females, Felicité (forty-six) and Rose Alpaide (fifteen) were of mixed blood; Marie Luce (thirty-two), Marie Rose (forty-three), and Louise (thirty-five) were listed as black. Frederic Bellot freed by gift the black female slave Louisonne, twelve, in 1825.[22]

John Baptist Lewis Birmingham was another who bore the expense of several manumissions, all thirty-six of them—twenty-one females and fifteen males—by gift. The manumissions took place in 1822 (fourteen slaves, eleven females and three males); 1823 (eight slaves, four females and four males); and in 1824 (fourteen slaves, six females and eight males). Jenaille (alias "Assez" and freed in 1822) was the only slave whose age was recorded (twelve years). She was of mixed blood. Among the other females freed in 1822 were Rose (alias "Lor"), Marie Joseph, Marie Francoise, Raine Rose, Adelaide, Zelie, Marie Adele, Marie Adrinette, Marie Joseph, and Rosiette. All were coloreds except for Marie Francoise and Adelaide. The first Marie Joseph was freed together with Jean Parfait, a male slave. Most slaves were freed individually in Antigua. Others were freed in pairs and, frequently, in larger groups of mixed gender. Among the females freed in 1823 through J. B. L. Birmingham, Marie Alexandrine was freed together with the male slave Augustin Beaubrun, and Clernena and Sophie were freed together. In 1824 the females Marie Ambroisine, Angelique, Augustine, Agnise, Rose, and Eleanore obtained their freedom. Marie Ambroisine, Agnise, and Rose were coloreds.[23]

For whatever reasons, several slave-owners were not able or willing to be as generous as Randall Righton and J. B. L. Birmingham in giving freedom as a gift to their slaves. Freedom was purchased from some, frequently at a slave's appraised value. The price paid for the "Redemption" of such slaves is recorded in the manumission lists next to the name of the person who bore the expenses of manumission. Such transactions were in a minority from 1821 to 1826. There were many more manumissions by gift than by purchase or for a nominal price. The highest price recorded for a male slave set free (the black person Samuel Charles, alias "Sam Doig") was £330 Antigua currency in 1824, while the corresponding price for a female slave (Susannah Evanson, of mixed blood) was £120 that same year. In 1821 the Rev. James Coull paid the year's highest price for freeing a female slave: £165 for Isabella Thomas. Also in 1821, William Thebud paid the expenses (£125) to free Elizabeth Felix, a black, while the highest price paid to free a male slave was £240 for Billy, also black, or William Danell, who was a cooper by occupation.[24]

There must have been great variation in the motivation of slave-owners or other persons who freed slaves, but such information is difficult to extract from the manumission lists. Here, too, slave registration lists might be helpful in some cases, but perhaps not as useful as reports about the operations of individual plantations, or wills, or other correspondence. One plantation report throws light on the manumission of Ann Conolly, mulatto or colored, in 1824 at the age of twenty-four. Ann was one of twenty-three mulatto slaves (thirteen females and ten males) attached to Sanderson's sugar plantation, where there were 233 slaves in all. The attorney for the plantation, which belonged to an absentee owner living in England, agreed to free Ann after it was proved that she had been held unlawfully for years. She should have been freed already because her father, a Mr. Connolly, who was white, had substituted another female slave for her. Connolly brought the case to the attention of the attorney, John Johnson, who had come out to Antigua from England to inspect the absentee owner's plantations. The black slave woman substituted for Ann, and the children to whom she had given birth, were all dead by this time. The case came before the courts, and Johnson finally agreed that "in justice" Ann was "entitled to her freedom" without "a shadow of doubt." He proposed that she be appraised, and he would free her for a fair price, set at £36. Conolly came up with the money, and his daughter, Ann, finally became a free person. However much she and her father may have desired her freedom, the view taken by the attorney, Johnson, was of critical importance. He was motivated to free Ann by more than the fact that she had been unjustly detained as a slave. "I can have no hesitation in stating," Johnson wrote, "that it would be beneficial to the Estate if the whole of the coloured women were disposed of, even at a smaller Sum; so useless are they in the first instance, and so materially do their bad examples affect the black slaves." Johnson was relieved to be able to get rid of Ann Conolly.[25]

Johnson's remarks imply that plantation owners placed great weight on operating their sugar-making enterprises with highly disciplined enslaved workers. Such owners did not normally deal with unruly slaves through manumission when they could resort to other harsh disciplinary measures, such as whipping.[26] It should therefore not be surprising that the overwhelming majority of slaves manumitted in Antigua and the rest of the British Caribbean colonies would not be field or plantation workers. None of the enslaved women freed at Antigua from 1820 to 1826, and whose occupations as slaves were recorded, was a field-worker, and most of them may have lived in the island's main town, St. Johns.[27] This means that most of Antigua's enslaved women worked in the cane fields, where they formed a higher proportion of the workforce overall than male field-workers, and lived out their lives in toil. Nonplantation females who lived in towns with their owners or by themselves had a far better chance to secure manumission, but that, of course, is not to say that the process was not without difficulties and frustrations, particularly for slaves.

Some enslaved women were fortunate enough to be freed for a nominal price, whether individually, along with another slave (male or female), or in a group of three or more, as with other forms of manumission. It is easier to identify cases of multiple manumission for a nominal price than similar cases of single manumissions from the official lists. In cases of multiple manumission, the price paid where more than one slave was involved frequently reveals a low average price per slave, especially if the total price paid was already low in relation to the number of slaves freed. In 1821 Neill Macdonald freed the colored slave Robert Beckles Husbands together with Caroline Cessegelsey, also colored, for only 10 shillings. That same year, Ann Jackson Roscoe freed Sally and Maria, both of whom were black, for only £1. Henry Hodges and his wife also freed one colored male and two colored female slaves in 1821 for only 5 shillings: Nicholas (twelve), Eliza (ten), and Mary. Samuel Byam followed the Hodges that year and freed six slaves (three females and three males) for only £36; Dorothy was black, and Sarah, Ann, Edward, Thomas Norbury, and Mathew were colored.[28] There is no clear evidence of a tendency to manumit aged, infirm, and otherwise incapacitated slaves at low prices between 1821 and 1826.

Some enslaved women actually found ways to purchase their own freedom and that of others. These women were not only resourceful in raising the amount of money that was involved but also fortunate that their owners were willing to free them. At least five cases of such unusual manumission are recorded in the list of slaves freed from 1821 to 1825. In 1824 Nancy, forty and black, paid £45 for her freedom. She was listed as a house-servant. That year, too, Maria, also black, purchased her freedom. She paid only £5, which may have been a nominal price. Three other cases of enslaved women who bought their freedom occurred in 1825. Hetty, a remarkable colored woman whose occupation was listed as "Lady's Maid," secured her freedom at fifty, together with that of her colored daughters Jane (twenty), Eliza (seventeen), and Georgianna (fifteen), all for £100. Here, too, it would appear that these manumissions were for a nominal price. Hetty and her three daughters were freed together on the same day. Another case of self-purchase in 1825 was the black woman Beckey, who paid £23.3s.6d. The third case in this category of manumission for 1825 was another black woman, Jane, who paid £33. Occupations for Beckey and Jane were not listed.[29]

When Nancy, Maria, Hetty, Beckey, and Jane obtained freedom through self-purchase, they, like other females who became free, accomplished a goal that was very important to them. The road to freedom must have been extremely difficult in some cases. Even the lucky ones freed by gift had already paid a price in that they had first endured a period of enslavement. However difficult the route to manumission may have been, many enslaved women sought, struggled for, and won that cherished prize. The slave Mary Prince tried hard to persuade her master and his wife to free her in Antigua, "but their hearts were hard—too hard to consent," she revealed in her autobiography. At one point, her mistress Mrs. Wood "was very angry—she grew quite outrageous—she called me a black devil, and asked me who had put freedom into my head." Mary Prince, who by then (1826) had already boldly married a free black man, Daniel James, without permission from her owners, replied, "'To be free is very sweet.'" That direct, intelligent, and politically subversive retort caused Mrs. Wood to "change colour" and leave the room where the exchange had taken place between slave and mistress. Mary Prince did not join the ranks of manumitted women in Antigua who, like her, regarded freedom as "very sweet."[30]

But if obtaining freedom was so satisfying to enslaved women, how did they fare later in preserving or extending what they had achieved? Slave society in Antigua was organized socially, economically, and politically around the centrally important relations between masters and slaves.[31] In such a society, free nonwhites generally struggled to carve out a tolerable existence. Whites regarded them as not far removed from the status and condition of slaves and deprived them of full civil rights, which only whites enjoyed. For free nonwhites, the struggle to live in Antigua was very real, and some did better than others. Still, in the face of the difficulties attached to a "free" existence, slave women and men in the colony preferred to carry the burdens of freedom than those of slavery.

A better appreciation of the fuller contexts of manumission for enslaved women can be obtained from information about their prospects after they were set free. The data are derived from a report prepared in 1827 by the Antigua registrar of deeds in response to instructions received from the imperial government in London for an account of all manumissions from 1820 to 1826.[32] The Antigua government issued a proclamation that required all persons who were manumitted during that period to report to the Office of the Private Secretary. They were given only three days to do so.[33] The report, presented in tabular form, lists female and male slaves separately and shows, to judge by the additional entries made for only a few persons, that only a small number of the long list of manumitted slaves recorded must have actually turned up (table 4.4).

We have, therefore, only a sample of the manumissions, but the information that is presented is of great importance. In five columns the report collected information in the following categories: "Name and Computed Age," "Whether Black or Coloured," "Former Occupation as a Slave," "Present Occupation as a Free Person," and "Present State of Comfort, arising from individual Industry." Table 4.5 presents the data for female slaves freed from 1821 to 1826. The

Table 4.4. Number of Manumitted (1821–26) and Newly Recorded (1827) Females and Males

Year	Females		Males		Total Manumitted	Total Newly Recorded
	Manumitted	Newly Recorded	Manumitted	Newly Recorded		
1821	96	5	72	4	168	9
1822	86	4	56	2	142	6
1823	109	6	78	12	187	18
1824	92	10	76	5	168	15
1825	84	7	72	4	156	11
1826	82	6	50	5	132	11

Sources: Gov. Patrick Ross to Sec. of State Bathurst, June 6, 1826, no. 17, enclosure, *Colonial Record Office 7/14*, Public Record Office, Kew, Surrey, England; and Ross to Sec. of State Goderich, July 12, 1827, no. 36, enclosure, and Sept. 27, 1827, enclosure, both in *Colonial Record Office 7/20*, Public Record Office, Kew, Surrey, England.

entries, although mere fragmentary references to more involved and historically important processes related to individual and collective lives, nonetheless open several windows into some of the contexts that surrounded the manumission of female slaves.

It is not clear why the thirty-eight females who responded to the government proclamation in 1827 did so although most females did not. The most illuminating information recorded about them is related to their occupations as slaves and after they were freed and how well they were then able to support themselves. Their occupations as slaves included lady's maid, huckster, domestic, seamstress, washer, housekeeper, house servant, and housemaid. Several females changed or expanded their occupations after their manumission, but it is not possible to tell how soon this occurred, nor in response to what particular set of circumstances. In general, however, they must have responded as best they could to the need to make a living—and in that some were more fortunate than others. Some were forced to fend for themselves in the harsh, racially polarized social and economic climate of Antigua slave society, while several others could rely on some support from benefactors, including former owners or other persons who had helped free them. The limited range of occupations that manumitted females held as slaves was similar to the range under freedom, but there were shifts within that range as these people moved from slavery to freedom. It is difficult to determine whether they tried out several occupations after gaining freedom.

Sally Green was among the females doing well enough six years after manumission in 1821. She was freed for £52.10s at forty years of age. Her occupation as a slave had been that of lady's maid. In 1827 she was listed as a baker who supported herself "in comfort." Clarissa, twenty-seven when freed by gift, still followed the occupation of huckster and supported herself and her mother comfortably "by her industry." Sally Green, who was probably a young child

Table 4.5. Females Manumitted (1821–26) in Antigua and Newly Registered (1827)

Year	Name	Age (Freed)	Color	Occupation Slave	Occupation Free	Condition in Freedom
1821	Sally Green Green	40	Colored	Lady's maid	Baker	"Supports herself in Comfort"
		—	?	None	None	"Supported by her Mother in Comfort"
	Eliza	10	Colored	None	None	"Supported by the Bequest of Mr. Symes, former owner"
	Phillis	50	Black	Huckster	—	"Unable to support herself from Infirmity"
	Clarissa	27	Black	Huckster	Huckster	"Supports herself & Mother in Comfort by her Industry"
1822	Margaret	75	Black	Domestic	None	"In a state of absolute destitution"
	Mary Jane	18	Colored	Seamstress	Seamstress	"Supports herself by her Industry & Assisted"
	Marinda	55	Black	Domestic	Domestic	"Supports herself comfortably by income allowed to her"
	Penelope	50	Black	Washerwoman	Washerwoman	"The same as when a slave"
1823	Charlotte Hoskins	18	Colored	Seamstress	Seamstress	"Supports herself by her Industry"
	Eliza Harvey	30	Colored	Seamstress	Seamstress	"Supports herself by her Industry in comfort"
	Fanny	49	Black	Washerwoman	Washerwoman	"Supports herself in comfort by her Industry"
	Ellen	32	Colored	Lady's maid	Lady's maid	"Supported by her former Mistress in Comfort"
	Dorothy Doig	35	Black	Housekeeper	Housekeeper/ washerwoman	"Supports herself decently & comfortably, also her granddaughter (free child)"
	Ann Putland	23	Colored	Seamstress	Seamstress	"Supports herself in comfort by her Industry"

Table 4.5. Cont.

Year	Name	Age (Freed)	Color	Occupation		Condition in Freedom
				Slave	Free	
1824	Lucy James	34	Black	Lady's maid	Washerwoman/seamstress	"Supports herself in Comfort by her Industry"
	Ashey	65	Black	Domestic	—	"Could not support herself without Assistance; supported by her Son a slave belonging to Adml. Tollemarche"
	Frances	18	Black	Domestic	Washerwoman/huckster	"Supported by her Father (free black) partly & by her own Industry"
	Sally	34	Colored	Washerwoman	Washerwoman	"Supported by her Industry and assisted by her Husband"
	Jenny	32	Black	Domestic	Huckster	"Sufficient for her Maintenance"
	Maria Evans	11	Colored	None	None	"Supported by her Mother"
	Nancy	40	Black	House servant	Huckster	"Supports herself in comfort"
	Hope James McKay Nanton	19	Black	Domestic	Domestic	"Supported in Comfort by her former mistress"
	Mary Player	30	Colored	House servant	Retail huckster	"Supports herself in Comfort by her Industry"
1825	Ann Burke	30	Colored	Domestic	Huckster	"Supports herself and child in Comfort"
	Hetty	50	Colored	Lady's maid	Seamstress	"Able to support herself & daughters decently"
	Jane	20	Colored			Hetty's daughters: "Assist their Mother in her occupation"
	Eliza	17	Colored			
	Georgianna	15	Colored			
	Ophelia	42	Black	Washerwoman	Washerwoman/huckster	"Supports herself in Comfort"

Table 4.5. Cont.

Year	Name	Age (Freed)	Color	Occupation Slave	Occupation Free	Condition in Freedom
	Moll (Mary Swift)	27	Black	Washer-woman	Washer-woman	"Supported by her Husband, Mr. Swift, in Comfort"
1826	Eliza Krogman	50	Colored	Seamstress	None	"Maintained by her former owner; unable to maintain herself"
	Penny Grant	24	Colored	Lady's maid	Seamstress	"Supports herself in comfort by her Industry"
	Mary Pemble	26	Colored	Housekeeper	House-keeper	"Comfortably supported by Mr. Hill, her former owner"
	Mary Ann Joseph	24	Black	Domestic	Seamstress	"Supports herself in comfort by her Industry"
	Phillis	28	Black	House servant	Huckster	"Supported partly by her Husband, a slave, & by her own Industry"
	Rebecca Seth	30	Black	Housemaid	Housemaid	"Former master supports her in comfort"

Source: Gov. Patrick Ross to Sec. of State Goderich, Sept. 27, 1827, no. 48, enclosure, *Colonial Record Office 7/20*, Public Record Office, Kew, Surrey, England.

when she was freed, was listed as having no occupation; her mother supported her well. Eliza was an older child of ten when she was freed. She was also listed without an occupation and was supported through the bequest of her former owner. The huckster Phillis, who at fifty was nearly twice the age of Clarissa when she was freed by gift, was unable to support herself because of infirmity six years later. One is left to wonder how healthy Phillis had been when she was freed. At fifty, however, she did accept the gift of freedom, believing perhaps that she still had a few years left to experience what it was like to be free while trying to support herself as a huckster. One manumitted female, Margaret, was badly off in 1827, and her age at manumission may have been a critical factor, as in the case of Phillis. Margaret, a domestic, was freed by gift in 1822 when she was seventy-five. Five years later she was described as being in "a state of absolute destitution." Eliza Krogman, fifty and a seamstress when she was freed in 1826, was a little more fortunate. One year later she was unable to support herself, and her former owner maintained her.

But age at manumission did not always work against a freed female slave. The case of a remarkable woman, Hetty, who had three daughters is illustrative. At fifty, Hetty, a lady's maid as a slave, purchased freedom for herself and her daughters in 1825 for £100. By 1827 she was listed as a seamstress and quite able to support herself and her daughters "decently." Her girls, now about two years older—Jane (twenty-two), Eliza (nineteen), and Georgianna (seventeen)—worked with her. Hetty brought herself and her girls out of slavery, raising money to pay for the manumissions herself, and she was doing well enough after freeing everyone to keep the family together.

Two other women were listed as having been freed in their fifties: Marinda at fifty-five and Penelope at fifty. Both were freed by gift in 1822. Marinda retained her occupation as a domestic and supported herself comfortably, not by her own labor solely but primarily by an "income allowed to her." This income probably rescued her from want. Penelope, too, retained her occupation as a washerwoman, and her condition was recorded to have been the "same as when a slave." Neither Marinda nor Penelope appears to have advanced in material well-being by her own efforts.

Like Marinda and Eliza Krogman, some freed females were able to depend on help from others, and among them were a few whose former owners still played important roles in their lives as free persons. Ellen, a lady's maid freed by gift in 1823 at the age of thirty-two, remained a lady's maid, most likely in the employ of her former owner, Ann Wilson Daniell, who supported her in comfort. The case of Hope James McKay Nanton, freed by gift at nineteen in 1824, was similar. Hope retained her occupation as a domestic with her former owner, Catherine Bladen Nanton, who supported her comfortably. The housekeeper Mary Pemble, freed at twenty in 1826, also retained her occupation, most likely in the employ of her former owner Nathaniel Hill, who supported her comfortably. Rebecca Seth, a housemaid when she was freed in 1826 at thirty, also retained her occupation with her former master, who supported her very well. That these females remained with their former owners after being freed suggests that a wide range of considerations must have influenced the path manumitted persons took after the most obvious chains of slavery were broken. It also suggests that the experience of slavery itself varied from slave to slave, not least in regard to relations with the slave-owner, male or female.

Some freed females received support from persons who were not their former owners, while others like Hetty and Clarissa were situated well enough to be able to support dependents. In the first category was a domestic, Ashey, freed by gift in 1824 at the age of sixty-five. One year later she was unable to support herself "without assistance," which came from her son who was still a slave. Her age was obviously a factor, but she was luckier than Phillis (fifty-six) and Margaret (eighty) in having someone, her son, to help her.

Freed persons often came to the aid of enslaved relatives and others, but the reverse was also not unusual. In roughly the same category as Ashey was a much younger female, Frances, a domestic who was also freed in 1824 at the age of eighteen. She changed her occupation to washerwoman and huckster. Unable to support herself fully, however, she relied on her father, free and black, for assistance. Sally, a thirty-four-year-old washerwoman, was freed along with her daughter Rebecca (ten) for £51 in 1824, and she remained in the same occupation, supporting herself with the help of her "husband." Maria Evans, freed that same year when only eleven, was listed as without an occupation three years later. Her mother supported her. Moll, also known as Mary Swift, was a washerwoman when she was freed for £150 in 1825 at the age of twenty-seven. She retained that occupation and was supported in comfort by her "husband," Mr. Swift, who was perhaps the same person (John Swift) who paid the expenses for her manumission. Another woman called Phillis, a house servant when she was freed in 1826 at the age of twenty-eight, changed her occupation to that of huckster. She was able to support herself in part by her own labor and in part with help from her "husband," who was still enslaved.[34]

Among the manumitted women besides Hetty and Clarissa who were able to support dependents were Dorothy Doig and Ann Burke. At thirty-five, Dorothy, a housekeeper, was freed by gift in 1823. She was later listed as a housekeeper and washerwoman who supported herself and her granddaughter, a free child, "decently & comfortably." Ann became free at thirty in 1825. She switched from the occupation of domestic to that of huckster and supported herself and her child comfortably.

Many manumitted women listed in 1827 were reported to be doing well enough to support themselves, several being noted as doing so "in Comfort" or "in Comfort by her own industry." Of course, several factors in combination would have shaped such an outcome after manumission, including age, occupation, racial background, employment opportunities, health, and good luck. Among these, occupation appears to have been of major importance. Of the occupations followed by thirty of the thirty-eight manumitted females listed in the report of 1827, that of seamstress was noted for ten persons and that of seamstress and washerwoman was noted once. All of these people were doing quite well. Nine of them were of mixed descent, and four had been seamstresses as slaves. They had therefore retained their occupation after manumission. These women included Mary Jane, who was freed in 1822 at eighteen for £82.10s; Charlotte Hoskins, who was also eighteen when she was freed in 1823 for £50; Elizabeth Harvey, who for £66 was also freed in 1823 at thirty; and Ann Putland, freed in 1823 as well, but by gift, at the age of twenty-three. All of them were less than thirty-five when they were freed. The remaining five colored females included Hetty, her three daughters, and Penny Grant. Hetty, fifty when freed in 1825, was much older than Mary Jane, Charlotte, Elizabeth, and Ann. Her three daughters ranged in age from fifteen to twenty when they, too, were freed in 1825 with their mother. Although their occupation as slaves was not listed, Hetty herself as a slave was a lady's maid. She changed her occupation to seamstress after manumission, and her daughters worked with her.

With young daughters to support, Hetty apparently chose her occupation well. Penny Grant, the other seamstress of mixed descent, who was freed in 1826 at the age of twenty-four, was by occupation a lady's maid when a slave. Like Hetty she switched occupations. There were two black seamstresses in the list of 1827. Lucy James, freed by gift in 1824 at thirty-four, worked as a lady's maid in slavery and after manumission took up the combined occupations of seamstress and washerwoman. The other black seamstress was Mary Ann Joseph, a domestic worker in slavery who was freed in 1826 at age twenty-four.

There may have been a color-occupation correlation among Antigua's free non-white population. Free women of mixed descent may have tended to monopolize more respectable occupations such as that of seamstress, which they could pursue in their own homes. While Hetty, Penny Grant, and Mary Ann Joseph worked at some domestic occupation as slaves, they set themselves up in a far better situation as seamstresses after they were freed. If Lucy James, who was black, worked both as a seamstress and washerwoman after attaining her freedom, she was probably responding to the racial and employment realities of Antigua society that dictated that her two occupations were a good combination. Both brought her work although washing was an occupation of lower status and involved much labor.[35] Sally was the only colored washerwoman listed in 1827. In slavery she held the same occupation. Three black washerwomen were listed, however, and four other black women (including Lucy James) combined that occupation with another. Frances, who had been a domestic slave, became a washerwoman and a huckster; Ophelia, forty-two and a washerwoman when she was freed in 1825, added the occupation of huckster; and Dorothy Doig combined the occupation of washerwoman with her old one of housekeeper. Among the three black women who carried on as washerwomen after they were freed were Penelope, Fanny, and Molly (or Mary Swift).

Mary Prince described the hardship connected to the occupation of washerwoman, basing the description on her own experience in that line of work in Antigua during the 1820s. Mary labored laundering bundles of clothes at the pond and at the tub. As a result of the frequency of drought on the island, residents built ponds that were put to great use. Mary believed that she became severely afflicted with rheumatism "by catching cold at the pond side, from washing in the fresh water."[36] Manumitted females at Antigua knowingly faced such risks to their health as well as the laborious work involved in being washerwomen because they were sure of regular if somewhat degrading work for survival.

Such women also gravitated, and for similar reasons, to the occupation of huckster or vendor of varieties of goods that they sold on their own account or for other persons who employed them. Some hucksters had small shops, and others plied their trade as itinerant vendors in towns and the countryside and to ships' crews. Enslaved women engaged in all forms of huckstering. Five hucksters were among the manumitted females listed in the report of 1827, one "retail" huckster, and two huckster/washerwomen. Four of the five hucksters were black: Clarissa, Jenny, Nancy, and Phillis. Clarissa had been a huckster as a slave, Jenny had been a domestic, and Nancy and Phillis had been house servants. All were doing well, but Phillis also received some support from her "husband," who was a slave. Some of the specifics of the manumission of Clarissa have been mentioned earlier. Jenny was thirty-two when she was freed in 1824 for £66, and Nancy, forty, was also freed that year for £45. The only huckster of mixed descent listed in 1827 was Ann Burke, freed in 1825. The two freed hucksters/washerwomen were the already-mentioned Frances and Ophelia, freed in 1824 and 1825, respectively.

And then there was Mary Play, freed for £41 at age thirty in 1824, who was listed as a "retail huckster." A colored woman who had been a house servant as a slave, Mary may have used such an occupational designation to distinguish herself from a common huckster. She, like Ophelia and Ann Burke, was able to support herself quite well. Most of the manumitted females of Antigua came face to face with the harsh realities of supporting themselves in an environment shaped by a heavy reliance on the labor of slaves on plantations and outside them. They discovered that freedom did not banish insecurity and that they had to cope as best they could, relying primarily on their will to survive.

In spite of the difficulties that freedom might bring, enslaved women in Antigua pursued it, finding ways to achieve that ultimate form of amelioration of their condition under slavery. To be free, as Mary Prince pointed out, was "very sweet," but in actuality the concrete sweetness of freedom varied with each manumitted female. By the 1820s many nonplantation female slaves optimistically took advantage of a growing climate of opinion among Antigua's residents, influenced to some extent by the antislavery campaign in Britain, that it was necessary to free their slaves or help them obtain freedom. A Methodist missionary at the neighboring colony of Montserrat interpreted these developments to mean that "the time to favor the servile progeny of Ham appears to be at hand."[37]

Some slave-owners freed their slaves by gift. Others, less generous, sold freedom for a nominal price. There were other slave-owners, too, who, fearing perhaps that general abolition of slavery might soon occur without just compensation to them, freed their slaves at or near their full appraised value. For such slave-owners humanitarianism was far less a motivation than economic and political considerations. But support for the amelioration of slavery in Antigua, and for manumission in particular, faced local opposition. The island legislature itself dragged its feet in passing enabling legislation, while some slave-owners expressed opposition in various ways.

John Osborn, a plantation attorney who took care of the affairs of the absentee Codrington family, opposed attempts to ameliorate slavery in general, and he was very critical of proposals and other efforts to manumit slaves. "The times are ominous and eventful" in Antigua, he wrote, fearful of the consequences of amelioration. Osborn felt that the amelioration of slavery as spelled out in the proposals of 1823 was misguided and that the scheme to improve the lives of slaves would do more harm than good if implemented too precipitately. Proper amelioration, he believed, would require time; it should be gradual. "The fact is," he wrote, "that the Negro mind has of late been constantly excited, and unsettled, and even goaded on to Freedom by troops of Sectarians, as well as by new laws" suggested by the imperial government. Osborn feared that such laws would "subvert subordination and discipline" among the slaves and "go great lengths to establish the rights of freedom, even before a compensation is offered" in the event of general emancipation. Osborn, greatly perturbed by the possible results of "unsettling the Negro mind," put some of the blame on the many "Sectarians" in Antigua, including the Methodist and Moravian missionaries who had been at work among the slaves, converting and educating them since about the late eighteenth century. The "more the mind is enlightened," Osborn complained, "the greater will be the desire for Freedom."[38]

Whether or not Osborn's claim was accurate in regard to manumission rates in Antigua remains to be demonstrated so far as the work of Methodists and Moravian missionaries is concerned. But the slaves of Antigua were enlightened more generally to seek freedom by existing conditions in support of amelioration. Encouraged by these conditions, female slaves in the colony exploited every opportunity for manumission, including perhaps those specifically related to gender, during the early and middle 1820s. By their determined push for individual freedom they showed willingness to grapple with the challenges of making a living as free persons. They would not have heeded the advice of people like Osborn who would have tried to discourage them. In the face of support for amelioration, not least from the female slaves themselves who sought or obtained manumission, a frustrated Osborn, who could not bear to see the old slave system undermined by amelioration, complained bitterly that manumission would not work because "a great bulk of the Coloured people and Blacks who have been emancipated in this Colony have returned to servitude in order to get their daily bread, and . . . many of both classes are employed and supported by our very Slaves." Manumission, it is true, was not without its problems, but the female slaves of Antigua regarded it as a worthwhile prize nonetheless during the 1820s.

Notes

1. J. H. Parry and P. M. Sherlock, *A Short History of the West Indies* (London: Macmillan, 1965), 182–83; Elsa V. Goveia, *Slave Society in the British Leeward Islands at the End of the Eighteenth Century* (New Haven: Yale University Press, 1965); Michael Craton, James Walvin, and David Wright, eds., *Slavery, Abolition, and Emancipation: Black Slaves and the British Empire* (London: Longman, 1976), 300–303, 310–15; David Barry Gaspar, "Slavery, Amelioration, and Sunday Markets in Antigua, 1823–1831," *Slavery and Abolition* 9 (May 1988): 1–28; David Barry Gaspar, "Ameliorating Slavery: The Leeward Islands Slave Act of 1798," in *The Lesser Antilles in the Age of European Expansion,* ed. Robert L. Paquette and Stanley L. Engerman (Gainesville: University Press of Florida, 1996), 241–58; J. R. Ward, *British West Indian Slavery 1750–1834: The Process of Amelioration* (New York: Oxford University Press, 1988); B. W. Higman, *Slave Populations of the British Caribbean, 1807–1834* (Baltimore: Johns Hopkins University Press, 1984), 348–78.

2. *Anti-Slavery Monthly Reporter,* Dec. 1827; Craton, Walvin, and Wright, eds., *Slavery, Abolition, and Emancipation,* 300–303; Gaspar, "Slavery, Amelioration, and Sunday Markets."

3. Gaspar, "Ameliorating Slavery." The Amelioration Act, "An Act More Effectually to Provide for the Support, and to Extend Certain Regulations for the Protection of Slaves," is Leeward Islands Act no. 36 in vol. 1 of *The Laws of the Island of Antigua Consisting of the Acts of the Leeward Islands, 1690–1798, and Acts of Antigua, 1668–1845,* 4 vols. (London: Samuel Bagster, 1805–46) (hereafter *Laws of Antigua*). I have consulted the copy of the act dated April 21, 1798, and printed in *House of Commons Sessional Papers of the Eighteenth Century,* ed. Sheila Lambert (Wilmington: Scholarly Resources, 1975), 122: 99–199.

4. "An Act to Repeal the Fortieth and Forty-First Clauses of an Act of This Island, Intituled, an Act for Attainting Several Slaves Now Run-Away from Their Masters' Services; and for the Better Government of Slaves, Dated the Ninth Day of December, in the Year of Our Lord One Thousand Seven Hundred and Twenty-Three; and to Make Persons Charged with and Found Guilty of the Murder of Slaves, Liable and Subject to the Same Paines and Penalties, as Are Inflicted for the Murder of Free Persons," Dec. 18, 1797, in *Laws of Antigua* 2: 285–88; "An Act for Settling and Regulating the Trial of Criminal Slaves by Jury," Feb. 28, 1798, in *Laws of Antigua* 2: 296–301. The clause or article in the Amelioration Act 1798 was number 12. See also "An Abstract of the Ameliorating Provisions of the Laws Last Enacted in Each of the British West India Colonies, for the Government and Protection of the Slave Population" (London, 1831), in Agents of the West Indian Colonies to Secretary of State Goderich, March 26, 1831, Colonial Office 318/110, p. 15, Public Record Office, Kew, Surrey, England (hereafter CO).

5. "An Act for the Further Prevention of Damages to the Harbours, and Abuses in Carrying on the Inland Trade of This Island; Regulating the Hire and Manumission of Slaves; and for Advertising Run-aways Committed to Gaol," Nov. 25, 1757, in *Laws of Antigua,* act no. 212, 1: 342–43, article 10.

6. Gaspar, "Ameliorating Slavery"; Gaspar, "Slavery Amelioration and Sunday Markets." Antigua did succeed in enacting a few other ameliorative regulations.

7. Antigua and Bermuda abolished slavery by legislative acts in 1834 without attaching a period of apprenticeship, as in other British colonies, to "prepare" the slaves for full freedom. See Wil-

liam A. Green, *British Slave Emancipation: The Sugar Colonies and the Great Experiment, 1830–1865* (New York: Oxford University Press, 1976), ch. 5, 129–61.

8. "An Abstract of the Ameliorating Provisions."

9. David Barry Gaspar, *Bondmen and Rebels: A Study of Master-Slave Relations in Antigua* (Baltimore: Johns Hopkins University Press, 1985), 162; Governor Patrick Ross to Secretary of State Bathurst, June 7, 1826, no. 18, CO 7/14; Antigua Census Data, CO 7/7; Higman, *Slave Populations,* 380–81. See also, on the free people of color in British Caribbean colonies, Arnold A. Sio, "Marginality and Free Coloured Identity in Caribbean Slave Society," *Slavery and Abolition* 8 (Sept. 1987): 166–82; Stephen Small, "Racial Group Boundaries and Identities: People of 'Mixed-Race' in Slavery across the Americas," *Slavery and Abolition* 15 (Dec. 1994): 17–37; M. G. Smith, "Some Aspects of Social Structure in the British Caribbean about 1820," *Social and Economic Studies* 1 (Aug. 1953): 55–79; David Lowenthal, "Free Colored West Indians: A Racial Dilemma," in *Studies in Eighteenth-Century Culture 3,* ed. Harold E. Pagliora (Cleveland: The Press of Case Western Reserve University, 1973), 335–53; and *Hints on the Propriety of Establishing by Law the Civil Rights of the Free People of Colour, in the British West India Colonies, as a Preliminary Step to Emancipating the Slaves and Preparing Them, by Enlightenment, for the Enjoyment of Civil Rights* (Newcastle upon Tyne, 1824).

10. Higman, *Slave Populations,* 379–86.

11. Ibid., 381.

12. Antigua Manumission Returns, Jan. 1, 1821–Dec. 31, 1825, in Governor Patrick Ross to Secretary of State Bathurst, June 6, 1826, no. 17, CO 7/14. The data are printed in *British Parliamentary Papers,* vol. 72: *Slave Trade* (Shannon: Irish University Press, 1969), 55–67. See also Antigua Manumission Returns, Jan. 1, 1821–Dec. 31, 1826, in Governor Patrick Ross to Secretary of State Goderich, July 12, 1827, no. 36, CO 7/20. This data is printed in *British Parliamentary Papers,* vol. 75: *Slave Trade,* 4–17. Additional data can be found in Antigua Manumission Returns, Jan. 1, 1808–Oct. 1, 1821, CO 7/7; and Jan. 1, 1817–Dec. 31, 1830, in Governor Patrick Ross to Secretary of State Goderich, Oct. 16, 1832, no. 61, CO 7/34.

13. Higman, *Slave Populations.*

14. Ibid., 383.

15. *Anti-Slavery Monthly Reporter,* Dec. 1827.

16. Higman, *Slave Populations,* 383; Sio, "Marginality and Free Colored Identity."

17. Letter from John Osborn, Antigua plantation attorney, Oct. 23, 1823, microfilm, reel no. 2, Codrington Papers, Nettie Lee Benson Latin American Collection, University of Texas at Austin; Gaspar, "Ameliorating Slavery"; Gaspar, "Slavery, Amelioration, and Sunday Markets."

18. Antigua Census 1821, CO 7/7; Ross to Bathurst, June 7, 1826, no. 18, CO 7/14.

19. Antigua Manumission Returns, Jan. 1, 1821–Dec. 31, 1825, in Ross to Bathurst, June 6, 1826, no. 17, CO 7/14.

20. Higman, *Slave Populations.* The Antigua triennial registration lists are in Treasury Department, Series 71 (T71): T71/245 (1817–18)-T71/250 (1832), Public Record Office, Kew, Surrey, England.

21. Antigua Manumission Returns, Jan. 1, 1821–Dec. 31, 1825, and Jan. 1, 1821–Dec. 31, 1826.

22. Ibid.

23. Ibid.

24. Ibid.

25. Report on Sanderson's Plantation (Antigua), in J. Johnson, "Reports Relating to Mr. Gordon's Estates in the West Indies, 1824," Beinecke Lesser Antilles Collection, Burke Library, Hamilton College, Clinton, N.Y.

26. Thomas W. Hyde to Methodist Missionary Society, Aug. 26, 1823, box 119, no. 137, Methodist Missionary Society Papers, Library of the School of Oriental and African Studies, London, England.

27. Antigua Manumission Returns, Jan. 1, 1821–Dec. 31, 1825, and Jan. 1, 1821–Dec. 31, 1826; Higman, *Slave Populations,* 382–83.

28. Antigua Manumission Returns, Jan. 1, 1821–Dec. 31, 1825, and Jan. 1, 1821–Dec. 31, 1826; "Female and Male Slaves Manumitted at Antigua 1820–1826," in Governor Patrick Ross to Secretary of State Goderich, Sept. 27, 1827, no. 48, CO 7/20.

29. Antigua Manumission Returns, Jan. 1, 1821–Dec. 31, 1825, and Jan. 1, 1821–Dec. 31, 1826; Manumission List for 1820–26 in Governor Patrick Ross to Secretary of State Goderich, Sept. 27, 1827, no. 48, CO 7/20..

30. Moira Ferguson, ed., *The History of Mary Prince: A West Indian Slave* (London: Pandora, 1987), 74–76. The autobiography of this woman was first published in London in 1831. See also Moira Ferguson, ed., *Nine Black Women: An Anthology of Nineteenth-Century Writers from the United States, Canada, Bermuda, and the Caribbean* (New York: Routledge, 1998), 47–66.

31. Gaspar, *Bondmen and Rebels;* Goveia, *Slave Society;* Smith, "Some Aspects of Social Structure"; Sio, "Marginality and Free Coloured Identity."

32. Manumission List for 1820–26.

33. *Weekly Register* [Antigua], Aug. 14, 1827.

34. Anglican ministers did not generally encourage slave marriages, and before 1837 marriages performed by Methodist and Moravian missionaries were not regarded as legal. Higman, *Slave Populations,* 369. In 1827 an Antigua official pointed out that "there is no existing law in this colony that makes marriage between Slaves a civil or religious contract, nor any law to prevent the separation of husband and wife." Antigua Colonial Secretary to Ross, May 23, 1827, in Governor Patrick Ross to Secretary of State Goderich, July 12, 1827, no. 36, CO 7/20.

35. Ferguson, ed., *History of Mary Prince,* 69.

36. Gaspar, *Bondmen and Rebels,* 117–18; Ferguson, ed., *History of Mary Prince,* 69.

37. Hyde to Methodist Missionary Society, Aug. 26, 1823, box 119, no. 137, Methodist Missionary Society Papers.

38. Letter from John Osborn, Antigua, Oct. 23, 1823, microfilm, reel no. 2, Codrington Papers.

CHAPTER 5

"Do Thou in Gentle Phibia Smile": Scenes from an Interracial Marriage, Jamaica, 1754–86

Trevor Burnard

The great crisis in the thirty-four-year relationship between Thomas Thistlewood, a white English immigrant to western Jamaica, and Phibbah, a native-born Jamaican slave, came in June 1757, three and a half years after Phibbah had established herself as his principal partner. Thistlewood had long been unhappy with his situation as an overseer on Egypt estate. He had had numerous arguments with his feckless employer, John Cope. Consequently, on June 18, 1757, Thistlewood agreed with "Mr John Parkinson to live at Kendal," an estate about ten miles further inland from Egypt in Westmoreland Parish. He was "to have an hundred per ann. the first year and afterwards to have my wages raised" as well as sundry provisions.[1]

Thistlewood's new situation had many advantages—increased wages, better conditions, and the severing of ties with Cope—but there was one major disadvantage. Thistlewood would now be physically separated from Phibbah, a woman, he lamented, who was "in miserable slavery."[2] Molly Cope, Phibbah's owner, was unwilling to sell or hire her to Thistlewood.[3] The parting was hard. "Phibbah grieves very much," Thistlewood noted five days before he was due to depart. He "could not sleep, but vastly uneasy."[4]

Thistlewood found Kendal estate in poor order and its slaves ill-disciplined.[5] He missed Phibbah terribly. After she visited, Thistlewood wrote: "Tonight very lonely and melancholy again. No person sleep in the house but myself and Phibbah's being gone this morning still fresh in my mind."[6] Phibbah's plight was worse, even if we know about her emotions only indirectly and from Thistlewood's perspective. Not only was she separated from a partner to whom she was emotionally attached but she was also in danger of losing some of her status as the privileged mistress of a white man if Thistlewood left Egypt permanently. Thus Phibbah found herself considering how to reestablish her relationship with Thistlewood and persuade him to return to Egypt. She had much to gain if she succeeded.

On the evening of their parting Phibbah gave Thistlewood a gold ring "to keep for her sake."[7] She proved her affection by constantly visiting Thistlewood and showering him with gifts. On July 13, 1757, she brought him a turtle, eggs, a pineapple, biscuits, and cashews. She also acted as an intermediary between Thistlewood and his former employer Cope, who very much wanted him back. Cope realized how difficult it was to hire experienced slave overseers. Phibbah ferried offer and counteroffer between the two men, taking the great risk in consequence of alienating her owner and losing her position as principal household slave at Egypt.

Phibbah faced several difficulties. First, Thistlewood was a noted philanderer who could replace her as his partner. At Kendal estate, indeed, Thistlewood took up briefly with a slave woman called Aurelia, making Phibbah jealous.[8] Second, Thistlewood resisted making a deal with Cope who often made reckless promises that he did not keep. Third, Thistlewood received several generous offers of work elsewhere. Finally, Thistlewood resented that Cope occasionally prevented Phibbah from coming to Kendal estate.[9]

Eventually, however, Thistlewood relented, and on June 27, 1758, he agreed to return to Egypt estate at a considerably increased salary and with the promise that Cope would hire Thistlewood's slaves. In part, Thistlewood returned because his conditions of employment had improved. But more important was his deep feeling for Phibbah. Her devotion had paid off. She and Thistlewood were never to part again. A relationship had been turned into a marriage, or at least the closest approximation of a marriage that was possible between a white man and a slave in eighteenth-century Jamaica. Moreover, Phibbah had established her own freedom. John and Molly Cope never again tried to dictate what Phibbah could or could not do. When Thistlewood left Egypt estate in 1767, John Cope did not object to Phibbah moving with Thistlewood to his new property at Breadnut Island.

Phibbah was not legally freed until 1792, six years after Thistlewood's death and after she was manumitted in Thistlewood's will, but her real freedom came in 1758 when Thistlewood decided to return to Egypt. That Phibbah was effectively free from 1758 hides the awkward fact that she was technically a slave during all of the forty years for which we have information about her. Without a formal documentation of emancipation, she was always liable to lose her privileges and "freedoms." Nevertheless, she did eventually become free in fact as well as in theory.

Phibbah was a typical freedwoman of eighteenth-century Jamaica, where slaves were most often freed because they were either the child or, like Phibbah, the mistress of a white man.[10] Phibbah was also like most Jamaica freedwomen in being native-born and a domestic by occupation.

We know about Phibbah because Thistlewood kept an extraordinary diary in which he jotted down his daily activities. The rich detail of the diary makes the contours of Phibbah's life uniquely accessible. Thistlewood's diary entries are nonetheless problematic.[11] We do not know what Phibbah looked like or anything about her ancestry. We see her only through the recorded observations of her lover, a lover who gave little attention to his own or Phibbah's interior life. We know that Phibbah was a Creole and that she had a sister, Nancy, who was a slave in a nearby parish. Phibbah was owned by William Dorril, a wealthy sugar planter and Thistlewood's first employer, who bequeathed her to his mistress, Elizabeth Anderson, who in turn left her to her natural daughter, Molly Dorrill, in 1754. By this date Phibbah herself had a daughter called Coobah. Assuming that Coobah was at least fifteen in 1762 when she had her first child, and that Phibbah was a similar age or older when she gave birth to Coobah, Phibbah's date of birth might be no later than the early 1730s. She was thus in her early to mid-twenties when she first became Thistlewood's partner. The last mention of Phibbah comes in 1792, when she was finally given the manumission promised her in Thistlewood's will. This means that Phibbah survived at least into her sixties. Besides Coobah, who was also alive in 1792, Phibbah gave birth to two more children, a still birth in 1755 that Thistlewood attributed to John Cope, and a son, John, in April 1760, who died, aged twenty, in 1780.

Our inability to flesh out more about Phibbah is a major historical problem in understanding her life. Nevertheless, all scholars of eighteenth-century enslaved women face similar problems with incomplete and biased sources, so we should be thankful we know as much about Phibbah as we do. That Phibbah achieved freedom as a result of her relationship with an often brutal white man makes it difficult to place her within the growing literature about freedwomen in the English-speaking world. It is still hard to think about interracial sexuality outside the prism of sexual exploitation. That is especially true for scholars who write about enslaved women and freedwomen in the American South. Black women's sexual interactions with white masters have been interpreted primarily as "part of a larger field of power relations in which masters expressed power sexually and viewed sexual activity as an expression of male power."[12]

Such emphasis on male patriarchal power and white men's sexual aggressiveness (both of which clearly characterized racial and sexual relations in eighteenth-century Jamaica) diminishes Phibbah, making her not the agent of her own destiny but merely a victim, or, even worse, a collaborator in the oppression of slaves. I believe that to understand Phibbah we need to move beyond viewing interracial sexual interactions solely through the very partial context of sexual exploitation. Phibbah was able to transcend the powerlessness of slaves through her privileged position as the mistress of a white man. That position enabled her to purchase property, advance the social status of herself and her family, and engage with Thistlewood on a more equal basis than any other slave. In doing so, she undermined the principle of black subordination and weakened assumptions of white dominance.[13] A study of how Phibbah secured individual and familial advantages as Thistlewood's long-term partner demonstrates how the personal agency of one actor disrupted seemingly rigid networks of social rules that were intended to secure the dominance of one group over another.

By asserting such a thesis, I am following lines of argument already well rehearsed by scholars of Caribbean slavery. Scholars of interracial sexual relations in North America see sexual relations between black women and white men and resulting miscegenation in almost wholly negative terms.[14] Caribbean historians, however, see interracial unions more positively. Edward Cox, for example, decries as "myth" the "fashionable" urge to "describe sexual relations between white males and free coloured and slave women as being of a fleeting nature without any degree of permanence."[15] Similarly, Barbara Bush exhorts us not to condemn all concubinage as sexual exploitation and notes that "many white men from all social ranks had fond and enduring relations with black and coloured women."[16]

The pronounced differences in the treatment of the Caribbean and North American experiences of enslaved women or free women of African descent are striking, given the existence of similar power relationships between white men and black women in both regions.[17] Thistlewood's diary shows that white Jamaican men had almost unfettered control over the lives of their black slaves. Their ability to punish was unrestricted by law or custom, and their opportunity for sexual adventure was unrestrained. In North America, white men who regularly violated black women sexually or lived with slave or free colored concubines faced considerable social stigma.[18] In the British West Indies, by contrast, white men had free sexual access to black women.[19] Patriarchy in Jamaica was the patriarchy of men who felt no need to temper their absolute powers with a concern for subordinates. The result was almost complete white male dominance and a slave system characterized by extreme brutality where slave-owners demonstrated singular indifference to the welfare and psychic well-being of their African charges.

Thistlewood was very much a Jamaican patriarch who adjusted very easily to the customs and mores of white men living among numerically dominant but socially subordinate black slaves. He was not a gentle master and often savagely flogged his slaves. Indeed, his first contact with Phibbah came when he gave her seventy lashes for harboring at her quarters a white man who had previously been supervisor on Egypt estate.[20] White Jamaican men were also notoriously self-indulgent, but Thistlewood was not as self-indulgent as some of them. He seldom drank to excess, he ate moderately, and he displayed in his remarkably methodical and extensive daily diary entries an intense desire to cultivate self-control.[21]

He did, however, devote himself to the pleasures of the flesh. Between 1751 and 1764 Thistlewood engaged in 1,774 sexual acts with 109 slave women.[22] He continued such philanderings, if on a less heroic scale, virtually until his death. Phibbah was far and away Thistlewood's most frequent sexual partner, but she had to share him with numerous others. Thistlewood was a quintessential sexual predator from whom no slave woman was safe. Like every other slave woman in eighteenth-century Jamaica, Phibbah had to cope with the constant fear of sexual molestation from other aggressively predatory white men who suffered no ill consequences from their actions.

The world in which Phibbah and other slave women attempted to forge some advantage for themselves and for their families was, therefore, highly skewed toward the interests of white men. Violence, exploitation, and instability marked the world of the slaves in eighteenth-century Jamaica. The brutality of Jamaican slavery may offer one explanation for the determination with which Phibbah and other relatively privileged domestic slaves pursued the furtherance of their interests through relationships with white men. These women did so in order to maintain their status within the slave community and to advance the likelihood that they and their children might be freed. The benefits of being the mistress of a white man were sufficiently enticing to encourage privileged black or colored women to detach themselves, at least sexually, from the company of slave men.

Jerome Handler has described the advantages that prolonged attachment to white men brought to Rachael Pringle Polgreen of early-nineteenth-century Barbados. Polgreen mixed almost entirely with whites in her successful career as concubine of two successive white benefactors and in her profession as a tavernkeeper.[23] An even more appropriate example, for our purposes, is that of Old Doll and her three daughters on Newton estate in eighteenth- and early-nineteenth-century Barbados. Hilary Beckles has found that these privileged household slaves used their positions and their many relations with white men to obtain substantial social authority within the slave community, to acquire some property of their own, and, above all, to prevent being relegated to the fields.

Old Doll and her daughters, in Beckles's view, had a strong perception of themselves as a slave elite with "rights" that were more often associated with free people than with slaves. They rejected arduous manual labor and socialized with free persons, both black and white, rather than with slaves. Their status was recognized by their access to slave assistants, whom they "owned." Most important, they adopted strategies that were explicitly intended to protect family interests. They worked hard to avoid being sent into the field, and when some family members were forced into such work "for degradation and punishment," they proved themselves such "nuisances" who "set the worst examples to the rest of the negroes" that managers of the estate reluctantly agreed to return them to house service. Just as important, they avoided any emotional or sexual involvement with slave men. Significantly, as they consolidated their positions as housekeepers and members of the slave elite, they also became lighter skinned; several generations of miscegenation transformed them from black to colored and from slave to free. When Old Doll died, her family had attained an enviable status both within the slave community and among whites, whom they increasingly resembled physically and socially. Fittingly, Old Doll's family buried her in a style normally reserved for whites. In part, Old Doll and her family rose in status by leaving their slave roots behind. But to view them as turncoats seems misplaced. As Beckles argues, they are better seen as "women—mothers and grandmothers—struggling to improve the intellectual and material lot of their families against reactionary plantation policies and the constraints imposed by the wider slave system."[24]

Phibbah and Old Doll were sisters under the skin. Both were privileged house slaves who increased their status and the position of their families through association with white men. In the process, both women separated themselves from the mass of slaves, even if both retained the confidence and respect of other slaves. Both women achieved freedom not through open resistance to slavery but through accommodation with white oppressors. Neither overtly challenged white power and white pretensions. Indeed, from a contemporary perspective both Old Doll and Phibbah may be seen as supporters of a monstrous system of oppression in which their partners were the primary perpetrators of violence against fellow blacks.

In a sense, Old Doll and Phibbah provided comfort to the oppressors of their people. Yet from another perspective, they posed insidious threats to the maintenance of a slave system based on the utter subjugation of one race and the absolute privileging of another. All blacks were meant to be inferior, enslaved, and incapable of reaching a measure of equality with whites. The support of privileged and elite slaves such as Phibbah was essential for the smooth functioning of Jamaica's slave system, but whites gained this support only by blurring divisions between black and white, slave and free. The story about Phibbah, an illiterate slave woman who became free, not only rescues from oblivion the life of an ordinary woman who belonged to a group whose lives we need to know more about but also helps illuminate some of the frictions and fissures that prevented Jamaican slavery from being completely closed to the possibility of individual social advancement.

The success of long-term interracial pairings in Jamaica depended very much on the character and status of the black mistress. Just as a wise planter made sure that his choice of a slave driver was a slave who could retain the respect of the slaves he was to control, so, too, a prudent white man chose as his long-term sexual partner a woman who carried authority in the slave community. To become the mistress of a white man accentuated a slave woman's status, but the exercise of that status fomented resentment within the slave community if she did not command respect. A mistress was less chosen by the master than she was co-opted with the tacit consent of other slaves. The slave mistress played a distinct leadership role within the internal hierarchy of the enslaved. She gained authority and prestige through her special access to the master. She was able to

intercede for slaves with masters and also provide information about the master to the slaves. With power came responsibility. If the master's mistress abused
her privileged status by lording it over other slaves, by playing favorites, or by
pleading too vigorously with her lover on the behalf of other slaves, she could
lose the respect of either the slaves or her master or both. From a master's perspective, a mistress who caused trouble with the slaves weakened his own authority over them. For slaves, their ability to negotiate with their master was
significantly reduced if they were unable to use the master's mistress as a reliable conduit of their concerns.[25]

Thistlewood was well aware of how an injudicious choice of a principal sexual
partner could disrupt slave management because he had himself once made a
poor choice. Thistlewood took Jenny, an African-born field slave who had little
status among slaves, as his "wife" between January 1752 and December 1753. It
was not a happy partnership. Jenny quarreled incessantly with Thistlewood and
with other slaves. The slaves evidently resented Jenny's rise in status as
Thistlewood's mistress. Quashe, a slave driver, was so bold as to make "impu-
dent" remarks about Jenny.[26] Unlike Phibbah, moreover, Jenny was not indifferent to the attractions of "negroe fellows," and Thistlewood had to reprimand
her for being "Concerned" with them and for "importuning for Sugar, Rum
etc."[27] Jenny's loyalties were all too clearly with her fellow slaves rather than with
Thistlewood; she found it difficult to resist the slaves' demands for assistance.
Thistlewood was not impressed, and several times he drove Jenny away on account of "her damn'd obstinate humour." He even gave her a sound whipping
on one occasion when he found that she had brought a knife with her to bed,
being "afraid" of her "intent."[28]

Jenny had to go. She was upsetting the slaves and disturbing Thistlewood.
If a mistress overplayed her hand with her lover or was unable to persuade other
slaves that she deserved her privileges, she was in danger of being displaced in
the master's bed, and she could be returned to the fields. What was perhaps
most remarkable about Jenny's replacement, Phibbah, was her ability to steer
a careful course between the Charybdis of overidentification with the values
of white society and the Scylla of too-close commitment to slave interests.
Phibbah was not a turncoat who worked against the slave community, even if
our understanding of her relations with fellow slaves is filtered through Thistlewood's perceptions.

Thistlewood seldom concerned himself with Phibbah's interactions with
other slaves. That in itself is revealing, for his concern about Jenny resulted from
Jenny's quarrels with other slaves. Phibbah evidently got on well with the other
slaves. As head domestic slave, she was the female equivalent of the slave driver.
Other slaves deferred to her. Phibbah assisted women when they gave birth, she
provided food from her provision grounds (and probably from Thistlewood's
larder) for slaves in need, and she participated in the ceremonies of the slaves.
Her connection with Thistlewood did not alienate her from their world. When

she was dangerously ill in 1768, "many Negroes came to see" her, and her dearest friends, house slaves Franke and Vine, and her adult daughter, Jenny Young, were extremely solicitous toward her. Similarly, when Mulatto John (Thistlewood and Phibbah's son) died, aged twenty, in 1780, many slaves from several plantations attended John's funeral and shared Phibbah's grief.[29]

Phibbah knew at least as much, probably more, about slave life as Thistlewood. When Thistlewood had sex with Eve rather than with Mountain Lucy (whom Phibbah had sent to him "to keep as a Sweetheart the Time she lies in"), Phibbah found out almost immediately. Thistlewood mused that he did not "know who could have told her." Phibbah obviously had her sources.[30] Phibbah was also aware, at least before she had become permanently attached to Thistlewood, of how slaves planned to frustrate his plantation management plans or intended to attack his person. Just after Christmas 1752, Thistlewood was caught unaware by a runaway, Congo Sam, who tried to murder him. Thistlewood barely escaped with his life. Reflecting on his narrow escape, Thistlewood noted that he had "reason to believe that many of the Negroes," including Quashe the slave driver and Phibbah, "knew that Sam had an intent to murder him" after hearing them "speak one day in the cookroom when I was in the back piaza reading."[31]

Slaves may not have shared such information with Phibbah after she became Thistlewood's mistress. Yet they continued to use her as a conduit to their master. Thistlewood often noted that Phibbah intervened on behalf of other slaves, three times expressing displeasure when she pushed their claims too far. In 1760, for example, Thistlewood reprimanded Phibbah "for intermeddling with Field Negroes business with me."[32] Phibbah's sphere of influence was the cookroom and did not extend, in Thistlewood's opinion, to the fields. Within the cookroom Phibbah reigned supreme, and Thistlewood allowed her to forgive those slaves for misdemeanors or punish them as she saw fit.[33]

As her willingness to punish slaves suggests, Phibbah's loyalties were divided. She undoubtedly provided Thistlewood with information about other slaves, even if he only rarely retailed such gossip to his diary. But it was natural that two people in a long-term intimate relationship would talk about the behavior and character of the slaves. Thus, Phibbah revealed to Thistlewood, when he was at Kendal estate, that Old Sambo had taken to "walking around Cabritto upper bridge with white men who promised to carry him to his country."[34] A slave mistress allowed entrée into the slave world. Phibbah was also privy to many white secrets, which she conveyed back to Thistlewood. She told him, for example, that Mrs. Cope had asked her "slyly" whether he "had made a will" after he had been very ill.[35]

Phibbah's contact with whites was extensive but not close. The social distance between whites and blacks in Jamaica was so great that she was seldom included in white social gatherings. Indeed, her involvement with whites was mostly limited to giving assistance, such as cooking for Molly Cope at christenings and weddings. She also assisted Molly in giving birth and helped out when the Cope children were ill.[36] By the 1770s, however, Phibbah's position as the established mistress of a local dignitary made her sufficiently respectable that white women allowed her to call on them. Thistlewood noted that Phibbah "went to see Miss Bessy Murray" in July 1771. In 1779 Phibbah reached the heights of her social respectability when she entertained two local grandees and their wives to "tea and porter under ye guinep tree in ye garden."[37] Such an event was extraordinary, and it suggests that James Stewart was right when he stated that late-eighteenth- and early-nineteenth-century white Creole women of Jamaica were willing to socially countenance entertaining the colored mistresses of family members.[38]

Yet if Phibbah was comfortable in the company of slaves and she occasionally mixed with whites, her preferred social network was among women of her own kind, the privileged house slaves and mistresses of white men. Phibbah interacted constantly during the 1750s and 1760s with her fellow domestic servants, House Franke and Egypt Lucy, and with Vine, the slave mistress of a white man on a nearby estate. When Phibbah gave birth to Mulatto John, House Franke came from Egypt to assist her, and Egypt Lucy gave "Phibbahs Child Suck." Similarly, House Franke contributed money (much of which she earned in economic partnerships with Phibbah and Egypt Lucy), as did Phibbah and Phibbah's daughter, Jenny Young (who had now changed her name from Coobah), to Young's white partner in order to secure the freedom of Phibbah's sister, Nancy, and that of Young's mulatto daughter.[39] When Egypt Lucy died at Egypt estate after a long illness in June 1772, Phibbah organized her burial. As in North America, "Adult female cooperation and interdependence was a fact of female slave life" in eighteenth-century Jamaica.[40]

Privileged black and colored women formed networks of friendship and mutual assistance. In 1765 Mrs. Bennett, a free colored who ran a school for colored children that Mulatto John later attended, gave "a negro wench named Bess to Phibbah for life and then to John." Bess, eleven, was put to work looking after Phibbah's stock, and later she assisted Phibbah in the cookroom.[41]

Privileged female domestics seldom associated with African-born male fieldworkers. If they did form liaisons with slave men they did so with light-skinned tradesmen or domestic servants. Phibbah's daughter, for example, had two mulatto tradesmen as partners. Phibbah herself does not seem to have ever been attached to a colored man. When she philandered, as seems certain she did, if to a much more limited degree than Thistlewood, it was with white men such as Thistlewood's employer John Cope or with Thistlewood's predecessor as overseer, John Filton.[42]

House slaves had little choice but to accept the sexual advances of white men. White men considered free sexual access to slave women to be their right, and they exercised that right often. House slaves had the most contact with white men and were, consequently, more likely than field slaves to be on hand when white men sought black women. After a night carousing, four friends of John Cope, "being heartily drunk," dragged Eve, a young house slave, from her bed "into the Water Room and were Concern'd with her[,] Weech 2ce [twice,] First and last."[43] To be a house slave was thus a mixed blessing. On the one hand, they enjoyed a much less arduous work regime than field slaves. Women like Old Doll and Phibbah had good reason to fear being sent to the cane fields. Most field hands were "trapped into a dehumanizing life of exhausting labor, debilitating disease, and demeaning social relationships."[44] House slaves were much better placed to survive the slave system. Their labor was easier, their life experiences were more varied, and their chances of manumission were considerably greater. As Barry Higman has demonstrated for early-nineteenth-century British Caribbean colonies, female domestics had the greatest chance of any slaves (except for head drivers, who were comparatively old when appointed to their position anyway) of reaching the "old age" of sixty.[45]

The frequent interactions of female domestics with white men certainly exposed them to sexual exploitation. Depersonalized, quasi-commercial sex between white men and slave women was pervasive and routine throughout the slave society of Jamaica, but it was particularly common between European migrants and slave domestics. House slaves were expected to provide sexual services for their masters as well as perform household chores. John Stedman candidly outlined in his narrative of his life in Suriname during the 1770s how it was customary for house slaves to combine the roles of housekeeper and concubine, although he transformed the tawdry commercial transactions between European men and adolescent girls into deeply romantic love stories. "The batchelors who live in this Climate," he opined, "all without Exception have a female Slave—mostly a creole—in their keeping who preserves their linnens clean and decent, dresses their Victuals with Skill, carefully attends them . . . during the frequent illnesses to which Europeans are exposed . . . [and] prevents them from keeping late Hours, knits for them, sows for them etc." Such attachments, Stedman claimed, were matters of such great pride to "these Girls," that "they hesitate not to pronounce as Harlots, [those] who do not follow them (if they can) in this laudable Example in which they are encouraged . . . by their nearest Relations and Friends."[46]

Stedman painted a rosy picture of institutionalized commercial arrangements of the late eighteenth and early nineteenth centuries through which "Relations and Friends" procured young women for European men.[47] "Relations and Friends" bargained away young women's capacity to choose their sexual partners in exchange for getting them positions as domestics. As the neighbor of Thistlewood and Phibbah, the wealthy sugar planter William Beckford, aptly put it, although working in the house with its "supposed indulgences" was "the more honourable" situation for slave women, "the most independent" slave women were those who worked in the fields "with its exaggerated labours."[48] Women who worked in the fields had some choice over whom they lived with, and they were able to exercise considerable cultural autonomy, retaining and enhancing African cultural practices.[49]

Much more than field slaves, female domestics, through continual interaction with whites, weakened their commitment to traditional African customs. Edward Long's observations that white women "insensibly adopted" the modes of dress, manners, and "drawling dissonant gibberish" of their black domestics also operated in reverse. The "sable handmaids" of white women were the most extensively creolized and Europeanized black slaves.[50] Whereas field hands practiced African religious ceremonies virtually undisturbed, the cultural options of female domestics were closely monitored. Consequently, black mistresses and house slaves risked some exposure to cultural isolation. Thistlewood disapproved of "African superstitions" and punished slaves for their involvement in such practices.[51] Phibbah, too, distanced herself from these activities. When she heard that her daughter Coobah had held two *myall* (African) dances in her house at Paradise estate, Phibbah immediately informed Thistlewood, who reprimanded Coobah severely the next time he saw her.[52] That Thistlewood discovered Coobah's secret is in itself revealing about how much more knowledge whites had about house slaves and their families than they did about field hands. In the privacy of the slave quarters, field slaves were probably able to practice obeah without Thistlewood's knowledge. House slaves did not have that degree of cultural freedom.

The advantages that slave women gained through sexual association with white men were often offset by their powerlessness over the actions of their partners. When slave women were unhappy with the treatment that their slave partners meted out to them, they could always complain to their masters. Thus, when London molested Hannah in 1755, Thistlewood "upon Hannah's complaint Whipp'd London."[53] But slave women had no higher authority to which to turn when their white partners mistreated them. White men could act with mind-numbing savagery and get away with it, as when Harry Weech decided to "cut off the lips, upper lip almost close to her Nose, off his Mulatto sweetheart, in Jealousy, because he said a Negroe should never kiss those lips he had."[54] Weech suffered no penalty for such barbarity. Phibbah's friend, Miss Sally, a free mulatto who lived with Thistlewood's neighbor, Mr. Wilson, was also ill-used by her partner, and she was forced to accept her beatings in silence. Thistlewood recorded Miss Sally to have been beaten by Wilson three times between 1775 and 1781. On the first occasion, Sally fled to Phibbah after Wilson cut her cheek with a cowskin. Sally declared that "She could never agree with his temper." Wilson visited Thistlewood the next day. Thistlewood noted without comment that Wilson refused to agree to a request from Sally's mother that Sally be allowed to return to her parents.[55] Sally was at least better off than Sappho, the mulatto mistress of Dr. Francis Ruecastle. He "beat etc his Wife sadly" and as a result Sappho died.[56]

Phibbah was comparatively fortunate. Thistlewood recorded only one act of violence he directed at Phibbah in the thirty-four years of their relationship. On

December 6, 1755, he gave her "some correction."[57] Thistlewood was never violent to Phibbah again. Indeed, their relationship became increasingly more harmonious. One must conclude that Phibbah bore considerable affection for Thistlewood despite the disparities in power between them and despite Thistlewood's persistent philanderings.

The most obvious manifestation of the physical bond between them was their vigorous sex life. Thistlewood never confined himself to one woman, but his infidelities did not lessen his attachment to Phibbah. His passion for her was most intense early in their relationship. In 1754 Phibbah and Thistlewood had sex 234 times (amounting to 88 percent of Thistlewood's sexual encounters in that year). Such intense sexual activity cooled in time, reaching a low of twenty-four sexual congresses in 1762 (26 percent of Thistlewood's sexual encounters in that year). But 1762 was an exceptional year. Most years during the 1760s and 1770s saw Thistlewood and Phibbah having sex often. In 1767 Thistlewood, forty-seven, had sex with Phibbah, who was probably in her late thirties, eighty-seven times by Thistlewood's own calculations.[58] Ten years later the couple still had sex four times a month, and sex with Phibbah accounted for more than two-thirds of Thistlewood's sexual activity.[59] Phibbah and Thistlewood continued an active sex life virtually to the end of Thistlewood's life. His last sexual encounter with her (and his last recorded sex with anyone) occurred on September 12, 1786, just two months before his final illness. Their vigorous sex life was not all at Thistlewood's insistence. Phibbah exerted a good measure of control. Of all the female slaves under Thistlewood's care, she alone did not always comply with his sexual demands. Several times he recorded that Phibbah "keep away" following a quarrel and when she was displeased with him.[60] It seems fair, therefore, to conclude that Phibbah and Thistlewood engaged in sex that was mostly consensual.

Like all lovers Thistlewood and Phibbah quarreled. In July 1754 Thistlewood recorded that Phibbah was "offended at my giving Jenny [his former mistress] a little Sugar." A few months later the two "had great words . . . in bed" over what Thistlewood believed was Phibbah's overfamiliarity with John Cope.[61] In time, quarrels between the two declined in frequency and intensity. Both became more assured of the other's constancy and emotional commitment. Indeed, by the 1760s it seems clear that Phibbah and Thistlewood cared deeply for each other. She grieved in March 1765 when Thistlewood's nephew accidentally drowned. Thistlewood noted that he felt "Strangely, pain all over me and can eat nothing," and, he added, Phibbah was also "ill" with grief.[62] Thistlewood demonstrated the depth of his feelings toward Phibbah by his close attention to her when she was sick. In November 1768 Phibbah "was so restless, and violent ill" that Thistlewood "thought she would have died." He "got up and tended her . . . getting no rest in the evening." The next day he called a doctor who bled her, but she did not get better despite Thistlewood's many ministrations that he hoped "would be a great service to her."[63]

By the time Thistlewood moved to Breadnut Island in 1767, the nature of his relationship with Phibbah was like that between husband and wife. His few complaints about her increasingly concerned minor domestic upsets. He grumbled, for example, in 1772 that the bad behavior of their son, John, was due to the fact that "His mother promotes his Ruin, by excessive indulgences and humoring him beyond all bounds."[64] Another cause for complaint came in 1776 when Thistlewood ruefully related that Phibbah had allowed herself to be tricked into giving more money than she should to a slave who "she was Weak enough to believe."[65]

Phibbah gained affection and emotional support from her involvement with Thistlewood, but there were other good reasons, including economic advancement and the interests of her family, why she would want to continue to be his mistress. Slave mistresses benefited enormously in financial ways from their attachment to white men. Attaining a measure of economic independence seems to have always been a priority for Phibbah, and she in large measure did so. By Thistlewood's death and by the time of her manumission, Phibbah was a wealthy woman of color, owning her own patch of land with her own livestock. In gaining property of her own, Phibbah achieved a limited independence for herself and, more important, for her family. Economic and family advancement went hand in hand. Her aim seems to have been to establish herself as an independent proprietor, and she realized the best way to achieve that was to take advantage of the opportunities that attachment to a white man afforded. She passed on her strategy for success to her children and sister, encouraging them to use their contacts with whites to further their own interests. Phibbah's involvement with Thistlewood, therefore, was more than just romantic. Her commitment to the interests of her flesh and blood was at least as strong as her devotion to Thistlewood. Through her attachment to Thistlewood she managed to advance those interests and to ensure that her family moved out of the dependence and uncertainty that characterized the slave condition into the comparative independence and security of free society.

A principal difference between slavery in the Caribbean and in most parts of North America was the much greater independent economic production of Caribbean slaves. They were expected to produce their own food on their own provision grounds and encouraged to market the surplus through the highly developed internal marketing systems of the islands where they lived. Slave and freedwomen played a vital role in this internal system of exchange. They replicated customs in the Caribbean that were important in West Africa, where women did most of the trading of goods at local markets. In eighteenth-century Jamaica probably a majority of slave "hucksters" were women. They were employed as small-scale itinerant vendors of agricultural products and retailers of clothing and other imported or locally processed goods.[66] Women like Phibbah had a strong competitive advantage as hucksters. Phibbah was able to draw on the resources of Thistlewood in developing her huckster trade. She could trade gifts from him in order to purchase livestock and other goods.

Thistlewood gave her gifts because he felt warmly toward her, but he also gave her goods because of her household expertise. Phibbah was an accomplished seamstress, and she earned a considerable income through the sale of her sewing to both blacks and whites. Thistlewood recognized her needlework skills even before he took up with her, giving her, for example, 8 bits for making him a waistcoat and breeches soon after he arrived at Egypt estate.[67] In this instance Phibbah made money on her own account. She continued to earn money that way for many years. Increasingly, however, she combined with Thistlewood in order to profit from her skill with a needle. Thistlewood provided her with cloth and buttons, and Phibbah turned those raw materials into finished products, passing only a portion of the profits to Thistlewood. Thistlewood began "subcontracting" Phibbah when he was at Kendal estate in 1757, giving her "goods worth £5 that she was to sell and give me the money."[68] By the 1770s these informal arrangements had been regularized. Thistlewood arranged for cloth and cloth-making materials to be sent to him, and Phibbah then turned them into clothes that she sold at local markets.[69]

Through these activities Phibbah earned a considerable amount of money. In August 1761 Thistlewood reported that he held nearly £67 on her behalf. This sum amounted to more than two years' salary for a white bookkeeper. It was sufficient to purchase seven or eight head of cattle. Phibbah even had enough money to lend to Thistlewood. He noted in 1769 that he owed Phibbah more than £27; in 1773 his debt to her amounted to £14.[70] Most of her income was derived from sewing, baking, and selling provision goods.[71] She earned additional money by buying and selling livestock. As early as 1758 she purchased a mare and arranged for a slave driver to look after it in return for every third foal from the mare. By 1760 she was able to sell one of the mare's progeny for £7, and she sold others in 1765, 1767, and 1772.[72]

When Thistlewood died, Phibbah was a substantial proprietor. She possessed at least three forms of property: land, slaves, and livestock. By 1783 Thistlewood formalized longstanding arrangements whereby Phibbah had her own estate on his property, arranging to fence in her ground and have a gate put in.[73] He confirmed Phibbah's right to her own land in his will, ordering his executors to "lay out the sum of One Hundred Pounds current money . . . in the purchase of a Lot or piece of land for the said Phibba wherever she shall choose and that they do build thereon a dwelling-house for the said Phibbah suitable to her station so that land and house do not exceed the said sum of One Hundred pounds." In his will Thistlewood also made legal Phibbah's status as a slave-owner, formally bequeathing to her "my negroe woman slave named Bess and her child named Sam," aged thirty-three and seven, respectively.[74] Her slaves would have helped Phibbah cultivate her land and care for her horses, cattle, and fowl. Among the livestock was a cow the appraisers of Thistlewood's estate in early 1787 noted had been claimed by "the old negro that lives with Mr Thistlewood."[75]

In effect, Phibbah had a family estate where she and her family could support themselves through subsistence production. Thus she and her family had been able to transform themselves from slaves to what Sidney Mintz has evocatively called "proto-peasants," or subsistence farmers engaged in independent production on lands they were able to call their own.[76] Central to this process of transformation was the family. As Mintz has insisted, slave and proto-peasant food production was a family enterprise and organized around the labor of family members.[77] Family estates were not just economic units. They were also "the basis for the creation of family lines and the maximization of kinship ties, in contrast to the kinlessness of the enslaved."[78] Phibbah's determination to forge an independent estate for herself showed her deep concern for the preservation and consolidation of her family lineage. Economic advancement was a principal way to ensure family survival.

Phibbah's strong commitment to her family and close friends pervades Thistlewood's revelations of her life in his diary entries. That Phibbah was able to maintain a vibrant, emotionally charged family life is in itself remarkable in light of the chaos and destruction that characterized Jamaican slavery and strongly militated against the formation of stable slave families. Orlando Patterson has stressed the extent to which Jamaican slaves faced a physical and cultural holocaust when they moved from Africa to Jamaica and the dramatic effects this had on family formation. Not all scholars agree with Patterson, but the depiction of slavery recorded by Thistlewood offers ample evidence that the world of slaves was one of great uncertainty and brutality that weakened solidarity among them and made slave family and community life highly dysfunctional.[79] Perhaps because Phibbah was both a household slave and a Creole she was insulated to a degree from the dehumanizing tendencies of slavery that produced for African field hands enormous cultural dislocation. Just as important, her involvement with Thistlewood provided protection for her family. A slave-owner was unlikely to sell or separate slave children from their mother if that mother was his mistress. Moreover, the mistress could expect her paramour to give favors to her kin, and she would hope for more for the children they had together.

Phibbah's family was small but close-knit. It comprised Phibbah; her sister, Nancy; her two children, Coobah (alias "Jenny Young") and John; and probably her close friend, House Franke. The four women in particular shared especially strong ties, visited each other frequently, and engaged in business together. Phibbah did her best to advance the interests of the other women. She sought favors for them from Thistlewood, tried to purchase their freedom, give them gifts, and assisted them in their work. She was especially solicitous of the interests of her two children. Coobah followed her mother as both a house slave and as the mistress of white men, but her experiences were more varied than her mother's and indicate that she was a woman of character and independence. The first mention of Coobah was, as for Phibbah, inauspicious: Thistlewood noted that he saved her from being raped in 1758 by his white bookkeeper who got her "into the Boiling-Room by Strategem" and "Attempted to Ravish her, Stopp'd a handkerchief into her mouth etc."[80] Coobah was probably still a child at the time. Three and a half years later she became the waiting maid of Mrs. Molly Cope and was due to have a child. Thistlewood thought that the child's father was either her husband, Mulatto Davie, a slave driver, or John Cope.[81] Through either the good offices of Thistlewood or Phibbah, Coobah never suffered the torments of fieldwork.

More than Phibbah, Coobah alternated between the world of privileged slaves and that of whites. She had several lovers, both mulattos and whites. In addition to Mulatto Davie and John Cope, she was involved with two overseers—slaves named Dago and Tom—before settling into a permanent relationship in November 1776 with Jimmy Stewart, a mulatto from the New Hope estate.[82] With these partners Coobah had six pregnancies that resulted in only two children who survived infancy: a mulatto, Nancy, to whom Thistlewood gave a dollar for Christmas in 1784, and a son named after his father, Jimmy, but who died at nearly six years of age in 1786.[83] Although she retained an association with African customs such as myall, Coobah was more Europeanized than her mother. Unlike Phibbah, she converted to Christianity in 1771 and changed her name to Jenny Young.[84] She and her husband, Jimmy Stewart, were Christian converts well before black baptism became popular or even acceptable in Jamaica among either blacks or whites.[85] Her conversion may have resulted from the experience that most differentiated her from the mass of Jamaican blacks: a year-long trip to England as the servant of John and Mary Cope's young son, William Dorrill Cope.[86] Such an experience surely helped Coobah achieve a better understanding of Europeans and their society.

Coobah visited Phibbah frequently and was particularly helpful in times of stress. When her half-brother John died in 1780, Coobah stayed with her mother for two weeks. Thistlewood increasingly welcomed her and began to treat her as his own daughter. He employed her to make clothes, sold her livestock, and gave her gifts when she was ill.[87] His affection for his stepdaughter was an important step in his own maturation. According to Hall, Thistlewood's open and affectionate association with Phibbah and Coobah encouraged him to temper his behavior toward his slaves and provided him with a greater appreciation of their world.[88] In this way creolization was a two-way process. Coobah "Africanized" Thistlewood, and at the same time her involvement with Thistlewood and other whites increased her "Europeanization."[89]

Part of the reason that black women attached themselves to white men in Jamaica concerned the considerable benefits they gained for the children produced in these relationships. Slave mistresses of white men were reputed by some observers to be indifferent parents. It was argued that "even a mulattoe child interrupts their pleasures" and that they used "certain herbs and medicines, that free [them] from such an incumbrance."[90] But the same observers who castigated black women for their failings as mothers also claimed that such women were notorious schemers on behalf of their kindred and burdened their lovers with a "spurious race of children" whose maintenance cost their white fathers dearly.[91] It seems likely that white men's concubines aspired to have mulatto children, and that they fought hard to gain as many advantages as possible for their children.[92] Certainly, Phibbah was a warm and affectionate mother who cared deeply for her children. When Mulatto John was ill, she looked after him; when he needed clothing, she made what he needed; when she went to see friends, she took him with her; and when John angered his father, she tried to help him.[93] When he came down with the fever that killed him, Phibbah walked a long distance to attend to him and bring him home. She was inconsolable after his death.[94]

Phibbah also helped persuade Thistlewood to provide for John's future. John received many favors from Thistlewood, the most important of which was his freedom in 1762.[95] Thistlewood taught his son to fish and hunt. He arranged for him to be sent to school from the age of five until he was twelve. He also had John apprenticed as a carpenter and fitted him out as a member of the colored militia. Unfortunately, John did not take full advantage of all Thistlewood provided. His apprenticeship proved especially disastrous. He absconded from work several times, misused his tools and those of others, and got drunk at his master's house. He was also nearly discharged from his indentures.[96] Thistlewood became so exasperated with John's failure to remain at work that he resorted to inflicting punishments usually reserved for slaves, flogging him and putting him in the stocks for an evening.[97] Nevertheless, Thistlewood retained affection for his son and took his death very hard. A week after John's burial, Thistlewood wrote "I am exceeding dejected and low spirited etc a parched mouth and great inward heat."[98]

The privileges given to John—freedom, education, and settlement in a trade—were powerful incentives for Phibbah to stay attached to Thistlewood. Had her son lived and grown out of his teenage delinquencies, he might have become a member of Jamaica's brown elite and enjoyed a standard of living and a status several steps above the mass of African slaves and superior to what Phibbah had attained for herself.[99] By inheriting property from Thistlewood and by attaining property through his own efforts, John would have been able to build on Phibbah's success and consolidate the family estate that she had laboriously put together. By "whitening" her children, Phibbah thus did the best she could for the future of her family.[100]

How then should we make sense of Phibbah? Like most slaves who became free, she fits uneasily into a historiography that persists in viewing slaves either as victims of oppression or as determined rebels whose "every willed response . . . to bend the system in their favor, to secure space for themselves, could be interpreted as resistance." But "such responses can also be interpreted as adaptation."[101] To place Phibbah within the prism of slave resistance risks trivializing the notion of resistance itself. If everything that does not actually directly aid planter oppression of slaves can be seen as resistance, then, as Michel-Rolph Trouillot laments, it is difficult to know whether resistance is a term that "stands for an empirical generalization, an analytical category, or a vague yet fashionable label for unrelated situations."[102]

Phibbah as resister stretches the concept of slave resistance too much. She may have expressed hostility to the monstrous system that entrapped her and other slaves in conversations with friends, but no evidence of such hostility toward slavery ever emerges in Thistlewood's diary observations. Apart from a single reference where Thistlewood tellingly describes Phibbah as "in miserable slavery," Phibbah's feelings about slavery are not revealed.[103] Much of what Thistlewood recorded, moreover, suggests that Phibbah was, if anything, a collaborator in the subjugation of slaves. She herself became a slave-owner. She was not averse to punishing slaves under her care, and she revealed slave delinquencies to her master.[104] Phibbah sought out the company of whites and other privileged slaves, and she abandoned African cultural practices. Perhaps significantly, Thistlewood did not mention her at all when he referred to the great slave rebellion of 1760 that came close to destroying white rule in Westmoreland Parish.[105] Most important, Phibbah was the principal comforter and support of the mortal enemy of the slaves, Thomas Thistlewood. Her love and counsel may have tempered Thistlewood's behavior toward his slaves, but it contributed primarily to his personal well-being, and as such it hindered the efforts of the slaves to resist his authority and power.

It is better to see Phibbah not as a collaborator but as an accommodator.[106] Neither victim nor heroine, she shows how effectively a resourceful, intelligent, and determined woman could become the agent of her own fortune. Through hard work and assiduous cultivation of her involvement with Thistlewood, Phibbah acquired a life of her own and sufficient prosperity that gave her dignity within a system where slaves were usually stripped of honor. What is most valuable about the Phibbah, and which we see through Thistlewood's eyes, is that she was a real woman, one capable of love and disdain, strong but sometimes foolish, a loyal friend, a devoted partner, a fond mother, and a resourceful entrepreneur. To see her from that vantage point does not decrease awareness of the destructiveness and immorality of slavery. Instead, recognition of how Phibbah "coped with slavery, survived it, and built from it and within it" brings with it the realization that Phibbah's life was "a remarkable achievement worth recognizing and celebrating as a triumph of the human spirit."[107]

Phibbah accommodated herself to slavery so well that in the end she transcended it and gained freedom. She transcended slavery in a more metaphysical way, demonstrating through her life and personality that the belief of slaveholders that slaves were utterly dependent and without honor was a lie. In that respect Phibbah delivered a more telling blow to the integrity of Jamaica's slave system than the resolute rebel. It was Phibbah rather than the rebel Tacky who did most harm to the conceptions of white Jamaicans about race and slavery. Her activities blurred the distinctions that whites believed naturally existed between whites and blacks. Her involvement with Thistlewood made her less African, and it also made him less European; her acquisition of a family estate denied the concept of slaves as propertyless and utterly dependent; and her production of a freed mulatto son and her eventual freedom complicated the easy equation that existed between white and free and slave and black. Messy reality softened and disturbed rigid theories about what slaves should do and be. Challenges to slavery could thus come just as easily and more effectively through gentle Phibbah's smile, as the execrable exotic ode to black womanhood, the "Sable Venus," had it, as through violent resistance.[108]

Notes

1. June 18, 1757, Monson 31/8. The Thistlewood diaries are in the Monson Deposit 31/1–31/37, Lincolnshire Archives, Lincoln, England. I am indebted to John Monson, Eleventh Lord Monson, for permission to quote from the Monson Deposit. The quotation in the title of the chapter is from (Rev. Isaac Teale), "The Sable Venus—An Ode," (Jamaica, 1765) in Bryan Edwards, *The History, Civil and Commercial, of the British Colonies in the West Indies*, 5 vols. (London, 1801), 2: 28.

2. July 17, 1757, Monson 31/8.

3. "Begged hard of Mrs Cope to sell or hire Phibbah to me, but she would not; he was willing." June 22, 1757, Monson 31/8.

4. June 19, 1757, Monson 31/8.

5. June 24, 1757, Monson 31/8.

6. July 4, 1757, Monson 31/8.

7. June 23, 1757, Monson 31/8. That Phibbah had genuine regard, perhaps love, for Thistlewood can also be seen in how deeply she grieved when Thistlewood's nephew, John, accidentally drowned. April 1, 1785, Monson 31/16.

8. July 3, 1757, Monson 31/8.

9. Jan. 10, Feb. 5, and April 23, 1758, all in Monson 31/9.

10. An analysis of grants of manumission made in Jamaica in 1748 and 1767 show that 55 percent of manumitted slaves were mulattoes (mostly children) and that 65 percent of adult manumitted slaves were females. Of fifty-nine slaves set free by will in St. Andrew Parish from 1720 to 1778, twenty-eight were women, twenty-three were children, and only eight were adult men. Internal evidence from wills strongly suggests that most freedwomen were domestics or mistresses or a combination of both. Manumissions, vols. 5 and 7, Jamaica Archives, Spanishtown; Wills, Island Record Office, Twickenham, Jamaica.

11. The biases and deficiencies of Thistlewood's diaries are beyond the scope of this essay. Briefly, Thistlewood wrote his diaries (an entry a day for nearly thirty-eight years) as part of a systematic record-keeping that also included commonplace books and weather journals. They were part of his passion for collecting facts and were intended as a way of ordering his life. Their major weakness is their lack of introspection. Unreflective about his own motives, Thistlewood was unconcerned with the feelings of others and noted their presence in his diaries merely as they coincided with his world and his concerns. The picture of Phibbah, therefore, is one that has to be pieced together from short, laconic, and often uninformative references to her in a very long text. For more

on the diary, see Douglas Hall, *In Miserable Slavery: Thomas Thistlewood in Jamaica, 1750–1786* (London: Macmillan, 1989).

12. Kathleen M. Brown, *Good Wives, Nasty Wenches, and Anxious Patriarchs: Gender, Race, and Power in Colonial Virginia* (Chapel Hill: University of North Carolina Press, 1996), 356.

13. Phibbah was thus what Eugene Genovese terms a "heroic accommodator"—a slave who acquiesced to her master's demands but exercised her plantation privileges to benefit her enslaved compatriots. Eugene Genovese, *Roll, Jordan, Roll: The World the Slaves Made* (New York: Pantheon, 1974), 327–98.

14. Some representative quotations: "Miscegenation under slavery was above all an indignity to the female slaves," in Thelma Jennings, "'Us Coloured Women Had to Go through a Plenty': Sexual Exploitation of African-American Slave Women," *Journal of Women's History* 1 (Winter 1990): 60; "[an interracial union] was deeply threatening and disturbing to the slave community," in Ann Paton Malone, *Sweet Chariot: Slave Family and Household Structure in Nineteenth-Century Louisiana* (Chapel Hill: University of North Carolina Press, 1992), 221; "the enormous disparities [in status] ensured that almost any sexual relationship would be exploitative," in Adele Logan Alexander, *Ambiguous Lives: Free Women of Color in Rural Georgia, 1789–1879* (Fayetteville: University of Arkansas Press, 1991), 66; "there was a strong depth of feeling against racial intermixture" and "female slaves confronted a limited choice in sexual matters involving their masters," in Peter Bardaglio, *Reconstructing the Household: Families, Sex, and the Law in the Nineteenth-Century South* (Chapel Hill: University of North Carolina Press, 1995), 50, 56; and "racial relations invariably occurred in a climate of sexual domination and despotic rule," in Ann Ducille, "'Othered' Matters: Reconceptualizing Dominance and Difference in the History of Sexuality in America," *Journal of the History of Sexuality* 1 (July 1990): 120.

15. Edward L. Cox, *Free Coloreds in the Slave Societies of St. Kitts and Grenada, 1763–1833* (Knoxville: University of Tennessee Press, 1984), 1533–54.

16. Barbara Bush, *Slave Women in Caribbean Society, 1650–1832* (Bloomington: Indiana University Press, 1990), 114.

17. Differences may be due to the greater influence of feminist thought in North American slave historiography; to the greater historical and contemporary acceptance of interracial sexual relations in the Caribbean than in the United States; and to the absence in North America of the concept of an intermediate racial category of mulatto. The existence of a mulatto class of "browns" who had greater privileges and higher status than blacks is a distinctive feature of Caribbean society, both during and after slavery.

18. Bertram Wyatt-Brown, *Southern Honor: Ethics and Behavior in the Old South* (New York: Oxford University Press, 1982), 307–24; Catherine Clinton, "'Southern Dishonor': Flesh, Blood, Race, and Bondage," in *In Joy and in Sorrow: Women, Family, and Marriage in the Victorian South, 1830–1900*, ed. Carol Bleser (New York: Oxford University Press, 1991), 57–64.

19. See, for example, the outraged comment by Maria, Lady Nugent after talking to the mistress of a "civil, vulgar, Scotch officer, on half-pay": "The overseer's chere amie, and no man here is without one, is a tall black woman, well made with a very flat nose, thick lips, and a skin of ebony, highly polished and shining . . . The marked attention of the other women, plainly showed her to be the favourite Sultana of this vulgar, ugly, Scotch Sultan." *Lady Nugent's Journal of her Residence in Jamaica from 1801 to 1805*, ed. Philip Wright (Kingston: Institute of Jamaica, 1966), 29.

20. May 4, 1752, Monson 31/3.

21. This essay forms part of a larger project about Thistlewood and his world. For other aspects of Thistlewood's life and diaries see Trevor Burnard, "Thomas Thistlewood Becomes a Creole," in *Varieties of Southern History: New Essays on a Region and Its People*, ed. Bruce Clayton and John Salmond (Westport: Greenwood Press, 1996), 99–118; Trevor Burnard, "'They Do Not Like Their Will to Be Thwarted': The Household and Household Violence in Thomas Thistlewood's Jamaica," in *Over the Threshold: Intimate Values in Early America, 1640–1865*, ed. Christine Daniels and

Michael V. Kennedy (New York: Routledge, 1999); and Trevor Burnard, "The Sexual Life of An Eighteenth-Century Jamaican Slave Overseer" in *Sex and Sexuality in Early America*, ed. Merril D. Smith (New York: New York University Press, 1998).

22. Figures derived from Mike Peck, "Unequal Relationships: An Historical Enquiry into Master-Slave Relations as Featured in the Journals of Thomas Thistlewood," M.A. thesis, University of Canterbury, 1995, 130–46.

23. Jerome S. Handler, "Joseph Rachell and Rachael Pringle Polgreen: Petty Entrepreneurs" in *Struggle and Survival in Colonial America,* ed. David G. Sweet and Gary B. Nash (Berkeley: University of California Press, 1981).

24. Hilary McD. Beckles, *Natural Rebels: A Social History of Enslaved Black Women in Barbados* (New Brunswick: Rutgers University Press, 1989), 65–68.

25. Genovese, *Roll, Jordan, Roll,* 359–61; William Dusinberre, *Them Dark Days: Slavery in the American Rice Swamps* (New York: Oxford University Press, 1996), 190–99.

26. June 29, 1752, Monson 31/3.

27. May 10, and Oct. 8, 1752, both in Monson 31/3.

28. Jan. 27, and May 26, 1753, both in Monson 31/4.

29. Nov. 20, 1768, and Sept. 7, 1780, both in Monson 31/19, 31/31.

30. Aug. 21–22, 1755, Monson 31/6.

31. Dec. 27, 1752, Monson 31/3.

32. Jan. 11, 1760, Monson 31/11; July 10, 1755, Monson 31/6; and June 16, 1781, Monson 31/32.

33. For punishments, see Aug. 7, 1770, Monson 31/21, and Nov. 2, 1771, Monson 31/22; for leniency, see June 16, 1781, Monson 31/32.

34. Jan. 4, 1758, Monson 31/9.

35. Nov. 1, 1755, Monson 31/6.

36. Jan. 21, 1759, Monson 31/10; Jan. 26, 1779, Monson 31/30. The most notable example of her attachment to the Cope family was her devoted service to the Cope's young son, Haughton, who died in 1774. Phibbah, along with her daughter and two other Egypt estate house slaves, sat up with Haughton on his deathbed. May 27, 1774, Monson 31/25.

37. July 13, 1771, Monson 31/21; Feb. 16, 1779, Monson 31/30.

38. James Stewart, *View of the Past and Present State of the Island of Jamaica* (Edinburgh: Olives and Boyd, 1823), 173.

39. April 29, May 1, 1760, Monson 31/11; April 8, 1776, Monson 31/27. For evidence that Phibbah, House Franke, and Egypt Lucy combined their economic endeavors, see Sept. 3, 1769, Monson 31/20, which deals with Thistlewood returning the £27.2s.6d. he borrowed from the three women.

40. Deborah Gray White, *Ar'n't I a Woman? Female Slaves in the Plantation South* (New York: W. W. Norton, 1985), 119.

41. July 24, 1765, Monson 31/16.

42. May 4, 1752, Monson 31/3; Oct. 3, Nov. 15, and Dec. 22, 1754, Monson 31/5; Aug. 5, 1755, Monson 31/6.

43. May 12, 1755, Monson 31/6.

44. Richard S. Dunn, "The Story of Two Jamaican Slaves: Sarah Affir and Robert McAlpine of Mesopotamia Estate," in *West Indies Accounts: Essays on the History of the British Caribbean and the Atlantic Economy in Honour of Richard Sheridan,* ed. Roderick A. McDonald (Kingston: University Press of the West Indies, 1996), 207; see also Richard S. Dunn, "'Dreadful Idlers' in the Cane Fields: The Slave Labor Pattern on a Jamaican Sugar Estate, 1762–1831," *Journal of Interdisciplinary History* 17 (Spring 1987): 795–822; and Richard S. Dunn, "Sugar Production and Slave Women in Jamaica," in *Cultivation and Culture: Labour and the Shaping of Slave Life in the Americas,* ed. Ira Berlin and Philip D. Morgan (Charlottesville: University of Virginia Press, 1993), 49–72.

45. B. W. Higman, *Slave Populations of the British Caribbean 1807–1834* (Baltimore: Johns Hopkins University Press, 1984), 332–36, 667–70.

46. John Gabriel Stedman, *Narrative of a Five Years Expedition against the Revolted Negroes of*

Surinam, transcribed for the first time from the original 1790 manuscript and edited with an introduction and notes by Richard Price and Sally Price (Baltimore: Johns Hopkins University Press, 1988), 47–48.

47. Stewart, *View of Jamaica,* 325; [Anon.], *Marly; or, A Planter's Life in Jamaica* (Glasgow: Griffin, 1828), 133.

48. William Beckford, *Remarks upon the Situation of Negroes in Jamaica* (London: T. & J. Egerton, 1788), 13.

49. Michael Mullin, *Africa in America: Slave Acculturation and Resistance in the American South and the British Caribbean, 1736–1831* (Urbana: University of Illinois Press, 1992), 159–73, 271–73.

50. Edward Long, *History of Jamaica; or, General Survey of the Antient and Modern State of That Island: With Reflections on Its Situations, Settlements, Inhabitants, Climate, Products, Commerce, Laws, and Government,* 3 vols. (1774, reprint London: Frank Cass, 1970), 2: 278–79.

51. On obeah and *myall,* see Dec. 29, 1780, Monson 31/31. In 1764 Thistlewood noted, "There is an information against Mr. Samuel Say of Cabaritta Estate for permitting a Negro play (for Vine's mother, who is lately dead) last Sunday Afternoon." Vine was Say's mistress. White authorities chided whites like Say who allowed their slaves such cultural latitude. May 5, 1764, Monson 31/15.

52. March 22, and April 16, 1769, both in Monson 31/20.

53. June 30, 1755, Monson 31/6.

54. Dec. 31, 1765, Monson 31/16.

55. Nov. 20–21, 1775, Monson 31/26; July 31, 1778, Monson 31/29; Oct. 8, 1781, Monson 31/32.

56. Aug., 1782, Monson 31/33.

57. This excludes the flogging that Thistlewood gave Phibbah on February 22, 1752, before Phibbah became his partner (Monson 31/3).

58. Dec. 31, 1767, Monson 31/18.

59. Indeed, Phibbah maintained her share of Thistlewood's sexual attentions over time. Between 1754 and 1764 she was his partner in 65 percent of his sexual encounters.

60. See, for example, Feb. 25, 1753, Monson 31/4; April 17, Oct. 4, and Nov. 19, 1754, Monson 31/5; Feb. 2, Feb. 7, July 6, Aug. 26, 1755, Monson 31/6; and Aug. 13, Aug. 17, and Aug. 31, 1759, Monson 31/10.

61. July 5, and Oct. 3, 1754, Monson 31/5.

62. April 1, 1765, Monson 31/16.

63. Nov. 18–24, 1768, Monson 31/19; see also May 27–June 3, 1775, Monson 31/26.

64. Aug. 21, 1772, Monson 31/23.

65. Jan. 7, 1776, Monson 31/27.

66. See, inter alia, Sidney Mintz and Douglas Hall, *The Origins of the Jamaican Internal Market System* (New Haven: Yale University Press, 1960); Roderick McDonald, *The Economy and Material Culture of Slaves: Goods and Chattels on the Sugar Plantations of Jamaica and Louisiana* (Baton Rouge: Louisiana State University Press, 1993); Mary Turner, ed., *From Chattel Slaves to Wage Slaves: The Dynamics of Wage Bargaining in the Americas* (Bloomington: Indiana University Press, 1995), 48–78; and Ira Berlin and Philip D. Morgan, eds., *The Slaves' Internal Economy: Independent Production by Slaves in the Americas* (London: Frank Cass, 1991).

67. June 6, 1752, Monson 31/3; see also March 24, 1752, Monson 31/3; and Dec. 31, Sept. 2, 1753, Monson 31/4.

68. Dec. 5, 1757, Monson 31/8.

69. See, for example, March 23, 1774, Monson 31/25; March 9, 1776, Monson 31/27; May 5, 1777, Monson 31/28; April 22, 1778, Monson 31/29; and Sept. 5, 1779, Monson 31/30.

70. Aug. 31, 1761, Monson 31/12; Sept. 3, 1769, Monson 31/20; May 19, 1773, Monson 31/24.

71. Jan. 10, 1773, Monson 31/24.

72. May 27, 1758, Monson 31/9; April 5, 1760, Monson 31/11; March 22, 1765, Monson 31/16; Sept. 27, 1767, Monson 31/18; May 17, 1772, Monson 31/23.

73. Hall, *In Miserable Slavery,* 296.

74. Bess had been given to Phibbah by Mrs. Bennett on July 24, 1765 (Monson 31/16). As a slave, however, Phibbah could not legally own a slave, and Bess had always been "given in" by Thistlewood as his own. Wills 52 (1786), 77, Island Record Office, Twickenham, Jamaica.

75. Inventories, 71 (1787), 200, Jamaica Archives, Spanishtown.

76. Sidney W. Mintz, *Caribbean Transformations* (Chicago: Aldine, 1974).

77. Sidney W. Mintz, "The Jamaican Internal Marketing Pattern: Some Notes and Hypotheses," *Social and Economic Studies* 4 (1955): 95–103; Sidney W. Mintz, "Was the Plantation Slave a Proletarian?" *Review* 2 (1978): 81–98; Mintz and Hall, *Origins of the Jamaican Internal Market System*, 1–26.

78. Jean Besson, "A Paradox in Caribbean Attitudes to Land," in *Land and Development in the Caribbean*, ed. Jean Besson and Janet Momser (London: Macmillan, 1787), 18.

79. Orlando Patterson, *The Sociology of Slavery: An Analysis of the Origins, Development and Structure of Negro Slave Society in Jamaica* (London: Macgibbon and Kee, 1967). For modifications of Patterson, see in particular Sidney W. Mintz and Richard Price, *The Birth of African-American Culture: An Anthropological Perspective* (Boston: Beacon Press, 1992); Mullin, *Africa in America;* and Barry Higman, "African and Creole Slave Family Patterns in Trinidad," *Journal of Family History* 3 (Summer 1978): 163–80.

80. Feb. 19, 1758, Monson 31/9.

81. Aug. 24, 1761, Monson 31/12.

82. Coobah had remarkable independence in sexual matters, if an anecdote reprinted by Thistlewood in 1768 is anything to go by. Coobah marked up a smock with the names of three men with whom she was involved and wrote underneath (implying, of course, that she had a high degree of literacy for a slave) "Here's Meat for Money, If you're fit, I'm ready, But take Care you don't fish [flash] in the pon [pan]." Oct. 1, 1768, Monson 31/19.

83. Dec. 6, 1784, Monson 31/35; Jan. 5, 1786, Monson 31/37.

84. Nov. 13, 1771, Monson 31/22.

85. The conversion of blacks to Christianity did not become general until the second decade of the nineteenth century. Thomas Coke, *A History of the West Indies, Containing the Natural, Civil, and Ecclesiastical History of Each Island*, 3 vols. (Liverpool: Nuttall, Fisher, and Dixon, 1808–11); Mary Turner, *Slaves and Missionaries: The Disintegration of Jamaican Slave Society, 1787–1834* (Urbana: University of Illinois Press, 1982), 6–18.

86. May 9, 1767, Monson 31/18; Jan. 31, 1768, Monson 31/19.

87. July 12, Aug. 23, 1777, Monson 31/28; Jan. 3, 1782, Monson 31/33.

88. Hall, *In Miserable Slavery,* 215. Thistlewood's fuller involvement with slaves does not demonstrate a change in his thinking toward slaves and slavery, nor does it indicate that he concerned himself overmuch with slaves as human beings. His "Africanization," his increasing familiarity with slaves, and his relative humanity toward his slaves in his later years result as much from his increased confidence in his ability to control slaves and from his movement away from the harsh labor regime of a sugar estate as it did with his involvement with Phibbah. Nevertheless, his dealings with Phibbah and Coobah reveal a more humane and kindly Thistlewood than the brutal overseer of the 1750s.

89. For the process of creolization, see Edward Braithwaite, *The Development of Creole Society in Jamaica, 1770–1820* (New York: Oxford University Press, 1971), 296–305.

90. Janet Schaw, *Journal of a Lady of Quality; Being the Narrative of a Journey from Scotland to the West Indies, North Carolina, and Portugal, in the Years 1774 to 1776,* ed. Evangeline Walker Andrews and Charles McLean Andrews (New Haven: Yale University Press, 1923).

91. Thomas Atwood, *The History of Dominica* (1791, reprint London: Frank Cass, 1971), 209–10.

92. Thistlewood's nephew, John, noted in his brief diary an episode where a woman "came to persuade me if possible to lay with her," arguing that "she wanted to have a child for (her) master" but feared her master was impotent." Feb. 3, 1765, Monson 31/16; John Thistlewood's diary, Monson 31/38.

93. For sickness, see Feb. 14, 1764, Monson 31/15; for clothing John, see Sept. 27, 1767, Monson 31/18, Aug. 29, 1774, Monson 31/25, and March 9, 1776, Monson 31/27; for visiting, see March 1, 1771, Monson 31/22; and for helping John, see Sept. 26, 1779, Monson 31/30.

94. Sept. 1–16, 1780, Monson 31/31.

95. Oct. 3, 1761, Monson 31/12; May 25, 1762, Monson 31/13.

96. Jan. 31, June 28, July 2, Oct. 28, 1777, Monson 31/28; Jan. 6, May 6, July 31, Dec. 29, 1778, Monson 31/29; May 26, 1779, Monson 31/30.

97. May 8, July 3, July 8, Dec. 29, 1778, Monson 31/29.

98. Sept. 13, 1780, Monson 31/31.

99. Gad Heuman, *Between Black and White: Race, Politics, and the Free Coloreds in Jamaica, 1792–1865* (Westport: Greenwood Press, 1981).

100. Bush, *Slave Women in Caribbean Society*, 116.

101. David Barry Gaspar, "Antigua Slaves and Their Struggle to Survive," in *Seeds of Change*, ed. Herman J. Viola and Carolyn Margolis (Washington, D.C.: Smithsonian Institution Press, 1991), 131.

102. Michel-Rolph Trouillot, "In the Shadow of the West: Power, Resistance, and Creolization in the Making of the Caribbean Region," in *Born Out of Resistance: On Caribbean Cultural Creativity*, ed. Wim Hoogbergen (Utrecht: ISOR Press, 1995), 9.

103. July 17, 1757, Monson 31/8.

104. July 10, 1755, Monson 31/6; Jan. 4, 1758, Monson 31/9; Nov. 2, 1771, Monson 31/22; Dec. 19, 1776, Monson 31/27.

105. May 1760, Monson 31/11.

106. Genovese, *Roll, Jordan, Roll*, 327–98. For an insightful analysis of the tension between accommodation and resistance see Sidney W. Mintz, "Slave Life on Caribbean Sugar Plantations: Some Unanswered Questions," in *Slave Cultures and the Cultures of Slavery*, ed. Stephan Palmie (Knoxville: University of Tennessee Press, 1995), 12–23.

107. Gaspar, "Antigua Slaves and Their Struggle to Survive," 131.

108. "The Sable Venus—An Ode," in Edwards, *History, Civil and Commercial*, 2: 28.

CHAPTER 6

The Fragile Nature of Freedom:
Free Women of Color in the U.S. South

Loren Schweninger

In 1813 Lucinda, a free woman of color, petitioned the Virginia General Assembly for relief. Following her owner's death, she explained, she and a number of other slaves had been manumitted by the owner's last will and testament. According to the will, they were required to leave the state. Their owner knew that if they remained in Virginia they would be returned to slavery under an 1806 statute that required freed slaves to emigrate from the state within a year or be reenslaved.[1] "[A]ll the slaves so emancipated (except your petitioner) were removed this year to the State of Tennessee," Lucinda wrote, "but your petitioner declined going with them, as she had a husband belonging to Capt. William H. Hooe in King George county, from whom the benefits and privileges to be derived from freedom, dear and flattering as they are, could not induce her to be separated." The question for Lucinda was not whether she was willing to sacrifice her freedom for her "marriage" but rather who would become her new owner. She feared being sold to someone who might "remove her to a place remote from the residence of her husband." She therefore asked the Virginia General Assembly to allow her to become a slave of her husband's owner (Appendix A).[2]

Other free women of color in the U.S. South shared Lucinda's dilemma during the late eighteenth century and the first six decades of the nineteenth century. They, too, confronted increasingly hostile and restrictive laws and faced wrenching decisions about their families as they struggled against economic, political, and legal barriers. Laws varied from state to state, but by the 1820s most states in the Upper South required manumitted slaves to emigrate or face a return to slavery; most in the Lower South prohibited manumission altogether except by a special act of the legislature. Lawmakers also passed codes to restrict the movement of free blacks, prohibiting them from assembling with slaves and requiring them to carry proof of their status ("freedom papers") on their persons at all times. How free black women (in this essay a term used interchange-ably with "free women of color") responded to these restrictions reveals a great deal about their tenuous status in southern society, the brittle nature of free-dom, and how far some of them were willing to go in order to maintain the integrity of their families.[3]

With a few exceptions, historians have neglected the plight of free women of color in the U.S. South.[4] Although devoting substantial attention to slave women, including their work routines, family and household structure, relationships with whites, and other dimensions of slave life, scholars have not examined the women who attained freedom with the same intensity.[5] This essay explores the difficulties free women of color confronted as they struggled as wives and moth-ers to preserve their family relationships. It does so by using a primary source that scholars have largely ignored: petitions to southern legislatures. Although relatively few in number, these legislative petitions articulate the values, attitudes, and mores of free black women, individually and collectively, as they lived out their lives a few steps away from being returned to bondage.[6]

During the period from the American Revolution to the Civil War, free women of color occupied a unique place in southern society. They were manumitted in greater numbers than their male counterparts, they represented a larger portion of the free black population, and they controlled a significant percentage of the black wealth. Their freedom came more readily because white men who took slave women as sexual partners sometimes provided them with deeds of manu-mission. As a result, in most communities they outnumbered free men of color. That was especially true in towns and cities where free blacks tended to congre-gate. For a variety of reasons—selective manumission, high male mortality, and large female slave populations—women dominated the urban free black popu-lation. By 1860, in towns and cities with 2,500 or more inhabitants, they consti-tuted 57 percent of the free black population; in the largest cities with popula-tions of ten thousand or more they constituted 58.5 percent.[7]

In towns and cities, most free black women worked as laundresses, maids, seamstresses, cooks, midwives, venders, and servants. In a few cases they man-aged small businesses, including hairdressing shops, confectioneries, bakeries, coffee houses, and boardinghouses. During the 1820s Susan Jackson of Savan-nah, Georgia, ran a popular pastry shop in Reynolds Ward, the leading business section of the city, and during the next decade Eliza Seymour Lee owned a popu-lar hotel in Charleston, South Carolina. One observer described Lee as "a very obliging and civil colored woman who is extremely desirous of accommodating us to our minds." Such enterprises, however, were unusual and tended to be more numerous in cities of the Lower South, especially New Orleans, where white men offered assistance to a few free black women. In most cities the vast majority of free black women found employment at the bottom of the economic ladder.[8]

Despite their low occupational status, free women of color gradually acquired small amounts of property. During the early nineteenth century, when many among them had only recently emerged from slavery, the number who owned property remained tiny. Following 1830, however, the number of black female property-owners increased rapidly. In 1830 in Petersburg, Virginia, a typical small town in the Upper South, only seven black females owned lots (compared with sixteen black men); by 1860, the number of black women who owned real estate had risen to ninety-two, nearly 40 percent of the black realty-owners. As in others towns, most of their holdings were valued at only a few hundred dollars, but by the eve of the Civil War free black women owned 22 percent of the total wealth controlled by free blacks in the region. Although there were significant differences in average holdings between the Upper and Lower South, that large proportion pointed to the independent role of free women of color. It also suggested that some women controlled property for both themselves and their slave husbands.[9]

Among the most difficult problems confronting free women of color was how to maintain their families. Women manumitted late in life, or who, as slaves, had started a family, or who married slave men, often found themselves confronting wrenching personal decisions regarding themselves and their loved ones. It is impossible to know exactly how many free black women faced such situations, but it is clear that a significant proportion of them remained closely tied to slaves and thus constantly faced possible separation from their spouses and/or children. It is true that in the Lower South small enclaves of prosperous free people of color intermarried and separated themselves as much as possible from other free blacks and slaves. Many of them owned slaves for commercial purposes. But they were not the norm, even in the lower states. Free blacks and slaves came together in the workplace, in church, at social gatherings, and in marriage.[10] Indeed, with the relatively small number of available free black men, free women of color were often left with few alternatives except to "marry" slaves.

One way for free women of color to obtain marital stability was to purchase husbands out of slavery. Except in Georgia, there were no legal barriers to such a purchase.[11] In most cases, however, costs were prohibitive, and even when enough money could be saved, or paid out over a period of years, the final transaction depended on the willingness of slave-owners to part with their property. And even when full payment was made, the owner could renege and sell the man if no legal agreement had been signed. Even if there were such an agreement, contracts between blacks and whites were sometimes not upheld in the courts.[12]

If everything went smoothly, women then faced the problem of freeing their husbands by deed or legislative act. Doing so presented additional obstacles because state laws either made it difficult, at times virtually impossible, to manumit slaves or required freed slaves to emigrate. But at a minimum, purchasing a husband meant that a wife could at least hold the man in "nominal slavery" during her lifetime. Priscilla Jessup of South Carolina purchased her husband, John, from Nathaniel Marion of Abbeville District in 1834. Unable to secure an act of emancipation, she held him in "nominal servitude" for more than a decade.[13]

It took Jemima Hunt of Virginia six years to pay for her husband. In 1805 she contracted with his owner to purchase him, promising to pay £10 a year. By the time she made the final payment in 1811 the couple had a large number of free-born children.[14] She then asked the General Assembly to grant him his freedom. "Be it enacted by the General Assembly, That when Jemima Hunt (a free woman of colour) of the county of Southampton, shall have regularly emancipated her husband, named Stephen, whom she purchased," an act of the assembly read, "he is hereby permitted to remain in this commonwealth."[15] During the 1790s Madelene St. Rigue of North Carolina arranged to purchase her husband, Major, from his owner, a man who lived in Edenton; she paid the final amount in 1801 and then petitioned the Assembly for his freedom. The General Assembly did not pass an act, but at the bottom of the docket page of her petition the word "granted" was written.[16]

The ambiguous result of Madelene St. Rigue's petition symbolized the difficulties free women of color confronted in seeking redress from state legislatures. Those who were successful usually presented strong arguments about how they had saved to purchase loved ones over many years, or they showed that their husbands as slaves had always been industrious, hard-working, and obedient. Even then, depending on the political climate or the level of fear among whites concerning slave unrest, forcefully argued and well-reasoned petitions might be rejected. As with Jemima Hunt, successful petitions occurred primarily during the late eighteenth and early nineteenth centuries. By the 1830s and 1840s, as sectional conflict intensified, it was highly unusual for free women of color to receive favorable consideration from state legislatures.

Most freedwomen, of course, did not possess the financial resources to purchase their husbands. If during the early nineteenth century it was very difficult to save the purchase price, as time passed it became virtually impossible. The price of a young male slave in 1800 ranged from $350 in Richmond to $500 in New Orleans; by 1837 the prices in those two cities rose to $900 and $1,300, respectively, and by 1856 to $1,300 and $1,500.[17] Unable to buy their slave husbands, women who remained in a state longer than the law allowed following their emancipation petitioned legislatures to remain with them. Rebecca of Sullivan County, Tennessee, was elderly when she finally obtained freedom. At the estate sale following the owner's death, all of her children, save one, were sold to distant markets. Rebecca petitioned the legislature in 1837 for permission to remain with her slave husband and her single remaining child, who was now an adult.[18] Like Rebecca, other black women asked general assemblies for permission to live near or with their slave husbands.[19]

How far some women were willing to go in this regard is illustrated by the case of Nelly Hoomes of Richmond, Virginia, who, with her daughter, was manumitted in the 1830s by William Marshall in his will. She continued to live in the state illegally and gave birth to three more children, Bartlett, Sam, and Pleasants, who were born free. The problem was that her husband, Bartlett Hoomes, was a slave who lived and worked in Richmond. If she could obtain permission to remain in Virginia eight or ten more years, she explained in 1833, she could save enough to purchase his freedom. Indeed, she had already started to save for that purpose, and she was confident that she could earn enough to make the purchase. She would then immediately leave the state with her husband.[20]

It was not only husbands that free women of color sought to protect but also children. In her petition to the North Carolina Assembly in 1791, Grace Davis noted that her son had "cheerfully turnd out during the war in defence of his Country." She had "a number of other Children" who were, like her son and herself, ostensibly free, but she wished to make their freedom "perfect" with "a special act in behalf of herself and her children."[21] During the same period, Amelia Green of Craven County, North Carolina, purchased and emancipated her daughters, Nancy Handy and Princess Green. She then asked the county court to "set free and emancipate them, and vest them with all powers, privileges and advantages which free people of color enjoy."[22] In Virginia during the early 1800s, Jenny Parker, even as a slave, assisted her children in obtaining their freedom. When, as an old woman, she finally acquired her own freedom, one of her children owned real estate and had purchased two of Parker's other children.[23] Most women who succeeded in freeing their children did so after many years of struggle.[24]

When it was not feasible to manumit children, mothers made every effort to avoid separation. Sometimes that was not possible because owners refused to release children from bondage, or traded them to neighbors, or sold them to distant markets. Even when slave-owners were amenable to assisting mothers, restrictive laws made it difficult to remain with offspring. Texas free black Fanny McFarland was manumitted by the last will and testament of her owner in 1835 for "long and faithful services." She acquired some "little property," she said, but was required by law to leave the state. Her four children, however, were slaves. She had neither the means nor the time to purchase them out of bondage. Leaving them would be a fate worse than death she confessed. She simply could not bear the thought of spending the "few remaining days of her life" without her children.[25]

Even when a mother and children obtained freedom, it was difficult to leave family members and friends. One Virginia woman explained that traveling to an unknown land, "in the midst of Strangers, cut off from the society & aid of relations & friends," would be unbearable.[26] "'Tis with anxious and trembling forebodings then that Your Petitioner presents herself before the Legislature," Elvira Jones of Richmond, Virginia, said in her 1823 petition, "to supplicate of their liberality and clemency, permission to herself and children to live and die in the Land of their nativity."[27] She explained that she had purchased herself and her two children, Julie Ann and William. Nashville slave Temperance Crutcher also purchased her freedom, and she, too, said she did not wish to search for a home "in the land of Strangers." She desired to remain near "kindred and friends."[28] The nine children of Sophia Towns of Nacogdoches County, Texas, asked the legislature of the Republic of Texas for an exemption from the emigration law. Louisa and Eliza Towns, the two eldest, were married and had five children. They and the others, ages four to twenty-six, had endeavored "to improve their condition by the acquisition of some little personal property." They also sought "to Demean themselves in a proper and becoming manner."[29] Agnes Earhart's eleven children in Mississippi were similarly not slaves, but they, too, were of various ages, and if required to leave the state, as she was informed was necessary by law, it would cause wrenching separations from various members of their families.[30]

Only a small proportion of the women who sought to protect their families by petitioning legislatures succeeded. As the years passed, especially following the Denmark Vesey slave conspiracy in South Carolina in 1822 and the Nat Turner slave revolt in Virginia in 1831, petitioners confronted increasingly hostile anti-free black laws and attitudes. Most states passed new comprehensive slave codes, and many slave-owners argued that free blacks provided a bad example for slaves. They were, a group of Chester District, South Carolina, whites asserted, "indolent, lazy, improvident, destitute of forethought, and totally incapable of self government."[31] By the 1840s and 1850s even states such as Delaware, which had a small black population, passed highly restrictive statutes.[32] In 1849 free blacks from outside Delaware were permitted to visit friends and family in the state for a maximum of sixty days. Previously, the visiting period had been six months. Authorities checked travelers closely. Two years later, in 1851, nonresident free blacks were prohibited from entering the state entirely.

As onerous as these attitudes and statutes were for free women of color, even more so was the determination of some whites to push them back into slavery. Indeed, many lived in constant fear that some "ill disposed person or persons" would return them to slavery. One woman confessed that she was virtually powerless against "Evil disposed Persons" who, without justification or provocation, might take her away as a slave.[33] They not only feared for themselves but also for their loved ones. What calamity could be worse, one mother agonized, than having children "taken up and sold." She could not think about it without terror in her heart.[34] During the 1820s and 1830s, as slave prices rose in the Deep South, free black women in the upper states remained constantly on guard to fend off slave traders or kidnappers who might sell them as slaves to plantation owners in the lower Mississippi river valley.

For Sarah Greene of Fairfax County, Virginia, the terror became a reality during the 1780s. Promised her freedom by an owner who died before he could execute his promise, Sarah was granted nominal freedom by the owner's widow. She and her four children enjoyed virtual freedom for many years, even after the widow remarried. But when the widow's second husband died, one of his male relatives kidnapped two of Sarah's children, carried them to "Carolina," and sold them as slaves. In 1784 he returned and was attempting to capture Sarah and her two other children. Sarah then petitioned the Virginia legislature for "an act to confirm to herself and Children that Freedom which it was the wish and intention of their Master that they should enjoy" (Appendix B).[35]

One of the most revealing cases concerning the problems that might confront free women of color involved the Vass slaves of Halifax County, Virginia. In his 1831 will, Phillip E. Vass provided that a group of his slaves should be given $2,000 and assisted in buying a farm and livestock in North Carolina. The slaves—Mary, Patsey, Samuel, Matilda, Jacob, and Meriwether—however, were kept in slavery for eight years following Vass's death.[36] The heirs argued that free blacks were not allowed to enter North Carolina, and therefore Vass's will was invalid. Even after Mary and the others sued in *forma pauperis* and won their freedom, the black family was unable to claim its inheritance.[37] They could not travel to North Carolina, nor could they remain in Virginia, without being reenslaved.[38] Patsey petitioned the Virginia Assembly in 1842 to remain in the state with her children, who were slaves, and with her husband, Terry Daniel, a free black shoemaker. She was fifty-five and to leave them, she said, would cause her unbearable pain and suffering. The petition, however, was rejected.[39]

The cases of Sarah Greene and Mary, Patsey, Samuel, Matilda, Jacob and Meriwether Vass reveal how relatives of slave-owners could thwart the wishes of masters who wished to manumit their slaves. In fact, the Virginia law that permitted slaves to sue for their freedom had less to do with providing blacks with an avenue to freedom than with protecting the desire of owners to dispose of their property as they wished. Sarah Greene and her children and the Vass slaves were not the only ones who struggled to extricate themselves from the greed of heirs or others determined to keep them in bondage. In 1783 a mother and her daughter petitioned the Virginia Legislature to protect them from heirs who were "laying claim" to them as slaves.[40] Another manumitted woman spent a "considerable portion of her time" hiding in the District of Columbia to avoid reenslavement. She rarely saw her husband and children.[41] Four other Virginia slaves, Cloe, Lotty, David, and Daniel—freed in the will of Emanuel Fentress because of their "honesty, fidelity, and good conduct"— feared being sold by Fentress's brothers, who sought to nullify his will.[42] Tennessee slaves Lizy and her six children—Bob, Susan, Violet, Reynolds, Jacob, and Ellie—were promised their freedom by a slave-owner in Stewart County, but shortly before his death in 1848 they fell into the hands of "false and pretended friends" who kept them enslaved. They, like the Vass slaves, instituted a suit for their freedom. Although the suit was eventually successful, they were then forced by law to emigrate to West Africa. At age sixty-five Lizy suffered from a number of ailments; Bob's health was also poor; and Susan was an invalid, cared for by her brothers.[43]

The contradictions in the lives of free women of color were perhaps nowhere more evident than in their relationships with whites. During the nineteenth century, South Carolina, Georgia, Florida, and Alabama enacted guardianship laws that required free blacks to obtain white guardians in much the same manner as parentless or propertied children would secure patrons to handle their legal affairs. No specific laws were passed in the upper states, but free blacks were often forced to secure white "protectors," people in the community who then would vouch for their good character. Free women of color who lived alone or with their children sometimes paid a heavy price for such "protection." They could be forced into an unwanted sexual relationship with their "protectors"; they could also be forced to work without pay to gain the good graces of a white family; and, whatever their feelings, they were obliged to act deferentially and humbly before whites. Free colored women fully realized that defiant or aggressive behavior might spell disaster.[44]

Nonetheless, many free black women relied on whites to assist them in finding suitable employment and protect them in times of racial unrest. "I take pleasure in recommending her as an honest and industrious Woman," George Burke wrote in 1850 from Ravensworth Plantation in Virginia about Sarah Dixon, a free woman of color. "She is a good Cook and a first rate washer and Ironer." Nor was there any doubt that she would give satisfaction in any undertaking, because she was not only skilled but "particularly suitable in her disposition."[45] Others said the same thing: Sarah was "a very respectable Girl—Honest, faithful and respectful to *all*."[46] She was "quite a good Cook, and would no doubt be a useful servant in almost any family." "I have always found her quiet and orderly, Civil and Respectful in her demeanor," one slaveholder said, "and in her general deportment amiable and well disposed[.]"[47] In other cases, too, white men described free black women as honest, industrious, dependable, and loyal. She always "conducted herself well and Earned her living by Honest Industry," a group of Texas men said about laundress Zylpha Husk, and another free woman of color, Jenny McFarland, was deemed a "good and usefull Citizen."[48] Another conducted herself "in an upright Honest industrous & respectable manner, with Credit to a person of her Couler."[49] Similar "certificates" said that black women were orderly, submissive, and trustworthy. Such recommendations meant the difference between employment and joblessness, family unity and separation, and sustenance and impoverishment.

Free women of color sought references for themselves and their husbands. Priscilla Jessup of Abbeville District, South Carolina, who purchased her husband out of slavery, asked a white man named N. McCants to trace her husband's history so she would have a record to prove his status. For six years he had been owned by McCants's stepfather, Nathaniel Marion, McCants said; he had never heard anyone speak against him, and he believed his conduct was good. Moreover, he had witnessed his stepfather sign the bill of sale conveying "the boy John" to Priscilla "for a Valuable Consideration."[50] Priscilla then obtained similar recommendations from other whites: they had known John for "a number of years and have never heard or known any thing disrespectful of His Character." "We believe him to be an honest upright boy and has the Confidence of his neighbours."[51]

Besides their efforts to assist their husbands and protect their children, free black women occasionally approached state legislatures about other matters, usually in unison with free black men. In 1825 a group of black women (and men) in Charleston, South Carolina, complained about a new tax placed on individuals who owned or rented houses "inhabited by negroes or persons of color" or who worked as mechanics (as did a number of free people of color in the city). The tax, $10 a year, was designed to help defray the cost of the municipal guard, which spent so much time seeking to control the black population. The women argued that the tax was unfair, unjust, and inequitable; it was tantamount to leveling a surcharge on black property owners and mechanics.[52] In Virginia, emancipated slave Henrietta of Warren County also lodged a complaint with her general assembly. In 1837 she asserted that local officials had denied her due process by rejecting her petition to remain in the state. A recent law, she said, permitted freed slaves to stay in Virginia if three-fourths of a county's magistrates voted in favor of such residency. In her county, however, county officials admitted that she could not remain under any circumstances. It was "impolitic to grant the leave in any instance in said county," the magistrates had declared, "in consequence of the number of free negroes in the county." Thus, Henrietta and her family were denied their rights under the law because it was "impolitic," a clear violation of their right of due process.[53] In another case of 1823, a group of free women of color in Richmond, Virginia, along with their husbands and others, petitioned the legislature for permission to erect a Baptist African Church. "It has been the misfortune of your petitioners to be excluded from the churches, meeting Houses and other places of public devotion which are used by white persons," they explained. As a result, they were "compelled to look to private Houses, where they are much crowded and where a portion of the Brethren are unable to hear or to partake of the worship which is going on." Thus, they sought to build their own church. They promised that its preachers would be fully acceptable to city fathers and that they would never hold night services.[54] This fervent plea, like the request for tax relief in Charleston in 1825 and Henrietta's plea for Virginia residency in 1837, was ignored. Nonetheless, as these cases show, free women and men of color presented arguments to the highest legislative tribunals in South Carolina and Virginia during the 1820s and 1830s.

Free black women faced many obstacles in their attempts to seek legislative redress. Those who sat in judgment over their petitioners were often unsympathetic slaveholders. Indeed, a substantial number of legislators wished to expel free blacks from the South, "return" them to West Africa, or, during the 1850s, reduce them to slavery. The women also faced a legislative process that was cumbersome. Petitions were read to the house or senate, sent to committee, returned to the floor, and voted up or down; at any time the requests might be tabled, amended, or rejected. In addition, illiterate women were dependant on whites to articulate their views and formulate their arguments. Although that was sometimes ably done, at other times whites who offered assistance knew little about the law or how to plead a case. Thus, in the midst of a society in which many whites sought to stifle free black aspirations, free women of color presented their pleas nevertheless. It is little wonder, then, that they usually failed and that their pleas to secure "justice" for themselves and their loved ones went unheeded. It is surprising indeed that they continued to seek redress through state legislatures.

A few free women of color gave up the struggle and opted to return to slavery, a route that only a handful among the tens of thousands of free black women in the South chose. Most, unlike Lucinda in Virginia in 1813, did so on the eve of the Civil War, when some whites were arguing that all free people of color should be reenslaved.[55] Fear, anxiety, economic hardship, and the suffering of children prompted most of them to seek out whites who would agree to become their owners. In 1861 Kissiah Trueblood, a twenty-three-year-old North Carolina free black, asked to become the slave of her employer, Dr. H. P. Ritter, in what could be termed voluntary enslavement. She was "destitute and without protection." She promised that any children she might have in the future would also become Ritter's slaves.[56] In 1860 Roseanna, a free woman of color in Hinds County, Mississippi, asked the legislature to pass a law making her the slave of Calvin Boles, a farmer.[57] That same year, several other free black women in Mississippi, rather than taking unwanted steps to emigrate, asked to become slaves.[58] One of them, Emmarilla Jeffries, wanted to remain "in the service of a gentleman who has Kindly provided for her wants" so she could be near her husband and sisters.[59]

Among the most heartrending examples of the efforts of free women of color to become slaves again was the case of Lucy Andrews, the daughter of a white woman and a slave in Lancaster District, South Carolina. At age sixteen in 1858, she asked to "go voluntarily into Slavery, and select her own Master" because "Slaves are far more happy, and enjoy themselves far better, than she does, in her present isolated condition of freedom." Toting her infant child, she wandered about from place to place in search of employment, but she could neither provide for herself nor her child. When her petition was denied, she again, in 1861, asked to become a slave, this time mentioning the name of W. Henry Duncan, "a Kind benevolent man, Kind as well to his slaves as to his neighbors." After a second denial, Lucy again petitioned to become Duncan's slave, finally revealing her true motives. Duncan owned her husband, Robbin. Although her first child had died, she now had two other children, Emily and Robbin, and now lived with her husband and their children on the Duncan farm. If she were permitted to become a slave she could remain with her husband. Despite her persistent efforts, however, Lucy Andrews was not successful in becoming a slave (Appendix C).

In some ways the pleas of free women of color were similar to those of free black men who tried to protect spouses, obtain freedom for family members, and remain within a state. Indeed, in a few cases, women joined with men to request some basic rights. Yet free women of color confronted particular burdens, especially with regard to protecting their children. Most of their petitions, like the ones by Lucinda in Virginia in 1813 and Lucy Andrews in South Carolina in 1858, were rejected, but the petitions themselves remain valuable documents because they reveal a great deal about the difficulties free women of color faced in seeking to maintain family stability in the midst of the oppositional forces of slave society. During the decades from the 1780s to the eve of the Civil War, free black women of the U.S. South struggled to sustain themselves and protect their husbands and children against onerous laws and the unsympathetic attitudes of most whites. That some would choose slavery over freedom rather than relinquish their ties with loved ones who remained in slavery bears witness to their deep commitment to family stability and to the fragile nature of freedom in the U.S. South.

Appendix A: Petition of Lucinda to the Virginia General Assembly

To the Legislature of the Commonwealth of Virginia,

The petition of Lucinda, lately a slave belonging to Mary Matthews of King George county respectfully sheweth.

That the said Mary Matthews, by her last will and testament, among other things, emancipated all her slaves, and directed that they should be removed by her executor to some place where they could enjoy their freedom by the laws there in force. That all the slaves so emancipated (except your petitioner) were removed this year to the State of Tennessee; but your petitioner declined going with them, as she had a husband belonging to Capt. William H. Hooe in King George county, from whom the benefits and privileges to be derived from freedom, dear and flattering as they are, could not induce her to be separated: that, in consequence of this determination on her part, a year has elapsed since the death of her late mistress Mary Matthews, and your petitioner, is informed that the forfeiture of her freedom has taken place under the law prohibiting emancipated slaves from remaining in this State; and that the Overseers of the Poor might now proceed to sell her for the benefit of the Poor of the county: Your petitioner, still anxious to remain with her husband, for whom she has relinquished all the advantages of freedom, is apprehensive that, in case of a sale of her by the Overseers of the Poor, she may be purchased by some person, who will remove her to a place remote from the residence of her husband: to guard against such a heart rending circumstance, she would prefer, and hereby declares her consent, to become a slave to the owner of her husband, if your honorable body will permit it; and for that purpose she prays that you will pass a law vesting the title to her in the said William H. Hooe and directing that all proceedings on the part of the

Overseers of the Poor for King George county to effect the sale of her may be perpetually staid;

And your petitioner will pray &c
Nov: 27th, 1813   *Lucinda*

Source: Petition of Lucinda to Legislature of the Commonwealth of Virginia, Nov. 27, 1813, King George County, Library of Virginia, Richmond. The petition was tabled.

Appendix B: Petition of Sarah Greene to the Virginia General Assembly

To the honourable the Speaker and Members of the house of Delegates of Virginia

The Petition of Sarah Greene humbly sheweth That your petitioner tho born in Slavery has never felt the hardships of that miserable State, it having been her Lott to fall into the hands of one of the best of Masters, the Reverend Charles Greene, late of the County of Fairfax deceased. That having had the good fortune to recommend herself to the favour of her said Master by many years of faithful service he had determined to reward your petitioner with Liberty to herself and Children. your petitioner is informed that the laws of this Country at that time would not admit of her masters liberating her by Will. and Death prevented him from putting in execution (by legal means) his benevolent Intentions towards your petitioner and her two Children. but that in his last Illness he exacted a promise from his Lady that she would fulfill those intentions after his death. Your petitioner further begs leave to show to your honble House that her said Master left his whole fortune in this Country to his Widow Mrs Sarah Greene who in the year 1767 intermarried with Doctor William Savage lately deceased, that previous to the said marriage Doctor Savage executed a Bond to George Washington and Bryan Fairfax Esquires obliging himself to pay a certain sum annually for the use of the said Mrs Greene during her life. That when the Bond was prepared and before it's [*sic*] execution Mrs Greene insisted that a clause should be inserted enabling her to set free your petitioner and Children. that Doctor Savage agreed that your petitioner and Children should be set free, but to save the trouble of drawing the bond over again promised that he would after the marriage execute an Instrument of writing empowering and enabling his said intended wife to emancipate your petitioner and her two Children, and called upon Witnesses to take notice of his said promise and your petitioner has been informed that he actually executed an Instrument of Writing for that purpose. Some unhappy Differances having arisen between Doctor Savage and his Lady he carried her to Ireland about the year 1769 and left her he returning to Virginia. after this time your petitioner and her Children were suffered to enjoy their Liberty for many Years. When a Mr Rice said to be a Relation of Doctor Savage took by force from your petitioner her two Children and carried them to Carolina, and has lately attempted to carry off your petitioner and two other Children since born, and still threatens to take the first opportunity of forcing them into Slavery, which your petitioner fears he will do unless your honble House will be pleased to interpose in their favour And as it was the intention of their Master to give them freedom and as Doctor Savage assented to his Lady's having that power. it is presumable that Mrs Savage (who your petitioner is informed died in obscurity and great poverty in Ireland without leaving any Relations) did direct them to be set free by her last Will. Tho even if she did not your petitioner humbly hopes that your honble house will pass an act to confirm to herself and Children that Freedom which it was the wish and intention of their Master that they should enjoy. and to which Doctor Savage had himself assented as part of his marriage Contract.

> And your petitioner as in duty bound will ever pray &c
> [signed] Sarah Greene

Source: Legislative Petitions, Petition of Sarah Greene to the Virginia House of Delegates, Fairfax County, Dec. 3, 1784, Library of Virginia, Richmond. The petition was tabled.

Appendix C: Petition of Lucy Andrews to the South Carolina Legislature

To the Honorable, the Senate, and House of Representatives, of the Legislature, of the State of South Carolina—

The humble Petition of Lucy Andrews, a free Person of color, would respectfully represent unto your Honorable Body, that she is now sixteen years of age, (and the Mother of an Infant Child) being a Descendant, of a White Woman, and her Father a Slave; That she is dissatisfied with her present condition being compelled to go about from place to place, to seek employment for her support, and not permitted to stay at any place more than a week, or two, at a time, no one caring about employing her—That she expects to raise a family, and will not be able to support them—That she sees, and knows, to her own sorrow, and regret, that Slaves are far more happy, and enjoy themselves far better, than she does, in her present isolated condition of freedom; and are well treated, and cared for by their Masters, whilst she is going about, from place to place, hunting employment for her support. That she cannot enjoy herself, situated as She now is, and *therefore* prefers Slavery, to freedom, in her present condition. Your Petitioner therefore prays that your Honorable Body, would enact a law authorizing and permitting her to go voluntarily, into Slavery, and select her own Master, and your Petitioner will, as in duty bound, ever pray &c-

> *her*
> *Lucy X Andrews*
> *mark*

Source: Records of the General Assembly, Lucy Andrews to the Senate and House of Representatives of South Carolina, ca. 1858, South Carolina Department of Archives and History, Columbia. Referred to Committee on Colored Population. No act was passed.[60]

Notes

My deep appreciation goes to Marguerite Ross Howell, who assisted in the preparation of this essay. The petitions cited below are part of the Race and Slavery Petitions Project at the University of North Carolina, Greensboro. The project has received generous financial support from the National Historical Publications and Records Commission at the National Archives, The National Endowment for the Humanities, and The Charles Stewart Mott Foundation. The originals of petitions cited, as well as other extant legislative petitions on race and slavery, can be found in the microfilm edition entitled "Race, Slavery, and Free Blacks: Petitions to Southern Legislatures, 1777–1867" and published by University Publications of America.

1. Any slave emancipated after May 1, 1806, who remained in the Commonwealth more than twelve months could be seized and sold back into slavery. *A Collection of All Such Acts of the General Assembly of Virginia, of a Public and Permanent Nature as Have Passed since the Session of 1801* (Richmond: Samuel Pleasants, Jr., 1808), 97. For the implementation of this law in practice, see John H. Russell, *The Free Negro in Virginia, 1619–1865* (Baltimore: Johns Hopkins University Press, 1913), 156; Ira Berlin, *Slaves without Masters: The Free Negro in the Antebellum South* (New York: Oxford University Press, 1974), 146–47; and Loren Schweninger, "The Underside of Slavery: The Internal Economy, Self-Hire, and Quasi-Freedom in Virginia, 1780–1865," *Slavery and Abolition* 12 (Sept. 1991): 16. The proceeds from the sale of free blacks went into what was called the "Literary Fund" to provide for the education of white children. *Fifth Annual Report of the Library Board of the Virginia State Library* (Richmond: Davis Bottom, 1908), 13.

2. Legislative Petitions, Petition of Lucinda to the Legislature of Virginia, Nov. 27, 1813, King George County, Library of Virginia, Richmond (hereafter LVA). Although the legislature responded to several requests concerning slaves during its next session, it failed to take action on Lucinda's petition. *Acts Passed at a General Assembly of the Commonwealth of Virginia, Begun and Held at the Capitol in the City of Richmond, on Monday the Tenth Day of October, in the Year of Our Lord, One Thousand Eight Hundred and Fourteen . . .* (Richmond: Thomas Ritchie, 1815), passim; see also *Acts Passed at a General Assembly of the Commonwealth of Virginia, Begun and Held at the Capitol in the City of Richmond, on Monday the Fourth Day of December, in the Year of Our Lord, One Thousand Eight Hundred and Fifteen . . .* (Richmond: Thomas Ritchie, 1816), passim. "Marriages" between free blacks and slaves, of course, had no legal standing.

3. Peter Kolchin, *American Slavery 1619–1877* (New York: Hill and Wang, 1993), 89–90, 128; *A Collection of All Such Acts of the General Assembly of Virginia, of a Public and Permanent Nature as Have Passed since the Session of 1801* (Richmond: Samuel Pleasants, Jr., 1808), 97; *Acts and Resolutions of the General Assembly of the State of South-Carolina Passed in December 1800* (Columbia: Daniel and J. J. Faust, 1801), 39–41; *Acts and Resolutions of the General Assembly of the State of South-Carolina, Passed in December, 1820* (Columbia: D. Faust, 1821), 22–24. The Upper South includes Delaware, Maryland, Virginia, North Carolina, Kentucky, Tennessee, and Missouri; the Lower South includes South Carolina, Georgia, Florida, Alabama, Mississippi, Arkansas, Louisiana, and Texas.

4. The exceptions include, among others, Cheryl Fish, "Voices of Restless (Dis)continuity: The Significance of Travel for Free Black Women in the Antebellum Americas," *Women's Studies* 26 (Oct. 1997): 475–95; Whittington B. Johnson, "Free African-American Women in Savannah 1800–1860: Affluence and Autonomy amid Adversity," *Georgia Historical Quarterly* 76 (Summer 1992): 260–83; Suzanne Lebsock, *The Free Women of Petersburg: Status and Culture in a Southern Town, 1784–1860* (New York: W. W. Norton, 1984); Adele Logan Alexander, *Ambiguous Lives: Free Women of Color in Rural Georgia, 1789–1879* (Fayetteville: University of Arkansas Press, 1991); Kent Anderson Leslie, *Woman of Color, Daughter of Privilege: Amanda America Dickson, 1849–1893* (Athens: University of Georgia Press, 1995); Judith Kelleher Schafer, "'Open and Notorious Concubinage': The Emancipation of Slave Mistresses by Will and the Supreme Court in Antebellum Louisiana," *Lou-*

isiana History 27 (Spring 1987): 165–82; and Loren Schweninger, "Property-Owning Free African-American Women in the South, 1800–1870," Journal of Women's History 1 (Winter 1990): 13–44.

5. Among the numerous works about slave women are John Campbell, "Work, Pregnancy, and Infant Mortality among Southern Slaves," Journal of Interdisciplinary History 14 (Spring 1984): 793–812; Elizabeth Clark, "Matrimonial Bonds: Slavery and Divorce in Nineteenth-Century America," Law and History Review 8 (Spring 1990): 25–54; Mary Ellison, "Resistance to Oppression: Black Women's Response to Slavery in the United States," Slavery and Abolition 4 (March 1983): 56–63; Elizabeth Fox-Genovese, Within the Plantation Household: Black and White Women of the Old South (Chapel Hill: University of North Carolina Press, 1988); Paul Finkelman, ed., Women and the Family in a Slave Society (New York: Garland Publishing, 1989); David Barry Gaspar and Darlene Clark Hine, eds., More Than Chattel: Black Women and Slavery in the Americas (Bloomington: Indiana University Press, 1996); Herbert Gutman, The Black Family in Slavery and Freedom, 1750–1925 (New York: Pantheon Books, 1976); Thelma Jennings, "'Us Colored Women Had to Go through a Plenty': Sexual Exploitation of African-American Slave Women," Journal of Women's History 1 (Winter 1990): 45–74; Sally G. McMillen, Southern Women: Black and White in the Old South (Arlington Heights: Harlan Davidson, 1992); Ann Patton Malone, Sweet Chariot: Slave Family and Household Structure in Nineteenth-Century Louisiana (Chapel Hill: University of North Carolina Press, 1992); Leslie A. Schwalm, "A Hard Fight for We": Women's Transition from Slavery to Freedom in South Carolina (Urbana: University of Illinois Press, 1997); Marli F. Weiner, Mistresses and Slaves: Plantation Women in South Carolina, 1830–1880 (Urbana: University of Illinois Press, 1998); Carole Shammas, "Black Women's Work and the Evolution of Plantation Society in Virginia," Labor History, 26 (Winter 1985): 5–28; Deborah Gray White, "Female Slaves: Sex Roles and Status in the Antebellum Plantation South," Journal of Family History 9 (Fall 1983): 248–61; Deborah Gray White, Ar'n't I a Woman? Female Slaves in the Plantation South (New York: W. W. Norton, 1985); Betty Wood, Women's Work, Men's Work: The Informal Slave Economies of Low Country Georgia (Athens: University of Georgia Press, 1995); and Wilma King, Stolen Childhood: Slave Youth in Nineteenth-Century America (Bloomington: Indiana University Press, 1995).

6. Only eighty-nine (3 percent) of the approximately 2,975 extant legislative petitions concerning race and slavery were presented by black women. An additional twenty-one petitions were presented by black men and women together. This essay focuses on those 110 petitions. In all, black men and women, slave and free, presented 426 petitions, or 14 percent of the extant documents. There are significant numbers of surviving petitions for only seven states: Delaware, Mississippi, North and South Carolina, Tennessee, Texas, and Virginia, with a scattering for Alabama, Florida, Missouri, and only one each for Louisiana and Georgia. No extant legislative petitions have been uncovered for Maryland, Kentucky, or Arkansas. Despite this, the surviving documents offer a good geographic balance for the East and West, Upper and Lower South. They also offer a representative sample of the views of free black women across the South on the subjects addressed in this essay.

7. Wilbert L. Jenkins, Seizing the New Day: African Americans in Post-Civil War Charleston (Bloomington: Indiana University Press, 1998), 2; Berlin, Slaves without Masters, 177.

8. Register of Free Persons of Color, Chatham County, Georgia, 1823–26, Georgia Historical Society, Savannah; Juliet E. K. Walker, "Racism, Slavery and Free Enterprise: Black Entrepreneurship in the United States before the Civil War," Business History Review 60 (Autumn 1986): 350; Frances Anne Kemble, Journal of Residence on a Georgia Plantation in 1838–1839 (1863, reprint edited by John A. Scott, Athens: University of Georgia Press, 1984), 41.

9. Schweninger, "Property-Owning Free African-American Women," 22.

10. See, for example, Gary Mills, Forgotten People: Cane River's Creoles of Color (Baton Rouge: Louisiana State University Press, 1977); David O. Whitten, Andrew Durnford: A Black Sugar Planter in Antebellum Louisiana (Natchitoches: Northwestern Louisiana State University Press, 1981); Michael P. Johnson and James L. Roark, Black Masters: A Free Family of Color in the Old South (New York: W. W. Norton, 1984); Larry Koger, Black Slaveowners: Free Black Slave Masters in South Carolina, 1790–1860 (Jefferson, N.C.: McFarland, 1985); and Loren Schweninger, Black Property Own-

ers in the South, 1790–1915 (Urbana: University of Illinois Press, 1991), ch. 4. For contrast with the Upper South, see T. Stephen Whiteman, *The Price of Freedom: Slavery and Manumission in Baltimore and Early National Maryland* (Lexington: University Press of Kentucky, 1997); and Tommy L. Bogger, *Free Blacks in Norfolk, Virginia, 1790–1860: The Darker Side of Freedom* (Charlottesville: University Press of Virginia, 1997).

11. *Digest of the Laws of the State of Georgia* (Milledgeville: Grantland and Orme, 1822), 467–69.

12. The issue of slaves making "contracts" for their freedom is discussed in Thomas D. Morris, *Southern Slavery and the Law, 1619–1860* (Chapel Hill: University of North Carolina Press, 1996), 380–85.

13. Records of the General Assembly, Petition of Priscilla Jessup to the South Carolina Legislature, Nov. 15, 1845, no. 33, South Carolina Department of Archives and History, Columbia (hereafter SCDAH).

14. Legislative Petitions, Petition of Jemima Hunt to the Virginia Legislature, Dec. 9, 1811, Southampton County, LVA.

15. *Acts Passed at a General Assembly of the Commonwealth of Virginia, Begun and Held at the Capitol, in the City of Richmond, on Monday the Second Day of December, in the Year of our Lord, One Thousand Eight Hundred and Eleven . . .* (Richmond: Samuel Pleasants, 1812), 137–38.

16. General Assembly, Session Records, Petition of Madelene St. Rigue to the North Carolina General Assembly, Nov. 28, 1801, Emancipation Petitions, Chowan County, North Carolina Division of Archives and History, Raleigh (hereafter NCDAH).

17. Ulrich Bonnell Phillips, *The Slave Economy of the Old South: Selected Essays in Economics and Social History,* ed. Eugene D. Genovese (Baton Rouge: Louisiana State University Press, 1968), 142.

18. Legislative Petitions, Petition of Rebecca to the General Assembly of Tennessee, Nov. 10, 1837, Tennessee State Library and Archives, Nashville (hereafter TSLA).

19. Legislative Petitions, Petition of Judy Johnson to the Virginia General Assembly, Dec. 11, 1835, Fairfax County, LVA. The reverse was also true. Anna Shelton, a slave who had married a free man of color, Peyton Shelton, discovered after her manumission that she had to leave "her husband, her home & her friends." She petitioned the legislature to remain in the state, but the petition was rejected. Legislative Petitions, Petition of Anna Shelton to the Virginia General Assembly, Dec. 19, 1823, Fluvanna County, LVA.

20. Legislative Petitions, Petition of Nelly Hoomes to the Virginia General Assembly, Feb. 5, 1833, Richmond City, LVA.

21. General Assembly, Session Records, Petition of Grace Davis and Richard Davis, her son, to the North Carolina General Assembly, Dec. 14, 1791, Brunswick County, NCDAH.

22. Petitions of Amelia Green to the Craven County Court, March 1795, Sept. 1796, Dec. 1801, Craven County Slaves and Free Negroes File, NCDAH; Petition of Nancy Handy, Princess Green, and John C. Stanly to the North Carolina General Assembly, Nov. 27, 1796, NCDAH; Loren Schweninger, "John Carruthers Stanly and the Anomaly of Black Slaveholding," *North Carolina Historical Review* 67 (April 1990): 188. For similar efforts by women in other North Carolina families, see General Assembly, Session Records, Petition of Rose to the North Carolina General Assembly, Dec. 7, 1808, Chowan County, NCDAH; and Petition of Hannah Allen to the North Carolina General Assembly, Dec. 5, 1817, Brunswick County, NCDAH.

23. Legislative Petitions, Petition of Jenny Parker to the Virginia Legislature, November 23, 1813, Surry County, LVA (includes Certificate, John Wilson et al., Nov. 23, 1813, and Certificate, Charles Graves et al., Nov. 23, 1813).

24. Legislative Petitions, Petition of Dilsy Gallego and Hembro Gallego to the Virginia General Assembly, 1813, Richmond City, LVA; Petition of Charity to the Virginia General Assembly, Nov. 28, 1815, Rockingham County, LVA (includes Certificate, A. Smith, Benjamin Cravens et al., Nov. 28, 1815).

25. Records of the Legislature, Memorials and Petitions, Petition of Fanny McFarland to the Senate and House of Representaives of the Republic of Texas, Oct. 30, 1840, Texas State Library, Archives Division, Austin (hereafter TSL-AD).

26. Legislative Petitions, Petition of Nancy to the Virginia General Assembly, Dec. 7, 1813, Cumberland County, LVA (includes Nancy's manumission in Copy of Last Will and Testament of Henry Holloway, Amherst County, Aug. 5, 1808, and Certificate, Thomas M. Deane, May 28, 1813).

27. Legislative Petitions, Petition of Elvira Jones to the Virginia General Assembly, Dec. 5, 1823, Richmond City, LVA. For other examples in Virginia, see Petition of Mary to the Virginia House of Delegates, Dec. 20, 1810, Stafford County, LVA; Petition of Betty, Franky, Billy, John, Henry Dean et al. to the Virginia General Assembly, Dec. 4, 1811, Amherst County, LVA; Petition of Nancy to the Virginia General Assembly, Dec. 7, 1813, Cumberland County, LVA; Petition of Hannah to the Virginia General Assembly, Dec. 8, 1825, Rockbridge County, LVA; Petition of Hannah to the Virginia General Assembly, Dec. 7, 1826, Russell County, LVA; Petition of Betsey and John to the Virginia General Assembly, Dec. 28, 1828, Richmond City, LVA; and Petition of Judy Johnson to the Virginia Senate and House of Delegates, Dec. 11, 1835, Fairfax County, LVA.

28. Legislative Petitions, Petition of Temperance Crutcher to the Tennessee General Assembly, Dec. 2, 1837, TSLA.

29. Records of the Legislature, Memorials and Petitions, Petition of Louisa Towns, Eliza Towns, Peter Towns, Matilda Towns, Delia Downs et al. to the Senate and House of Representatives of the Republic of Texas, Oct. 18, 1840, TSL-AD. For other examples in Texas, see Petition of Lavinia Mansel et al. to the Congress of the Republic of Texas, Dec. 23, 1844, and Petition of Nancy and Thomas Flournay to the Texas General Assembly, Dec. 25, 1847, both in TSL-AD.

30. Legislative Papers, Petitions and Memorials, Petition of Agnes Earhart to the Mississippi Legislature, 1859, Mississippi Department of Archives and History, Jackson (hereafter MDAH). In 1831 the Mississippi legislature passed a law requiring all adult free Negroes to leave the state. Charles Syndor, "Free Negro in Mississippi before the Civil War," *American Historical Review* 32 (July 1927): 785; Charles Syndor, *Slavery in Mississippi* (1933, reprint Baton Rouge: Louisiana State University Press, 1966), 203.

31. Records of the General Assembly, Petition of Citizens of Chester District to the South Carolina Legislature, ca. 1859, ND no. 1843, SCDAH.

32. *Laws of the State of Delaware, Passed at a Session of the General Assembly, Commenced and Held at Dover, on Tuesday the Fifth Day of January, in the Year of Our Lord, One Thousand Eight Hundred and Forty Nine* (Dover: S. Kimmey, 1849), 319; *Laws of the State of Delaware, Passed at a Session of the General Assembly, Commenced and Held at Dover, on Tuesday the Seventh Day of January, in the Year of Our Lord, One Thousand Eight Hundred and Fifty-One* (Wilmington: Johnson, Chandler and Harker, 1851), 591–92.

33. General Assembly, Session Records, Petition of Charlotte Green to the North Carolina General Assembly, Dec. 11, 1792, NCDAH.

34. General Assembly, Session Records, Petition of Rose to the North Carolina General Assembly, Dec. 7, 1808, Chowan County, NCDAH.

35. Legislative Petitions, Petition of Sarah Greene to the Virginia General Assembly, Dec. 3, 1784, Fairfax County, LVA. The petition was tabled. Cited earlier in another context, free black Priscilla Jessup also expressed fears about being cast into slavery. Records of the General Assembly, Petition of Priscilla Jessup to the South Carolina Legislature, Nov. 15, 1845, no. 33, SCDAH.

36. Copy of Last Will and Testament of Philip E. Vass, Aug. 8, 1831, in General Assembly, Session Records, Petition of Jacob, Mary, Patsey, Meriwether, and Matilda to the Legislature of North Carolina, Dec. 20, 1844, in Senate Committee Reports, Nov. 1844–Jan. 1845, box 4, NCDAH. Vass died in 1832.

37. General Assembly, Session Records, Copy of Petition of Jacob, Mary, Sam, Meriwether, Patty, and Matilda to the Superior Court, Halifax County, Virginia, April 3, 1840, with Petition of Jacob, Mary, Meriwether, Patsey and Matilda to the Legislature of North Carolina, Dec. 20, 1844, in Senate Committee Reports, Nov. 1844–Jan. 1845, Box 4, NCDAH. The petition was addressed "To the Honorable William Leigh Judge of the Circuit Superior Court of Law & Chancery for the County of Halifax." A Virginia law of 1795, updated from 1818 to 1820, permitted persons believ-

ing themselves illegally held as slaves to file a legal complaint against the person who assumed ownership. Magistrates were required to issue a warrant summoning the presumed owner to answer the complaint. Defendants were commanded to give bonds with security "equal at least to the full value of such complainant" and appear before the next session of the superior, county, or corporation court. Complainants without funds could sue in *forma pauperis,* and the same strictness "as to *form,*" one judicial decision explained, "is not required in actions for freedom as in other cases." When people brought such an action for themselves as well as for children, the declaration of trespass and assault, formal in other cases, could in these instances be informal. *Digest of the Laws of Virginia, which Are of a Permanent Character and General Operation; Illustrated by Judicial Decisions* (Richmond: Smith and Palmer, 1841), 869–71.

38. Legislative Petitions, Petition of Mary, Patsey, and Jacob to the Virginia General Assembly, Dec. 15, 1841, Halifax County, LVA. The petition to remain in the state was rejected.

39. Legislative Petitions, Petition of Patty Daniel to the Virginia General Assembly, Dec. 14, 1842, Halifax County, LVA.

40. Legislative Petitions, Petition of Ann Rose and Margaret Rose to the Virginia General Assembly, Dec. 5, 1783, no county, LVA (includes Copy of Last Will and Testament of Walter Robertson, Dec. 1, 1778, and Deed of Manumission, Thomas Hope, May 16, 1783).

41. Legislative Petitions, Petition of Mary to the Virginia House of Delegates, Dec. 9, 1813, Stafford County, LVA.

42. Legislative Petitions, Petition of Cloe, Lotty, David, and Daniel to the Virginia General Assembly, Oct. 14, 1814, LVA.

43. Legislative Petitions, Petition of Lizy, Bob, Susan, Violet, and Reynolds to the Tennessee General Assembly, 1855, TSLA.

44. Berlin, *Slaves without Masters,* 215n59; Marina Wikramanayake, *A World in Shadow: The Free Black in Antebellum South Carolina* (Columbia: University of South Carolina Press, 1973), 151; Legislative Petitions, Petition of Milley to the Virginia General Assembly, Jan. 25, 1836, Richmond City, LVA; see also Legislative Papers, Petitions and Memorials, Petition of Ann Caldwell to the Mississippi Legislature, 1859, MDAH.

45. Legislative Petitions, Certificate, George Burke, Feb. 15, 1850, with Petition of John Edward Dixon and Sarah Dixon to the Virginia General Assembly, March 13, 1850, Fairfax County, LVA.

46. Legislative Petitions, Certificate, James D. Kerr, March 7, 1850, with Petition of John Edward Dixon and Sarah Dixon to the Virginia General Assembly, March 13, 1850, Fairfax County, LVA.

47. Legislative Petitions, Certificate, A. M. Fitzhugh, March 1850, with Petition of John Edward Dixon and Sarah Dixon to the Virginia General Assembly, March 13, 1850, Fairfax County, LVA.

48. Records of the Legislature, Memorials and Petitions, Certificate, J. W. Moreland, John W. Moore et al., Dec. 16, 1841, with Petition of Zylpha Husk to the Senate and House of Representatives of the Republic of Texas, Dec. 16, 1841, TSL-AD; Records of the Legislature, Memorials and Petitions, Certificate, Robert Wilson, J. W. Moreland et al., Oct. 30, 1840, with Petition of Fanny McFarland to the Senate and House of Representatives of the Republic of Texas, Oct. 30, 1840, TSL-AD.

49. Legislative Petitions, Certificate, Seymour Scott, Parke Bailey et al., Dec. 1, 1813, with Petition of Nancy, woman of color, to the Virginia Assembly, Dec. 7, 1813, Cumberland County, LVA; see also Legislative Petitions, Certificate, John Wilson, Samuel Wilson, and James Wilson, Nov. 23, 1813, with Petition of Jenny Parker to the Virginia General Assembly, Nov. 23, 1813, Surry County, LVA.

50. Records of the General Assembly, Certificate of N. McCants, John R. Tarrant, Nov. 4, 1845, Records of the General Assembly, with Petition of Priscilla Jessup to the South Carolina Legislature, Nov. 15, 1845, no. 33, SCDAH.

51. Certificate, Larkin Reynolds, W. Harris, W. Chiles et al., Nov. 14, 1845, with Petition of Priscilla Jessup to the South Carolina Legislature, Nov. 15, 1845, no. 33, SCDAH.

52. Records of the General Assembly, Petition of Catharine Hyams, Mary Williamson, Elizabeth Robertson, John Burk, Hiliare Barreau et al. to the South Carolina General Assembly, 1825, SCDAH.

53. Legislative petitions, Petition of Henrietta, Edward, and Adam to the Virginia General Assembly, Jan. 4, 1838, Warren County, LVA (includes Copy of County Court Record, Warren County, Aug. 24, 1837).

54. Legislative Petitions, Petition of Teanah and Richard Dye, Mary and Humbrey Tompkins et al. to the Virginia House of Delegates, Dec. 3, 1823, Richmond City, LVA. Although the petitioners say they were excluded from white churches, Luther Porter Jackson notes that many Richmond blacks "enjoyed a certain freedom of movement in the white church." Luther Porter Jackson, "Religious Development of the Negro in Virginia from 1760–1860," *Journal of Negro History* 16 (April 1931): 200.

55. In North Carolina in 1858, for example, bills were introduced in the house and senate "to permit free persons of African Descent to select their own masters and become slaves." John Hope Franklin, *The Free Negro in North Carolina, 1790–1860* (Chapel Hill: University of North Carolina Press, 1943), 214–16.

56. General Assembly, Session Records, Petition of Kissiah Trueblood to the North Carolina General Assembly, Pasquotank County, Petitions, Nov. 1860–Feb. 1861, NCDAH.

57. Legislature Papers, Petitions and Memorials, Petition of Roseanna to the Mississippi Legislature, 1860, MDAH.

58. Legislative Papers, Petitions and Memorials, Petition of Ann Archie to the Mississippi Legislature, Jan. 12, 1860, MDAH.

59. Legislative Papers, Petitions of Memorials, Petition of Emmarilla Jeffries to the Mississippi Senate and House of Representatives, Jan. 19, 1860, MDAH.

60. On two subsequent occasions Lucy Andrews petitioned the South Carolina Assembly to become a slave, but she was denied each time. Records of the General Assembly, Petition of Lucy Andrews to the Senate and House of Representatives of South Carolina, Nov. 20, 1861, and Nov. 25, 1863, no. 97 and no. 11, SCDAH (includes Certificate, J. R. Hunter et al., ca. 1861; Report Committee on Colored Population, ca. 1861; and Statement, R. S. Beckham, Nov. 25, 1863).

PART 2

Making a Life
in Freedom

CHAPTER 7

Out of Bounds: Emancipated and
Enslaved Women in Antebellum America

Wilma King

Βy the onset of the Civil War, African American women made up slightly more than 50 percent of the free black population in the United States. Unlike most of their enslaved sisters, large numbers of free women left a variety of published and unpublished records in private collections and the public domain that elevate many of these women above the mass of free persons. These sources can be used to probe into relationships between free black and bound women of color across class and geographical lines.[1] This chapter explores why some emancipated women ignored southern customs and boundaries and risked their own freedom to fight for the liberty of enslaved women and also why many free black northern women ignored gender conventions and subjected themselves to social criticism in pursuing similar objectives.

At the close of the period related to the American Revolution, northern states had either abolished slavery or had made provisions to do so. Northern legislatures freed tens of thousands of slaves without regard to distinctions based on their gender and color or the class of their former owners. In the post-Revolutionary War South slavery became more firmly entrenched. Individual emancipations there were often linked to special circumstances connected to personal relationships between slaves and their owners or to the economic status of slaveholders. By the nineteenth century, most northern blacks were presumed to be free, whereas most of those of the South were presumed to be slaves.[2]

The free black population increased from a few thousand in 1750 to 59,466 by 1790. Fewer than one-half—27,109—of free blacks lived in the North; the remainder were in the South. Between 1790 and 1810 the overall increase in the number of free blacks exceeded the increase among slaves when these populations reached 186,446 and 1,191,362, respectively. After 1810 the largest growth among free blacks in the United States was recorded in 1830, when their numbers reached 319,599, or 13.7 percent of the total black population. The percentage declined to 11 percent by 1860, when there were 488,070 free blacks and 3,953,760 slaves.[3] The number of free black women swelled from 120,790 in 1820 to 253,951 in 1860, when the total number of free persons was 488,070. In that same period the number of slave women increased from 750,010 to 1,971,135. Although the number of free black women outdistanced that of free black men, the number of slave women lagged behind that of enslaved men. From these data it can be argued that more opportunities probably existed for the development of associations between slave and free women because more women than men crossed over from slavery to freedom.[4]

In any case, slavery and freedom were intertwined to the extent that few free women could not claim a relative or friend who had been enslaved or one who remained in bondage. Some of the more pathetic examples come from antebellum Baltimore, where "masters could free a slave prospectively, let her unborn children be born as slaves for life, and then sell those children to the freedwoman or her husband." This was contrary to statutes by which children were to follow the legal condition of their mothers. It is not surprising, however, that thwarting the statute occurred in Baltimore, where the slave population declined from 4,700 to 4,100 between 1810 and 1830 while the free black population soared from 5,600 to more than 14,000. Because Baltimore was essentially a free-labor city in the midst of a slaveholding region, slave-owners preserved bondage through "term slavery," an arrangement made with owners whereby slaves received their freedom at a specific time. Under the circumstances, owners could and did demand that children born to term slaves would become bondservants as payment for their upbringing until they reached twenty-one or twenty-five years of age or older. These conditions made the liberty of mothers less than complete because it maintained legal distance between them and their children.[5]

Any form of separation and disengagement from relatives and acquaintances kindled a wrenching fear of never being reunited among those involved. For example, distance and status separated the slave-born Matilda Skipwith (known as Matilda Lomax following her 1848 marriage to Samuel B. Lomax) from her family and friends. The Virginia planter John Hartwell Cocke emancipated Matilda and her parents in 1833 and relocated them to Liberia. After nearly twenty years in Africa, Lomax still missed her kinfolk sorely. "Nothing could afford me more pleasure," she wrote in 1851, "than to visit again the scenes of childhood & look upon those faces which were once familiar to me." Lomax's longing was no different from that of many other free black women who were disconnected by distance, great or small, and by legal entanglements.[6] If separated, to what extent could the women maintain their relationships? Were southern free women at liberty to befriend their enslaved sisters? Could these free women afford to establish meaningful relationships with slaves if whites abhorred the unsettling idea of open exchanges between free persons and slaves, which they believed would raise aspirations for freedom?

The historian Ira Berlin addressed these questions, in part, when he wrote that "standing a step above the slave, these freemen [and women] could see how their status might degenerate and they knew whites needed only the flimsiest excuse to grab their liberty . . . and they were not willing to surrender . . . [precious benefits] without a guarantee of something better. Slaves were in no position to offer such an assurance. Freedom within the context of slavery thus pushed freemen [and women] and bondmen [and women] apart." Free Upper South women and men, continued Berlin, found themselves in the unenviable position of lacking enough confidence in their own status to lend a hand to their enslaved sisters and brothers. Michael P. Johnson and James L. Roark also argued that free women and men in the South remained aloof from their bonded contemporaries, largely because they feared the loss of their own independence. Their freedom, these historians maintained, was "eggshell-thin, and its fragility caused . . . constant concern."[7]

But even a cursory review of more recent writing suggests that there are enough deviations from these interpretations to warrant more systematic study of interactions between enslaved and emancipated persons. Whittington B. Johnson, whose study of black Savannah overlaps in time with the work by Berlin, Johnson, and Roark, asserted that "social lines between free African-Americans and slaves were blurred." Lois Virginia Gould's investigation of New Orleans, Pensacola, and Mobile between 1769 and 1860 showed that the conditions under which black women lived in those Gulf port cities were fluid enough for slaves to pass as free and for blacks to pass as whites. Furthermore, slave women sometimes won liberty based upon presumptions of freedom. Tommy L. Bogger's examination of free blacks in Norfolk, Virginia also notes that interactions between slave and free persons were common. Finally, Bernard Powers's study of Charleston does not equivocate in saying that free blacks and slaves "interacted freely and naturally."[8]

In determining the extent to which bound and free black women interacted, and the nature of their relationships, the distance between enslavement and emancipation becomes significant. In all probability, newly freed women had more relatives and friends in bondage than persons who were born into families that had enjoyed freedom over several generations. Also, their economic status and geographical locations must be considered. In any case, activities associated with the comings and goings of southern blacks in bustling urban centers and thriving port towns made it more difficult to maintain strict lines of distinction between persons who were slaves and those who were not. In 1856 a visitor to a New Orleans market observed "an assemblage of productions from every clime, of animal and vegetable." She recalled seeing "negroes, mulattos, and whites, Spanish, French, Creole, and American, Jews, Chinese, and Indians, all dressed

in different costumes & speaking their various languages." Under the circumstances, it was impossible for her to determine which person of African descent
was enslaved or free.[9] In antebellum Baltimore, where the slave population
reached an "all-time high of 4,672" in 1810 and the free population escalated
beyond twenty-five thousand in 1850, bondage was practically unsustainable. The
likelihood of passing oneself off as free in such a city was great. In the countryside, however, it was a different matter generally, not so much because there were
far fewer free persons overall but because they were scattered over a greater area.
Consequently, free persons were more likely to be known by local residents than
in places of dense populations such as Baltimore and New Orleans.[10]

In general, slaves and free persons socialized both openly and covertly when
opportunities presented themselves. Free persons who lived in the cities sometimes hid fugitive slaves or helped them fade into oblivion. Sometimes their
paths also crossed in daily activities around the race track, in the market place,
and at church. Other opportunities for interaction abounded. On Sunday af-
ternoons, for example, from the turn of the nineteenth century until the Civil
War, blacks in New Orleans congregated with limited interference at Congo
Square, also known as Place Congo, located near present-day St. Ann, Rampart,
and St. Claude streets. Their drumming, dancing, and singing attracted white
onlookers who gazed upon the crowds ranging from a few hundred to several
thousands. A reporter wrote that "they assembled . . . to renew old loves, and
to gather new friendships; to talk over affairs of the past week, and lay new plans
for enjoyment in the coming ones."[11]

Although the collective activities at Congo Square between 1800 and 1862 are
described as slave gatherings, it is reasonable to suppose that free persons were
among the multitudes. After all, what were the visual differences between enslaved and emancipated revelers? In February 1819 Benjamin Henry Latrobe
observed that at Place Congo of the "5 or 600 persons assembled in an open
space or public square" all of them "seemed to be *blacks*."[12] Latrobe added, "I
did not observe a dozen yellow faces." Could one safely assume that persons with
skin color that was nearly white or some shade of yellow were free, while persons of a darker color were slaves? Would newly freed women shun their enslaved sisters and not capitalize upon a ready opportunity to come together
socially? Would free women erase or ignore their interests in an obvious connection to their African homeland following the stroke of a pen that declared
them to be free?[13]

The probability that slave and free women would come together at Place
Congo in New Orleans is great, but specific supportive evidence is not easy to
find. Public records show, however, that blacks mingled in other urban areas.
According to an ordinance passed in Richmond, Virginia, in 1853, "no negro shall
keep a cook-shop within said city, under the penalty of stripes, at the discretion of the mayor." The rationale for such legislation was explained: "Cook-
shops kept by free negroes, being in effect . . . taverns of the lowest description,

and liable to become sources of infinite disorder and corruption among the black population, slave as well as free, the propriety of regulating or wholly interdicting them in the city of Richmond, must be apparent to all."[14] Clearly, uninhibited exchanges between slaves and free persons were, to southern legislators, potentially dangerous.

Similarly, the case of *Smith v. Commonwealth,* heard by a Kentucky court in 1845, implied that slaves and free persons socialized together "from time to time" at a grocery. There was no testimony in the case to verify that women and men who frequented the establishment were in the "habit of cursing, swearing, and making noise, to the annoyance and disturbance of the neighbors," yet Smith was charged with keeping a "disorderly house," a phrase meant to include prostitution. It was argued that "keeping of a grocery, at which that class [free and enslaved blacks] of the community are habitually allowed to assemble, and buy whisky and tipple and drink at pleasure" had the potential to corrupt their morals and entice them into petty theft to support their drinking habits. The court further implied that the gathering of such merrymakers created opportunities for the obstruction of the "good government, well being and harmony of society."[15]

Whether the anxiety in Virginia or Kentucky was real or imagined is of less importance than the well-known fact that slave and free persons frequented cook-shops, groceries, and "disorderly houses." What is less well known is the extent to which black women patronized the groceries or owned them. To be sure, "underground" social activities were "distinctly masculine," yet it would be presumptuous to think that Nancy Anderson, a free black indicted in 1856 for keeping a "disorderly house" described as a possible "center of interracial socializing" in Granville County, North Carolina, was entirely unique. An untold number of women and men operated dram shops and other underground attractions, but they left no paper trail unless they were arrested, indicted, tried, or sentenced.[16]

Many legal records exist, however, that are related to the ownership of slaves and reveal more about relations between free black and enslaved women. The number of black slaveholders was small, one in ten, when compared to their white counterparts, as was also true of the numbers of slaves owned by blacks. Nevertheless, black women were represented in the ranks of slaveholders as early as the 1650s in Virginia, and they were in the majority among black slaveholders in Charleston, South Carolina, between 1820 and 1860.[17]

Questions often arise regarding the connection between the skin color of African American slaveholders and the treatment of their chattel. The northern freeborn Eliza Potter, who observed slavery firsthand during her travels in the South, offers some insight into the matter in her 1859 autobiography. In writing about a black woman from Cincinnati who became a slaveholder in New Orleans, Potter claimed that she was the "most tyranical, overbearing, cruel taskmistress that ever existed." Potter believed that the owner's color was an impor-

tant factor in an explanation of the way that she treated her slaves. "The pro-
pensities are the same," Potter wrote, "and those who have been oppressed themselves, are the sorest oppressors." Finally, Potter added, "It is a well known fact,
those who are as black themselves as the ace of spades will, if they can, get
mulatoes [*sic*] for slaves, and then the first word is 'my nigger.'"[18] This anecdotal
reference is not sufficient, however, to round out a portrayal of black
slaveholding women. It does not consider the reasons for owning slaves, nor does
it take regional differences into account. To be sure, in the Lower South many
African American slaveholders had linkages to white relatives or benefactors. It
is erroneous to assume, however, that these women were cruel or had uniform
mixtures of European and African blood. Public records often add "fwc" (free
woman of color) to the names of free women of mixed blood, but that says little
or nothing about the actual coloration of their skin. In any case, color appears
to be less significant in assessing the treatment of slaves than the reasons for
owning slaves among free female slaveholders of African descent.

These women owned slaves for familial and financial reasons, which could
make a difference in whether they were benevolent or brutal owners. Relatives
and friends sometimes bought slaves to avoid separations or to circumvent state
laws that required freed persons to leave the state or face reenslavement. Free
persons sometimes held slaves as security. This appears to have been the case
with the North Carolinian Molly Horniblow, which prompted her grandson
John S. Jacobs to write, "It may seem rather strange that my grandmother should
hold her son a slave; but the law required it. She was obliged to give security that
she would never be any expense to the town or state before she could come in
possession of her freedom. Her property in him was sufficient to satisfy the law;
he could be sold at any minute to pay her debts."[19] Why Mary Spies, a successful Savannah washerwoman, owned five adult women whom she purchased in
the 1820s is not entirely clear. In all probability, they assisted her in her laundering work, but it is also possible that they were relatives.[20] There is little doubt,
however, about the South Carolinian Margaret Mitchell Harris's reasons for
owning slaves. Unlike Spies, Harris inherited twenty-one slaves from her father,
Robert Michael Collins, and sixteen other slaves from Elizabeth Holman Collins,
her mother. In the 1840s the value of Harris's estate, which included a
Georgetown District plantation of nearly a thousand acres, more than doubled.
By 1849 she produced 240,000 pounds of rice annually for an 18.43 percent rate
of return on her capital investment. Although she was a successful planter, Harris
"had a premonition of the coming disaster" of the Civil War and general emancipation. She sold all of her slaves in 1860 and then invested $35,000 from the
sale in stocks and bonds. Clearly, for Harris financial considerations were of
primary concern.[21]

Similarly, the last will and testament of Betsy Sompayrac, a free woman of
color, in Natchitoches, Louisiana, reflected an economic interest in chattel.
Sompayrac, a small slaveholder and mother of four, dictated her final wishes to

the parish judge on January 15, 1845. Obviously concerned about the financial consequences of her approaching death and its impact on the welfare of her minor children, Sompayrac sought to guarantee a degree of economic security by parceling out chattel among them. Her son, Daniel, inherited one slave, the "boy Alexander." A "boy" James, along with another "boy" Solomon, became the property of Sompayrac's son Stephen. The "little negro girl named Elizabeth" and the woman Jane were set aside for Sarah Ann Sompayrac. There were differences in the legacies that go beyond Sompayrac's sons receiving male slaves and her daughter receiving females.[22] Intricate stipulations in the will did not allow Sarah and Stephen to benefit from their inherited slaves permanently. The boy Solomon was Stephen's property only until he reached thirty-five years of age in consideration of his status as Sompayrac's godson. Obviously, Solomon's mother and Sompayrac shared a friendship across legal boundaries. Being a godparent could carry a serious responsibility involving trust and respect. To accept guardianship, if necessary, meant a commitment to the child's emotional, physical, and religious well-being, as if that child were the guardian's own. Sompayrac cared about Solomon, but her sentiments for him were not as strong as for her own children.[23] Even more striking than Solomon's treatment were the conditions affecting Jane, who would become Sarah's property only after liquidation of Sompayrac's debts. Rather than request the sale of her real and personal property, Sompayrac asked her executors to rent her home and to hire Jane out to pay off her debts. Later, Sarah could take possession of Jane but not of her progeny. The dying woman requested that any offspring would belong to her son Benjamin, who lived away from Natchitoches when she dictated the will, if he returned.[24]

What was the true relationship between these women and the nature of their interactions? Aside from the veiled distance between Sompayrac and Solomon's mother, there is Sompayrac's calculated indifference toward Jane, who could only look forward to working to pay off Sompayrac's debts, and to giving up her unborn children. There were no provisions to protect Jane's family from a possible separation should Benjamin return to Natchitoches, collect his inheritance, and leave again. Sompayrac's will gives credence to the view of historians that in the Lower South, free blacks of means "demonstrated little interest in those in bondage except perhaps as property."[25]

Without a doubt there were exceptions. Some women jeopardized their own well-being and crossed boundaries designed to separate slave from free persons. In general, the most meaningful and long-lasting interactions were based on family connections. It is no surprise that free women, including Marie Therese, née Coincoin, of Natchitoches, Louisiana, worked for decades to emancipate their offspring and other kin. Coincoin paid for the liberty of her two children largely out of an annuity, and then she forfeited a "guaranteed" pension in her declining years. Beyond the financial costs, there were the mental liabilities in seeing her children freed by their white father in a niggardly fashion. Certainly, it must have been difficult to see Nicholas Augustine, born January 22, 1768, freed in 1792, while his twin sister Marie Suzanne remained in slavery nearly twenty-five years longer. These are poignant examples which underscore the economic and emotional costs of liberty. Coincoin and Alethia Tanner, two successful businesswomen, may be compared in that both women purchased and manumitted their kin. Tanner, unlike Coincoin, bought her own freedom. Afterward, she purchased twenty-two relatives and friends, whom she emancipated. Coincoin differed from Tanner in that her primary concern was in purchasing and emancipating members of her immediate family.[26]

Hannah Jackson, a washerwoman and resident of Alexandria, Virginia, was of the same ilk. In April 1816 she submitted several affidavits and deeds to the U.S. Circuit Court that revealed much about the laundress's integral connection to the enslavement and emancipation of family members. One of the affidavits freed Emanuel, a child of six or seven. He was the son of Johanna Weaver, Hannah Jackson's daughter. Another affidavit certified that Hannah Jackson had given William Newton $65 in hand and $230 over a period of time for the child Ann Weaver, presumably Johanna Weaver's daughter and Hannah Jackson's granddaughter. No doubt Jackson intended to emancipate the child. Hannah Jackson later offered liberty to other members of her family. She manumitted her forty-five-year-old sister, Esther, who was also a washerwoman, along with her four children (three girls and a boy) ranging in age from one to eleven years old. William Hepburn sold the family to Jackson on February 1, 1816, for $1,000. How Jackson raised the sum is unknown. In all probability, the sisters worked together and pooled their resources. It would have been nearly impossible for either of them to accomplish this feat alone. It was common among free women to buy and liberate enslaved family members. According to recorded deeds for 1856, 1858, and 1860 in Washington, D.C., and its surrounding area where Tanner and Jackson lived, relatives were responsible for 10 percent of manumissions. Tanner was unusual in that she liberated such a large number of slaves, absorbing the cost of several certificates of manumission, which increased from $20 to $50 each by 1851 and thus made freedom more precious.[27]

Aside from the purchase and manumission of relatives and friends, other interactions between enslaved and emancipated black women deserve attention. A good example is the relationship between the North Carolinian Molly Horniblow and her enslaved granddaughter, Harriet Jacobs, who hid herself in the older woman's attic between 1835 and 1842. Such a response from a family member is understandable, but what motivated other women who helped Jacobs? Both Sally, identified as one who "could be trusted" with Jacobs's secret, and the "kind lady," who offered to "conceal her for a time," were as important as Betty, who led Jacobs to safety. The text surrounding the nameless and faceless "kind lady" suggests that she was white, while the speech patterns of the women who shielded and helped Jacobs suggests that they were slaves. Jacobs gives voice to the "lady" who cautioned against ruining herself and her family. The other women do not express fear of repercussions if they are exposed. Notwithstanding these differences, the evidence of interlocking associations of long duration makes it clear that each woman put herself at risk for a friend.[28]

There are also similarities in the behavior of free Charlestonians who assisted the slave-born Nancy Weston's son Archibald Grimké in 1862. They harbored a fugitive and put themselves in danger of losing their own freedom. Grimké lived in the home of one family until that situation became too dangerous. He then fled, with the assistance of his mother, to the home of her distant free relative Thomas Cole. Grimké stayed with the Coles more than two years, until the fall of Charleston in February 1865. No doubt the wife of Thomas Cole was instrumental in protecting the runaway who depended upon her for meals and clothes. She remains silent in the Grimké biography, but readers must ask whether she considered this unusual responsibility an extra burden. It is also reasonable to wonder about the emotional costs of harboring a fugitive. What did this woman and her family have to lose through their actions? Finally, would she have been willing to assist a fugitive who was not a relative? These questions are also applicable to Harriet Jacobs's grandmother. Both Horniblow and Cole jeopardized their own well-being in the interest of others. Their actions were like those of Harriet Tubman but differed in scope. Tubman, who liberated herself by running away in 1849, returned to the South repeatedly and rescued scores of others from bondage. As was the case with Cole and Horniblow, Tubman's family members were among the beneficiaries of her daring leadership.[29]

Discussions of familial or fictive kin reveal nothing about relationships beyond these linkages. It is generally assumed that southern black women, who enjoyed freedom over a long period of time, perhaps generations, and those whose economic standing offered some measures of security were less likely to involve themselves in any behavior that might threaten their liberty. That impression comes from studies focusing particularly on the well-known freed South Carolinian William Ellison and the freed Mississippian William Johnson along with Charleston's Free Brown Society. This area of historical inquiry needs further attention to illuminate interactions between free and slave women who were not connected by familial ties.[30]

Consider the following extracts from letters written in 1857 by two women whose husbands either bought or would soon buy domestic servants for their households. On July 11, 1857, Emma Hoggatt of New Orleans wrote to her aunt, Ann Battles Johnson, "Now for me to tell you about a woman that jeff bought today. She seems to be a woman very willing. Says she can make homemade bread, buscuits, pies and do everythin thats wanting abut the house and if she suits I will be just fixed wich I hope she will." Several months later, on December 27, 1857, Tryphena Fox of Jesuits Bend, Louisiana, wrote to her mother, Anna Rose Holder, "She [the slave woman] came & worked two days, so we could see what she was capable of doing, and I find her a good washer & ironer and pastry cook & able to cook plain, every day meals. . . . How much trouble she will give me, I dont know, but I think I can get along with her, passable well any how." That one letter was written by a black woman and the other by a white woman are of no consequence here. The primary concerns of these two women were whether the slaves would perform domestic work satisfactorily and add to the quality of their own lives. At the outset, this is nothing more or less than a mistress-maid association.[31]

In all probability, Hoggatt's aunt, the freed mulatto wife of William Johnson (a prosperous Natchez, Mississippi, barber) and mother of ten children, had a similar relationship with the women her husband owned. Diaries kept by Ann Battles Johnson's husband between 1835 and 1851 reveal his views about relations between the free apprentices whom he hired and their enslaved acquaintances. "Fraternization with slaves," Johnson's biographers wrote, "was out of the question—or so he thought." The slave-born barber grumbled about the interest the apprentice showed in attending "darkey parties" arranged by slaveholders. Ostensibly, Johnson's disparaging description reflects his repulsion at the thought that free persons and slaves would socialize freely. A closer reading of Johnson's diaries suggests that his aversion to "darkey parties" had much to do with moral standards. The possibilities of intimacy between young unmarried persons, slave and free, was more disturbing to him than the crossing of legal boundaries. Neither Johnson's diaries nor his wife's letters include anything about her thoughts regarding the festivities. Readers must consider, however, whether she shared her husband's views about the matter.[32]

Similar questions arise about how the freedwoman Matilda Ellison, wife of William Ellison, a prosperous freed mulatto planter and ginwright in Statesboro, South Carolina, interacted with or thought about the women her husband owned. The gender ratio among Ellison's slaves should have caused her some concern. Adult men always outnumbered women, but the gender bias was more pronounced among the children. Of the eight youngsters Ellison owned in 1840, five were boys. Ten years later he owned ten children. Only one was a girl. In 1860 fifteen of the twenty enslaved children were boys. Johnson's pattern of owning slaves defies explanation related to natural increase, and historical records do not show that Ellison freed or gave the children to his own heirs. It appears that he sold off the girls to raise capital to purchase adult men for work in his gin shop. If that is true, Matilda Ellison witnessed slave mothers being separated from their daughters in extraordinary numbers over an extended period. How Ellison responded to this occurrence within her own household remains unknown. But the general response of slave women who faced such horrifying events is known. Some mothers consoled their offspring and prepared them to accept the inevitable. Others interfered by running away, hiding their children in the woods, or threatening to kill them. A small number of women arranged for buyers to keep their offspring nearby. In short, the women did whatever they believed would prevent separations, including appeals to the wives of slaveholders to use their influence. Sometimes they succeeded.[33]

Matilda Ellison, at least twenty-one and the mother of a five- or six-year-old when her husband purchased and emancipated her, was not so far removed from slavery that she was oblivious to the pain involved in the separation of mothers from their children. Nevertheless, if slave women sought her influence and she agreed, it was of very little or no consequence because the number of girls among the children remained unusually low between 1840 and 1860. This, of course, is speculation, and without substantial evidence one will never know the true relationship between Matilda Ellison and the females her husband owned or sold.

By contrast, records left by Mary Peake during the 1860s, and by Jane Crouch during the 1880s, reveal much about the association with slaves of these two freeborn Virginians. Peake, a teacher, lived in Hampton. Crouch, also a teacher, made her home in Alexandria. Crouch admitted that she "took care not to [admit] any slave children." Although her "will was good to do so," she feared arrest, which would "make it doubly hard" to maintain the school; therefore, she chose "not to run the risk." As a child, she had attended a school which local police closed, an event that no doubt influenced her decision.[34] There is a sharp difference in the case of Mary Peake, who opened a school in 1847 to black girls and boys without regard to their legal status. She had as much to lose as Crouch if the statutes that prohibited meetings of free blacks with the intent to teach slaves to read and write were enforced, yet Peake persevered. Southern free blacks faced the possibility of losing rights and privileges, even their own liberty, if they aligned themselves too closely with slaves. Many, like Crouch, concluded that the risks were too great. Systematic investigation is necessary to determine the extent to which other free women were of the same mettle as Mary Peake.[35]

This free woman, however, along with an untold number of unheralded individuals, worked for the mental and physical liberation of slaves. Frances Ellen Watkins explained the exigency of the matter in 1852 when she wrote, "The Condition of our people, the wants of our children and the welfare of our race demand the aid of every helping hand." Without fanfare or membership in antislavery organizations, black women lent a hand to destroy slavery when opportunities arose. If "Whites became abolitionists out of choice," historian Waldo E. Martin, Jr., has observed, "blacks were abolitionists out of necessity."[36] The freeborn Sarah Mapps Douglass, who came of age in a middle-class Philadelphia home, seemed oblivious at first to the condition of enslaved blacks and admitted that she had "formed a little world" of her own and "cared not to move beyond its precincts." When the Pennsylvania legislature debated an 1832 bill that would have required free persons of color to carry passes, it shattered the tranquility and security of Douglass's realm. Now, she plainly saw the tyrannical "iron hand" lurking at the border of her "peaceful home." As a result, "the cause of the slave became my own," she wrote.[37]

Abolitionists, black and white, female and male, attacked slavery through the press, from the pulpit, and on the lecture platform. They wrote letters to antislavery newspapers or journals and spoke publicly against bondage. Some participated openly in mass demonstrations against the more stringent Fugitive Slave Act of 1850, while others assisted runaways. The form of protest, whether organized and formal or spontaneous and informal, mattered little to antislavery advocates. Their primary objective was to end slavery. Eliza Potter told a slave whom she met in Louisville all she knew about Canada and provided specific directions for relocating there. Potter saw herself as the "humble means of unloosing the shackles of one upright and manly soul." In all probability, she would have also assisted the man's sister had that person not already fled from slavery. In any case, Potter was ultimately arrested and tried as an accessory. When questioned, she did not deny complicity in directing the slave's "footsteps to a new world." In fact, she was quite indignant at the charges against her. "I said in reply to those who examined me," Potter wrote, "that I recognized no crime in what I had done." She denied emphatically that her intent was to break any law. Unlike Harriet Tubman and many others who assisted fugitives, Potter went to jail for three months for "doing what [she] conscientiously felt to be a Christian deed." Comparing herself to the biblical Job, Potter "adhered to [her] integrity to the last," preferring "to be tried . . . and die rather than shrink from owning" that she "had boldly aided in rescuing the soul of an oppressed fellow-being." Potter believed that her truthful response aided in winning an acquittal.[38]

Although Potter did not join organized groups or speak out publicly against slavery, she may be compared to the freeborn Maria W. Stewart, the first woman to address a "promiscuous" audience about slavery in 1833. Both Potter and Stewart held strong convictions about bondage and defended their actions fearlessly. Stewart went further than Potter in that she crossed gender boundaries by stepping out of bounds in the interest of freedom and equality. "Who," she asked, "shall go forward and take off the reproach that is cast upon the people of color? Shall it be a woman?" She was willing to sacrifice her life for black liberty and equality. "Resistance to oppression was, for Stewart, the highest form of obedience to God." Her bold public stance placed her clearly beyond the boundaries society set for women. Familial expectations did not circumscribe Stewart, a childless widow who was orphaned at an early age. Nor did her religion confine her. As a "free" woman, she spoke without equivocation. In an address delivered on February 27, 1833, at Boston's African Masonic Hall she asked, "Is it blindness of mind, or stupidity of soul, or the want of education that has caused our men who are sixty or seventy years of age, never to let their voices be heard, nor their hand be raised in behalf of their color? Or has it been for the fear of offending the whites?" In the same breath, Stewart challenged men to "throw off . . . fearfulness, and come forth in the name of the Lord" to make themselves "useful and active members in society." She ended the address by noting that "African rights and liberty is a subject that ought to fire the breast of every free man of color in these United States, and excite in his bosom a lively, deep, decided, and heartfelt interest."[39]

Stewart's daring remarks of 1833 were like David Walker's chilling appeal published in 1829, calling upon "Heaven . . . to awaken in the breasts of . . . afflicted, degraded and slumbering brethren" an active spirit against misery and wretchedness. The difference was in the reception of words written by a man and those spoken by a woman. Stewart was out of bounds not only in speaking before a mixed audience but also in violating gender conventions that required deference to men. She berated them publicly and questioned their manliness, and some in the audience responded by disrupting the meeting, pelting her with vegetables, and denouncing her criticisms.[40] By the end of 1833 Stewart decided to leave Boston. In her farewell address she defended her right to speak in public. "What if I am a woman?" she asked. Moreover, she suggested that the "hissing" and contempt from outraged men tested her constitution but did not break her spirit. She admitted making herself "contemptible in the eyes of many," but it was in the interest of a greater cause. Stewart bowed out, but she established a precedent for other women, including Frances Ellen Watkins, Sarah Parker Remond, Mary Ann Shadd, Ellen Craft, and Sojourner Truth, to speak out publicly against slavery.[41]

To be sure, gender conventions prohibited women from active participation in some facets of American social and political life. The urgency to eliminate bondage, however, was too great for them to consider social customs when liberty was at stake. That was especially true with many free black northern women who did not distance themselves from issues related to the loss of freedom. These black women, who made up a large percentage of the northern free urban populations, worked as washerwomen and domestic servants and thus enjoyed some flexibility in the use of their time and in their actions. As a result, they were more readily available to watch out for slavecatchers in their midst who might seize fugitive slaves and free blacks alike. In 1847 a group of free black women led by the prominent Bostonian Nancy Prince successfully thwarted a slavecatcher at a Smith Court home. According to an observer, the men were away at work, but "there were those around that showed themselves equal to the occasion." Before the kidnapper "could fully realize his position, [Prince] with the assistance of the colored women that had accompanied her, had dragged him to the door and thrust him out of the house." The commotion drew a large number of women and children together, who pelted the would-be kidnapper with stones and other missiles under Prince's direction and chased him away.[42]

Nearly a decade before, in 1836, black women were also in the forefront of a rescue in Boston that involved two alleged fugitives, Eliza Smalls and Polly Ann Bates. Following a hearing, the judge declared that Smalls and Bates were free to leave, but women in the crowd feared for the safety of the "freedwomen." Matthew Turner, an agent for the Baltimore slaveholder who claimed to own Smalls and Bates, indicated that he would pursue the women under the 1793 Fugitive Slave Law. In the midst of what became known as the "Abolition Riot," a "rush was made, and the liberated prisoners were born [*sic*] out by the colored females in attendance, and not by the colored men." As the women saw it, their duty was to protect themselves and others against the loss of liberty. After all, "OPPOSITION TO TYRANTS," as proclaimed an 1834 broadside that warned New Yorkers to beware of kidnappers, was "OBEDIENCE TO GOD."[43]

The *Colored American*, a newspaper published by blacks in New York City between 1837 and 1841, looked askance at the behavior of black women who attempted to rescue fugitives. "Everlasting shame and remorse seize upon those females," wrote the editor, who "so degraded themselves" in such tumults. The editor begged the women's husbands "to keep them at home and find some better occupation for them." It was clear, of course, that these women and any person they might save from bondage cared more about freedom than "proper" behavior. Free black women continued their direct action on behalf of fugitive slaves. In 1859 Harriet Tubman was the "mastermind" behind the rescue of a fugitive in Troy, New York, according to her biographer Sarah H. Bradford. Amid the pandemonium created as the crowd swelled, Tubman forced her way through, tore the fugitive away from the officer, and held on to him until they reached safety. Tubman emerges as the heroine of the event, but she could not have carried out the daring rescue without the assistance of many others, including free black women.[44]

These free black women viewed their efforts as fulfilling a Christian duty that required strong moral conviction as well as the will to overlook sexist remarks, dismiss gender conventions, and ignore local customs. Free black women, whatever their geographical location in antebellum America, faced similar challenges. At the onset of the Civil War in 1861, Frances E. Watkins said that their future was "bound up in one great bundle of humanity." In explaining the relationship between free blacks and their enslaved contemporaries, she wrote, "Our fates seem linked together, our destiny entwined with theirs, and our rights are interwoven together." Watkins and other free women understood that they could never be truly free until all blacks were free. But would that ever come to fruition? What could be done to make freedom a reality? A generation earlier Maria W. Stewart had asked, "Who shall go forward and take off the reproach that is cast upon the people of color? Shall it be a woman?"[45]

Over the years many free women had weighed their options and decided that freedom was more ephemeral than real as long as slavery and threats of enslavement existed. As a result, they willingly lent a "helping hand" to remove the "reproach" cast upon the people of color in a variety of ways that ranged from hiding runaway slaves to speaking on abolitionist platforms. Regardless of the method they chose, free black women answered Stewart's question with a resounding "Yes!"

Notes

My thanks to Shirley Yee, Norrece T. Jones, Jr., Stanley Harrold, Victoria Bynum, and Pero Dagbovie for their critical readings and useful comments on a version of this chapter before its presentation at the 1998 Organization of American Historians' conference in Indianapolis.

1. Fannie Jackson Coppin, *Reminiscences of School Life, and Hints on Teaching* (Philadelphia: A. M. E. Book Concerns, 1913); Zilpha Elaw, "Memoirs of the Life, Religious Experience, Ministerial Travels and Labors of Mrs. Zilpha Elaw," Julia A. J. Foote, "A Brand Plucked from the Fire: An Autobiographical Sketch by Mrs. Julia A. J. Foote," and Jarena Lee, "The Life and Religious Experience of Jarena Lee," all in *Sisters of the Spirit: Three Black Women's Autobiographies of the Nineteenth Century*, ed. William L. Andrews (Bloomington: Indiana University Press, 1986), 49–160, 161–243, and 25–48; "A Faithful Report of the Trial of Doctor William Little, on an Indictment for an Assault and Battery, Committed upon the Body of His Lawful Wife, Mrs. Jane Little, a Black Lady," in *Free Blacks, Slaves and Slaveowners in Civil and Criminal Courts: The Pamphlet Literature*, ed. Paul Finkelman, ser. 6, vol. 1 (New York: Garland Publishers, 1988), 103–11 ("A Faithful Report" is a compilation of the indictment, jurors' names, and sworn testimony, along with an appendix containing letters from Dr. Little to his wife, Jane, and a copy of their marriage license); Frances E. Watkins, *Poems on Miscellaneous Subjects* (Nendeln, Liechtenstein: Krause Reprint, 1971); Rebecca Jackson, *Gifts of Power: The Writings of Rebecca Jackson, Black Visionary, Shaker Eldress*, ed. Jean McMahon Humez (Amherst: University of Massachusetts Press, 1981); Harriet Jacobs, *Incidents in the Life of a Slave Girl: Written by Herself*, ed. Jean Fagan Yellin (Cambridge: Harvard University Press, 1987); Michael P. Johnson and James L. Roark, eds., *No Chariot Let Down: Charleston's Free People of Color on the Eve of the Civil War* (New York: W. W. Norton, 1984); Elizabeth Keckley, *Behind the Scenes; or, Thirty Years a Slave, and Four Years in the White House* (New York: Oxford University Press, 1988); Gerda Lerner, ed., *Black Women in White America: A Documentary History* (New York: Vintage Books, 1973); Eliza Potter, *A Hairdresser's Experiences in the High Life* (New York: Oxford University Press, 1991); Nancy Prince, *A Black Woman's Odyssey through Russia and Jamaica* (New York: Markus Wiener Publishing, 1990); Amanda Berry Smith, *An Autobiography: The Story of the Lord's Dealings with Mrs. Amanda Smith, Colored Evangelist; Containing an Account of Her Life Work of Faith, and Her Travels in America, England, Ireland, Scotland, India and Africa, as an Independent Missionary* (Chicago: Afro-Am Press, 1969); Maria W. Stewart, *Maria W. Stewart, America's First Black Woman Political Writer: Essays and Speeches*, ed. Marilyn Richardson (Bloomington: Indiana University Press, 1987); Dorothy Sterling, ed., *We Are Your Sisters: Black Women in the Nineteenth Century*, (New York: W. W. Norton, 1984); Charlotte Forten Grimké, *The Journals of Charlotte Forten Grimké*, ed. Brenda Stevenson (New York: Oxford University Press, 1988); Sojourner Truth, *Narrative of Sojourner Truth: A Bondswoman of Olden Time Emancipated by the New York Legislature in the Early Part of the Present Century with a History of Her Labors and Correspondence Drawn from Her Book of Life* (1875, reprint, Chicago: Johnson Publishing, 1970); Phillis Wheatley, *The Collected Works of Phillis Wheatley: The Schomburg Library of Nineteenth-Century Black Women Writers*, ed. John C. Shields (New York: Oxford University Press, 1988); Harriet Wilson, *Our Nig; or, Sketches from the Life of a Free Black in a Two-Story White House, North, Showing That Slavery's Shadows Fall Even There* (1859, reprint, New York: Vintage Books, 1983).

2. An exception existed in New Hampshire, where ambiguity existed in the state's 1783 Declaration of Rights. One interpretation held that only slaves born after adoption of the declaration were free rather than all slaves in the state. The legislature clarified the matter in 1857. Arthur Zilversmit, *The First Emancipation: The Abolition of Slavery in the North* (Chicago: University of Chicago Press, 1967); Gary B. Nash, *Forging Freedom: The Formation of Philadelphia's Black Community, 1720–1840* (Cambridge: Harvard University Press, 1988); Gary B. Nash, *Freedom by Degrees: Emancipation in Pennsylvania and Its Aftermath* (New York: Oxford University Press, 1991). See also Kimberly S. Hanger, "Avenues to Freedom Open to New Orleans' Black Population, 1769–1779,"

Louisiana History 31 (Summer 1990): 237–64, which includes a discussion regarding the emancipation of *pardo* (light-skinned) and *moreno* (dark-skinned) slaves in Spanish New Orleans.

3. *Population of the United States in 1860: Compiled from Original Returns of the Eighth Census by Joseph C. G. Kennedy* (Washington: Government Printing Office, 1864), 2; William Loren Katz, ed., *Negro Population in the United States, 1790–1915* (New York: Arno Press and the New York Times, 1968), 53.

4. Katz, *Negro Population in the United States,* 54–55.

5. Stephen Whitman, "Diverse Good Causes: Manumission and the Transformation of Urban Slavery," *Social Science History* 19 (Fall 1995): 335, 346–48.

6. Randall Miller, ed., *"Dear Master": Letters of a Slave Family* (Ithaca: Cornell University Press, 1978), 106; Whitman, "Diverse Good Causes," 347, 348.

7. Ira Berlin, "The Structure of the Free Negro Caste in the Antebellum United States," *Journal of Social History* 9 (Spring 1976), 298, 308–9; Michael P. Johnson and James L. Roark, "Strategies of Survival: Free Negro Families and the Problem of Slavery," in *In Joy and in Sorrow: Women, Family, and Marriage in the Victorian South, 1830–1900,* ed. Carol Bleser (New York: Oxford University Press, 1991), 89.

8. Whittington B. Johnson, *Black Savannah, 1788–1864* (Fayetteville: University of Arkansas Press, 1996), 1–2, 4; Lois Virginia Meacham Gould, "'In Full Enjoyment of Their Liberty': The Free Women of Color of the Gulf Ports of New Orleans, Mobile, and Pensacola, 1769–1860," Ph.D. diss., Emory University, 1991, 8, 56, 58, 72, 107–17; Tommy L. Bogger, *Free Blacks in Norfolk, Virginia, 1796–1860: The Darker Side of Freedom* (Charlottesville: University of Virginia Press, 1997); Bernard E. Powers, Jr., *Black Charlestonians: A Social History, 1822–1885* (Fayetteville: University of Arkansas Press, 1994), 61. See also Victoria E. Bynum, *Unruly Women: The Politics of Social and Sexual Control in the Old South* (Chapel Hill: University of North Carolina Press, 1992), 39–40; and Kimberly S. Hanger, *Bounded Lives, Bounded Places: Free Black Society in Colonial New Orleans, 1769–1803* (Durham: Duke University Press, 1997).

9. Tryphena Blanche Holder Fox (hereafter TBHF) to Anna Rose Holder (hereafter ARH), Nov. 9, 1856, Fox Papers, Mississippi Department of Archives and History, Jackson (hereafter MDAH).

10. Orville Vernon Burton, "Anatomy of an Antebellum Rural Free Black Community: Social Structure and Social Interaction in Edgefield District, South Carolina, 1850–1860," *Southern Studies* 21 (Fall 1982): 294, 299, 303; Whitman, "Diverse Good Causes," 336. Baltimore's free population in 1800 was 2,771; in 1810, 3,973; in 1820, 10,326; in 1830, 14,790; in 1840, 17,967; and in 1850, 25,442. Randall M. Miller and John David Smith, eds., *Dictionary of Afro-American Slavery* (New York: Greenwood Press, 1988), 76, 261.

11. Gary A. Donaldson, "A Window on Slave Culture: Dances at Congo Square in New Orleans, 1800–186," *Journal of Negro History* 69 (May 1984), 63–72; Whitman, "Diverse Good Causes," 352; Hanger, *Bounded Lives, Bounded Places,* 94. George W. Cable, "The Dance in Place Congo," *Century Illustrated Monthly Magazine* 31 (1886): 517–32.

12. Benjamin H. Latrobe, *The Journals of Benjamin Henry Latrobe, 1799–1820: From Philadelphia to New Orleans,* ed. Edward C. Carter, II, John C. Van Horne, and Lee W. Formwalt (New Haven: Yale University Press, 1980), 3: 203 (emphasis in the original).

13. Donaldson, "A Window on Slave Culture," 68.

14. Helen Tunnicliff Catterall, ed., *Judicial Cases Concerning American Slavery and the Negro* (Washington: Carnegie Institute of Washington, 1936), 1: 233.

15. Catterall, ed., *Judicial Cases,* 1: 371–72.

16. Bynum, *Unruly Women,* 79.

17. Letitia Woods Brown, *Free Negroes in the District of Columbia, 1790–1846* (New York: Oxford University Press, 1972), 19; Powers, *Black Charlestonians,* 49.

18. Potter, *A Hairdresser's Experience,* 159.

19. Jacobs, *Incidents in the Life of a Slave Girl,* 262n; Michael P. Johnson and James L. Roark, *Black Masters: A Free Family of Color in the Old South* (New York: W. W. Norton, 1984), 101–6.

20. Whittington B. Johnson, "Free African-American Women in Savannah, 1800–1860: Affluence and Autonomy amid Diversity," in *"We Specialize in the Wholly Impossible": A Reader in Black Women's History,* ed. Darlene Clark Hine, Wilma King, and Linda Reed (Brooklyn: Carlson Publishing, 1995), 243.

21. Larry Koger, *Black Slaveowners: Free Black Slave Masters in South Carolina, 1790–1860* (Jefferson: McFarland, 1985), 124–25; Loren Schweninger, *Black Property Owners in the South, 1790–1915* (Urbana: University of Illinois Press, 1990), 116, 190.

22. Betsy Sompayrac, Last Will and Testament, Jan. 15, 1845, Office of the Parish Clerk, Natchitoches, Louisiana. See also Kimberly S. Hanger, "Patronage, Property and Persistence: The Emergence of a Free Black Elite in Spanish New Orleans," in *Against the Odds: Free Blacks in the Slave Societies of the Americas,* ed. Jane G. Landers (London: Frank Cass, 1996), 51–52.

23. The selection of godparents and sponsors varied by color and status. For example, in 1854 the North Carolina slave-owner Mary Ruffin Smith stood as sponsor at the baptism of Lucy Battle Smith, a relative of Cornelia Smith whom she owned. The Rev. Henry T. Lee served as rector of the Chapel of the Holy Cross, Chapel Hill, North Carolina, from 1856 to 1858. He baptized Ann Elisa, Henry, Patsy Alice, and Rufus, the children of Lissy and Sam, on Easter Sunday, March 23, 1856. Their sponsors, Mrs. William Horn Battle and her invalid daughter Susan Catherine, also sponsored eight other children baptized on the same day. Furthermore, Reverend Lee baptized George, a youngster owned by the Chaves family. Records indicate that an enslaved woman was his sponsor. Mary Arthur Stoudemire, "Black Parishioners of the Chapel of the Cross, 1844–1866," *North Carolina Genealogical Society Journal* 9 (May 1983), 78–84.

24. Sompayrac, Last Will and Testament; Michael P. Johnson and James L. Roark, "'A Middle Ground': Free Mulattoes and the Friendly Moralist Society of Antebellum Charleston," *Southern Studies* 21 (Fall 1982): 253.

25. Berlin, "The Structure of the Free Negro Caste," 312.

26. All references to the Coincoin-Metoyer children are found in Gary B. Mills, *The Forgotten People: Cane River's Creoles of Color* (Baton Rouge: Louisiana State University Press, 1977); Gary B. Mills, "Coincoin: An Eighteenth-Century 'Liberated' Woman," *Journal of Southern History* 42 (May 1976): 203–22; and Constance McLaughlin Green, *The Secret City: A History of Race Relations in the Nation's Capital* (Princeton: Princeton University Press, 1967), 16. Hanger's studies focus on colonial Louisiana, where laws were quite different from those in antebellum North Carolina and South Carolina. The fact remains, however, that families crossed boundaries to help their relatives.

27. Sara Revis, *Hannah Jackson: An African American Woman and Freedom,* Alexandria Archaeology Publication no. 33 (Alexandria: Office of Historic Alexandria, 1985), 1; Green, *The Secret City,* 16; Mary Beth Corrigan, "'It's a Family Affair': Buying Freedom in the District of Columbia, 1850–1860," in *Working toward Freedom: Slave Society and Domestic Economy in the American South,* ed. Larry E. Hudson, Jr. (Rochester: University of Rochester Press, 1994), 177–79, 186. See Loren Schweninger, "A Slave Family in the Antebellum South," *Journal of Negro History* 40 (January 1975): 29–44.

28. Jacobs, *Incidents in the Life of a Slave Girl,* 57, 96, 97, 99–100; Bethany Veney, *The Narrative of Bethany Veney: A Slave Woman* (1889, reprint, Luray, Va.: Page County Historical Association, 1998), 23–24.

29. Dickson D. Bruce, Jr., *Archibald Grimké: Portrait of a Black Independent* (Baton Rouge: Louisiana State University Press, 1993), 14–16.

30. William Ransom Hogan and Edwin Adams Davis, eds., *William Johnson's Natchez: The Ante-Bellum Diary of a Free Negro* (Baton Rouge: Louisiana State University Press, 1951); Edwin Adams Davis and William Ransom Hogan, *The Barber of Natchez* (Baton Rouge: Louisiana State University Press, 1954); Johnson and Roark, *Black Masters;* Johnson and Roark, "'A Middle Ground,'" 247nn5,6; Robert L. Harris, Jr., "Charleston's Free Afro-American Elite: The Brown Fellowship Society and the Humane Brotherhood," *South Carolina Historical Magazine* 82 (Oct. 1981): 289–310.

31. E. Hoggatt to Dear Aunt, July 11, 1857, William T. Johnson and Family Memorial Papers, Louisiana and Lower Mississippi Valley Collections, Louisiana University, Baton Rouge; TBHF to ARH, Dec. 27, 1857, MDAH.

32. Edwin Adams and William Ransom Hogan, *The Barber of Natchez* (Baton Rouge: Louisiana State University Press, 1998), 54–68, 241. See also Hogan and Davis, eds., *William Johnson's Natchez*.

33. Johnson and Roark, *Black Masters*, 131–33. It was not unusual for enslaved women to appeal to slaveholding women in an attempt to mitigate their condition. See Frances Anne Kemble, *Journal of a Residence on a Georgian Plantation in 1838–1839*, ed. John A. Scott (Athens: University of Georgia Press, 1984), 108, 214, 222–23; Lavinia to Dear Missis, Lawton Family Papers, University of South Carolina, Columbia.

34. Jane A. Crouch, First Summer School File, Hampton University Archives, Hampton, Va.; Johnson and Roark, *Black Masters*, 14–15, 23, 64–65; *Two Black Teachers during the Civil War: Mary S. Peake, the Colored Teacher at Fortress Monroe* [by] *Lewis C. Lockwood. Life on the Sea Islands* [by] *Charlotte Forten* (New York: Arno Press and the New York Times, 1969).

35. June Purcell Guild, *Black Laws of Virginia: A Summary of the Legislative Acts of Virginia Concerning Negroes from Earliest Times to the Present* (Richmond: Whittet and Shepperson, 1936), 175–76; Michael Eggart, "Anniversary Address," in Michael P. Johnson and James L. Roark, "'A Middle Ground': Free Mulattoes and the Friendly Moralist Society of Antebellum Charleston," *Southern Studies* 21 (Fall 1982): 262–64.

36. William Still, *The Underground Rail Road. A Record of Facts, Authentic Narratives, Letters, & c., Narrating the Hardships, Hairbreadth Escapes and Death Struggles of the Slaves in Their Efforts for Freedom, as Related by Themselves and Others, or the Largest Stockholders, and Most Liberal Aiders and Advisers, of the Road* (Philadelphia: Porter and Coats, 1872), 757; Waldo E. Martin, Jr., *The Mind of Frederick Douglass* (Chapel Hill: University of North Carolina Press, 1984), 25. Following the Nat Turner insurrection in 1831 it was more difficult for blacks to hold meetings of any kind. As a result, open gatherings by free blacks to discuss matters related to slavery jeopardized their own liberty. Interest in assisting slaves to gain their freedom was manifested in other ways.

37. Sterling, ed., *We are Your Sisters*, 126–27.

38. Potter, *A Hairdresser's Experience*, 17–19.

39. Stewart, *Maria W. Stewart*, 9, 20, 57, 64 (quotation); Gerda Lerner, *The Grimke Sisters from South Carolina: Pioneers for Woman's Rights and Abolition* (New York: Schocken Books, 1971).

40. David Walker, *David Walker's Appeal, in Four Articles: Together with a Preamble, to the Coloured Citizens of the World, but in Particular, and Very Expressly, to Those of the United States of America*, ed. Charles M. Wiltse (New York: Hill and Wang, 1965), 2; Shirley J. Yee, *Black Women Abolitionists: A Study in Activism, 1828–1860* (Knoxville: University of Tennessee Press, 1992), esp. chapter 5, "Breaking Customs," 112–34; Shirley J. Yee, "Organizing for Racial Justice: Black Women and the Dynamics of Race and Sex in Female Antislavery Societies, 1832–1860," in *Black Women in America*, ed. Kim Marie Vaz (Thousand Oaks: Sage, 1995), 48.

41. Stewart, *Maria W. Stewart*, 72, 73.

42. Sterling, ed., *We Are Your Sisters*, 222.

43. Ibid., 221; Leonard W. Levy, "The 'Abolition Riot': Boston's First Slave Rescue," *New England Quarterly* 25 (March 1952): 85–89; Jane H. Pease and William H. Pease, *They Who Would Be Free: Blacks' Search for Freedom, 1830–1861* (New York: Atheneum, 1974), 207; Benjamin Quarles, *Black Abolitionists* (New York: Oxford University Press, 1969), 205.

44. Sterling, ed., *We Are Your Sisters*, 222–23; Willi Coleman, "Architects of a Vision: Black Women and Their Antebellum Quest for Political and Social Equality," in *African American Women and the Vote, 1837–1965*, ed. Ann D. Gordon et al. (Amherst: University of Massachusetts Press, 1997), 35–36.

45. Sarah Bradford, *Harriet Tubman: The Moses of Her People* (1869, reprint New York: Corinth Books, 1961), 120.

CHAPTER 8

Free Black and Colored Women in Early-Nineteenth-Century Paramaribo, Suriname

Rosemarijn Hoefte and Jean Jacques Vrij

During the period of slavery, Paramaribo, capital of the colony of Suriname, was the only urban center in a society dominated by plantation agriculture. When the Dutch took over the colony from the English in the late seventeenth century, Paramaribo was scarcely more than a hamlet. Fifteen years later it still consisted of no more than fifty or sixty houses, but during the following years its growth was steady.[1] J. D. Herlein, who lived in the colony during the first decades of the eighteenth century, reported in 1718 that Paramaribo consisted of about five hundred wooden houses.[2] In 1772 there were 867 houses in town, and ten years later the number rose to 1,015.[3] By 1821 there were 1,382 houses.[4] All of these counts probably failed to register the modest accommodations that could be found in most yards (*erven*) behind the main buildings. Here the majority of town slaves and also some impoverished free people had their living quarters. In 1821 the number of these dwellings was reportedly three times that of regular houses.[5]

Eighteenth- and nineteenth-century residents and visitors alike characterized Paramaribo as a charming town. "La plus belle & a cause de son climat, la plus saine de l'Amérique" was the perhaps overly chauvinistic appraisal of David Isaac Cohen de Nassy, the eighteenth-century historian of Suriname's Sephardic Jewish community.[6] Most contemporary authors remarked on the cosmopolitan character of Paramaribo's population. Even when blacks and coloreds are excluded, the diversity was striking. The white segment of the population included Germans, Ashkenazi and Sephardic Jews, Dutch (including a substantial number of naturalized French Huguenots), and smaller numbers of French, Scandinavian, and Anglo-Saxon residents.[7]

John Gabriel Stedman was a captain in an expeditionary force sent out to fight the maroons of Suriname.[8] He lived there from 1773 to 1777 and left a colorful description of Paramaribo:

> Paramaribo is a very lively place, the Streets being crowded with Planters, Sailors, Soldiers, Jews, Indians, and Negroes, while the river Swarms with Canoes, barges, yoals, Ships boats &c constantly going and coming from the different Estates and crossing and passing each other like the wheries on the Thames, and mostly accompanied with bands of Musick [...] I might Still add the number of Carriages, Saddle Horses, and Profuseness in dress, which is truly magnificent Silk Embroidery Genua-Velvets diamonds Gold, & Silver-Lace being dayly wear, not so much as a Captain of a trading Ship appearing in less than Solid Gold buckles to his Stock, breeches &c, nor are they less refined at their tables where every thing that can be call'd deelicate is produced at any price, and served up in the newest fashion'd Silver-Plate and Japan-China—But nothing so much displays the Luxury of the inhabitants of Surinam, as the Quantity of Slaves that constantly attend them, sometimes in one family to the number of 20 and greatly upwards.[9]

The riches that Stedman mentioned grew out of the profits made on the many sugar, coffee, and cotton plantations of Suriname.[10] During the 1650s English colonists and Sephardic Jewish refugees from Brazil (arriving in two groups in 1652 and later in 1666) introduced the cultivation of sugar. When the Dutch took over the colony from the British in 1667, about fifty sugar plantations were in operation. Following an initial decrease in the number of estates, the production of sugar increased steadily, followed later by coffee and then by cotton and cacao on a smaller scale. By 1745 there were 154 sugar and 140 coffee plantations in operation with slave labor. By the second half of the eighteenth century, when Stedman lived in the colony, Suriname was experiencing halcyon years. By 1770 more than four hundred plantations exported coffee and sugar; the export value of the tropical products was highest between 1770 and 1789. The number of plantation slaves may have been as high as sixty thousand.[11]

At this time the numerical imbalance between whites and slaves was extreme. "Nowhere in the world," Gov. Jan Nepveu wrote in 1769, perhaps slightly exaggerating, "neither in ancient nor in modern times, has there ever been heard of such a large disproportion as exists in the colony of Suriname, where the number of whites, including planters, free burghers, employees, soldiers, no one excepted, can only be brought at one to fifteen [slaves] at the most, as there are as much as sixty to seventy thousand slaves against three to four thousand whites, everyone included."[12] The situation was most dramatic in the plantation area (as opposed to Paramaribo), where around 1774, according to Alex van Stipriaan's calculations, there were sixty-two slaves for every white person.[13] The ratio became less skewed subsequently.[14] The population imbalance, however, nurtured an atmosphere of fear and insecurity among whites, particularly when plantations were under attack from the maroon communities in the interior. Yet the colony did not experience many slave rebellions that have been recorded.

Several scholars have suggested that the fear and insecurity of Suriname whites contributed greatly to the existence of relatively smooth relations between them and the free blacks and coloreds of the colony. Keeping free blacks and coloreds at a social distance from whites was evidently not as pronounced a policy in the colony as it was elsewhere in the Caribbean. Harry Hoetink, Orlando Patterson, and Gert Oostindie have attributed that to the need of Suriname whites for allies who would support them against the overwhelming majority of slaves.[15]

As Hoetink did not fail to notice, however, several factors prevented whites from keeping free blacks and coloreds at arm's length. One was the growth of the free colored and black population concentrated in Paramaribo. Their history has been largely neglected. With few exceptions, contemporary observers as well as later scholars have tended to focus on plantation agriculture, slavery, and maroon societies at the expense of the urban environment of Paramaribo. Rosemary Brana-Shute, a notable exception to the rule, has called this sort of focus "agricultural myopia."[16]

The urban society of Paramaribo, probably more subject to change than the plantation economy, deserves careful study, and this chapter will focus particularly on free black and colored women during the early nineteenth century, when social patterns had crystalized. A colonial census of 1811 provides valuable insight into Suriname society of the time. The discussion will draw on the poll census and other sources to examine the slave background of the free black and colored women of Paramaribo, their role as "housekeepers" in free or common-law unions, and their means of existence. Because the meaning of the words *black* and *colored* varies over time and place, it must be stressed that these were quite unambiguous terms in early-nineteenth-century Suriname. "Black" (*zwarte* or *neger*) designated those of unmixed African origin; those of mixed ancestry were called "colored" (*couleurling* or *kleurling*). The only major ambivalence existed in regard to the so-called *karboegers,* with one white and three black (*neger*) grandparents (making them the equivalents of Sambo in the anglophone Caribbean), who were categorized either as blacks or coloreds.

According to the 1811 census, 2,029 individuals were registered as whites and 3,075 as free coloreds and blacks. The data, however, cannot be taken at face value. A number of persons of mixed descent were categorized as whites, and several individuals failed to turn in their census forms. Among that category were plantation managers and their aides, who lived on estates. It is certain that some of these persons were colored or black, but most free plantation residents were white at the time. It still is highly probable that nonwhites formed close to 50 percent of Suriname's free population.[17] In Paramaribo itself, free nonwhites outnumbered whites by at least 3:2.

During the initial stages of the emergence of Paramaribo there were few, if any, free blacks and coloreds. As a rule, free people were white, and blacks and persons of mixed ancestry were slaves. For the first century or so, the data about the size of the nonwhite free population are sketchy. Census returns for 1762 record 1,623 names of white inhabitants and 258 names of free blacks and coloreds, but similar reservations apply here as for the census of 1811.[18] The number of free blacks and coloreds for 1762 should therefore be considered a minimum. The same can be said of the number (739) of free colored and black residents of Paramaribo (148 men, 323 women, 132 boys, and 136 girls) listed in March 1781.[19] The number of white residents was placed at 1,107 that same year, but that number is almost certainly much too low.[20] During the period from 1788 to 1811, the number of white town-dwellers seems to have hovered around two thousand.[21] Probably during the last two decades of the eighteenth century in Paramaribo the number of free nonwhites surpassed that for whites. According to a report of 1791, Suriname had 1,760 free nonwhite inhabitants, the great majority of whom lived in Paramaribo.[22] By 1805 there were reportedly 2,889 free coloreds and blacks in the colony as a whole.[23] Perhaps at least 2,500 of them lived in town, and most were women—1,328 adult females as opposed to only 640 adult males.[24]

Slavery and Manumission

The great majority of free blacks and coloreds were former slaves who had benefited from manumission. Brana-Shute analyzed all manumissions in Suriname for the period from 1760 to 1828 and estimated that about four thousand slaves were manumitted during that time.[25] Between 1797 and 1802, when the manumission rate was relatively high, at least 762 slaves joined the free population.[26] Increased rates of manumission caused authorities some concern. In December 1803 and July 1804 the Court of Policy and Criminal Justice, the policymaking body of Suriname, tightened regulations regarding financial guarantees and raised taxes on manumission from 50 guilders (for women and children) and 100 guilders (for men) to 250 guilders (for children) and 500 guilders (for women and men).[27] Evidently, colonial officials noticed a connection between a decline in the subordination of town slaves and the growing number of persons who crossed the line between slavery and freedom. Officials also doubted that freed persons could maintain their own livelihoods. Children of deceased mothers in particular often became a burden on the colony.[28]

From as early as 1733, manumissions were considered invalid unless they were reviewed and sanctioned by the court. Thereafter, concerns about the social repercussion of manumission shaped nearly all new legislation, almost up to the abolition of slavery in 1863.[29] Despite regulations that made it increasingly difficult (theoretically) for slaves to achieve free status, the number of manumissions over the long run continued to grow.[30] That trend can be explained in part by what may be called "chain manumission" as manumitted persons became manumitters themselves—and often of members of their own family.[31]

Scholars have often remarked that an urban environment was congenial to freedom in the slave societies of the New World. Suriname was no exception. Few plantation slaves were manumitted.[32] The ones who were generally belonged to a minority group—house servants. Frequently they were women who, by rendering domestic service and fulfilling the role of concubine, had gained the affection of the plantation manager. Most freed plantation slaves, however, were the children of these women and white managers.

Plantation managers were hired by estate owners, who, if they lived in Suriname at all, preferred to reside in Paramaribo rather than on their plantations. As a rule, managers were bachelors; many had come to Suriname as soldiers.[33] They were financially unable to maintain a family in a "decent" (*burgerlijke*) way. Plantation owners and their agents or administrators often objected to women "from outside" (lawful spouses or otherwise) living on estates. Such women were a financial burden, and, moreover, owners and agents recognized that there were advantages in the creation of closer ties between managers and female slaves.

G. P. C. van Breugel, a Dutch plantation owner who visited his possessions in Suriname in 1823–24, returned from the colony with a rather teleological perspective on the matter. There was more than met the eye to an "ancestral custom" that dictated that a new manager should immediately pick out a domestic servant in order to cohabit "in a Suriname way"—or so he understood. A relationship with a female slave gave a new manager insight into the lives of the slaves and the problems and conflicts of the labor force. The habit of taking a slave concubine became so entrenched that introducing a woman from outside almost inevitably led to unrest among domestic and field slaves.[34] It was certainly not an entrenched habit, however, that a manager would purchase and then free his concubine and/or their children. When managers switched plantations, as often happened, they would then chose a new concubine. According to Van Breugel, the former partner would live with the manager's successor, and the children would remain slaves on the plantation.[35] Of course, there were exceptions, and they are of particular interest because they would become part of the free black and colored population.

There are cases of managers who manumitted all or a few of their children but not the children's mothers. Sometimes these freed children then purchased and freed their mothers and/or other siblings. The manager of 't Eyland Plantation, Frederik Hoth, had five children with the black slave Mimie. He then became manager of St. Barbara Plantation, but his relationship with Mimie continued. He would have slaves from St. Barbara pick up Mimie by boat at night, and she would be returned to 't Eyland in the early morning. This mobility, however, was prohibited by law; when it was discovered, Hoth had to pay a fine and Mimie was flogged.[36] Hoth lawfully owned Emanuel, one of his children with Mimie. The boy was sent to Europe when he was six, returning to Suriname in 1780 as Emanuel Fredrik Hoth and becoming financially successful.[37] He managed to purchase his mother, Mimie, and his only surviving sister, Antje, both of whom he manumitted in 1795.[38] In 1811 Antje, a seamstress, lived in Paramaribo with her mother and her two boys, Jacob and François, who were in school.

Occasionally, a manager might purchase and free a substantial number of family members. Hans Joachim Emicke, manager of Kortevreugd and Kleinshoven Plantation, bought his four daughters by the black slave Carolina and manumitted them in 1796.[39] After his death in 1800, his will revealed that Carolina was to be bought and manumitted as well, which happened in 1803.[40] Carolina, however, had another daughter from a previous relationship, the black slave Johanna, who by 1800 had three children of her own. Hans Joachim Emicke's will directed that money from his estate should be used to purchase and free Johanna and her children.[41]

Eight years later, Johanna was indeed manumitted, but it remains unclear whether Emicke's money was used in the transaction. More important seems to be the fact that Johanna followed in her mother's footsteps and became the concubine of Emicke's successor at Kortevreugd and Kleinshoven, Johan Peter Joseph Pohl. The couple had at least five children, four born while Johanna was still a slave. Pohl became the owner of Johanna and their children as well as two of her children from a previous relationship, all of whom he manumitted in two stages in 1808 and 1812.[42]

Thus within a period of sixteen years Carolina, her five daughters, and six of her grandchildren were freed. At the time of the census of 1811, she and four daughters lived in Paramaribo. The youngest lived with her mother, in all likelihood in the house left them by Emicke, and the three others lived as common-law wives with white men. Their cousin Louisa, the eldest daughter of Johanna, was the common-law wife of the co-owner and administrator of Kortevreugd and Kleinshoven Plantation. In contrast, Johanna and her children with Pohl remained at the plantation where she used to work as a slave. That was exceptional. Most freed concubines of plantation managers moved, along with their children, to Paramaribo, if only because the children could go to school there. It is likely that not much later Johanna came to town as well, when Pohl repatriated to Germany. He married there in 1817 and never did return to the colony. He did, however, legitimize his offspring, and Johanna received an annual stipend for life. She died in 1839.[43]

The cases described are not representative in one aspect: The great majority of the freed population originated from the slave population of Paramaribo and not from rural plantation slaves. That does not necessarily mean, however, that these freed people had lived in Paramaribo all their lives. Some were born in Africa and others on a Suriname plantation. Slaves were moved regularly from plantations to Paramaribo. Sometimes their stay in town was only temporary, to learn a skill, for example, or receive medical treatment. The duration of the stay could be indefinite, however, if owners or administrators residing in town wanted their services or if they were considered less useful on the plantation.[44]

In 1791 eight thousand slaves were estimated to live in Paramaribo. According to the census of 1811, there were 9,714 private (*particuliere*) slaves in Suriname, nearly all of whom lived in town.[45] White, urban residents numbered approximately two thousand in both years, and the free population of Paramaribo as a whole was in the range of three to five thousand. The numerical disproportion between slaves and white/free people was thus less pronounced in town than in the plantation area. Still, the high number of slaves in Paramaribo often drew criticism.[46] That criticism was leveled generally against households with more slaves than could usefully be employed.

Urban slaves fully employed in the households or businesses of their owners and those who were redundant could gain freedom albeit through different ways. A number of house slaves, most often women who had loyally served their owners for many years and assisted them through difficult times such as illness or death, were granted freedom. In 1772 Anna, the black slave of Jean Philippe Peneux, a Suriname-born white, accompanied her owner to the Dutch Republic. She was baptized there and became a member of the Reformed church. In a notarized deed Peneux then gave Anna her freedom because she had served him and his family for a long time and had nursed him through a major illness. In 1773 the newly named Anna van Peneux and her former owner returned to Suriname.[47] In the census of 1811, Peneux's white son registered Anna and declared that he took care of her because she was too old to work.

The loyalty and service of a slave during an owner's infancy and childhood, or when family members died, were often rewarded with freedom. David d'Aron Jesserun freed the slave Porcia, a present from his mother, because she had raised him.[48] Jan Nepveu (who would later become governor) and his first wife, Johanna Agatha Audenrogge, declared in their will that, after they died, their slaves Cornelia and Nanoe, who had been the wet nurses of their children, should be manumitted. Nepveu's wife died five years later, in 1765, and on her deathbed she requested the freedom of the slave Constantie, who had tended her during her last days. Nepveu manumitted Constantie and her children in 1773. He also freed Cornelia even though both female slaves had already enjoyed de facto freedom for some time. Nanoe and her son, Valentijn, were freed after the death of the governor in 1779.[49] At the time of the census of 1811, only Nanoe's son and two of Constantie's children, all of them mulattos, were still alive. Nanoe's son, now known as Jan Louis Valentijn, and Jan Philip Zeeman, Constantie's son, were both carpenters. In the wooden town of Paramaribo theirs could be a profitable trade. In the case of Zeeman, it clearly was. He owned thirty-five slaves, nearly all of them carpenters. In 1814 he earned three times as much as a plantation manager.[50] Johanna Elisabeth Saraatje Zeeman, Constantie's daughter, earned her living as a knitter. She had a long relationship with Johannes Stuger, a German who came to Suriname as a soldier and later became a merchant and plantation owner. In 1811 Stuger had already died, but he left Johanna some of his possessions. Their six children were heirs to half of his estate.[51]

Owners who had more slaves than they actually needed in their households or businesses often compelled them to earn a living. Every week they handed over a fixed amount in cash to their master. It was often left up to the slaves themselves how they would earn their money. Of course, that could lead to criminal behavior and was therefore legally prohibited. Nevertheless, the practice was common in Paramaribo.[52] The wage system gave some slaves opportunity to save money and ultimately buy their freedom. It was also possible for them to borrow money to purchase themselves from their owners and ultimately obtain manumission. Thus slaves mortgaged themselves and paid off their creditors in installments. That was the strategy followed by Fortuna, a black slave originally from Woudvlied Plantation. In 1777 Catherina van Weijne (herself manumitted in 1754) loaned Fortuna 800 guilders to enable her to pay off her owner. After doing so, Fortuna finally obtained her letter of manumission in 1801.[53]

Several redundant female slaves earned a living by becoming the common-law wife or "housekeeper" of a free man. They were able to use their situations as paths to freedom. When he died in 1763, the former colonial official Ephraim Coomans Scherping left dozens of domestic slaves, including a number of women who had been hired out to citizens of Paramaribo. At least four of them—Nanie and Maria, both black, and Aaltje and Mariana, both mulattas—were the "housekeepers" of the mulatto Christiaan Pokorna and of the white residents Jan Emanuel Vieira, Antoine Imbert, and Pieter Hendrik de Bije, respectively. Imbert, De Bije, and Vieira bought and manumitted their concubines and their joint offspring during their lifetimes; Vieira bought Maria and her seven mulatto children for 4,000 guilders.[54] The manumission of Nanie and her children was included in Pokorna's will.

In regard to "racial relations" between whites and free coloreds/blacks, Suriname's colonial policy was comparable to that of other slave societies of the Americas in its attempts to maintain both a legal and socioeconomic distance between white and nonwhite free people. Its professed objective was to contain the expectations of the slaves. Even when free, coloreds and blacks would still be considered inferior to whites, an unalterable status. Nonetheless, the gap between whites and free blacks and coloreds began to close.[55] An economic crisis and subsequent wave of white emigration during the 1770s depleted the white population, and as a result free colored men filled positions once monopolized by whites. This occupational shift changed the social hierarchy, and daily reality moved increasingly away from the ideal of white people on top, free people below, and slaves at the very bottom.

The multiethnic composition of the white population may have reinforced these social changes. It was often common for the government or a private employer to prefer, for instance, a Christian colored man with a Dutch education to a German or a Jew. Thus, coloreds in particular could take advantage of divisions within the white population. As a consequence, "ethnic protectionism" did not develop in the same way as in the anglophone and francophone Caribbean with their more ethnically homogeneous white population. Keeping free blacks and coloreds at a distance was not possible for another reason: domestic relations. The shortage of white women precluded endogamy in Suriname, and the resulting intimate relations between whites and nonwhites undermined official policy. As early as 1751, a military officer noticed that many Suriname dignitaries "preferred black women to their wives."[56] He observed that the awe in which blacks formerly held whites was rapidly decreasing.

Housewives and Housekeepers

The overwhelming majority of urban free men in Suriname had a nonwhite partner, most of them free women. As far as can be determined, no black or colored men had white partners in 1811.[57] That was probably also true for most white town-dwellers. In 1805 it was estimated that the colony had only 754 white women and 1,907 white men but 1,328 free black and colored women.[58] According to the census of 1811, the number of white women dropped to 441, but the number of free black and colored women went almost unchanged (1,330) and was almost three times the number of white women. Of the 1,330 free colored and black women in the census, only seventeen were married and twenty-one were widowed—2.9 percent. (By way of comparison, at least 268 of the 441 white women were married and 122 were widows—88.4 percent.)

If the white men were raised in societies where a legal marriage was standard, why were there so few marriages between whites and nonwhites? What kept white men from turning their nonwhite *huishoudster* (housekeeper or common-law wife) into a legal spouse or *huisvrouw* (housewife)? Was the social distance between whites and nonwhites sufficiently wide that a white man would lose status if he married a nonwhite woman?[59] There are indications that this indeed was the case in eighteenth-century Suriname. The much-discussed marriage of Elisabeth Samson, a wealthy black, to a white man caused much commotion, in part because the union would lower his status. Colonial officials declared that the idea of a mixed marriage up to that time (1764) had always been treated with contempt. It was suggested that if such legal unions could not be prevented, husbands should be declared "dishonorable" and excluded from all official functions.[60] That same year, a military officer who intended to marry a colored woman was threatened with dismissal, which did not deter the couple. They married in 1765.[61]

Undoubtedly, the mentality of whites had changed during the decades between the 1760s and the taking of the census of 1811. Several high-ranking officials, plantation owners, and administrators were unmistakably married to colored women. The fact that the former colonial official and plantation owner H. F. Matile was married to the colored widow of two ministers shows that even men of the cloth did not fear loss of social prestige when they married a non-white woman. Matile's wife, the mulatta Nanette Susanna Peterse, had been exceptionally well-raised and received her education at a distinguished French school in the Dutch town of Gouda. In 1784 she married a minister, J. S. C. B. Donkerman, and three years later another minister, A. A. Sporon.[62]

There is another reason why color codes alone cannot explain the dearth of legal unions. Colored and black men seem to have been even less willing than white men to marry women with whom they lived, even though they were often of the same complexion. In 1811 only seven of thirty-eight nonwhite married women were the housewives or widows of nonwhite husbands, whereas thirty-one had married a white man. Of course, socioeconomic and cultural differences that were not related to color may also have been obstacles to marriage, but these elements did not seem to have played a role in many nonlegal partnerships. Finally, as in Europe, the financial costs of a wedding might have been a reason to forgo the ceremony.[63]

The explanation of the low marriage rate, however, is probably to be found in the way people perceived the alternative to marriage. Concubinage was popularly called "Suriname marriage."[64] By the late eighteenth century, it was accepted by all social strata and by both sexes.[65] That colored and black women accepted Suriname marriages is not surprising; both civil and church marriages were European conventions. In the Old World, concubinage was punishable and labeled as "whoring." Of course, in Suriname Dutch law prevailed, but it was socially accepted.

Contemporary observers noted that women took liaisons with male partners seriously. As Stedman, for example, noted:

> I must describe this Custom which I am convinced will be highly censured by the Sedate European Matrons—and which is nevertheless as common as it is almost necessary to the batchelors who live in this Climate; these Gentlemen all without Exception have a female Slave—mostly a creole—in their keeping who preserves their linnens clean and decent, dresses their Victuals with Skill, carefully attends them—they being most excellent nurses—during the frequent illnesses to which Europeans are exposed in this Country, prevents them from keeping late Hours knits for them, sows for them &c—while these Girls are sometimes Indians sometime Mulattos and often negroes, naturally pride themselves in living with an European whom they serve with as much tenderness, and to whom they are Generally as faithfull as if he were their lawfull Husband.[66]

The concubines who figure here in Stedman's description are invariably slaves. If a housekeeper was—and remained—a slave, however, that would constitute a fundamentally different kind of relationship from the one under consideration in this discussion. One may doubt the accuracy of Stedman's observations; even in his day during the mid-1770s many housekeepers were free women. In any case, slave concubines during the early nineteenth century were the exception rather than the rule.[67] Stedman did make some valid observations, however, particularly about the general acceptance of concubinage and the devotion of female partners. Writing fifty years later, Lammens noted that "many of these women are reputed to be very virtuous."[68]

A Suriname marriage certainly was not a random sexual relationship. There were conventions to be observed, the most important of which was obtaining the consent of the mother of the housekeeper or common-law wife. The mother also negotiated a brideprice or wedding present.[69] Van Breugel mentions, too, that a simple ceremony inaugurated a Suriname marriage to signify the "permanence" of the relationship. The mother, often accompanied by a female neighbor, would lead her daughter to the bedroom of the groom. The next morning mother and neighbor visited the room again and then announced that the marriage had been concluded.[70]

Suriname- and African-born women fully accepted the practice of Suriname marriage, and there seems not to have been much resistance from Europeans as well. Even the churches seem to have accepted reality and took no disciplinary action against congregation members who had common-law wives. In the late eighteenth century several deacons and ministers lived with housekeepers.[71]

A Suriname marriage could be an attractive option for Europeans who came out to the colony intending to make a fortune and then return home for good. Many, however, never repatriated. When they realized that they would probably remain in Suriname, many decided to legalize their ties with their housekeepers. One example is a German master mason, Christiaan Fyth. In 1804, at the age of fifty-eight, he married a mulatta, Antoinetta Smidt, forty-one. They were already the parents of two daughters, twenty-two and sixteen. Two months after their wedding the couple became grandparents for the first time. In the census of 1811 Antoinetta Smidt, by then widowed, was the owner of nineteen slaves, including seven adult African masons.[72] In another example, the mulatta Henriëtta Geertruida Sluyter, who in 1811 was registered as a housekeeper, married her Dutch partner Abraham van der Kamp in 1819. The newspaper announcement did not mention that the bride was forty and the groom fifty-two. Only one month later the newspaper announced that Mrs H. G. Sluyter, spouse of Abraham van der Kamp, had delivered a son, their ninth child.[73]

It was not only European men in Suriname who preferred concubinage to marriage. Lammens noted that coloreds and blacks feared that the ties of matrimony would make them unhappy. Teensta confirmed this by telling the story of a colored man who, in refusing a white man the hand of his daughter, Louisa, said that he could live with her but should not take away Louisa's freedom.[74] How is this attitude to be explained? First, it must be taken into account that the conditions of Suriname households could differ substantially. Most contemporary authors have only described those cases in which the man was the wealthier partner. He owned or rented the house in which the family lived and supported his housekeeper and children. The woman managed the household, and the main work was done by domestic slaves. If the man earned only a small wage, the woman would fulfill the tasks normally done by slaves (cleaning, washing, cooking, and sewing). When the partner was, or became, better-off, however, the woman's personal wealth could grow due to the "wedding present" and other gifts, such as houses, slaves, furniture, and money received over the course of the relationship.[75]

But the man was not always the more affluent partner. Lammens described destitute European immigrants who fled into the arms of "colored or black women, especially those who are established or have any means of income."[76] Willem Adriaan Koopman, who was colored, wrote in 1819 about a military officer called Nesselrode who stripped his rich legal wife of all her assets, then obtained information about colored women who possessed their own house and slaves, and finally moved in with Marie van den Bergh, a mulatta, where he enjoyed free board and lodging.[77]

In such cases, women were not always eager to marry. According to the Dutch laws of marriage, a married woman was subordinate to her husband and did not have legal competence (*handelingsbekwaamheid*). The husband was, in fact, his wife's legal guardian. He was entrusted with the management of her assets, and she needed his consent to dispose of her own capital and property or conclude any contract.[78] Wives thus risked the fate of the rich spouse of officer Nesselrode. Moreover, it was not easy to obtain a divorce; *incompatibilité d'humeurs* was not reason enough to leave a legal spouse. A Suriname marriage could thus be an attractive option for both partners.

The Census of 1811

In October 1811, Charles Bentinck, governor of Suriname under British rule, informed the public that he had received orders from London "to transmit without delay, to his Majesty's Ministers of State, an accurate statement and return of the population of this colony in general, and of each colour and sex in particular, including whites, free people of colour [& negroes] and slaves."[79] All free citizens were ordered to register themselves and their slaves before the end of November. Slaves were to be categorized as Africans, Creoles, or coloreds, and their type of work was to be specified. Free blacks and coloreds in particular were required to list their "means of subsistence, trade or profession." Even though it was not required of white citizens, some supplied that information anyway when they registered. The colonial administration received information about 5,104 free individuals, 9,714 non-plantation slaves, and 42,223 plantation slaves.[80]

Most registration forms contained information about more than one person. Often the individuals included on a single document formed a household, but some households filled out separate forms as in the case of Amimba van Gühl, a black, and a white baker, C. G. Gühl. From another source it is clear that these two persons actually lived together. In 1823 Amimba requested permission to continue Gühl's business when he had left the colony temporarily. She declared that she had lived with him for more than thirty years and had managed his household while he ran his bakery.[81]

The colonial administration later subdivided the census forms into two series, one for "white inhabitants" (983 forms) and one for "free coloured and black residents" (1,351 forms). Documents were included in the first set in cases where forms contained the name of at least one white individual. Jurjanus Sluyter, for example, was the only white person on his return, which also included the names of nine free coloreds and fourteen free blacks, but his form was placed among the "white" set. This procedure explains why the first set includes the names of many nonwhites. Moreover, nonwhites were included in the "white" set because a number of coloreds were registered as whites, according to a convention arrived at thirty years earlier. In 1781 a mulatto named Carel Rühle, the African-born son of a free black woman on the coast of West Africa, having first migrated to Amsterdam and then to Suriname, complained that he was assigned to the colored and black militia in Paramaribo. Other coloreds, he pointed out, served in the white militia, particularly Johan Adolf Esser, who had become a lieutenant despite being the legitimate son of Adolf Esser, a German, and Johanna van der Weg, a mulatta. Rühle's complaint forced the government to establish a clear-cut rule in such matters. The degree of miscegenation was the most important but not the only criterion. So-called octoroons, people who had one black great-grandparent (of eight) and were phenotypically hard to distinguish from whites, were now assigned to the white militia. Mulattos such as Rühle, having equally black and white ancestors, were without exception assigned to the black and colored militia. The most difficult case was related to quadroons (people who had one black and three white grandparents), who were divided into two categories. The first group included those born out of a legal marriage and therefore considered white; the other group included those born out of a Suriname marriage or any other nonlegal relationship and consequently categorized as colored.[82]

The classification of "colored" was important in militia matters but had no further practical social consequences except in censuses that listed the categories "white," "colored," and "black." That was, therefore, the case in 1811. A son born of a legal marriage, the watchmaker Daniel George Ney, son of Benjamin Ney, who was Swiss, and the mulatta Johanna Christina George, registered himself as white. A well-known teacher, Johannes Vrolijk, who was born of a nonlegal association between a white, Petrus Cornelis van Stuyvesand, and a mulatta, Coba from Groot Marseille Plantation, classified himself as colored.[83]

Not everyone, however, followed the regulation of 1781 to the letter. Christiana Wilhelmina Kalden, widow of Willem Hendrik Esser (a brother of Johan Adolf

Esser) was registered as colored, but her sisters Johanna Antonia and Martha Elisabeth Kalden, wives of the town carpenter Johan Carel Schönher and the teacher Hendrik Herman Arnzen, respectively, were classified as white. Yet all three were the offspring of the legal marriage between Louis Kalden, who was Dutch, and Anna Elisabeth Albregt, a mulatta.[84]

The majority of the colored women who in 1811 were married to—or widows of—white men were registered as white, even when they should have been classified as coloreds according to the regulation of 1781. One example is Carel Rühle's sister, Martha. She migrated to Suriname in 1770 and married Johannes Schneebeling, who was Swiss, that same year. In 1811 the widowed Martha listed herself as white.[85] Octoroons were sometimes listed as coloreds and sometimes as whites, often with the addition of the word *casties* (octoroon). Johanna Jacoba Henriëtte van der Zee, a quadroon, registered herself and her octoroon adult children as coloreds; consequently, her form is filed with those of "free coloured and black residents." The quadroon Adriana Agnetta Middellijn, a seamstress and landowner, however, filed her octoroon children as whites, so her form is included with the "white inhabitants" set. There was therefore in Suriname a twilight zone of coloreds who for various reasons were counted as whites. Even though their number cannot have been very large, it is nevertheless clear that the figures reported to London are not accurate.

The 1811 census returns yield a count of 1,330 free black and colored women, 1,212 of whom provided information on their means of subsistence. That count includes women registered as white but who were actually colored. The 1781 regulation is not followed in this study, and quadroons and octoroons born out of legal unions have been counted also as coloreds. The proportion of colored women was therefore 57.8 percent; for black women, it was 42.2 percent.

The census data on the means of subsistence of free colored and black women are based on information provided by the women themselves. Such information is not always reliable, although some women were very meticulous in their responses. Francina van Weijs, a free black, for instance, wrote that she enjoyed free housing and made her living by renting out two slaves and working as a seamstress and a domestic. Most women, however, reported only a single source of income, and in a number of cases this was questionable. Among the 1,056 women registered in the "free coloured and black residents" file, 403 were slave-owners. Among them, 221 owned one or two slaves, 110 owned three to five slaves, fifty-six owned six to ten slaves, eleven owned eleven to twenty slaves, and five owned more than twenty slaves. Undoubtedly, many of these slaves provided their free colored and black mistresses with additional income. That was most likely the case with the mason and two mason's apprentices who belonged to the mulatta Paulina de Montel. She also owned four African women—two domestics, one cook, and one woman in training to become a laundress. Paulina de Montel, however, did not list any source of income. Francina van Doesburg, a free colored, only reported for the census that she was a seamstress. She also owned fifteen slaves, however: two seamstresses, a carpenter, a gardener, two domestics, a cook, a knitter, four boys in the carpenter's trade, and the rest were too old or too young to work. At least ten of these slaves could earn money for her. Similarly, Johanna van Arden, a free black who was pastry cook, failed to list her slaves (a carpenter and two apprentices, a gardener, a cooper, and two domestics) as sources of income.

When other archival data are used in combination with the census of 1811, it may turn out that a large proportion of the free colored and black women had more sources of income than the ones they reported. In 1823, for instance, the same Paulina de Montel requested and obtained permission to continue operating the bakery of her deceased common-law husband J. S. Sanches. The business had enabled him, she stated in her request, to maintain herself and her children in a decent way. Because their eldest daughter was born in 1803, that probably would have already been the case in 1811.[86] Another example would be that of Johanna Christina Steeven, a free colored. She was registered as the

Table 8.1. Means of Subsistence, Trades, or Professions of Free Black and Colored Women in Paramaribo, Suriname, 1811

Source of Income	Colored Women	Black Women	Total
Textiles			
Manufacture	7	31	38
Seamstress	352	145	497
Apprentice	26	10	36
Washerwoman	19	72	91
Household work			
"Housekeeper"	113	53	166
Domestic servant	13	24	37
Domestic servant apprentice	2	—	2
Preparing food	2	5	7
(Market) vendor	1	16	17
Midwife	—	4	4
Teacher	1	—	1
Landowner	6	4	10
Coffee house keeper	2	—	2
Nursing of sick	—	1	1
Multiple sources of income	15	9	24
Income from capital, real estate, slaves	9	10	19
Idle			
Dependent on others	66	43	109
Old and sick	43	78	121
Without income	8	13	21
Unclear	2	7	9
Unknown	82	36	118
	769	561	1,330

Source: Public Records Office, Colonial Office, London, Census Suriname 1811. We have used the microfilm version deposited in the Dutch National Archives in The Hague.

huishoudster of the mulatto Adriaan Johannes Comvalius but actually owned one of the twelve slaves in the household, a cook. Other sources also reveal that she was a licensed rum-seller.[87]

Of the total number of 1,212 free colored and black women who provided information on their means of existence, almost half (47.1 percent) were employed in textiles, whether as seamstresses, apprentices, or manufacturers of cloth (knitters and weavers). The women of another category (16.9 percent) were employed in households. The majority of these women were huishoudsters, but the group also included a small number of domestics. The third-most-common means of subsistence was laundry work; 7.5 percent of the women were registered as washerwomen. More than one-fifth of the group (20.7 percent) were listed as not working. These women in all likelihood were financially supported by their families, former owners, or other persons who cared for them. One example is Bellona van Schelling, a free colored who on account of her age no longer could make a living. Her daughter Silvia, a laundress, and her grandson Jacobus Frans Haster, a tailor, probably looked after her.

Colored free women dominated some jobs but apparently shunned others. The majority of seamstresses (70.8 percent) and huishoudsters (68 percent) were colored free women, but few from this group were employed as laundresses and market vendors. These were typically "black jobs" performed by a majority of free black women—79.1 percent for laundresses, and 94.1 percent for vendors. Skilled seamstresses enjoyed higher status than unskilled laundresses and vendors. The occupation of vendor was held in particularly low esteem; many slave women also worked as market vendors. The same was true for domestic work (in 64.8 percent of the cases performed by fully black women), which was done mostly by slaves.

The small number of women, only 166, who stated that they were a huishoudster seems to contradict our contention that Suriname marriage was standard in the colony. It should be remembered, however, that the census requested information about a person's source of income. Apparently, some considered being a common-law wife a livelihood, although many did not. The mulatta Hendrina Elisabeth Vieira, for instance, was the huishoudster of a white Creole, Charles Abraham Lemmers Godefroy, for more than thirty years. Yet she reported in the census that she was a seamstress.[88] The census category "dependent on others" also included huishoudsters.

The census data reveal that free colored women were relatively better off than free black women and that some free colored women were quite well-to-do. Anna Hartog Jacobs, a mulatta registered as "living of her interest," owned thirty-two slaves. Anna, or Hanna as was her original name, was the daughter of Hartog Jacobs, a Jew, and his black slave, Princess. In 1770, when she was two, her father manumitted her together with her mother and brother. When Hartog Jacobs died in 1792 he left two plantations, and Hanna and his three brothers became co-owners. In his will he also left money to pay for Hanna's (possible) wedding, although she never did marry. She lived, however, with Hendrik Maurits Wolff, a prominent colonial official. When Wolff died in 1804, he left his common-law wife Anna 30,000 guilders and named their daughter his sole heiress. Anna Hartog Jacobs later benefited from more inheritances and bequests, including 100,000 guilders left by her daughter. Anna died in 1845, leaving two houses, thirty-one slaves, some land, and partial ownership of a coffee plantation.[89]

Of the ten landowning free women listed in the census, seven possessed town gardens rather than plantations. The other three women who declared themselves to be landowners (Anna Hartog Jacobs was not included in this group) were all of mixed blood.[90] One of them, Susanna Ostrehan, seems to have been a foreigner; it has not been possible to trace the source of her wealth. The other two, Susanna Muntz, née Goede, and Philippina Wijnbergen, née Albrecht, were both widows of white men. Both owned timber plantations with forty-one and nine slaves, respectively.

Some free women achieved their comfortable economic status on their own. The mulatta Elisabeth Meijerhof (the teacher in table 8.1) in 1817 ran a school with thirty-five pupils, boys and girls of all races. She taught them spelling, reading, writing, and, "female handicrafts" for a fee of 5 to 6 guilders a month. Elisabeth Meijerhof was the daughter of a black, Quasiba van De Loncour, and Lodewijk Meijer. In 1771, when she was eight, her father sent her to the Netherlands. She returned to Suriname in 1792, pregnant but unmarried. Her father seems to have taken care of her education, but that was all as far as material support was concerned.[91] Another example of such enterprise was the mulatta Elisabeth Wilhelmina de Montel, daughter of Salomon de Montel, a Sephardic Jew, and Dido, a free black and sister of Paulina de Montel. In 1781 when she was fifteen, Elisabeth married a Frenchman, Pierre Thuillier. Her dowry included four slaves and goods and cash worth more than 10,000 guilders. Two years later her husband gave her permission to rent and operate an inn, called the Surinaamsche Beurs (Suriname Exchange). This meant that from now on she enjoyed the status of acknowledged business woman (*openbare koopvrouw*). Elizabeth thus took advantage of the most important possibility in the marriage law to independently conclude commercial transactions. In 1811, by then the widow of a second husband, the North American Andrew Bunker, she was registered in the census as keeper of a coffee house. She also owned thirty-one slaves.[92]

Elisabeth Wilhelmina de Montel was, of course, an exception among free black and colored women in early-nineteenth-century Paramaribo. Even though the accuracy of the census of 1811 can be challenged, its data provide some indication of the means of existence of the 1,212 free black and colored women who supplied relevant information. Almost half of them were employed in the making of textiles and/or sewing. Occupations with the potentially highest earnings and least slavelike working conditions were the domain of colored women. There were free colored and black women who were relatively well-off, owning slaves, houses, and other real estate acquired through bequests and inheritances or their own labor. Many, however, probably lived in less comfortable circumstances, which can be partially explained by the women's slave background. Most former slaves lacked the education and/or training to do more than menial work. Moreover, many recently manumitted women (and men) were almost penniless. Even though town slaves in particular frequently worked outside the homes of their masters and were allowed to keep part of the wages they earned, more often than not such earnings were invested in purchasing their freedom, which did not leave much to set up a business. And the more years they spent in slavery, the fewer years remained to improve their lot.

This chapter has drawn attention also to the importance of the so-called Suriname marriage that the census of 1811 tended to obscure. These often long-lasting common-law relationships were an important element of Suriname colonial society. The low number of legal unions is not only to be explained on the basis of color codes. A Suriname marriage was accepted by all social strata (including the church) and by both sexes by the late eighteenth century. Originally, such alliances were often between a free male and a female slave, but, gradually, free colored and black women replaced slaves as concubines of free men. The scarcity of women of their own race give white colonists little choice but to tie the knot with colored or black women. After all, in early-nineteenth-century Paramaribo free nonwhites outnumbered white citizens by 3 to 2, and women formed the majority of free colored and black groups. The census of 1811 sheds some light on the lives of these women, but more research needs to be done in other archival sources.

Notes

1. G. W. van der Meiden, *Betwist bestuur: Een eeuw strijd om de macht in Suriname 1651–1753* (Amsterdam: De Bataafsche Leeuw, 1987), 55, refers to an account by Adriaan van Berkel, who lived in Suriname from 1680 to 1689. See also Rudolf van Lier, *Samenleving in een grensgebied: Een sociaal-historische studie van Suriname* (Amsterdam: S. Emmering, 1977), 21; Jan Jacob Hartsinck, *Beschryving van Guiana of de Wilde Kust in Zuid-America* . . . (Amsterdam: Greer Tielenburg, 1770), 647; and [David Nassy], *Essai historique sur la Colonie de Surinam* . . . *par les régens et réprésentans de ladite nation juive Portugaise* (Paramaribo: s.n., 1788), 2: 19.

2. J. D. Herlein, *Nauwkeurige beschrijvinge van Zuriname* (Leeuwarden: Meindert Injema, 1718), 46. Gov. Jan Nepveu questioned this estimate (Van Lier, *Samenleving*, 21).

3. C. L. Temminck Grol et al., *De architectuur van Suriname, 1667–1930* (Zutphen: De Walburg Pers, 1973), 360–63; see also Robert Cohen, *Jews in Another Environment: Surinam in the Second Half of the Eighteenth Century* (Leiden: E. J. Brill, 1991), 74–84. It seems that Cohen is mistaken when he gives a total of 811 houses in 1772.

4. H. Uden Masman, *Kort verslag van den zwaren brand te Paramaribo, hoofdplaats der kolonie Suriname op den 21 januarij 1821 voorgevallen* . . . (Amsterdam: G. S. Leeneman van der Kroe, 1821), 14.

5. Uden Masman, *Kort verslag*, 14.

6. [Nassy], *Essai historique*, 2: 19.

7. See, for example, Herlein, *Nauwkeurige beschrijvinge*, 48; A. F. Lammens, *Bijdragen tot de kennis*

van de kolonie Suriname, tijdvak 1816 tot 1822, ed. G. A. de Bruijne (Amsterdam: Vrije Universiteit Amsterdam, Geografisch en Planologisch Instituut, Vakgroep Sociale Geografie van Ontwikkelingen, 1982), 55; [J. D. Kunitz], *Surinam und seine Bewohner oder Nachrichten über die geographischen, physischen, statistischen, moralischen und politischen Verhältnisse dieser Insel während eines zwanzigjährigen Aufenthalts daselbst, gesamelt von J. D. Kunitz, ehemaligen Plantagendirekteur* (Erfurt: Beyer and Maring, 1805), 56–57; and M. D. Teenstra, *De negerslaven in de kolonie Suriname en de uitbreiding van het Christendom onder de heidensche bevolking* (Dordrecht: H. Lagerweij, 1842), 8, 17, 37. Teenstra complained that Germans pulled the strings in this Dutch colony.

8. Escaped slaves found refuge in the tropical rain forest, withdrawing behind natural obstacles such as waterfalls and rapids. Marronage seems to have occurred even during the English period before 1667. During the Dutch administration the maroon problem continued to grow, and soon these "runaways," who searched for weapons and new recruits, especially women, posed a military threat to plantations. From the 1670s, a citizens' militia was organized to hunt maroons and destroy their villages. In the eighteenth century larger military expeditions, including Amerindians and slaves, were organized. According to David Nassy, during the 1730s and 1740s Suriname had became "a theatre of perpetual war" (*Essai historique*, 1: 87). During this period, expeditions reached their maximum size and frequency. Nevertheless, most were unsuccessful. That lack of success and growing costs forced the colonial administration to change course. In the 1760s peace treaties were concluded with the three main groups of maroons: with the Ndyuka in 1760, the Saramaka in 1762, and the Matawai in 1767. The Ndyuka and Saramaka at that time numbered between 2,500 to three thousand each; the Matawai were a much smaller group of some three hundred. Maroons received autonomy and in turn pledged to refrain from acts of aggression against the colony. They kept the treaties, but the marronage problem continued to exist, and groups of runaway slaves continued to pose military threats to the plantation colony. For an introduction to the maroons, see Richard Price, *The Guiana Maroons: A Historical and Bibliographical Introduction* (Baltimore: Johns Hopkins University Press, 1976).

9. John Gabriel Stedman, *Narrative of a Five Years Expedition against the Revolted Negroes of Surinam*, transcribed for the first time from the original 1790 manuscript, edited and with an introduction and notes by Richard Price and Sally Price (Baltimore: Johns Hopkins University Press, 1988), 236. Lammens (*Bijdragen tot de kennis van de kolonie Suriname*, 63) describes the period from 1816 to 1822 and also points to the constant coming and going of people—whites, coloreds, blacks, and Amerindians—and the apparent general affluence. He observes that a newcomer might think that "Paramaribo is a city right out of *The Arabian Nights*."

10. As Cohen (*Jews in Another Environment*, 66–72) has remarked, the picture Stedman painted of Suriname as a land of milk and honey—at least for its white inhabitants—is somewhat superficial. Many whites had recently acquired their plantations and had only been able to do so by taking out a mortgage. Other planters had also borrowed heavily, with their estates as collateral. Soon, many proved unable to pay off their debts and ended up losing their property to the Dutch investment firms that had granted the loans. As a consequence, absentee ownership became more pronounced, and many whites left the colony. Those who stayed, mostly Jews, often lived in dire circumstances. In 1776 Governor Nepveu referred to "the great poverty now prevailing here . . . there are many whites who do not look it, but have to make do with a dry banana" (quoted in Cohen, *Jews in Another Environment*, 66).

11. For an overview of Suriname's plantation economy see Alex van Stipriaan, *Surinaams contrast: Roofbouw en overleven in een Caraïbische plantagekolonie, 1750–1863* (Leiden: KITLV Press, 1993), esp. 33–34 and 310–11. Van Stipriaan (28–32) places the Suriname plantation economy in a Caribbean context. Even though Suriname was one of the oldest and largest plantation colonies in the Caribbean, it was never among the most important. Its population size was comparable to that of Barbados rather than that of Saint Domingue, Jamaica, and, later, Cuba. The production and export of sugar in those last three colonies were also much higher.

12. National Archives (hereafter NA), The Hague, the Netherlands, Proprietors of the Colony

of Suriname (hereafter SvS) 337 folio (hereafter fol.) 384–88, Gov. Jan Nepveu to the Proprietors, March 28, 1769, appendix.

13. Van Stipriaan, *Surinaams contrast*, 313. In Jamaica, where according to Michael Craton the ratio was "the highest in the British West Indies," it was one to ten. Craton, "Jamaican Slavery" in *Race and Slavery in the Western Hemisphere: Quantitative Studies*, ed. Stanley L. Engerman and Eugene D. Genovese (Princeton: Princeton University Press, 1975), 254.

14. In 1791 there were forty-five thousand plantation slaves in Suriname against 1,360 white plantation residents—that is, a ratio of 33:1. In Suriname as a whole, however, there were fifty-three thousand slaves and 3,360 white civilians—a ratio of 16:1. When the military is taken into account, about 1,200 men, the ratio changes to 12:1. And when finally the 1,760 free blacks and coloreds are taken into consideration, the ratio is eight slaves to one free individual. J. Wolbers, *Geschiedenis van Suriname* (Amsterdam: De Hoogh, 1861), 442–43.

15. Harry Hoetink, "Surinam and Curaçao," in *Neither Slave nor Free: The Freedmen of African Descent in the Slave Societies of the New World*, ed. David W. Cohen and Jack P. Greene (Baltimore: Johns Hopkins University Press, 1972), 80–81; Orlando Patterson, *Slavery and Social Death: A Comparative Study* (Cambridge: Harvard University Press, 1982), 257; Gert Oostindie, "Voltaire, Stedman, and Suriname Slavery," *Slavery and Abolition* 14 (Aug. 1993): 20.

16. Rosemary Brana-Shute, "The Manumission of Slaves in Suriname, 1760–1828," Ph.D. thesis, University of Florida, 1985, 11.

17. According to the returns of the Suriname Census of 1811, there were 515 large and small plantations, and if the plantation management usually consisted of one or two free men, the number of white men not included in the census cannot have been higher than a thousand. The original census results are in the Public Records Office, Colonial Office, London, Census Suriname 1811. We have used the microfilm version deposited in the Dutch National Archives in The Hague.

18. NA, SvS 318, fol. 77ff.

19. NA, Raden van Politie (Court of Police and Criminal Justice, hereafter RvP), 113, appendix to minutes of March 12, 1781.

20. NA, RvP 113, minutes of May 14, 1781.

21. [Nassy], *Essai historique*, 2: 37; Wolbers, *Geschiedenis van Suriname*, 442–43; Census 1811.

22. Wolbers, *Geschiedenis van Suriname*, 442–43. The number of 1,760 free blacks and coloreds in 1791 seems rather high but not impossible. Assuming an average of fifty-seven manumissions each year (Brana-Shute, "Manumission of Slaves," 188), close to six hundred individuals might have been manumitted during the ten-year interval between 1781 and 1791. Furthermore, the number of 739 free blacks and coloreds in 1781 does not include those living in the plantation area, whereas the figure recorded in 1791 does. Finally, the two to three hundred black soldiers of the *vrije corps* (later called "Black Rangers") might have been included as well in 1791. These soldiers were former slaves whom the government purchased from their owners and then freed on the condition that they would fight the maroons. Therefore, these men were generally stationed in the plantation area and not in town.

23. J. F. E. Einaar, *Bijdrage tot de kennis van het Engelsch Tusschenbestuur van Suriname, 1804–1816* (Leiden: M. Dubbeldeman, 1934), 72n4.

24. Brana-Shute, "Manumission of Slaves," 342.

25. Ibid., 188. In the twenty-three samples, between 1,305 and 1,341 individuals were manumitted—an average of fifty-seven to fifty-eight persons a year. See also Brana-Shute, "Approaching Freedom: The Manumission of Slaves in Suriname, 1760–1828," *Slavery and Abolition* 10 (Dec. 1989): 42.

26. The years 1799 (127 manumissions) and 1802 (161 manumissions) were sampled by Brana-Shute ("Manumission of Slaves," 45). On the basis of Vrij's research notes, we can add 212 manumissions in 1797 and 1798 and 262 manumissions in 1800 and 1801. Additional sources used were NA, RvP 464–68, 959, 472–78, and 539.

27. Brana-Shute, "Manumission of Slaves," 43; Brana-Shute, "Approaching Freedom," 141–42.

Brana-Shute is slightly mistaken when stating that the person who vouched for the support of the manumitted (not necessarily the owner) should post a bond of 2,000 guilders. That was only the case when the bond person wanted to leave the colony. The increased taxes on manumission clearly represented large sums of money, almost equal to an average annual income. Compare the salaries listed in Einaar, *Bijdrage tot de kennis van het Engelsch Tusschenbestuur,* 201–18.

28. NA, RvP 149, minutes of Dec. 28, 1803. In these minutes of the Court of Policy, no mention is made of a need to raise government revenue. That had been the explicit motive for introducing taxes on manumission in 1788, and Brana-Shute ("Manumission of Slaves," 142–47) maintains that it also lay behind the resolution of 1804. It seems very likely, however, that the tax increase was primarily intended to be prohibitive.

29. For these laws and regulations see Brana-Shute, "Manumission of Slaves," 101–75. Beginning in 1843, it became less difficult to obtain manumission.

30. Brana-Shute, "Manumission of Slaves," 140, 146, 176–219. During the period from 1832 to 1863, 6,364 slaves were manumitted. Okke ten Hove and Frank Dragtenstein, *Manumissies in Suriname, 1832–1863* (Utrecht: CLACS and IBS, 1997).

31. Brana-Shute, "Approaching Freedom," 57, first compared this type of manumission to chain migration.

32. We are writing about those slaves that made the direct transition from plantation slavery to freedom, not about those who had been transferred to town, lived there for a period of time, and were then manumitted. Cf. Brana-Shute, "Manumission of Slaves," 267–70.

33. Van Heshuysen, as quoted in Einaar, *Bijdrage tot de kennis van het Engelsch Tusschenbestuur,* 172–73.

34. Royal Institute for the Tropics (KIT), Amsterdam, RG-89, G. P. C. Van Breugel, "Verhandelingen over Surinaamsche bezittingen zeer dienstig voor eigenaren van plantaadjes in de Westindien" (manuscript), 45–46, 63–64. See also KIT, RG-78, G. P. C. Van Breugel, "Journal van mijn vertrek naar, verblijf te, en terugkomst van de kolonie Suriname in de jaren 1823 en 1824" (manuscript), Feb. 7, 1824.

35. KIT, RG-89, 63–64. Teenstra (*De negerslaven in de kolonie Suriname,* 25–27), argues that limited financial resources prevented the average manager from manumitting his children and/or partner. Van Breugel, however, thought it was good policy to enable a director to buy his children and that, alternatively, the owner could give the children as a present to the director, which would help ensure the loyalty of the latter.

36. NA, RvP 825, fol. 218ff. Hoth died in Paramaribo in 1785.

37. When he died in 1810, he left two houses in Paramaribo and a timber plantation with twenty-two slaves. NA, Oud Notarieel Archief Suriname (Notarial Archives of Suriname before 1828, hereafter ONAS), 300, no. 13, 16; RvP 427, fol. 275ff; SvS 207, fol. 469; SvS 208, fol. 430.

38. NA, RvP 461, fol. 12ff.

39. NA, RvP 463, fol. 3.

40. NA, RvP 483, fol. 81.

41. NA, ONAS 78, no. 25.

42. NA, RvP 505, fol. 2; NA, RvP 521, fol. 44.

43. NA, Notarieel Archief Suriname (Notarial Archives of Suriname, 1828–1845, hereafter NAS), 35, no. 177, testament of J. P. J. Pohl, Coblenz, July 16, 1828. Heirs of five-sixths of Pohl's legacy were his five legitimized children born in Suriname.

44. Gert Oostindie, *Roosenburg en Mon Bijou: Twee Surinaamse plantages, 1720–1870* (Dordrecht: Foris Publications, 1989), 81, 114; Van Stipriaan, *Surinaams contrast,* 307. In the case of redundant slaves, it often concerned individuals of mixed blood who were generally not used in the fields—cf. Lammens, *Bijdragen tot de kennis van de kolonie Suriname,* 178; and E. J. Bartelink, *Hoe de tijden veranderen: Herinneringen van een ouden planter* (Paramaribo: H. Van Ommeren, 1916), 18—or slaves causing disciplinary problems.

45. Wolbers, *Geschiedenis van Suriname,* 442–43.

46. Van Lier, *Samenleving*, 110.

47. NA, SvS 207, fols. 213 and 578; Gemeente Archief Amsterdam (the Municipal Archives of Amsterdam, archief kerkeraad Hervormde Gemeente) 26, fols. 243, 249, and 250; NA, ONAS 735, act reg. December 8, 1781.

48. NA, RvP 539, fol. 27.

49. NA, ONAS 29, fols. 366–67, ONAS 42, fol. 79 ff.; RvP 410, fol. 16; RVP 427, fol. 46. Nepveu had also taken care of the housing, financial support, and education of the children.

50. NA, RvP 196, minutes of May 29, 1815.

51. NA, RvP 503 no. 81; RvP 487, fol. 19ff.

52. Herlein, *Nauwkeurige Beschrijvinge*, 48; Stedman, *Narrative*, 241; Van Lier, *Samenleving*, 110–12. The owner was allowed to rent out slaves on the basis of a contract between owner and lessee.

53. NA, RvP 478, fol. 39; NA, RvP 363, fol. 145.

54. NA, ONAS 215, fols. 350–54; NA, ONAS 42, fol. 415; ONAS 42, fol. 478, March 6, 7, 1769; Raad van Civiele Justitie (Court of Civil Justice) 497, *Imbert v. Crommelin*, c.s.; RvP 397, fol. 285; RvP 402, fol. 189; RvP 406, fol. 281; RvP 427, fols. 134, 282, and 416; RvP 428, fol. 45; RvP 445 fols. 38 and 39; RvP 456, fol. 33; RvP 463, fol. 35; RvP 537, fol. 3.

55. Hoetink, "Surinam and Curaçao"; Jean Jacques Vrij, "Jan Elias van Onna en het 'politiek systhema' van de Surinaamse slaventijd, circa 1770–1820," *Oso* 17 (1998): 130–47.

56. Quoted in Van der Meiden, *Betwist bestuur*, 118–19.

57. This does not mean, however, that such relations did not exist. There are contemporary suggestions that relationships between a nonwhite man and a white woman did exist even though that was considered not done. Lammens, *Bijdragen tot de kennis van de kolonie Suriname*, 102; Teenstra, *De negerslaven in de kolonie Suriname*, 2: 152. It seems, however, that social disavowal depended on the socioeconomic position of the male partner.

58. Brana-Shute, "Manumission of Slaves," 342.

59. This is the opinion of Van Lier (*Samenleving*, 53–58).

60. NA, SvS 321, fols. 321–25, Governor and Councils to Proprietors, Feb. 21, 1764. On the Elisabeth Samson case, see Rosemarijn Hoefte, "Free Blacks and Coloureds in Plantation Suriname: The Struggle to Rise," in *Against the Odds: Free Blacks in the Slave Societies of the Americas*, ed. Jane G. Landers (London: Frank Cass, 1996), 110–13.

61. NA, SvS 54, fol. 343, resolution dated Oct. 3, 1764; Oud-Archief Burgerlijke Stand (Civil Registers of Suriname before 1828, hereafter BS) 3, fol. 219.

62. NA, BS 2, fols. 181 and 203; SvS 207, fol. 469; SvS 208, fol. 387; Center for Genealogy and Heraldy (The Hague), Records of the Dutch Reformed Community of Gouda, Register of Church Members (copy), fol. 332, Certificates of Departure (copy), fol. 170. Nanette Susanna Peterse was the daughter of the white Creole Pierre Planteau and the black Lavallière van Bossé and related to Elisabeth Samson. For more on Nanette Peterse, see Jaap Versept and Jean-Jacques Vry, "Een Surinaamse Nederlander ut vroeger tÿd: Fredrik Petius Gisius Nanning (1798–1832)," in *Wi Rutis* 2, no. 1 (2002): 13–34.

63. Louise A. Tilly, Joan W. Scott, and M. Cohen, "Women's Work and European Fertility Patterns," *Journal of Interdisciplinary History* 6 (Winter 1976): 463–70. For the Netherlands, see Arie Theodorus van Deursen, *Plain Lives in a Golden Age: Popular Culture, Religion and Society in Seventeenth-Century Holland* (New York: Cambridge University Press, 1991), 93, and J. Kok, *Langs verboden wegen: De achtergronden van buitenechtelijke geboorten in Noord-Holland, 1812–1914* (Hilversum: Uitgeverij Verloren, 1991), 54–55, 97.

64. Van Lier, *Samenleving*, 56. The term was probably coined during the nineteenth century. G. P. C. Van Breugel, *Dagverhaal van eene reis naar Paramaribo en verdere omstreken in de kolonie Suriname* (Amsterdam: C. G. Sulpke, 1842), 32, based on experiences during his journey in 1823 and 1824; A. Kappler *Zes jaren in Suriname, 1836–1842: Schetsen en taferelen* (1854, reprint Zutphen: De Walburg Pers, 1983), 22. We have found the exact term *Suriname marriage* (*Surinaams huwelijk*) used only once in a contemporary test: in a letter from 1874 cited in Ellen Klinkers, *Op hoop van*

vrijheid: Van slavensamenleving naar Creoolse gemeenschap in Suriname, 1830–1880 (Utrecht: Vakgroep Culturele Antropologie, Universiteit Utrecht, 1997), 176–77.

65. See contemporary accounts by Van Breugel, *Dagverhaal*, 30; Lammens, *Bijdragen tot de kennis van de kolonie Suriname*, 82, 91–92; and Kappler, *Zes jaren in Suriname*, 23.

66. Stedman, *Narrative*, 47–48.

67. Lammens, *Bijdragen tot de kennis van de kolonie Suriname*, 93.

68. Ibid., 92.

69. Teenstra, *De negerslaven in de kolonie Suriname*, 48, 64; Lammens, *Bijdragen tot de kennis van de kolonie Suriname*, 109. Stedman relates that on February 22, 1773, "a negro woman offers me the use of her daugter [Johanna] while here, for a sertain soom [.] we don't agre[e] about the price" (*Narrative*, xxxii–xxxvi). Several months later he gave Johanna a number of presents, and she moved in with him.

70. Van Breugel, *Dagverhaal*, 30.

71. Examples are Hans Joachim Emicke, who as a deacon in the Lutheran church attended the baptism of his four daughters with the black Carolina. Another deacon and high-ranking colonial, Hendrik Maurits Wolff, had three children from different women. Ministers who had concubines included Jocobus Tallans, Paulus Snijderhans, and Johannes Christoffel de Cros (Stedman, *Narrative*, 47n.).

72. NA, BS 4, fol. 222; NA, BS 14, fols. 93 and 284.

73. NA, BS 8, Oct. 1819; collection of family announcements in Centraal Bureau voor Genealogie.

74. Lammens, *Bijdragen tot de kennis van de kolonie Suriname*, 109, see also 152–53; Teenstra, *De negerslaven in de kolonie Suriname*, 67.

75. Lammens, *Bijdragen tot de kennis van de kolonie Suriname*, 93; Van Breugel, *Dagverhaal*, 30, 32.

76. Lammens, *Bijdragen tot de kennis van de kolonie Suriname*, 92.

77. W. A. Koopman to Baron Van Lynden, June 30, 1819, copy in NA, Lammens Collection 16, no. 45, fol. 34. Marie van den Berg's actual name was Maria Elisabeth Scholtsborg, and in 1811 she was registered as a basket-weaver and huckster who then had twenty-three slaves.

78. Leonard Blussé, *Strange Company: Chinese Settlers, Mestizo Women and the Dutch in VOC Batavia* (Dordrecht: Foris Publications, 1986), 176, 201–2, 258; Donald Haks, *Huwelijk en gezin in Holland in de 17de en 18de eeuw: Processtukken en moralisten over aspecten van het laat 17de-en 18de-eeuwse gezinsleven* (Utrecht: Hes, 1985), 153.

79. NA, RvP 226, no. 130. The English occupied Suriname during the Napoleonic Era, from 1799 to 1802 and from 1804 to 1816.

80. Census Suriname 1811.

81. NA, RvP 718, no. 72.

82. NA, RvP 424, fols. 356ff and 112, Feb. 28, 1781.

83. The Dutch father of Vrolijk was a lawyer, plantation owner, and member of the Court of Policy and thus belonged to the Suriname elite. He gave his son a good education. Daniel George Ney had a part-time job at Vrolijk's school. Ney's mother, Johanna Christina Ney, was born out of a union between C. S. George and a free black, Bettie. She married Benjamin Ney, also a high colonial official, in 1781, but their marriage soon fell apart.

84. Anna Elisabeth Albregt was born in 1751, the daughter of Jürgen Albregt, who was white, and the free black Johanna Wilhelmina Augustus (a.k.a. Toetoeba). She married Louis Kalden, a bookbinder, in 1770.

85. For the Rühle family, see Michel R. Doortmont, Natalie Everts, and Jean Jacques Vrij, "Tussen de Goudkust, Nederland en Suriname: De Euro-Afrikaanse families Van Bakergem, Woortman, Rühle en Huydecoper," *De Nederlandsche Leeuw* 1 (2000): 400–561.

86. NA, RvP 720, no. 175; NA, BS 14, fol. 261.

87. NA, RvP 722 no. 128.

88. NA, BS 10, baptism of their daughter, Elisabeth Godefroy, Dec. 15, 1791; Department of Orphans and Unattended Goods, Suriname 1788–1828, 126, fol. 332.

89. NA, RvP 403, fol. 296; ONAS 67, no. 8; ONAS 87, no. 6; NAS, 74, nos. 126 and 131; *Surinaamse Almanak voor het jaar 1845,* 80.

90. We have placed two more landowners in other categories. Adriana Agnetta Middellijn stated that she derived income from her land and as a seamstress, and we have categorized her as having multiple sources of income. Hendrina Elisabeth Vieira registered as a seamstress, but the plantation data in the census reveal that she owned two timber plantations with twenty-eight and ten slaves, respectively. We have nevertheless categorized her as a seamstress because that was the only source of income she filed.

91. NA, RvP 697, no. 35; SvS 207, fol. 49; SvS 210, fol. 1011; BS 10, fol. 218.

92. NA, BS 10, fol. 93; BS 10 2, fol. 151; ONAS 129, fol. 8ff; ONAS 129, fol. 126.

CHAPTER 9

Ana Paulinha de Queirós, Joaquina da Costa, and Their Neighbors: Free Women of Color as Household Heads in Rural Bahia (Brazil), 1835

B. J. Barickman and Martha Few

In 1835 Ana Paulinha [*sic*] de Queirós, a sixty-year-old, never formally married, freeborn woman of mixed African and European ancestry
(*"parda"*), found herself heading a fairly prosperous household in São Gonçalo
dos Campos, a largely rural parish in the region known as the Bahian Recôncavo
in the province (now state) of Bahia in Northeastern Brazil. The census takers
who visited the household in that year listed Ana Paulinha's occupation as
"farming" (*lavoura*), which in São Gonçalo dos Campos almost certainly meant
that she grew tobacco for export in combination with food crops for home consumption and for sale in local markets. Ana Paulinha's household included her
thirty-six-year-old unmarried son as well as two male slaves and one female
slave. That same year, a few miles away, local census takers in the sugar-producing parish of Santiago do Iguape came upon what was no doubt the much more
modest residence of Joaquina da Costa, a fifty-year-old, Brazilian-born single
black woman (*"preta"*) and former slave. A laundress by trade, Joaquina shared
her household with Raimundo da Rocha, also a freed Brazilian-born black slave,
whose recorded occupation was "beggar" and who was surely very old—so old,
in fact, that the census takers listed his age at an implausible 120.[1]

As non-"white" free women, Ana Paulinha de Queirós and Joaquina da Costa
were not by any means anomalies in late-colonial and early-nineteenth-century
Brazil. Nor would it have been particularly unusual at the time that they headed
their own households. In contrast with the southern United States and several
other slaveholding regions of the Americas, free women of color in Brazil did
not represent a small minority within either the overall female population or

the population of African ancestry. On the contrary, freeborn and freed blacks and mulattos already accounted for perhaps one-fourth of Brazil's total population in the early 1800s; by 1872, the year of the country's first national census, they outnumbered both whites and slaves.[2]

Nevertheless, free women of color have seldom been the subject of specific historical research in the otherwise large and growing literature about women in colonial and nineteenth-century Brazil. The general lack of such research may be due in part to difficulties in identifying free non-"white" women in the sources. It may also reflect the fact that, until recently, historical research on Brazil has tended to focus on either race or gender rather than on the intersections of the two.[3] Yet they deserve attention—if for no other reason than research on free women of color can reveal much about how racial and gender hierarchies intersected in nineteenth-century Brazil.

This chapter, based chiefly on two manuscript censuses, examines freeborn and freedwomen in early-nineteenth-century Brazil, with particular focus on women such as Ana Paulinha de Queirós and Joaquina da Costa who served as household heads in rural areas of the Bahian Recôncavo during the mid-1830s. The Recôncavo at that time ranked as one of the oldest, most important slaveholding regions of not only Brazil but also the Americas.[4] Our largely exploratory work with the two censuses demonstrates that, by the 1830s, free women of color headed a significant share of all households in the Bahian countryside. In large part responsible for their own survival and also for the well-being of their households, these free non-"white" women found and created for themselves opportunities within the slave-based economy of the rural Recôncavo. The households they headed often had access to land and controlled other productive resources; in some cases they even owned slaves. But the censuses also suggest that free women of color in the Bahian Recôncavo, whatever measure of autonomy and authority they may have enjoyed as household heads, did not escape hierarchies based on race, color, gender, and ethnicity that permeated Brazilian society at the time. Indeed, for most free non-"white" women, household headship went hand in hand with poverty and insecurity.

The two censuses used in this chapter are among the few surviving results of a failed attempt to carry out a general population count in the Northeastern province of Bahia in 1835.[5] Organized by *fogo* (household), they provide a range of individual-level information about inhabitants of two largely rural parishes in the Recôncavo: Santiago do Iguape and São Gonçalo dos Campos.

Both parishes were located in the township of Cachoeira and no more than seventy-five kilometers from Salvador, Bahia's capital, largest city, and main port. Santiago do Iguape (or simply Iguape) stood out as one of the wealthiest sugar districts in Bahia. In the 1830s Iguape had twenty-one operating *engenhos* (sugar plantations with mills), which, measured by the number of slaves they employed, were among the largest in Brazil. Living in the parish at the same time were nearly a hundred sharecropping cane farmers (*lavradores de cana*). Although they generally worked rented land, most cane farmers used slave labor, typically owning between five and twenty-five slaves. Contemporaries often described Iguape as a thickly settled district dominated by slave-based sugar production and large plantations. Nevertheless, more than two hundred small farmers found room in the parish to grow food crops for domestic consumption and for sale. Artisanal and fishing households were also numerous.[6]

By contrast, tobacco, not sugarcane, was the chief crop in São Gonçalo dos Campos, which lay directly northwest of Iguape in an area that by the mid-seventeenth century had become the main center of tobacco production in Brazil. Tobacco from São Gonçalo dos Campos and other nearby parishes was exported to Europe and also to West Africa, where merchants used it in acquiring slaves for the transatlantic slave trade. Because this export staple could be grown nearly as efficiently on a few acres as on a large estate, a variety of rural establishments produced tobacco in the Recôncavo, ranging from peasant holdings that relied exclusively on family labor to large farms that employed as many as thirty or more slaves. By the 1830s, tobacco, generally in combination with food crops, was cultivated in São Gonçalo dos Campos on more than five hundred small and large *fazendas* and *sítios* (farms).[7]

The 1835 censuses for Iguape and São Gonçalo dos Campos indicate that the two parishes had a combined population of 18,816—7,410 in Iguape and 11,406 in São Gonçalo dos Campos. In the sugar parish of Iguape slaves made up just over half (53.8 percent) of the population, and in São Gonçalo dos Campos they represented 34.4 percent of the total population of the parish. "Whites" (*"brancos"*) in both parishes were a minority within the free population, comprising only 29.9 percent of all free inhabitants in São Gonçalo dos Campos and an even smaller proportion (17.2 percent) in Iguape. The rest of the free population in the two parishes consisted of freeborn and freed non-"whites," classified in the censuses as *"pretos"* ("blacks"), *"pardos,"* and *"cabras."* "Pretos" ("blacks") could be either Brazilian- or African-born; all the native Brazilian "blacks" listed in the two censuses had been born in Bahia. "Pardo" is usually translated as "mulatto" because it was the term most often used to describe individuals of mixed European and African ancestry. "Cabra" (literally "she-goat"), at least in principle, referred to the offspring of a mixed "pardo" and "black" couple or to the child of two "cabras." "Faded black" perhaps best captures in English the meaning of "cabra" because it designated a color perceived as somewhere between "preto" and "pardo."[8] In both Santiago do Iguape and São Gonçalo dos Campos, approximately 70 percent of all free non-"whites" were "pardos."

Women, according to the two censuses, headed 758 (27.8 percent) of the fogos in the two parishes. By far the majority (80.5 percent) of those female-headed households belonged to freeborn and freed women of color. Free "pretas," "pardas," and "cabras" headed 337 fogos, or 19.1 percent of all households, both male- and female-headed, in São Gonçalo dos Campos. In the sugar parish of

Iguape, 273 (28.3 percent) of all households belonged to such women. Free women of color thus accounted for a total of 610, or more than one-fifth (22.1 percent), of all *chefes de fogo* (household heads) in the two parishes. The 2,300 individuals who lived in the households belonging to those women, in turn, comprised more than 12 percent of the combined population of Iguape and São Gonçalo do Campos.

Elsewhere in the Americas, manumission practices seem to have played a significant role in giving rise to female-headed households within the free population of color. But only in part can such practices explain why so many free "pardas," "pretas," and "cabras" in these two parishes found themselves heading households and exercising related responsibility and authority. To be sure, in Brazil, as in other parts of the Americas, female slaves, when compared to male slaves, generally stood a better chance of earning their freedom through manumission. That pattern appears quite clearly in the two 1835 Bahian censuses. Women made up 55.9 percent of all freed slaves in São Gonçalo dos Campos and Santiago do Iguape in 1835; that amounts to a ratio of approximately 127 freed slave women for every one hundred freed male slaves. By contrast, in the combined slave population of the two parishes, there were 124 male slaves for every one hundred female slaves. The surviving notarial records for Iguape also confirm a tendency, where manumission was concerned, to favor women. In the records, females accounted for 66.3 percent of all slaves manumitted between 1831 and 1845. If we take the composition of Iguape's slave population in 1835 as the basis for a rough calculation, that percentage would imply that slave women were 2.8 times more likely to gain their freedom than male slaves.[9] It might then be assumed that the relatively low number of freed male slaves worked against the establishment of male-headed households within the free non-"white" population and forced many free women of color to assume headship.

Although no doubt valid for other regions of the Americas, an explanation along those lines cannot fully account for the large number of households headed by free women of color in Santiago do Iguape and São Gonçalo dos Campos. On the one hand, men headed not merely the majority (69.3 percent) of all non-"white" households but also the majority (60.1 percent) of households belonging to former slaves. On the other hand, fully 80 percent of the non-"white" women who served as chefes de fogo in those parishes were *ingênuas* (free by birth) (table 9.1). Some ingênuas were undoubtedly the daughters of freed slaves. But given that Portuguese settlers in Bahia had already begun using slaves imported from Africa as early as the mid-sixteenth century, it would not be at all impossible that, by 1835, as many as 250 years or approximately eight generations might separate a freeborn Bahian woman of color from her nearest enslaved or African-born ancestor.

Rather than being chiefly the product of manumission practices, household headship by free non-"white" women in Iguape and São Gonçalo dos Campos matches broader patterns in Brazilian society at the time. Research since the

Table 9.1. Distribution of Non-"white" Female Household Heads by Legal Status and
Color, Santiago do Iguape and São Gonçalo dos Campos, 1835

Legal Status and Color	Santiago do Iguape		São Gonçalo dos Campos		Both Parishes	
	Number	Percent	Number	Percent	Number	Percent
Freed	84	30.8	33	10.1	118	19.4
Freeborn	189	69.2	302	89.9	491	80.6
"Blacks"[a]						
African-born "blacks"	18	6.6	11	3.2	29	4.8
Bahian-born "blacks"	103	37.7	74	22.0	177	29.0
	121	44.3	85	25.2	206	33.8
"Cabras"	2	0.7	28	8.3	30	4.9
"Pardas"	150	54.9	224	66.5	374	61.3
Total non-"white" females[b]	273	100.0	337	100.0	610	100.0

Source: Endnote 1.
a. Regardless of birthplace.
b. Total includes one woman in São Gonçalo dos Campos for whom information on legal status is missing.

1970s has gone far in dismantling the once-common view that large extended households dominated by wealthy white (male) planters and landowners were the rule everywhere in colonial and nineteenth-century Brazil. Focusing mainly on Southeastern Brazil, that research has shown that women typically headed anywhere from 10 to 40 percent of all households. Among other factors, poverty, the instability of marriages and consensual unions, and male migration to frontier areas contributed to widespread female headship. Inheritance laws may have also played a role; in Brazil, a wife generally retained half of a couple's jointly owned property after her husband's death, and all children, male and female, inherited equally.[10]

Although well developed, the literature on female headship in Brazil does not, for the most part, directly address questions of race or color. Historians have, instead, tended to discuss women household heads generically. Even so, the few studies that do distinguish "white" and non-"white" women suggest that São Gonçalo dos Campos and Iguape were not exceptional and that, on the contrary, free women of color also made up a sizable share of all household heads in other well-settled areas of colonial and nineteenth-century Brazil.[11] That should not come as a surprise. After all, by the early or mid-1800s freeborn and freed blacks and mulattos already constituted a majority or near majority of the nonslave population in many parts of Brazil, including the parishes of Santiago do Iguape and São Gonçalo dos Campos and the province of Bahia as a whole.

Perhaps the only grounds for surprise lie in the fact that the findings presented here come from well-established centers of slave-based export agriculture in coastal Northeastern Brazil. That is, they refer to precisely the region that the older literature most closely associated with large patriarchal households domi-

nated by wealthy, white, male, slave-owning planters. Such households did exist in the two parishes, but they represented only a small share of all fogos listed
in the two censuses. In this regard it is noteworthy that fogos headed by free
women of color were proportionately more numerous in the sugar-producing
parish of Iguape than in São Gonçalo dos Campos.

The non-"white" women who headed households in the two parishes did not
constitute a homogeneous group. They differed not only by legal status (whether
freeborn or freed) but also by birthplace (and hence ethnicity) and color.
Twenty-nine of those women were freed African-born slaves (table 9.1). The
censuses list their place of birth as the "Coast of Africa" (*Costa d'África*), a ge-
neric term that obviously reveals nothing about their ethnic or regional origins.
But here we can turn to studies of the transatlantic slave trade, which have firmly
established that, in the late eighteenth and early nineteenth centuries, West Africa, and more specifically areas along and near the Bight of Benin, supplied the
bulk of all African slaves shipped to Bahia. Probate records from São Gonçalo
dos Campos and Santiago do Iguape for 1820 to 1839 also confirm the predominance of West Africans within the local slave population. Of African-born slaves
for whom the records provide information on ethnicity or regional origin, fully
86 percent were West Africans. Slaves designated as *nagôs* (Yorubas) formed the
single largest group of West Africans listed in the records (31.6 percent), followed
by *jejes* (Ewe-Aja-Fon) (24.0 percent) and *uçás* (Hausas) (15.5 percent). Therefore, most of the twenty-nine freed African women would have come from West
Africa and were, in all likelihood, nagôs, jejes, or uçás.[12]

Africans, however, made up only a small fraction (4.8 percent) of all free non-
"white" female household heads. Women classified as "cabras" were also few in
number. Far more numerous than either Africans or "cabras" were native
"pretas." Households belonging to such women numbered 103 in Iguape and
74 in São Gonçalo dos Campos and thus accounted for 29 percent of all fogos
headed by free women of color in the two parishes. Approximately two-thirds
(65.5 percent) of Bahian-born "preta" household heads were free by birth rather
than *libertas* (freed slaves). In turn, women designated in the censuses as
"pardas" accounted for an even larger share of all free non-"white" female
household heads in these rural districts: nearly 55 percent in Iguape and more
than 66 percent in the neighboring tobacco parish. The great majority (more
than 90 percent) of "parda" household heads had been born free and therefore
had no direct personal experience with enslavement.

Whether they were "pretas," "pardas," or "cabras," the non-"white" women
who headed households in São Gonçalo dos Campos and Santiago do Iguape
tended to be middle-aged or older; in this regard, they resembled "white" female household heads in the same two parishes. No more than 6.4 percent were
under the age of twenty-five; fewer than one-fourth were over fifty-nine. In both
parishes the majority (approximately 70 percent) had recorded ages between
twenty-five and fifty-nine; the mean age stood at roughly forty-four in Iguape

and at nearly forty-five in São Gonçalo dos Campos. Freeborn heads were on the whole younger than those who had gained their freedom through manumission (with average ages of 43.5 and 50.3, respectively). Indeed, freed African-born women displayed the highest average age (fifty-nine). Only one African was under forty; most were at least fifty. It makes sense that former slaves in general, and specifically freed African-born women, had higher average ages, because many of them, especially those who were African by birth, would have obtained their freedom only after reaching adulthood.[13]

Fairly high average ages did not, however, translate into widespread experience with formal marriage. Fully three-fifths of the 610 free women of color who served as chefes de fogo were listed as single (table 9.2). More than half (56.4 percent) of those single women were never-formally-married mothers living with at least one child. Widows, in turn, composed just over one-third of all non-"white" female household heads; an even smaller share consisted of married women living without their husbands.

Here some caution is required in interpreting the evidence from the 1835 censuses. In many areas of colonial and nineteenth-century Brazil, a legal, church-sanctioned marriage was the rule only among the wealthier and "whiter" segments of free society. For the rest of the free population, consensual unions often took the place of formal marriage. Although not recorded as such in the 1835 censuses, consensual unions would seem to have been common in the two Bahian parishes. Therefore, perhaps a sizable proportion of the free, never-married, non-"white" women who appear in the censuses as single mothers may not have been unwed mothers in any conventional sense. Rather, their partners may have already died by 1835, making them consensual-union widows, so to speak. There are, of course, other possibilities as well. For example, some women and their consensual-union partners may have chosen to live apart, for whatever reason. Others may have been involved in more or less stable and lasting but unconse-

Table 9.2. Marital Status of Non-"white" Female Household Heads and Those Living with Resident Children, Santiago do Iguape and São Gonçalo dos Campos, 1835

Legal Status and Color	Marital Status				Residing with Children
	Married	Widowed	Ever Married	Single	
Freeborn	4.5%	37.5%	42.0%	58.0%	66.9%
Freed	8.5	22.0	30.5	69.5	44.9
All non-"whites"	5.2	34.5	39.7	60.3	62.7
"Pardas"	5.1	41.0	46.1	53.9	69.2
"Cabras"	10.0	33.3	43.3	56.7	70.0
All "blacks"	4.9	22.8	27.7	72.3	49.5
Bahian-born "blacks"	5.1	22.0	27.1	72.9	53.1
African-born "blacks"	3.4	27.6	31.0	69.0	27.6

Source: Endnote 1.

Note: "Ever married" means married or widowed. Percentages for marital status exclude one freeborn "parda" in São Gonçalo dos Campos for whom information on marital status is missing.

crated relationships with male slaves who lived and worked on nearby plantations and farms.[14] Still other women may have chosen not to form unions at all.
The censuses suggest an association between formal marriage and legal status and color that roughly paralleled the prevailing social-racial hierarchies. Thus,
whereas only a minority of non-"white" female heads in Santiago do Iguape and
São Gonçalo dos Campos were married or widowed, the opposite held true for
"white" women who headed households in the two parishes. Nearly two-thirds
(65.3 percent) of all "white" female chefes were either married or widowed, with
widows far outnumbering married women. There are also differences among
non-"white" women (table 9.2). For instance, as might be expected, the censuses
register a higher proportion of ever-married women (i.e., wives residing without their husbands, and widows) among freeborn heads than among those who
were former slaves. Likewise and by an even wider margin, the proportion of ever-
married women was higher among "pardas" than among female chefes classified
in the censuses as "pretas." Widows, for example, made up more than two-fifths
of all "parda" heads but no more than 22.8 percent of the "pretas." In other words,
"black" women were on the whole much more likely to be single than their
"parda" neighbors and hence much less likely to become household heads as a
result of a husband's death, or formal widowhood.[15]

   Broadly similar patterns emerge in regard to the presence of children within
households headed by free women of color in the two parishes. All in all, 382
(roughly three-fifths) of those households contained resident children (table
9.2). The number of children present obviously varied, but more than 80 percent of the 382 households included fewer than five resident children. The average in both parishes stood at just under three (2.8 in Iguape and 2.9 in São
Gonçalo dos Campos). Not surprisingly, most (64 percent) of the 1,086 children
found in households belonging to free non-"white" women were fifteen or
younger; 23.6 percent were under nine. Yet the experience of living with an older
child was more common than such figures might suggest. More than one-third
(38 percent) of all households with children contained at least one daughter or
son aged twenty or older; 11.5 percent included a son or daughter who was more
than twenty-nine.

   Slightly more than one-half (54.2 percent) of the women who lived with children in the two parishes were listed in the censuses as single. But that should
not obscure the fact that widowed and married women in both São Gonçalo
dos Campos and Santiago do Iguape were more likely to head households with
children than single women; 72.3 percent of the married women and widows,
as opposed to only 56.4 percent of the single heads, lived with children. The
households of ever-married women also contained, on average, a larger number of resident children than those headed by single women (3.4 for married
women and widows and 2.4 for single women).[16]

   Other differences in the proportion of women living with children largely
overlap with those related to marital status (table 9.2). Fewer than one-third of

the 118 fogos belonging to freed, former slave women, for example, contained resident children. In the case of freed African-born women that proportion was even smaller, barely surpassing one-fifth. By contrast, two-thirds of all households headed by freeborn women included at least one child. That freedwomen in general, and African-born women in particular, should have been less likely to live with children makes sense. They tended to be older than their freeborn neighbors, which meant there was a greater chance that their children had reached adulthood and established their own households. In some cases freedwomen may have had still-enslaved children who lived on nearby farms and plantations.[17] It is also possible that freedwomen, as former slaves who in many cases would have experienced harsh living and working conditions while enslaved, may have suffered lower rates of absolute fertility.

Similarly, "black" women in general, including those born in Bahia, were less likely to reside with children than their "parda" and "cabra" neighbors. Nearly 70 percent of all parda-headed households contained children, but local census takers encountered sons and daughters in only one-half of the households belonging to "black" women. The disparity does not disappear when only never-formally-married women are considered. Although fully two-thirds (66.6 percent) of all single "pardas" lived with children, only 40.3 percent of single "black" women did so. Nor does the disparity disappear when we control for differences in legal status. Children were found in fewer than one-half (48 percent) of all freeborn "preta" households as opposed to 69.9 percent of all fogos headed by freeborn "pardas."[18]

In interpreting these findings we need to keep in mind an obvious but perhaps easily overlooked point: The ability to bring a pregnancy to term, to survive childbirth, and then to rear a child beyond infancy depended in large measure on the mother's health and economic well-being. The presence of children within a household can then indicate the relatively better health and greater economic security of the mother. At the very least, their presence would suggest that free non-"white" female heads whose fogos included sons and daughters had the wherewithal to sustain a child through its first years rather than abandon it on some neighbor's doorstep, turn it over to a friend or relative, or resort to infanticide.[19] Children could, moreover, represent an asset within a rural household. If they survived to six or seven, all the more so if they reached their teens, children could be employed not only in looking after younger siblings but also in tasks that ranged from caring for domestic animals to fetching water or firewood and helping with various types of fieldwork as well as artisanal activities such as spinning, weaving, and sewing. Resident daughters and sons, then, could make a significant contribution to a household's economic well-being and thereby increase its collective chances for survival.

Along the same lines, having and rearing a child might often constitute one of the very few, more or less secure guarantees on which free women of color could count against utter destitution in their old age. Take, for example, Joana de Cerqueira, a freed African slave and farmer in São Gonçalo dos Campos, who must have been quite old (census takers registered her age as one hundred). Living entirely alone and unable to rely on anyone within her fogo for help in planting and harvesting her crops, Joana de Cerqueira surely led an extremely precarious existence. If she happened to fall ill or become in some other way incapacitated, her survival would depend entirely on the goodwill of neighbors and nearby relatives. The insecurity of her daily life would have been familiar to many of the other 233 free women of color who lived alone in the two parishes; of those 233, approximately one-fifth (19.7 percent) were at least fifty-five.

The presence of children, particularly older children, could go far in mitigating such insecurity. The 1835 censuses yield numerous examples that point to the role children might play as a guarantee against wretched poverty in old age. Consider the case of Joana Maria da Conceição, a freeborn and single sixty-three-year-old "parda" household head in Iguape who had no declared occupation. Although Joana Maria apparently lacked any source of income she was not necessarily destitute. On the contrary, she could rely on her thirty-year-old resident son, Teodósio d'Araújo da Silva, whose occupation, "farming" (lavoura, i.e., growing food crops) would have guaranteed at least a minimum of well-being for the household.

If we do indeed take the presence of children as a rough and indirect indicator of a mother's relative economic security, then the evidence on this matter matches, with considerable consistency, the information on marital status. In both cases the 1835 censuses suggest a pattern of overlapping differences based on legal status, color, and birthplace that mirrored the social-racial hierarchy of the time. Within that hierarchy, freeborn women ranked above freed, former slave women, especially those born in Africa. Likewise, women classified as "pardas," occupying a relatively privileged position among non-"white" women, ranked above their presumably darker-skinned "black" neighbors, including those born in Bahia.

Whether or not they lived with children, and whatever their marital status or color, the free non-"white" female chefes of Santiago do Iguape and São Gonçalo dos Campos had to be concerned with sustaining themselves and the households they headed from one day to the next. Therefore, except where they depended entirely on charity to survive, those women and their households necessarily needed access to productive resources: land, labor (including their own), specialized skills, or some combination of the three. At the same time, if "parda," "preta," and "cabra" heads were to have any chance of retaining some autonomy, they also had to adapt their household survival strategies to conditions that prevailed in each parish. In effect, although the neighboring parishes of Santiago do Iguape and São Gonçalo dos Campos were both well-established centers of slave-based export agriculture, the opportunities open to free Afro-Brazilian women, and hence the household strategies they pursued, differed significantly in the two districts.

The census information on the head's "occupation" (*profissão*) provides only a very rough guide to those strategies for several reasons. By their very nature, the censuses do not for the most part allow us to detect cross-household ties; instead, they present apparently self-contained residential units. But, as members of a larger community, free non-"white" female chefes in the two parishes most certainly did establish and regularly rely on a wide variety of cross-household exchanges and contacts, not only with other Afro-Brazilians, whether free or not, but also with the local "white" population. Furthermore, census takers recorded multiple occupations for no more than a handful of individuals. Yet it is safe to assume that ensuring household survival often required women, particularly poorer women, to engage more or less regularly in a diverse mix of economic activities, some of which may have defied neat and easy classification. The census takers in other instances may not have considered some activities as legitimate "occupations." In this regard it is noteworthy that not a single woman of any color in either parish was listed as a *parteira* (midwife) or as a *curandeira* or *rezadeira* (roughly, folk healer). And it almost goes without saying that no non-"white" woman had a recorded occupation that linked her to Afro-Brazilian religious practices. Such practices were, after all, illegal and subject to repression. As a result, free women of color would have hardly volunteered to the census takers the information that they earned their livelihood in part as *mães de santo* (priestesses).[20] These considerations must be kept in mind in evaluating women who lacked recorded occupations and who, at least in Iguape, constituted a substantial share of all non-"white" female chefes.

If free women of color as individuals might draw their income and sustenance from various activities, the same held true for the households they headed. Therefore, the head's occupation, as recorded in the censuses, did not necessarily reflect the full range of activities that contributed to a household's survival. But here we confront a major difficulty with the sources. Like their U.S. counterparts in the nineteenth century, the census takers who surveyed the two Bahian parishes in 1835 incorporated into their population count a patriarchal bias. They at least implicitly assumed that a head's occupation sufficed to define the economic activities of the entire household. Bahian census takers further assumed that the other household members were best classified under the category "occupation" by their relationship to the head ("son," "daughter," "slave," etc.). As a result, census takers only irregularly listed occupations (in the sense of a conventional economic activity) for household members other than the head. Yet they did so in enough cases to make it clear that household members were sometimes involved in different and even totally unrelated activities.[21]

In any event, table 9.3 presents the recorded occupations held by the free women of color who served as chefes de fogo in the two parishes. The table shows that 280 (46.1 percent) of those women were listed as engaged in agriculture of one type or another. Although, as a rule, the censuses do not provide any direct information about ownership of rural property, agricultural produc-

Table 9.3. Occupations of Non-"white" Female Household Heads, Santiago do Iguape and São Gonçalo dos Campos, 1835

Occupation	Santiago do Iguape		São Gonçalo dos Campos		Both Parishes	
	Number	Percent	Number	Percent	Number	Percent
Farmer and farming[a]			259	77.1	259	42.5
Cane farmer	1	0.4			1	0.2
Growing food crops[b]	20	7.3			20	3.3
	21	7.7	259	77.1	280	46.0
Seamstress	123	45.2	55	16.1	178	29.3
Spinning (*fiadeira*)	15	5.5			15	2.5
Weaving (*tecedeira*)			2	0.6	2	0.3
Petty trade, "business," etc.[c]	5	1.8	19	5.7	24	3.9
Day laborer (*ganhadeira*)	20	7.4			20	3.3
Laundress (*lavadeira* and *lavandeira*)	8	2.9			8	1.3
Plantation nurse[d]	1	0.4			1	0.2
"Hoe" (*enxada,* i.e., fieldhand)	1	0.4			1	0.2
Beggar[e]	3	1.1	1	0.3	4	0.7
No recorded occupation	75	27.6			75	12.3
Total[f]	272	100.0	336	100.0	608	100.0

Source: Endnote 5.
a. *Lavradora* and *lavoura.*
b. *Roceira* and *lavoura.* On *lavoura* in Iguape, see B. J. Barickman, *Bahian Counterpoint: Sugar, Tobacco, Cassava, and Slavery in the Recôncavo, 1780–1860* (Stanford: Stanford University Press, 1998), ch. 5.
c. Includes *negócio* (business or trade), *negocia* (does business), *negociante* and *negociadeira* (engaged in business), and *mercadeira* (marketeer).
d. *Ocupada dos serviços das crias* (i.e., "employed in taking care of the child slaves," but which might also mean "employed in supervising the work done by child slaves").
e. *Mendiga* (beggar) and *esmola* (alms).
f. Totals exclude two women (one in each parish) for whom information on occupation is missing.

tion obviously required more or less stable access to land. That might mean renting or in some cases even owning it. It is also probable that many free non-"white" women who headed farming households were "tenants at will." As such, they would have occupied a small plot of land on an estate owned by a rural proprietor in exchange for odd services, loyalty, and occasionally a nominal rent in cash or kind. Tenants at will were in all likelihood significantly more common in Iguape, where a handful of sugar planters and well-to-do cane farmers owned nearly all rural property in the parish. Landownership tended to be far less concentrated in the tobacco districts of the Recôncavo.[22]

Whatever the arrangement for access to land, that access crossed color lines. If it is true that "pardas" made up nearly two-thirds (63.6 percent) of all women with farming occupations, then "pretas" and "cabras" composed more than one-third of those women. In fact, even freed slaves headed farming households; twenty-nine libertas, including eleven Africans, held occupations that identified them as farmers of one type or another. Gaining access to land, moreover, did not depend on formal marriage; approximately 47 percent of women with farming occupations were listed as single.

That 280 women were listed as engaged in farming almost certainly underestimates the number of households headed by free pardas, pretas, and cabras that had access to land and cultivated crops for domestic consumption, for sale, or for both purposes. In some cases, although the census takers did not register a farming occupation for the head of the household, they did so for its other members. Thus, in Iguape, Maria do Carmo, a fifty-year-old, freeborn "parda," whom the census takers listed as a "seamstress," headed a household that included her twenty-year-old son, Josino José Barreto. His occupation, according to the census, was "farming," which in Iguape would have meant growing mainly food crops. Clearly, then, Maria do Carmo's fogo depended in part on agriculture for its collective survival and therefore must have had access to land.

Likewise, it would be rash to assume that, even where the censuses do not register a son or other household member as being involved in agriculture, all households headed by seamstresses, marketeers, spinsters, and so forth had absolutely no access to land and relied entirely on purchased foodstuffs. São Gonçalo dos Campos and Santiago do Iguape were, after all, overwhelmingly rural parishes, and in Bahia, as in many parts of the Americas, even plantation slaves often had garden plots or provision grounds where they cultivated food crops for their own use and to sell.[23] Thus, although seamstresses, spinsters, weavers, and marketeers might draw most of their cash income from sewing, spinning, weaving, and huckstering, many of them may have had a *roça* (garden plot) behind their often modest dwellings. Such plots would have yielded cassava, maize, beans, and various green vegetables for home consumption and, in some cases, small surpluses for sale in local markets. The surpluses would have been larger where free women of color, including those without agricultural occupations, owned slaves and employed them in cultivating crops. Such women may have even used their slaves to produce export crops such as sugarcane and tobacco.

Yet even when we take into account such possibilities and keep in mind that the census category for "occupation" constitutes no more than a rough guide to household survival strategies, the category does, nevertheless, reveal a sharp contrast between the two parishes. In Iguape, the local census takers enumerated only twenty-one non-"white" female heads who drew livelihoods from one or another type of agriculture (table 9.3). Another eight women in the parish headed households that included at least one other member listed as engaged in agriculture. Thus, according to the census, commercial agriculture would have figured regularly and prominently in the survival strategies of no more than twenty-nine (11 percent) of the 273 households belonging to free women of color in Iguape. By contrast, fully 77 percent of all such women in São Gonçalo dos Campos had "farmer" or "farming" as their recorded occupations.

The contrast has much to do with the differences between tobacco and sugar. Tobacco was fully compatible with small-scale "family" farming. Not only could

it be grown efficiently on very small plots, but farmers could also combine tobacco cultivation with the production of food crops such as cassava, maize, and
beans. Where a household contained working-age children, they could be useful in many tasks directly related to tobacco production. Processing tobacco did
not require heavy investment in equipment and installations. As a result—and
provided their households had access to at least a few acres of land—small farmers, including freed and freeborn non-"white" women, could successfully engage
in tobacco production. At the same time, they could plant food crops for home
consumption and sale in local markets. In fact, women in the twentieth century
often assumed full charge of the daily work on tobacco farms in the Bahian
Recôncavo while their husbands worked in town or at nearby sugar plantations.[24]

The composition of farming households, which represented more than three-
fourths of all non-"white," female-headed households in São Gonçalo dos Campos, suggests a pattern of "family"-based farming in the tobacco parish. If heads
of households and slaves are excluded, individuals for whom the census takers
failed to note any kinship tie with the head made up 15.2 percent of the population of those fogos. For the most part these apparently unrelated household
members were classified as *agregados* and *domésticos,* literally, as "attached" or
"added-on persons" and "domestics." Although some domésticos and
agregados no doubt did housework, they should not be confused with domestic servants. Instead, the two terms were used more or less interchangeably (at
least in the 1835 censuses) to refer to individuals who had become in some way
dependent on a household head and hence subject to that person's "domestic"
authority.[25] Thus, into the catch-all categories of agregado and doméstico fell
boarders and lodgers, who no doubt often worked in exchange for their keep,
as well as informally adopted children, poorer relatives, and, occasionally, even
older sons and daughters. All of these dependent persons could contribute
through their labor to a household's survival.[26]

But far more numerous than agregados, domésticos, and the like were sons
and daughters. When heads and slaves are again excluded, resident children
accounted for nearly 85 percent of all free members in farming households belonging to free non-"white" women in São Gonçalo dos Campos. Children were
present in almost three-fourths (73.4 percent) of those households. For most
free non-"white" female chefes in São Gonçalo dos Campos, household survival
thus centered on the combined labor of a "family" unit. Working together with
their children, female chefes produced food crops for domestic use and to sell
in local markets as well as tobacco for export. Domésticos, agregados, and even
slaves in some cases augmented the household's labor supply. Yet for the daily
and yearly tasks of planting, weeding, and harvesting that ensured survival, most
free farming women of color in São Gonçalo dos Campos depended chiefly on
themselves and their children.

By comparison with tobacco, sugarcane as a crop was far less accessible to
poorer farmers. Owning and operating a plantation with a functioning sugar

mill lay well beyond the means of even the most prosperous free woman of color in Iguape and required an enormous investment in land, equipment, and labor (in the form of slaves). In Iguape the average engenho employed 123 slaves in 1835. Free women of color could, of course, grow sugarcane for delivery to a nearby engenho as sharecropping cane farmers. But that would mean surrendering to the owner of the engenho at least half their crop in exchange for having their cane milled. Cultivating cane was, moreover, exhausting and often dangerous work. The majority (77 percent) of all cane farmers in Iguape, whether male or female, were slave-owners, who on average could count on the labor of fourteen enslaved workers. It is quite telling in this regard that the one and only non-"white" female cane farmer in Iguape, Ana Joaquina de Lima, a freeborn and widowed "parda," owned ten slaves.

Unable, for the most part, to rely primarily on commercial farming, free women of color in Iguape turned to other non-agricultural pursuits to ensure household survival. Other than in agriculture, however, economic opportunities for women would seem to have been quite limited in the rural Recôncavo of the early nineteenth century. Marketeering and other forms of petty trade, which in urban areas of Brazil stood out as one of the most common occupations among poorer women, notably free Afro-Brazilian women, held few prospects in the countryside. Indeed, judging by the number of women listed as marketeers and as "doing business," opportunities to earn a livelihood from petty trade seem to have been greater in São Gonçalo dos Campos than in Iguape. Likewise, in contrast with many rural and semirural areas in the province of Minas Gerais in Southeastern Brazil, the Recôncavo in the 1830s lacked a well-developed domestic cloth-making industry. Although in Minas Gerais that industry provided full- or part-time employment for thousands of free and slave women, only seventeen of the 610 non-"white" female household heads in Iguape and São Gonçalo dos Campos, according to the censuses, were engaged in either spinning or weaving. Fifteen of them, all listed as *fiadeiras* (spinsters, i.e., those engaged in spinning), resided in Iguape, but they constituted fewer than 6 percent of the non-"white" female chefes in that parish. Thus free women of color in the Bahian countryside apparently could not, in any significant numbers, rely chiefly on domestic crafts to sustain themselves and their households.[27]

It is true that, much more so than in the tobacco-growing economy of the neighboring parish, Iguape's sugar economy generated demand for a wide variety of artisanal skills. Free blacksmiths, masons, sawyers, skilled sugar specialists, and the like were numerous in the parish. But prevailing gender conventions barred women from most of those artisanal activities with one key exception: sewing. Slave holdings on the sugar plantations and cane farms of the parish tended to be much larger than those on tobacco farms. As a result, free women of color had far greater chances to earn a more or less regular cash income by sewing the meager clothes worn by rural slaves in Iguape. "Seamstress" ranked as the single most common occupation among non-"white" female heads in the sugar parish. Concerns with respectability and propriety may have led some women to declare sewing as their occupation, but, for others, sewing may have been the one specific skill that they could claim and that the census takers would have recognized as a legitimate occupation. Even so, the contrast between the two parishes is striking. Although fewer than 17 percent of all "parda," "preta," and "cabra" household heads in São Gonçalo dos Campos reported "seamstress" as their occupation, 45.02 percent did so in Iguape. That is, proportionately, well over twice as many free women of color in Iguape apparently drew a major part of their livelihood from sewing as in the tobacco parish.[28]

Other women in the sugar parish had to resort to working as unskilled wage laborers, or they fell back on an ill-defined, and no doubt changing, mix of activities. Although not one free non-"white" female head in São Gonçalo dos Campos held a recorded occupation that clearly identified her as an unskilled wage-earner, twenty-nine women in Iguape did, including one "hoe" (*enxada*) or fieldhand, eight laundresses, and twenty day laborers (*ganhadeiras*). Employment for these women was undoubtedly less than steady. Moreover, as unskilled wage-earning women engaged in the heavy manual labor of activities such as laundering and fieldwork that were associated with slave status, they would have ranked at or near the very bottom of free society in the rural Recôncavo. That none of them owned even a single slave reinforces the conclusion that they led impoverished lives. It is perhaps not surprising that nineteen of the twenty-nine were former slaves, including four African-born women. All but three were classified as "pretas." In other words, when compared to the householding parish population of free "pardas," "pretas," and "cabras" as a whole, this group of unskilled wage-earners was, by a wide margin, disproportionately made up of "black" women, former slaves, and Africans.

Even more numerous in Iguape than unskilled wage laborers were women for whom the census takers noted no occupation. In São Goncalo dos Campos, all "preta," "parda," and "cabra" heads of household had recorded occupations. By contrast, women who had no declared occupations numbered seventy-five in Iguape and composed more than one-fourth of all free non-"white" female heads of households in the parish. But just because census takers failed to record an occupation for these women does not necessarily mean that all of them were idle or that their households belonged to "the non-working segments of the population."[29] Of the seventy-five such women of color in Iguape, sixteen were slaveholders who collectively owned forty-seven slaves; four of them owned six or more. How they employed their slaves cannot be determined from the census. Some may have rented out the slaves for work on neighboring sugar plantations and cane farms. Another eleven of the seventy-five women headed households that included at least one member who, according to the census, did exercise a gainful occupation.

That, however, still leaves forty-eight non-"white" female heads, or nearly 18 percent of all such women in Iguape, for whom census takers registered no occupation. Not all of them would have been necessarily indigent, but certainly many of the forty-eight confronted real hardship in their daily lives. Their households would have often survived, as best they could, from an odd mix of whatever small-scale, cash-earning activities presented themselves, including perhaps occasional wage labor, and from the food crops they managed to cultivate in small roças. When compared to all free non-"white" female heads in the parish, these women were, like those who worked as unskilled wage laborers, disproportionately "black" (58.3 percent), African by birth (18.9 percent), and former slaves (47.9 percent).

In sum, where free women of color are concerned, the evidence from the censuses about the occupations of heads of households would lead to the conclusion that Iguape's slave-based sugar economy, characterized by large plantations and cane farms and a highly concentrated pattern of land tenure, offered far fewer opportunities to non-"white" female chefes than the relatively more open tobacco-growing economy of São Gonçalo dos Campos, where many "pretas," "pardas," and "cabras" were able to sustain their households through "family" farming. As a result, free women of color in Iguape, especially those who were "black," African by birth, or former slaves, confronted greater poverty and economic insecurity in their daily lives than their counterparts in the tobacco parish.

Such a conclusion would not be wrong, but the contrast it suggests is overdrawn. It exaggerates the security and prosperity that free non-"white" farming women enjoyed in São Gonçalo dos Campos; it also underestimates the ability of free women of color to adapt their lives, domestic living arrangements, and households to the conditions they found in the sugar parish.

On the one hand, "family"-based farming did not by any means guarantee prosperity or eliminate insecurity from the lives of free women of color in São Gonçalo dos Campos. Indeed, as will be seen, the majority of all non-"white" women serving as chefes de fogo in the tobacco parish, including those who headed farming households, were poor; most must have led lives marked by a real measure of insecurity. Children, for example, were often too young to contribute in any significant way to a household's domestic economy. Moreover, whether male or female, heads of tobacco-growing households had no control over fluctuations in overseas markets or over droughts and excessively wet winters, both of which could easily ruin tobacco and food crops alike. The risks involved in farming would have been even greater for women without resident children of working age and without slaves; either they brought into their households agregados and domésticos or they fell back entirely on their own labor. Thirty-nine free non-"white" farming women in São Gonçalo dos Campos did in fact live alone, and nearly two-thirds of them were over the age of forty-nine. For the most part they must have just barely survived from one day to the next. When compared to the entire population of free non-"white" female household heads in the parish, solitary farming women were disproportionately "black"

(58.9 percent), more than twice as likely to be freed slaves, and nearly five times more likely to be African by birth.

On the other hand, the 1835 census suggests that free non-"white" women in Iguape found ways to reduce household economic insecurity and take better advantage of the parish's sugar economy and its setting along the River Paraguaçu and near the Bay of All Saints. The census takers, for example, did not record an occupation (in the sense of a conventional economic activity) for any of the more than 560 sons and daughters living in farming households headed by free women of color in São Gonçalo dos Campos; children, even those eighteen or older, were simply listed as "sons" and "daughters" in the column for "occupation." In farming households, it is reasonable to assume that most able-bodied, working-age children devoted the bulk of their labor time to agricultural tasks and domestic chores. The great majority of all resident daughters and sons in Iguape also lacked, at least in the census, occupations. But for three daughters and thirty-one sons in twenty-five different fogos in the sugar parish, census takers did record occupations (above and beyond "daughter" and "son"). The daughters included a seamstress, a laundress, and an ironess (*engomadeira*). In this context, however, the sons stand out because, if gender conventions barred women of whatever color from many trades, the same did not hold true for their male offspring. The thirty-one resident sons held occupations ranging from carpenter, cobbler, and blacksmith to fisherman, joiner, and mason.[30] When such sons were present, a more diverse household economy resulted in which the family's daily existence centered on a combination of related, or in some cases entirely unrelated, activities such as spinning and fishing. That was precisely the combination that census takers found in the fogo headed by the seventy-year-old Francisca Maria d'Almeida, a never-formally-married Bahian-born "black" woman and freed slave listed as a spinster. Living with Francisca Maria were her two sons, Antônio da Silva and Luís Gonzaga, both of whom were in their thirties and, according to the census, fishermen by trade.

The example of Francisca Maria and her sons points toward a strategy of pooling labor, diverse skills, and other resources within the fogo. A closer examination of household composition in the sugar parish yields further evidence pointing in the same direction. In Iguape, just as in São Gonçalo dos Campos, children figured prominently in the composition of households headed by free women of color. When heads of households and slaves are excluded, resident daughters and sons accounted for approximately two-thirds (67.1 percent) of all household members. The real difference between the two parishes lay in the presence of kin (other than sons and daughters) as well as domésticos, their dependants, and other apparently unrelated free household members. If heads of households and slaves are again excluded, such individuals composed 32.9 percent of all residents in those fogos as opposed to fewer than 16 percent in farming households belonging to non-"white" women in São Gonçalo dos Campos. Likewise, although fewer than 19 percent of those farming households contained extended kin, domésticos, and other free non-kin, nearly 29 percent of all non-"white," female-headed households did so in Iguape.

Incorporating more distant relatives and non-kin into the domestic unit increased a household's labor supply and thereby improved its collective chances for survival. Of course, where non-nuclear household members were very young or very old, their presence might easily amount to a burden. While representing more mouths to feed, they would have contributed little in the way of labor to the domestic economy. In Iguape, however, 54.5 percent of all free non-nuclear household members were between ten and sixty; more than one-third (37.5 percent) fell into the sixteen-to-forty-year-old age group and were therefore in their prime working years.[31] Such individuals contributed not only labor but also, in some cases, income-earning skills. As with resident children, most free-adult, non-nuclear household members lacked a recorded occupation (in the sense of a conventional economic activity) in the census. But for forty-nine of them, sixteen women and thirty-three men in forty different fogos, census takers did take the trouble to list specific occupations. Among the sixteen women were several seamstresses, a spinster, a day laborer, and two beggars. The men held an even wider range of occupations. They included eight carpenters, one wainman, two blacksmiths, one slave-driver, four cobblers, one sawyer, two sugar-masters, one assistant sugar-master, five fishermen, one tailor, five who engaged in small-scale farming, and one beggar.[32]

In part as a result, considerable complexity sometimes characterized households belonging to non-"white" women in Iguape. Two examples will suffice to make the point that although gender-based segregation excluded women of color (and also, for that matter, "white" women) in Iguape from many activities, their households were not always relegated to the margins of the local economy. The first example comes from the fogo of Felipa de Sá Barreto, a fifty-year-old, freeborn, widowed preta who had no recorded occupation and lived with her two Bahian-born "black" slaves. Felipa's household also included Cosme de Góes, a twenty-five-year-old freeborn "black" who, at least according to the census, lacked any kinship tie with Felipa, as well as Cosme's wife and the couple's three young children. Cosme was listed as a sugar-master (a highly skilled and all-male occupation) employed at the Engenho Vitória, a nearby sugar plantation, one of the largest in Bahia. Thus, through Cosme, Felipa de Sá Barreto's household had direct links with Iguape's sugar industry.

More complex in its composition was the household of Escolástica Maria, a forty-six-year-old and never-formally-married freeborn "parda," who, like Felipa de Sá Barreto, had no recorded occupation. Escolástica Maria lived with her three daughters and three sons. The eldest son, José Severino d'Almeida, was listed as a *roceiro,* a small farmer who grew food crops such as cassava and beans for sale in local markets. One of José Severino's brothers was a blacksmith, while the youngest of the three worked as a cobbler. Residing in the same household was Francisco de Macena, thirty and also a blacksmith by trade, together with his wife and their infant son. According to the census, neither Francisco de Macena nor his wife, both of whom were pardos, had any close connection through kinship with Escolástica Maria. The household also included a twenty-two-year-old unmarried doméstica, Antônia Sodré, a "parda," and her newborn daughter. Finally, the household contained six slaves. Even though the census furnishes no information about the type of work those slaves performed, it is clear that Escolástica Maria's fogo had multiple and varied links with the local economy. At the very least, smithing, shoe-making, and farming all contributed to the household's collective survival.

Iguape's sugar economy restricted the opportunities of free women of color who headed households in the parish, pushing many of them into poverty and, in some cases, into what must have been a precarious daily existence. But as the examples of Felipa de Sá Barreto and Escolástica Maria suggest, at least some of those women found ways to reduce household insecurity and take advantage of the sugar economy of the parish and its geographic setting. They did so by relying on resident children, other kin, and non-kin and by pooling labor and varied skills within their fogos.

Escolástica Maria and Felipa de Sá Barreto are also examples of free women of color who headed slave-owning households and therefore could claim the rights and privileges of slave-owners. That free Afro-Brazilian women who were the descendants of slaves, or in some cases former slaves themselves, should have held other Afro-Brazilians as slaves is not surprising. Slave labor underpinned nearly the entire Brazilian economy. As numerous studies have shown, slaveholding reached deep into the social structure of colonial and nineteenth-century Brazil. Slave-ownership thus stands out as perhaps the single best indicator of the prosperity that free non-"white" women and their households could achieve in the rural Recôncavo of the early nineteenth century. It also makes it possible to gauge the relative prosperity and poverty of those women against the wealth of other groups in the local free population.[33]

Slaves could be found in seventy-two households belonging to free non-"white" women in the two parishes: twenty-six in Iguape, the sugar parish, and forty-six in the adjacent tobacco parish of São Gonçalo dos Campos (table 9.4). As a group, the non-"white" women who headed those slave-owning households were much more likely to be either married or widowed than those who did not own slaves. Forty-eight of the seventy-two household heads were widows, and two were married women who lived without their husbands. Collectively, the seventy-two household heads owned a total of 254 slaves. That translates into an average holding of 3.5 slaves, correctly suggesting a pattern of small-scale slave-ownership. The majority (78.9 percent) of those women owned fewer than six slaves; more than half (56.9 percent) could claim ownership of no more than one or two. Yet even where they owned only one slave, that one slave would have certainly been their single most valuable possession and would have often represented a substantial investment. A healthy young adult male slave without

Table 9.4. Indexes of Slaveholding within the Free Population of Household Heads by Color, Sex, and Legal Status, Santiago do Iguape and São Gonçalo dos Campos, 1835

	Rate of Slaveholding[a]	Number of Slave-owners	Average Number of Slaves Owned[b]	Total Number of Slaves Owned[b]
"White" males				
Santiago do Iguape	57.1%	84	27.0	2,268
São Gonçalo dos Campos	81.6	346	7.2	2,491
Both parishes	75.3	430	11.1	4,759
"White" females				
Santiago do Iguape	54.5	24	26.6	638
São Gonçalo dos Campos	62.1	64	8.0	514
Both parishes	59.8	88	13.9	1,152
Non-"white" males				
Santiago do Iguape	12.9	99	4.0	393
São Gonçalo dos Campos	14.6	179	4.1	741
Both parishes	14.0	278	4.1	1,134
Non-"white" females[c]				
Santiago do Iguape	9.5	26	3.2	83
São Gonçalo dos Campos	13.6	46	3.7	171
Both parishes	11.8	72	3.5	254
"Parda" females				
Santiago do Iguape	14.0	21	3.7	77
São Gonçalo dos Campos	18.3	41	4.0	162
Both parishes	16.6	62	3.9	239
"Black" females[d]				
Santiago do Iguape	0.3	4	1.2	6
São Gonçalo dos Campos	0.4	3	1.7	5
Both parishes	0.3	7	1.6	11
Freeborn non-"white" females				
Santiago do Iguape	11.6	22	3.5	78
Sã Gonçalodos Campos	14.2	43	3.8	163
Both parishes	13.2	65	3.7	241
Freed non-"white" females				
Santiago do Iguape	4.8	4	1.3	5
São Gonçalo dos Campos	8.8	3	2.7	8
Both parishes	6.0	7	1.9	13

Source: Endnote 1.

Note: Does not include absentee slave-owners. The table uses households as units of slave-ownership. See B. J. Barickman, "As cores do escravismo: Escravistas 'pretos,' 'pardos' e 'cabras' no Recôncavo baiano, 1835," *População e família* (São Paulo), 2, no. 2 (1998): 7–62.

a. Defined here as the percentage of all households that owned slaves (e.g., the 57.1 percent for "white" males in Santiago do Iguape indicates that 57.1 percent of households headed by "white" males in that parish owned at least one slave).

b. In calculating averages, we have excluded those households where the head was absent, which numbered six in Iguape and eleven in São Gonçalo dos Campos. These were plantations and farms with absentee owners. At least five and probably all six of the absentee heads in Iguape were "white" males; it is also likely that most absentee heads in São Gonçalo dos Campos were also either "white" males or females. Because absentee slave-owners have been excluded here, the numbers of slaves shown in the last column for "white" and non-"white" male and female owners do not sum to the total slave population in the two parishes.

c. Includes one "cabra" slave-owner in São Gonçalo dos Campos.

d. Includes one African-born slave-owner in Iguape.

special skills fetched approximately Rs.370$000 (370 *mil-réis*) in Bahia in the early 1830s. That same amount at the time would have purchased slightly more than 337 bushels (*alqueires*) of cassava flour (*farinha de mandioca*), a basic and essential foodstuff in the local diet; 337 bushels would have been enough to provide thirty-seven adults with a full year's supply of flour.[34]

Moreover, among the seventy-two heads of households were seven women who possessed ten or more slaves and therefore would have ranked as fairly well-to-do slaveholders in the rural Recôncavo of the early nineteenth century. The seven women included the seamstress Isabel Maria da Visitação, forty, a single freeborn "parda" in Iguape who lived with her two teenaged daughters and Rodrigo Camilo de Brandão, her eighteen-year-old son described in the census as a small-scale merchant (*negocia*). Isabel Maria's fogo also contained eleven slaves, making her the wealthiest slave-owning free woman of color in the sugar parish. Even wealthier were three freeborn widowed parda farmers in São dos Campos: Isabel Maria da Conceição, Maria de Jesus, and Maria da Cunha, who owned thirteen, sixteen, and nineteen slaves, respectively—significantly more than the average holding for all slave-owning farmers, including "white" males, in the same parish (6.8 slaves).

The relative prosperity of these seventy-two slave-owning free women of color should not, however, be misinterpreted. They constituted a small minority within the householding population of non-"white" women in the two parishes. Nearly nine-tenths (88.2 percent) of those women did not own slaves. That was also true in São Gonçalo dos Campos, where slaves were present in fewer than 14 percent of all non-"white" female-headed households, and where 220 (84.9 percent) of the 259 farming households belonging to free women of color did not possess even a single slave.

These data gain added significance when set against those for other groups within the free population living in the two parishes. In effect, the distribution of slave holdings in Santiago do Iguape and São Gonçalo dos Campos closely matched the hierarchies based on color, gender, legal status, and ethnicity of the time (table 9.4). Not surprisingly in terms of slave-ownership, "white" males occupied the highest rank within local society. "White" men not only owned the majority of all slaves living in the two parishes but also displayed the highest rates of slaveholding of any group. Nearly three-quarters (72.1 percent) of all fogos headed by "white" males included at least one slave, as opposed to only 11.8 percent of all households belonging to free women of color. Likewise, in combined returns for the two parishes the average "white" male slave-owner held 11.1 slaves, or more than three times the average for non-"white" women. Not a single free woman of color in the two parishes possessed twenty or more slaves, but more than one-tenth (11.2 percent) of all "white" male slave-owners could claim such holdings. No "parda," "preta," or "cabra chefe" in either Iguape or São Gonçalo dos Campos came even close to matching the wealth of sugar planters such as Manoel Inácio de Lima or Colonel Domingos Américo da Silva, both of whom were "white." In 1835 Col. Domingos Américo kept a labor force of 237 slaves at his two adjoining sugar plantations, while Lima Pereira's nearby estate, the Engenho da Praia, had a resident population of 250 enslaved workers.

Within this ranking based on slave-ownership, "white" males were closely followed by "white" women and then, at a much greater distance, by "pardo," "preto," and "cabra" males. At the very bottom of the ranking, with the lowest average number of slaves and the lowest rates of slaveholding, were free women of color. In other words, when wealth is measured by slave-ownership free non-"white" women as a group constituted the poorest segment of the householding population in both Santiago do Iguape and São Gonçalo dos Campos.[35]

Table 9.4 also reveals differences among those women. As might be expected, those who were freeborn had higher rates of slaveholding and possessed more slaves on average than former slaves. Of the seven freedwomen who owned slaves, six were Bahian by birth. That is, in the two parishes, only one of the twenty-nine freed African female household heads was a slave-owner: the fifty-year-old Joaquina Maria, whose occupation was listed as "does business" and who owned a single African-born male slave.[36] Likewise, and again as might be expected, women classified as "pardas" in the censuses were more likely to head slave-owning households than "black" women; the presumably lighter-skinned "pardas" also owned more slaves on average than their "black" neighbors. In fact, not only did "pardas" account for 86.1 percent of the non-"white" slave-owning women in the two parishes, but the great majority (94 percent) of all slaves held by such women belonged to pardas. The thirteen non-"white" women with six or more slaves were all, without exception, freeborn "pardas."

The evidence for slaveholding once again suggests that, by comparison with other free non-"white" women, "pardas" and especially freeborn "pardas" occupied a relatively privileged position within the overlapping racial and ethnic hierarchies that ran throughout Brazilian society in the early nineteenth century. But that higher rank should not be exaggerated. Even when compared to "white" women, "pardas" demonstrated low rates of slaveholding. Indeed, slaves were entirely absent from over four-fifths (83.4 percent) of all "parda"-headed households. Thus, if we measure wealth in terms of slave-ownership, most "parda" women, like the majority of their preta and cabra neighbors, oversaw households that must be classified as belonging to the poorest segments of the free population.

Thus the 1835 censuses reveal a social landscape in rural Bahia where free women of color frequently headed households and exercised the authority and responsibility that headship entailed. On their own, they sustained themselves and reared their children. Where necessary and when possible, they brought into their households the skills and labor of more distant kin, non-kin, and other dependants. The censuses also reveal that the "pretas," "pardas," and "cabras" of Iguape and São Gonçalo dos Campos found a place for themselves and their households in the Recôncavo's slave-based agricultural economy. They took in sewing and washing, they farmed the land and cultivated crops not only for home consumption but also for local and export markets, they spun and wove cotton cloth, they handled small-scale trade, and they worked as day laborers. Through sons as well as through male domésticos and the like, these women, at least in Iguape, established an even wider range of links between their households and the local economy. To be sure, the result was seldom prosperity or even a moderately comfortable and secure existence. The adjective *prosperous* would apply perhaps only to the small minority of non-"white" women who presided over slave-owning households and, more precisely, to the even smaller minority who owned six or more slaves. But at the very least, the majority managed both to survive and retain a measure of household autonomy.

In some ways the very existence of free non-"white" women household heads, whether they were poor or prosperous, challenged the prevailing racial and gender ideologies that were so intimately linked with slaveholding not only in Bahia, but in Brazil as a whole during the early nineteenth century. Authority and responsibility within those ideologies were attributes that properly belonged to free adult men and, whenever possible, to freeborn adult men and, more specifically, adult white men. Nevertheless, as they surveyed the two Bahian parishes and as they confronted on the ground a diversity of domestic living arrangements, the 1835 census takers repeatedly found themselves forced to assign household headship—and hence authority and responsibility—to "parda," "preta," and "cabra" women and even to former slave women born in Africa. And again, although scant, the comparative evidence suggests that São Gonçalo dos Campos and Santiago do Iguape were not, in this regard, anomalies. Elsewhere in early-nineteenth-century Brazil women of color made up a large share of the free population and were often heads of households. Clearly, Brazilian slave society could accommodate the presence of free non-"white" women as chefes de fogo and even, in some cases, as the heads of slave-owning households.

Accommodation of such women within the existing slave-based social structure did not, however, necessarily weaken either slavery or the broader social structure. On the contrary, the 1835 censuses indicate that free women of color who headed fogos in the Bahian countryside lived out in their daily lives the overlapping racial, gender, ethnic, and color hierarchies that permeated Brazilian society at the time. They did so in the poverty that characterized the majority of all free non-"white," female-headed fogos and in the relative likelihood that they had become household heads through formal widowhood or did or did not live with children. The same hierarchies further impinged on their lives in the occupations they held and in their experiences with slavery, whether as former slaves, as slave-owners, or as both, all of which helped create the differences that distinguished freedwomen from their freeborn neighbors, Africans from Bahians, and pardas from pretas.

Yet perhaps the most critical questions must remain unanswered. What did household headship mean for these women? Did they embrace and value the responsibilities that headship implied—and the corresponding freedom from direct control and "protection" by husbands, fathers, and other male kinfolk? Can we even speak about autonomy in any meaningful way when, for the majority of free women of color, poverty accompanied headship and when, as women and regardless of their legal status or income and unlike free non-"white" males, they had no right to any voice in formal politics? The question Donald Ramos has raised in a similar context is pertinent here: Was the "existence of so many female-headed households an indication of the exploitation or the independence of these women"? The 1835 censuses provide no information to answer such questions. The problem does not, however, lie only or chiefly in the shortcomings of the censuses as sources. It also stems from the diversity found among the free women of color who headed households in the Bahian countryside. Although useful for many analytical purposes, the general category *mulheres livres de cor* (free women of color) may also be misleading insofar as it encompassed, in Brazil, women who had a wide range of very different life experiences.[37]

That range of experiences, in turn, makes it difficult to supply any single answer or set of answers to the questions we have raised. Ana Paulinha de Queirós, the freeborn "parda" introduced at the beginning of this chapter, headed a moderately prosperous farming household that included her adult son and three slaves. By contrast, Joaquina da Costa, the freed "black" slave, had to make do with whatever she earned as a laundress while looking after the 120-year-old beggar with whom she shared her fogo. At first view it might seem obvious that Ana Paulinha, who was able to command the service of three slaves and count on her son's help, would have assigned a greater positive value to headship than Joaquina da Costa and that, for Joaquina, poverty virtually annulled any autonomy she enjoyed as a household head. But is it, in fact, at all obvious that the sixty-year-old Ana Paulinha preferred the daily responsibilities and duties of overseeing a slaveholding farm to having at her side her son's deceased or departed father? For all we know, although the census takers recognized Ana Paulinha as the household's head, she may have, in practice, turned over those responsibilities and duties to her son. Likewise, is it truly self-evident that the poverty Joaquina experienced outweighed in her mind the freedom she had gained through manumission? If the 1835 censuses fail to supply the answers, they do at least allow us to raise such questions.

The censuses also force us to recognize that the history of Afro-Brazilian women cannot be reduced to the history of slave women. By the late eighteenth and early nineteenth centuries, a flourishing slave-based economy, which drew on the coerced labor of hundreds of thousands of captive women and men of African birth and ancestry, coexisted in Brazil with a large and growing free population of color. It should be more than obvious that despite common traits and despite solidarities that in some cases may have bridged the slave-free divide, vast differences often separated the lives of enslaved women from those led by free pardas, pretas, and cabras in Bahia and elsewhere in Brazil.[38] Likewise, and even more forcefully, the censuses also make it clear that research on the history of free women within Brazilian slave society cannot be restricted to the study of white women. On the contrary, more often than not investigating that history means delving into the lives of freed and freeborn women of color. It involves reconstructing the story of how free pretas, pardas, and cabras, whether household heads or not, attempted to survive in often very different economic settings. To reconstruct that story also requires exploration of how women such as Ana Paulinha de Queirós and Joaquina da Costa created spaces for themselves in those often different settings while at the same time they daily confronted the overlapping gender, racial, ethnic, and color hierarchies that characterized Brazilian society, which ranked not only as the oldest and longest-lasting slave societies in the Americas but also as one of the largest.

Notes

We thank Karen Anderson, Sharla Fett, Donna Guy, Elizabeth Kusnezof, Maria Inês Côrtes de Oliveira, Elizabeth Santos, and Laura Tabili for comments and suggestions on earlier versions of this chapter. Special thanks to Armando Sarmento Tavares for providing logistical support.

1. "Relação do Numero de Fogos, e moradores do Districto da Freguezia de Sant-Iago Maior do Iguape, da Comarca da Villa da Cachoeira da Provincia da Bahia" (1835), and "Relação do Nº de Fogos e moradores do Districto da Freguezia de São Gonçallo da Vã da Cachoeira" [1835], both in Arquivo Público do Estado de Bahia (Salvador), Seção Histórica (hereafter APEB, SH), 6175–1 and 5683.

2. Dauril Alden, "Late Colonial Brazil," in *The Cambridge History of Latin America*, ed. Leslie Bethell, 11 vols. (New York: Cambridge University Press, 1984–95), 2: 607; Herbert S. Klein, "Nineteenth-Century Brazil," in *Neither Slave nor Free: The Freedman of African Descent in the Slave Societies of the New World*, ed. David W. Cohen and Jack P. Greene (Baltimore: Johns Hopkins University Press, 1972), 313; Thomas W. Merrick and Douglas H. Graham, *Population and Economic Development in Brazil, 1800 to the Present* (Baltimore: Johns Hopkins University Press, 1979), 52, 70.

3. On historical research about women in Brazil, see *História das mulheres no Brasil*, ed. Mary del Priore and Carla Bassanezi (São Paulo: Editora Unesp and Contexto, 1997), which does not include articles specifically about free women of color; and Rachel Soihet, "História das mulheres," in *Domínios da História: Ensaios de teoria e metadologia*, ed. Ciro Flamarion Cardoso and Ronaldo Vainfas (Rio de Janeiro: Campus, 1997), 275–96. Slave and freedwomen (but not freeborn women of color) have received some attention in the literature. See Mary Karasch, "Anastácia and the Slave Women of Rio de Janiero," in *Africans in Bondage*, ed. Paul Lovejoy (Madison: University of Wisconsin Press, 1986), 79–105; Mary Karasch, "Slave Women on the Brazilian Frontier in the Nineteenth Century," in *More Than Chattel: Black Women and Slavery in the Americas*, ed. David Barry Gaspar and Darlene Clark Hine (Bloomington: Indiana University Press, 1996), 79–96; Maria Inês Côrtes de Oliveira, *O liberto: O seu mundo e os outros, Salvador, 1790/1860* (São Paulo: Corrupio, 1988); Sonia Maria Giacomini, *Mulher e escrava: Uma introdução histórica ao estado da mulher negra no Brasil* (Petrópolis: Vozes, 1988); Luciano Figueiredo, *O avesso da memória: Cotidiano e trabalho da mulher em Minas Gerais no século XVIII* (Rio de Janeiro: José Olympio; Brasília: UNB, 1993); Eduardo Paiva França, *Escravos e libertos nas Minas Gerais do século XVIII: Estratégias de resistência através dos testamentos* (São Paulo: Annablume, 1995); Kathleen J. Higgins, "*Licentious Liberty*" *in a Brazilian Gold-Mining Region: Slavery, Gender, and Social Control in Eighteenth-Cen-*

tury Sabará, Minas Gerais (University Park: Pennsylvania State University Press, 1999); Sandra Lauderdale Graham, *Caetana Says No: Women's Stories from a Brazilian Slave Society* (New York: Cambridge University Press, 2002); and Júnia Ferreria Furtado, *Chica da Silva e o contratador dos diamantes: O outro lado do mito* (São Paulo: Companhia das Letras, 2003). More generally, see the pioneering studies of A. J. R. Russell-Wood and Herbert S. Klein in *Neither Slave nor Free: The Freedman of African Descent in the Slave Societies of the New World*, ed. David W. Cohen and Jack P. Greene (Baltimore: Johns Hopkins University Press, 1972), 84–133, 309–34. Neither author discusses women in detail. Elsewhere in the Americas historians have profitably used notarial records to examine free women of color. See Susan M. Socolow, "Economic Roles of the Free Women of Color of Cap Français," in *More Than Chattel: Black Women and Slavery in the Americas*, ed. David Barry Gaspar and Darlene Clark Hine (Bloomington: Indiana University Press, 1996), 279–97; and Suzanne Lebsock, *The Free Women of Petersburg: Status and Culture in a Southern Town* (New York: W. W. Norton, 1984), ch. 4. As some of the studies cited demonstrate, freed African slaves in Brazil and, less frequently, freed native-born slaves sometimes identified themselves as such in their wills. Of course, not all freed slaves filed wills. Moreover, using notarial records to investigate the free population of color in Brazil more generally poses considerable difficulties. In Bahia and probably in the rest of Brazil, at least from the late eighteenth century on, wills, contracts, and post-mortem inventories seldom mention color. Hebe Maria Mattos, *Das cores do silêncio: Os significados da liberdade no Sudeste escravista, Brasil século XIX* (Rio de Janeiro: Nova Fronteira, 1998), esp. 93–103.

4. Although focusing mainly on the U.S. experience, Clare Robertson provides several key insights into the general phenomenon of non-"white" female headship in "Africa in the Americas? Slavery, Women, the Family, and the Gender Division of Labor," in *More Than Chattel: Black Women and Slavery in the Americas*, ed. David Barry Gaspar and Darlene Clark Hine (Bloomington: Indiana University Press, 1996), 3–40. For comparative purposes, see also Lebsock, *The Free Women of Petersburg*, esp. ch. 4; Jay Kinsbruner, *Not of Pure Blood: The Free People of Color and Racial Prejudice in Nineteenth-Century Puerto Rico* (Durham: Duke University Press, 1996), esp. chs. 3–5; and Loren Schweninger, "Property-Owning Free African-American Women in the South, 1800–1870," in *"We Specialize in the Wholly Impossible": A Reader in Black Women's History*, ed. Darlene Clark Hine, Wilma King, and Linda Reed (Brooklyn: Carlson Publishing, 1995), 253–79. On the Recôncavo, see Stuart B. Schwartz, *Sugar Plantations in the Formation of Brazilian Society: Bahia 1550–1835* (New York: Cambridge University Press, 1985); and B. J. Barickman, *A Bahian Counterpoint: Sugar, Tobacco, Cassava, and Slavery in the Recôncavo, 1780–1860* (Stanford: Stanford University Press, 1998). In this essay, references to women and female household heads, unless otherwise qualified, should be understood as meaning free women of color who served as household heads. Likewise, we use "free" to refer to both freeborn and freedwomen.

5. Unfortunately, some sheets are missing from the census of São Gonçalo dos Campos, and the entire last section (for the subdistrict of the Capela dos Humildes) is too fragile for use, as are several sheets for the other subdistricts. Thus, the figure of 11,406 used here for the parish's total population derived from a direct count of the nominal lists for the 1,760 households on the sheets that could be examined. In the independent Empire of Brazil, parishes served as both ecclesiastical and political-administrative units.

6. See, on Iguape, Barickman, *A Bahian Counterpoint*, chs. 5–6, and, on the Bahian sugar industry more generally, Schwartz, *Sugar Plantations*. Arlene Díaz and Jeff Stewart, using the 1835 census, examine the general phenomenon of female-headed households in Iguape in "Occupational Class and Female-Headed Households in Santiago Maior Do Iguape, Brazil, 1835," *Journal of Family History* 16 (1991): 299–313. Although it raises interesting issues, their study suffers from several problems. Díaz and Stewart focus on occupation, more specifically on occupations of household heads, but for reasons not explained they exclude from their analysis several occupations held by household heads: fieldhand (*enxada*); wage-earning day laborer (*ganhadeira*); beggar, cobbler, sawyer, and runaway slave-catcher (*capitão de entradas*); spinster (*fiadeira*); and no-

tary (*escrivão de paz*). They also do not use a residual category such as "other" to encompass these occupations. Díaz and Stewart, again without explanation, also include in their analysis "boxmakers," an occupation not held by any individual (household head or not) listed in the census. The apparently arbitrary exclusion of certain occupations and the inclusion of a nonexistent occupation would seem to distort any analysis of "occupational class."

7. Barickman, *A Bahian Counterpoint*, chs. 2, 5, 6, 7.

8. Joao José Reis, *Slave Rebellion in Brazil: The Muslim Uprising of 1835 in Bahia*, trans. Arthur Brakel (Baltimore: Johns Hopkins University Press, 1993), 121 (for "faded black"). Three other points should be noted. First, "pardos" were not necessarily the offspring of a mixed white-Afro-Brazilian couple. They might also be (and often were) the children of two "pardos." Second, no individual of indigenous ancestry was listed as such in the censuses. Third, when appropriate, we employ in the text the feminine forms, *parda* and *preta;* the term *cabra* is used for both men and women.

The terms for color (*qualidade*) used in the 1835 censuses, it bears stressing, should not be taken as an infallible guide to ancestry or pigmentation or as necessarily reflecting self-identification by color. Rather, they should be understood as categories census takers used within a preconceived four-way scheme. In part as a result, considerations of social and legal status, wealth, and reputation would have influenced how a specific individual was classified. B. J. Barickman, "As cores do escravismo: Escravistas 'pretos,' 'pardos' e 'cabras' no Recôncavo baiano, 1835," *População e família* (São Paulo) 2, no. 2 (1998): 7–62, which also cites other relevant works on color classification in Brazil. Therefore, throughout this chapter, the four color terms appear with quotation marks whenever they refer to categories used in the censuses. Because "cabras" made up only a small share of all non-"white" female heads in the two parishes (table 9.1), we have, for the most part, not dealt specifically with "cabras" in this chapter. Moreover, both within and across parishes, use of the term is inconsistent in the 1835 censuses, which is perhaps not surprising given the term's derogatory connotations. On cabras in the 1835 censuses, see Barickman, "As cores de escravismo."

9. "Livro de notas de escrituras: Santiago do Iguape, 1831–1845," Arquivo Regional da Cachoeira, Cachoeira, Bahia, Brazil (hereafter ARC), contains manumission records involving eighty-three slaves. For references to the extensive literature on manumission in Brazil, see Mieko Nishida, "Manumission and Ethnicity in Urban Slavery: Salvador, Brazil, 1808–1888," *Hispanic American Historical Review* 73 (Aug. 1993): 363n6. On manumission and female headship elsewhere, see, for example, Lebsock, *The Free Women of Petersburg*, ch. 4.

10. Elizabeth Anne Kuznesof, "The Role of the Female-headed Household in Brazilian Modernization: São Paulo, 1765–1836," *Journal of Social History* 13 (Summer 1980): 589–613; Elizabeth Anne Kuznesof, "An Analysis of Household Composition and Headship as Related to Mode of Production: São Paulo, 1765–1836," *Comparative Studies in Society and History,* 22 (Jan. 1980): 78–108; Donald Ramos, "City and Country: The Family in Minas Gerais, 1804–1838," *Journal of Family History* 3 (1978): 361–75; Donald Ramos, "Single and Married Women in Vila Rica, Brazil, 1754–1838," *Journal of Family History* 16 (1991): 261–82; Maria Odila Leite da Silva Dias, *Quotidiano e poder em São Paulo no século XIX: Ana Gertrudis de Jesus* (São Paulo: Brasiliense, 1984); and Eni de Mesquita Samara, *As mulheres, o poder e a família: São Paulo, século XIX* (São Paulo: Marco Zero, 1989). On inheritance laws, see Linda Lewin, "Natural and Spurious Children in Brazilian Inheritance Law from Colony to Empire: A Methodological Essay," *The Americas* 48 (Jan. 1992): 351–96. In the revisionist literature, it is common to cite as the main source for the older view Gilberto Freyre, *Casa-grande & senzala: Formação da família brasileira sob o regime patriarcal,* 22d ed. (1933, reprint Rio de Janeiro: José Olympio, 1983). But that is misleading. See B. J. Barickman, "Revisiting the *Casa-grande:* Plantation and Cane-farming Households in Early Nineteenth-Century Bahia," *Hispanic American Historical Review* (in press). On revisionist literature, see Ronaldo Vainfas, *Trópico dos pecados: Moral, sexualidade e inquisição no Brasil* (Rio de Janeiro: Campus, 1989), 107–20; and Sheila de Castro Faria, *A colônia em movimento: Fortuna e família no cotidiano colonial* (Rio de Janeiro: Nova Fronteira, 1998), 45–52.

11. Black and "parda" women, for example, accounted for 38.1 percent of all female heads of households in the city of São Paulo in 1804 and 39.5 percent in 1834 (or 16.0 percent and 12.8 percent of all heads, male and female, in 1804 and 1834, respectively). Calculated from Dias, *Quotidiano*, 21–22. In five districts in Minas Gerais in 1831 and 1835, non-"white" women headed 24.9 percent of all households and 64.4 percent of the female-headed households. Ramos, "Single and Married," 372.

12. Based on slave appraisals in a sample of sixty-four postmortem inventories (dated between 1820 and 1839) of estates belonging to planters and farmers in the two parishes. APEB, Seção Judiciária, Inventários e Testamentos (hereafter IT) and ARC, IT. The inventories provide information on the ethnic or regional origins of 411 African slaves. (Another 155 African-born slaves were described simply as "Africans.") Also see Reis, *Slave Rebellion*, 139–41; Schwartz, *Sugar Plantations*, 339–48; and Maria José de Souza Andrade, *A mão-de-obra escrava em Salvador, 1811–1860* (São Paulo: Corrupio, 1988), 97–108. On the slave trade, see Pierre Verger, *Fluxo e refluxo do tráfico de escravos entre o Golfo de Benim e a Bahia de Todos os Santos dos séculos XVII a XIX*, trans. Tasso Gadzanis (São Paulo: Corrupio, 1987).

13. The average age of "white" women heads was 45.4 years in Iguape and 48.4 in São Gonçalo dos Campos. "Age-heaping" is a problem in the 1835 censuses—that is, the recorded ages for a disproportionate number of individuals end with the digits 0 or 5, which suggests that those ages are estimates.

14. Suggestive of this possibility is the fogo headed by Clemência, a freed African. She lived with her legitimate African-born husband, Jerônimo, a slave owned by a sugar planter, who had apparently allowed the couple to live in an odd corner of his estate and away from the main slave quarters. Also suggestive are cases in the censuses where freedwomen are listed as wives of male slaves and as residing in the slave-owner's household. On marriage and consensual unions, see Maria Nizza da Silva, *Sistema de casamento no Brasil colonial* (São Paulo: T. A. Queiroz/Edusp, 1984), 36–58; Elizabeth Kuznesof, "Sexual Politics, Race, and Bastard-bearing in Nineteenth-Century Brazil: A Question of Power or Culture?," *Journal of Family History* 16 (1991): 241–45; Katia M. de Queirós Mattoso, *Família e sociedade na Bahia no século XIX* (São Paulo: Corrupio, 1988), 78–88; Luciano Raposo de Almeida Figueiredo, *Barrocas famílias: Vida familiar em Minas Gerais no século XVIII* (São Paulo: Hucitec, 1997); and Dain Borges, *The Family in Bahia, Brazil, 1870–1945* (Stanford: Stanford University Press, 1992), 79–81.

Although the matter has not received adequate attention in the literature, it would seem that, unlike legitimately married widows, consensual-union widows as such did not enjoy formal, legal rights to one-half of the couple's property when their partners died (Mattos, *Das cores*, 61). But it would not be surprising if, informally, community practices conceded comparable rights to both legitimate and consensual-union widows. Investigating the matter will, however, prove difficult. On the one hand, informal practices, almost by definition, do not appear in formal probate records. On the other hand, within the poorest segments of the free population, in which presumable consensual unions were more common, surviving spouses, consensual-union partners, and heirs often failed to take on the bother and expense of carrying out a postmortem inventory.

15. The statement remains valid even when, to control for differences in legal status, we restrict our attention to freeborn "pardas" (40.7 percent and 22 percent widows, respectively) and "pretas" (55 percent and 71.7 percent single, respectively). Perhaps the only deviation from the expected pattern comes from African-born women who displayed higher rates of formal marriage than Bahian-born "blacks." But the difference between the two groups was small, in fact much smaller than the difference between "black" women in general and "pardas" (table 9.2).

16. Averages do not include households without children. For similar findings elsewhere in Brazil see Ramos, "Single and Married," 267–68, 271; and Mattoso *Família*, 88. The following paragraphs focus on differences across groups in the proportion of women living with children. Differences across groups in the average number of resident children follow roughly similar patterns.

17. The possibility (fully compatible with everything known about slavery in nineteenth-century Brazil) is suggested by two 1845 cases in Iguape, where mothers bought the freedom of their children. "Livro de notas," ARC, fols. 139–40 and 142–43.

18. For similar findings elsewhere in Brazil, see Ramos, "Single and Married," 275–76.

19. On child abandonment in Brazil see Kuznesof, "Sexual Politics"; Mattoso, *Família*, pp. 94–97; and Renato Pinto Venâncio, "Maternidade negada," in *História das mulheres no Brasil*, ed. Mary del Priore and Carla Bassanezi (São Paulo: Editora Unesp and Contexto, 1997), 189–222. Here, in stressing the positive aspects of residing with children, we certainly are not minimizing the possibility—indeed, likelihood—that some or many free women of color had become mothers as a result of sexual exploitation of one type or another. But the censuses provide no means to measure the frequency with which that was the case.

20. Tercina Barbosa Vergolino (Integrated Master's Program in Sociology and Economics, Federal University of Pernambuco) reports (in a personal communication, April 1998) finding in her fieldwork with poorer groups in rural Northeastern Brazil during the 1980s and 1990s that household heads, even those with specialized skills, often had to resort to more than one occupation to survive.

On midwives, curandeiras, and Afro-Brazilian religious specialists, see Luiz Felipe de Alencastro, "Vida privada e ordem privada no Império" and Luiz Mott, "Cotidiano e vivência religiosa: Entre a capela e o calundu," both in *História da vida privada no Brasil*, ed. Fernando A. Novais, 4 vols. (São Paulo: Companhia das Letras, 1996–98), 2: 68–70, 2: 72 (fig. 49) and 1: 155–220; Karasch, "Anastácia," 90; Karasch, "Slave Women," 89; João José Reis, "Magia Jeje no Bahia: A Invasão do Calundu do Pasto de Cachoeira, 1785," *Revista Brasileira de História* 8 (1988): 57–81; Kim D. Butler, *Freedoms Given, Freedoms Won: Afro-Brazilians in Post-Abolition São Paulo and Salvador* (New Brunswick: Rutgers University Press, 1998), 192–99; and Ruth Landes, *The City of Women*, intro. Sally Cole, 2d ed. (1947, reprint Albuquerque: University of New Mexico Press, 1994). On black and mulatto female healers elsewhere in Latin America, see, for example, Martha Few, *Women Who Live Evil Lives: Gender, Religion, and the Politics of Power in Colonial Guatemala* (Austin: University of Texas Press, 2002), 69–89.

Research on urban areas of colonial and nineteenth-century Brazil often calls attention to prostitution. Although some free women of color in the two Bahian parishes may have earned part of their living as prostitutes, it seems unlikely that many did so or that many relied chiefly on prostitution to sustain themselves. These were, after all, predominantly rural parishes. Moreover, like their U.S. counterparts, the 1835 census takers did not regard strictly domestic, noncash-earning labor as an "occupation" even though such labor might be critical to a household's survival and often involve heavy work.

21. Cf. Díaz and Stewart, "Occupational Class." Although they work with both individual- and household-level data from the 1835 census of Iguape (311–12n1), Díaz and Stewart do not acknowledge that heads and nonheads of households might have different occupations (whether recorded or not). Instead, they use the head's occupation to characterize the entire household. For example, they state that "only 5.4 percent of the entire population, male and female, were dedicated to subsistence agriculture" (309). Although apparently referring to the proportion of individuals engaged in agriculture, the figure of 5.4 percent in fact refers to the share, as calculated by Díaz and Stewart, of individuals living in households headed by "small farmers" ("Occupational Class," 303, table 1). But households in Iguape sometimes sheltered individuals who had completely unrelated occupations. Likewise, individuals engaged in small-scale farming could be found in fogos belonging to heads of households with nonfarming occupations and even those with no recorded occupations. On U. S. census-taking practices, see Margo Anderson, "The History of Women and the History of the Statistics," *Journal of Women's History* 4 (Spring 1992): 14–36; and Margo Anderson, "(Only) White Men Have Class: Reflections on Early Nineteenth-Century Occupational Classification Schemes," *Work and Occupations* 21, no. 1 (1994), 5–32.

22. Barickman, *A Bahian Counterpoint*, ch. 5. For the expression "tenants at will" (often called

moradores or *agregados* in Brazil), see John MacGregor, *Commercial Statistics: A Digest of . . . of All Nations*, 2d ed., 5 vols. (London: Whittaker, 1850), 4: 179 (quoting M. A. de Mornay, a French engineer who lived in Northeastern Brazil during the 1840s).

23. B. J. Barickman, "'A Bit of Land, which They Call *Roça':* Slave Provision Grounds on Sugar Plantations and Cane Farms in the Bahian Recôncavo, 1780–1860," *Hispanic American Historical Review* 74 (Nov. 1994): 649–87.

24. Barickman, *A Bahian Counterpoint*, esp. chs. 6–7. Specifically on women and tobacco in the twentieth century, see Walter Alberto Egler, "Aspectos gerais da cultura do fumo na região do Recôncavo da Bahia," *Boletim Geográfico* 10, no. 111 (1952): 681; Ariadne Soares Souto Mayor, "Comentário do mapa da produçao de fumo da Bahia," *Boletim Geográfico* 11, no. 112 (1953): 90; and Sylvia dos Reis Maia, "Dependency and Survival of Sapeaçu Small Farmers—Bahia, Brazil," Ph.D. diss., Boston University, 1985, 91, 96–98, 166–67. We do not assume that either "family"-based farming or other collective household survival strategies always produced harmonious relationships among family and other free household members. Nor do we assume that those strategies generally resulted in an equal or even distribution of workloads and consumption among free members. The censuses do not, for the most part, allow us to address such issues directly.

25. Cf. Díaz and Stewart, "Occupational Class," (303, table 1, 304, 309), in their study based on the 1835 census of Iguape, regard "doméstico" as referring to a specific occupation, comparable to "carpenter," "laundress," or "seamstress" and, more specifically, meaning wage-earning domestic servant. But, like agregado (or "daughter," "son," and "wife," all of which appear in the column for "occupation"), "doméstico" referred to a relationship to the household head and not to a specific occupation. (Those few free domestic servants that appear in the census are described as *criados.*) And some domésticos were listed as holding conventional occupations such as blacksmith, fisherman, or sawyer. Some even owned slaves.

26. Use of the terms *agregado* and *doméstico* varies within the censuses. Census takers in Iguape used "doméstico" almost exclusively, but in São Gonçalo dos Campos they employed both terms. Their preference for one term or the other, however, varied by subdistrict within that parish. Barickman, *A Bahian Counterpoint*, ch. 6; B. J. Barickman, "Reading the 1835 Censuses from Bahia: Citizenship, Kinship, Slavery, and Household in Early Nineteenth-Century Bahia," *The Americas* 59 (Jan. 2003): 287–324; Martha Few, "Gender, Race, and Export Agriculture in Nineteenth-Century Brazil: A Tobacco-growing Parish," given at a meeting of the Pacific Coast Council on Latin American Studies, Phoenix, Oct. 1992.

Census takers used the two terms to classify what would seem to be—and in some cases most certainly were—female consensual-union partners in male-headed households. Moreover, we refer to agregados and domésticos as being apparently unrelated to household heads. Yet some no doubt were related and even perhaps close relatives despite the lack of any recorded indication of kinship in the censuses. (Brazilian naming practices in the past often make it difficult to determine kinship from surnames. In addition, the censuses often fail to list surnames, even for some household heads.) Finally, no nonnuclear kin, listed as such, appear in the farming households of free women of color in São Gonçalo dos Campos. Extended kin do, however, appear in nonfarming households in that parish and in non-"white" female-headed *fogos* in Iguape.

27. On petty trade, see Maria Odila da Silva Dias, "Nas fímbrias da escravidão urbana: Negras de tubuleiro e de ganho," *Estudos Econômicos* 15, special issue (1985): 89–109; Dias, *Quotidiano*, 114–26; and "Relação dos Africanos libertos na Freguezia de Santa Anna" (1849), APEB, SH, 2898. On cloth-making in Minas, see Douglas Cole Libby, "Proto-Industrialisation in a Slave Society: The Case of Minas Gerais," *Journal of Latin American Studies* 23 (Feb. 1991): 1–35.

Also see, on textile and other craft activities in female-headed households in São Paulo, Kusnezof, "The Role of the Female-Headed Household," 597; and Dias, *Quotidiano*, 81–112. The 1835 censuses do not specify the type of cloth produced by the spinsters and weavers in two parishes, but it was almost certainly cotton cloth. Although apparently not grown in either São Gonçalo dos Campos or Iguape, cotton was cultivated on a commercial scale in nearby parishes and townships. "Mappa Statistico da Freguezia de Santo Estevão de Jacuipe dos anos 1826 e 1827 . . ." and "Mappa Statistico das Povoaçoens que tem esta Freguezia de Santa Anna do Camizão . . ." [1825], both in ARC, papéis avulsos; Domingos José Antonio Rebello, "Corographia, ou abbreviada historia geographica do Imperio do Brasil" (1829), *Revista do Instituto Histórico e Geográfico da Bahia* 55 (1929): 166.

That relatively few women of color in the two parishes held artisanal occupations other than sewing does not necessarily mean that such women did not engage in small-scale domestic craft production (e.g., lace-making, embroidery, preparing preserved fruits, or mat-making). It merely suggests that they did not rely chiefly on those activities for their livelihoods.

28. The higher proportion of artisanal and fishing households in Iguape may have also contributed to a greater demand for the services of seamstresses.

29. Díaz and Stewart, "Occupational Class," 309, classify such households as "non-working."

30. The sons included four carpenters, two blacksmiths, nine small-scale farmers (lavoura and *roceiro*), one joiner, one cane farmer, one mason, nine fishermen, two cobblers, one tailor, and one "does business" (*negocia*, i.e., a petty trade or small-scale merchant).

31. The evidence here can—and should—also be read from the opposite direction, that is, as indicating that many working-age free adults in Iguape lacked the resources to establish their own households and therefore found it necessary to "attach" themselves to other households.

32. Díaz and Stewart, in studying "white" and non-"white" female headship in Iguape based on the 1835 census, argue that a spatial pattern of "gender segregation" characterized the parish with "male fishing hamlets around the rivers and male dominated trades households surrounding the sugar mills," while "in areas of marginal subsistence, . . . female-headed households predominated" ("Occupational Class," 311). That argument, for which the authors provide no evidence, finds little support in the 1835 census. On the one hand, fishermen did live in female-headed households. More generally, Díaz and Stewart ignore the presence of sons or male domésticos (including males over the age of twenty-one) in such households. At the same time, whatever the phrase "areas of marginal subsistence" might mean, both "white" and non-"white" female-headed households could be found interspersed between plantations in the main, cane-growing areas of the parish. Indeed, households headed by "white" women included large cane farms and even a few sugar plantations. On the other hand, wives, daughters, and female domésticas were present in the households of male artisans and fishermen. Whether or not slaves are included, roughly 47 percent of all residents in fogos headed by fishermen were women. It is difficult to construe a roughly 47 percent female population as constituting a gender-segregated "male fishing hamlet."

33. The seminal work on widespread slave-ownership in Brazil is Stuart B. Schwartz, "Patterns of Slaveholding in the Americas: New Evidence from Brazil," *American Historical Review* 87 (Feb. 1982): 55–86; also see Francisco Vidal Luna and Iraci del Nero da Costa, "Posse de escravos em São Paulo no incío do século XIX," *Estudos Econômicos* 13 (1983): 211–21. Although several studies have dealt with slaveholding by former slaves in Brazil, research on slave-ownership among free (i.e., freed and freeborn) Afro-Brazilians is scant. But see Herbert S. Klein and Clothilde Paiva Andrade, "Slave and Free in Nineteen-Century Minas Gerais: Campanha in 1831," *Slavery and Abolition* 15 (April 1994): 1–21, esp. 15–16; Francisco Vidal Luna and Herbert S. Klein, *Slavery and the Economy of São Paulo, 1750–1850* (Stanford: Stanford University Press, 2003), ch. 7; and Barickman, "As cores do escravismo." At least in some cases, free African Americans in the U.S. South apparently owned loved ones, relatives, and friends as slaves to circumvent local legislation restricting manumission. But no comparable legislation existed in Brazil, where before 1871 manumission was essentially a private matter. Owners were entirely free to manumit their slaves if they wished. See Manuela Carneiro da Cunha, "Silences of the Law: Customary Law and Positive Law on the Manumission of Slaves in Nineteenth-Century Brazil," *History and Anthropology* 1 (1985): 427–43. Therefore, non-"white" slave-owners must be regarded as being in every sense slave-owners. Unlike some early-nineteenth-century censuses in Southeastern Brazil and mid-century censuses in the United States,

the 1835 Bahian household lists provide no information on estimated income or value of property owned.

34. Barickman, "As cores do escravismo." We set aside dealing with the occupations held by these women except to list them: thirty-nine farmers, five seamstresses, and two women engaged in petty trade in São Gonçalo dos Campos and, in Iguape, eight seamstresses, one cane farmer, one woman engaged in petty trade, and sixteen with no recorded occupations.

35. If, however, we were to distinguish among different groups of non-"white" males, then this statement would need to be modified to take into account the complex interplay of color, gender, and ethnicity. "Parda" women, for example, would out-rank "black" males.

36. The low rate of slaveholding among African-born women (and also, for that matter, men) in the two parishes should not be ascribed to any general reluctance among freed Africans to acquire slaves. Evidence from other areas, although scant, indicates that freed Africans in Brazil did own slaves when they could afford to do so. "Relação dos Africanos libertos . . ." (1845), APEB, SH, 2898; Oliveira, *O liberto,* 35–36, 40–45; Klein and Andrade, "Slave and Free," 4, 15–16; Nishida, "Manumission," 389–90. Rather, at least in part, the explanation lies in the largely rural economy of these two parishes, which would have restricted opportunities for Africans first as slaves, when most of them would have been fieldhands, and then after manumission.

37. Ramos, "Single and Married," 279; also see Lebsock, *Free Women of Petersburg,* 102–3; and Robertson, "Africa in the Americas?" 9–20. In Imperial Brazil, freed Brazilian-born male slaves could vote in the first round of the two-tiered election system provided they met the income requirements. Freeborn Brazilian males, including blacks and mulattos, could also vote in the second round if they met the higher income requirements. On the category "free men [women] of color" in Brazil, see Manuela Carneiro da Cunha, *Negros, estrangeiros: Os escravos libertos e sua volta à África* (São Paulo: Brasiliense, 1985), 17–100, esp. 22–24.

38. Freed and freeborn women represented 48.1 percent of all Afro-Brazilian women in Iguape and 59.1 percent in São Gonçalo dos Campos. In combined returns for the two parishes, 54.7 percent of all women of color were free.

CHAPTER 10

Libertas Citadinas: Free Women

of Color in San Juan, Puerto Rico

Félix V. Matos Rodríguez

In 1824 Balbina Alonso, a *liberta* (free woman of color) who lived in San Juan, Puerto Rico, was accused of having an illicit love affair with Don Antonio Cordero. Church authorities complained that although she had been banned to the small town of Patillas on Puerto Rico's southeastern shore, Alonso was still in San Juan, enjoying the company of Cordero, who was married.[1] Alonso wrote to the governor to defend her innocence, honor, and good name. She demanded that her ecclesiastical accusers take her to court to substantiate their claims. The trial never materialized. The governor instead asked Cordero to behave in an honorable way, and he exiled Alonso to the nearby town of Loíza. The governor's rationale for this action was based on the fact that Cordero had fathered Alonso's son. Thus, although Alonso's presence was a scandalous nuisance, placing her in Loíza allowed the father to be nearby to help raise the child. This proximity, however, angered church officials, who claimed that Alonso's exile to Loíza only forced Cordero to travel a few additional miles to continue to engage in the sinful practice of concubinage.

The incident illustrates some of the realities that free women of color faced in nineteenth-century San Juan. First, Alonso embodied the stereotype of the seductive temptress, the *mulatta*. She should therefore be driven away or cast aside so that the honorable marriage of Cordero and his wife could be protected. The presence of this woman of color in San Juan caused fear. Both church and state joined forces in upholding gendered and racist notions of public morality.[2] Alonso, however, fought against her unjustified exile with all the resources available to a woman of her class and race. That a woman of color wrote to the governor and challenged the powerful dean of the Cathedral Chapter, Don Nicolás Alonso de Andrade, to take her to court so she could defend her good name publicly was a strong indication of Alonso's resolve and courage. Denied that legal recourse, she then relied on an alternative strategy: She resisted and defied the law and continued to see Cordero and care for their son.

As a result of the attention scholars in the Americas have given to women's history in general and the history of colored women in particular since the 1980s, stories such as Alonso's are being brought to light.[3] Who were the free women of color in Puerto Rico? How many of them were there in mid-nineteenth-century San Juan? How important were they for the city's socioeconomic development? Other questions emerge as well from the social, political, and economic context of the lives of free women of color in mid-nineteenth-century San Juan. How did changes in the slave trade, in slave prices, and in overall labor supply affect the lives of urban free women of color during the 1840s, 1850s, and 1860s? How did the abolition of slavery in other parts of the Caribbean affect the treatment that elite *sanjuaneros* and *sanjuaneras* and government officials gave free women of color? What roles did libertas play in such changes as emancipation that the city experienced in the second half of the nineteenth century? This essay will focus on the period between around 1800, which marks the emergence of large-scale, slave-run plantations in Puerto Rico, and 1873, the year of the abolition of slavery there. Most demographic data come from the 1833 and 1846 manuscript censuses available for San Juan.

Libertas in the City

San Juan was the administrative and military center of Spanish colonialism in Puerto Rico. Founded in 1521 on the westernmost third of a little barrier island at the entrance of a well-protected harbor, San Juan was always a small city. By 1782 the city proper was completely surrounded by a defensive wall and by several fortifications. The intramural sector measured 682 meters long and 430 meters wide and was divided into four barrios—Fortaleza (also called San Juan), Santa Bárbara, Santo Domingo, and San Francisco—using Luna and Cruz streets as the dividing markers.[4] A fifth barrio, Ballajá, was created by the mid-nineteenth century. By this time, the city was compact, with few open spaces available for construction. The defensive walls provided a boundary that limited the real estate and commercial expansion of the city into the rest of the barrier island.

The population of San Juan grew at a modest rate during the mid-nineteenth century after a period of significant growth occurred during the late eighteenth and early nineteenth centuries. A sluggish economy and the physical constraints of the walled city combined to limit the rate of expansion of the sanjuanero population (table 10.1).[5] Still, Spanish immigrants, African slaves, freed persons from nearby Caribbean islands, and people from towns in San Juan's hinterland continued to move, or to be moved, into the city during the first two-thirds of the nineteenth century. San Juan's role as Puerto Rico's capital city and most important commercial center helped attract newcomers.

Table 10.1. San Juan's Population, Selected Years

Year	Population	Rate of Growth
1776	6,605	—
1783	6,462	—
1803	7,835	21.2%
1816	8,907	13.6
1827	11,484	28.9
1845	13,000	13.2
1859	13,627	4.8
1865	17,930	31.5
1874	21,847	21.8

Sources: Aníbal Sepúlveda Rivera, *San Juan: Historia ilustrada de su desarollo urbano* (San Juan: Carimar, 1989), 162, table 6.6; Adolfo de Hostos, *Historia de San Juan: Ciudad Murada* (San Juan: Instituto de Cultura Puertorriqueña, 1983), 21; Archivo General de Puerto Rico, Colecciones Particulares, Colección Scarano, CP-3, Sept. 19, 1803.

Puerto Rico's free colored population was very large. Indeed, it was, proportionately, far larger than the colored populations of the United States, Cuba, Jamaica, and Barbados throughout the nineteenth century.[6] Free people of color made up between 31 and 38 percent of the population in San Juan throughout the nineteenth century. In 1802, for example, they composed 31 percent of San Juan's population, a percentage that increased to 34 percent in 1828 and peaked at 38 percent in 1865. In 1867, just six years before the abolition of slavery, free coloreds accounted for 32 percent of San Juan's total population.[7]

Like other societies of the Americas heavily influenced by slavery, Puerto Rico developed a taxonomy that combined legal and social perceptions of race, color, and hierarchy. In the Puerto Rican case, Jay Kinsbruner has provided a brief but illuminating description of racial classifications for the eighteenth and nineteenth centuries: "Puerto Ricans recognized degrees of blackness, generally descending from white to *pardo,* to *moreno,* to *negro. Pardos* almost always were the free people of color of lightest skin color; *morenos* were darker skinned, and *negros* the darkest of all. These, nevertheless, were flexible terms, variously used."[8]

As in other parts of the Spanish empire, laws and social customs limited the opportunities available to free coloreds in Puerto Rico. Free people of color were not authorized to hold positions in the local *cabildo* (town council), nor were they allowed to obtain a university education. As plantation slavery intensified in Puerto Rico throughout the nineteenth century and abolition occurred in other Caribbean societies, the fear of slave revolt led local officials to impose new restrictions on free coloreds.[9] Still, people of color in Puerto Rico enjoyed some rights that separated them from the slave population, for example, the rights to belong to colored militias, travel freely, and pursue artisan and domestic occupations.

Around the mid-nineteenth century Spanish colonial officials and the city's elites enacted policies that pushed people of color from within the city limits into the extramural barrios surrounding San Juan. Women, the majority of both slave and free colored populations, were particularly affected by these policies of urban construction and relocation. The Spanish government developed the extramural barrios of La Marina and Puerta de Tierra for poor and colored people, many of whom were forced there by high rents within the city.

For colonial officials and members of the elite the relocation accomplished desirable goals. First, poor and colored workers would still be accessible to San Juan's intramural labor pool because of the proximity of the extramural barrios. Second, the government could pursue the construction of several military and civic installations in areas previously inhabited by San Juan's marginal classes. These areas of huts and shacks were considered an eyesore to the reform-oriented members of the city's upper classes. Finally, moving colored and poor people outside the city walls solved a security problem in a city where racial fears ran high.[10]

Several authors have shown that San Juan was a city of economic opportunity for free people of color.[11] Women, of course, benefited from the economic space that the peculiarities of the city's demographic and economic development provided. During the nineteenth century, urban centers such as San Juan profited from many services that women traditionally performed, among them cooking, cleaning, washing, sewing, gardening, nursing, and caring for the sick, old, and young. The services of free women of color were also associated with small-scale enterprises related to retail, housing, and transportation. In providing such services, free colored women commonly worked side by side with slaves.

Free colored women seem to have been well represented among owners of very small grocery shops and among street vendors in nineteenth-century San Juan. They operated numerous *ventorillos, fondas,* and other small establishments. Ventorillos sold low-quality spirits and fruit and vegetables produced in the city's hinterland. The 1846 census shows that women of color often operated these shops. One of these *ventorilleras* was Gertrudis Tanco, a thirty-four-year-old widow who was black.[12] Another ventorillera listed in that census, Juana de los Santos, was twenty-six, black, and single. Both Tanco and Santos lived in the Santa Bárbara barrio. Angela Belse, another ventorillera, lived in the San Francisco barrio. She was a single, twenty-seven-year-old free *parda* (mulatta) who lived alone in a room she rented from Doña María Antonia Pizarro.

Fondas, like ventorillos, were small establishments that catered to poor and working-class customers. The fondas depended on the solidarity and patronage of artisans, slaves, travelers, peons, and construction workers, among others. City residents and transients came looking not only for food and drink but also for entertainment, relaxation, and companionship. Fondas and other similar businesses were often family operations. The case of Catalina Munero is a good example. Munero, a seventy-year-old parda widow, was a *fondera* in San Juan. A native of Santo Domingo, she ran her business with the help of her five grandchildren, with whom she also lived.

Mondonguerías were another example of food-selling establishments controlled by women. *Mondongo* (tripe) is a type of stew prepared with the intestines and other inner parts of cows and pigs. In San Juan most mondongueras—women who prepared mondongo—were free women of color. Many of them were partners or relatives of butchers, most of whom lived near or in the Santa Bárbara barrio. The slaughterhouse was located next to this barrio on the outside part of the city's wall.[13] The town council designated an area contiguous to the slaughterhouse for mondongueras to conduct their sales, and women who ran these shops paid taxes to the municipal authorities to operate them.[14] Other mondongueras sold their product from their homes or in small roadhouses outside the city walls.

Feliciana Cueto was a forty-six-year-old black mondonguera who was married to a butcher.[15] She and her husband, José María, lived in their house along with one guest and four female slaves, all of whom were listed also as mondongueras. Another mondonguera was Lucía de Jésus, who resided on San Sebastían Street in the Santa Bárbara barrio, a street known in the nineteenth century as the "street of the mondongueras."[16] De Jésus, forty, was a mulatta and married to Juan Francisco Regis, for whom no occupation was listed in the 1846 census. She had three children aged nineteen, ten, and six.[17] In the same barrio as De Jésus lived a number of free colored women who raised the pigs that would be used to make the mondongo. Juana González and María Petrona Mosquera were listed as *puerqueras* (pig-raisers) in the census.[18] González, thirty-three, was a single mother of three infants. Mosquera, forty-eight and the mother of one, was married, but her husband was not listed in the census. Both women were mulattas.

Spanish authorities were always suspicious of mondonguerías because they were frequented by blacks, mulattos, libertos, and other "questionable characters." Colonial officials and elite members of society feared that racial and anti-Spanish conspiracies might be hatched in mondonguerías and watched them closely. Yet regardless of repeated harassment by authorities, mondonguerías remained popular establishments among the city's poor and colored residents.

Although the historical record does not offer much direct evidence, Spanish officials and elite sanjuaneros also suspected that prostitution was pursued at the various establishments patronized by the city's colored community. San Juan, with a high proportion of transient and military populations, was always a city in which the services of prostitutes were in high demand. For white sanjuaneros, the racist belief in the "natural" lasciviousness of people of color made the connection between nocturnal gatherings by free coloreds and illicit sex very probable. Several authors have speculated that the city's high numbers of mulattos and pardos—particularly slaves—could be explained by the widespread practices of concubinage and prostitution among the white and colored populations.[19] Although more research is needed before that argument can be accepted, there is no doubt that nineteenth-century colonial authorities were convinced that women of color, particularly those who were free, caused the problem of prostitution in San Juan.

It was common for free women of color to sell food and other items in the city's streets. Even when some had other forms of employment such as domestic service, they still sold food on the street or door-to-door in order to supplement their incomes. Both free and slave women were active as *revendonas* (street vendors). If it is true that many slave women used their earnings as street vendors or domestics to help pay for their manumissions, it is easy to assume that once they became free they continued in the same type of work. In that sense San Juan would be typical of other Caribbean urban centers where women of color flocked to street corners, trying to sell various goods, and urban slave-owners supplemented their earnings by allowing their slaves to sell their services and other goods door-to-door. In Kingston, Jamaica, for example, the practice was so common that officials repeatedly passed legislation prohibiting people of color from selling in the city's streets.[20] Female street vendors and hucksters also played conspicuous roles in other large Caribbean towns such as Bridgetown (Barbados), Havana (Cuba), Paramaribo (Surinam), and Saint-Pierre (Martinique).[21]

Most street vendors listed in San Juan's mid-nineteenth-century censuses were women of color, evidently either single persons or widows. At the time of the 1846 census, the revendona Ana Gabiel, who lived in the Santa Bárbara barrio, was a thirty-five-year-old single black slave who rented her own room and lived alone. Another revendona was Carmen Dorado, a widow. She was sixty, African-born, and black.[22] Ana María Guzmán, Guadalupe Rijos, Emilia Cristina, Rafaela, and Josefa all walked the city streets, trying to sell foodstuffs. A native of Curaçao, Guzmán, forty, was a black, single head of a household and had four young children to provide for.[23] Some of the other vendors seemed to have been young single women who were trying to make ends meet. Rafaela, for example, lived with a large household as an *agregada* (farmhand or domestic living on another farm or in another household) and was forty, single, and black. Emilia Cristina, a parda, was also forty and single.

Free women of color also went door-to-door as domestics, although some worked exclusively for one family and did not venture into the streets to secure additional clients. Laundry work was one of the most common forms of domestic employment.[24] Laundresses could provide full-time help at an elite family's house or at a state, church, or military institution. Others provided washing and ironing services to several individual clients. The women usually collected clients' clothing and took it away for washing. The vast majority of the women of San Juan who worked as laundresses were women of color, about two-thirds of them free and the other third slaves. The typical laundress in San Juan was a young, single, free woman of color.

Dorotea Ramos was, perhaps, a typical sanjuanera laundress. In 1846 she was listed as a single, twenty-three-year-old, free parda.[25] Ramos rented a room from

Don Manuel Valdez in the San Francisco barrio and had two young children. Bibiana Torres, another laundress with two children, lived in the San Francisco barrio.[26] She was black, single, and twenty-seven. Juana Ríos, also a laundress, was a twenty-two-year-old single mulatta who lived with her mother and two sisters on Cruz Street.[27] Her mother, Josefa, rented a room from another free woman of color, Ignacia Cisneros. Both Cisneros and Ríos's mother were seamstresses. Although most laundresses tended to be young, older free colored women followed this occupation as well, for example, María de la Encarnación, a free black.[28] She was forty-four and resided in an apartment with other free black women who worked as candy makers and laundresses. All data about these individuals come from the 1846 manuscript census for San Juan.

Until the abolition of slavery, it was customary in San Juan for other household domestics such as servants, cooks, and maids to be female slaves, but free women of color were also to be found among domestics. Manuela Escalera, for example, was a cook in the household of the influential Spanish merchant Don José J. Arranzamendi. Escalera, fifty, was a married parda.[29] Her husband is not listed in the 1846 census, but Escalera lived with two sons, one a carpenter and the other a shoemaker. Arranzamendi also had a female slave cook named Catalina. María Jacinta and Manuela Barriga were also cooks in the household of a seventy-two-year-old widow, Doña Feliciana Velazco.[30] Jacinta, eighteen, was a single free parda. Barriga was older (fifty-four), black, and not married. Domestic servants, for the most part, were slaves. Occasionally, a free woman of color such as Lucia Meclen worked as a servant. She was a single, twenty-eight-year-old parda who lived with the family of Don Ramón Cedeño on Tanca Street.[31]

Real estate was an important element in the urban economy of the walled city of San Juan. Military restrictions prevented the construction of buildings of more than two or three floors. I have shown elsewhere that women owned a significant amount of the real estate property in San Juan.[32] Business and inheritance practices appear to be among the main reasons for between 34 and 37 percent of the real estate properties in San Juan between 1820 and 1859 being owned by women.[33] These data are derived from city property lists, which, unfortunately, do not provide information on the property owner's racial origin. Still, evidence from the notary records shows that free women of color did own significant amounts of real estate in nineteenth-century San Juan.

More free colored than white women owned homes in the northeastern barrio of Santa Bárbara, where there was, as Jay Kinsbruner has argued, a substantial degree of house ownership.[34] Furthermore, more free colored than white women in this barrio owned real estate. House ownership numbers for free people of color in the other three intramural barrios—Fortaleza, Santo Domingo, and San Francisco—were quite small. In the selection of cases I have mentioned, many properties were located on the part of Sol Street connected to the Santa Bárbara barrio. The fact that, proportionately, more free women of color than white women owned the house in which they lived could also be tied to the high percentages of female-headed households among women of color.[35]

María Dolores Torres, for example, owned a small one-floor house on Sol Street in 1844; she was a free black widow in her sixties.[36] Also in 1844 and on the same Sol Street, Hilaria Torres sold her one-story stone house to Pedro Atencio for 500 pesos. Torres, also a widow, had inherited the house from her deceased husband, Juan Pablo Latorre.[37] At the time of the sale, Torres, a free *morena*, could not sign her name. In 1829, María de la Concepción Ramos, a free parda, sold half of her house to Fernando Sierra for 200 pesos.[38] The house, built on land that belonged to the town council, was also in the section of Sol Street located within the Santa Bárbara barrio.

Former slaves owned real estate in San Juan. Such was the case for María de la Cruz Morales, a black who at the time of the writing of her will could not provide the notary with her parents' names, "given the sad condition in which my countrymen left [Africa]." Morales, a seventy-year-old widow at the time she drafted the will in 1861, left her one-story house located next to the Carmelite convent to the three sons of a friend.[39] Some free colored women also rented houses and rooms to others. Bernarda Baez, a mulatta widow, rented a one-story house on San Sebastían Street to Pablo Abadía, a married mulatto tailor, thirty-three, who lived with his wife Vicenta Megías and had no children.[40]

The free women of color of San Juan who were actively involved in the small retail, street vending, and domestic work of the city's economic life did not ordinarily experience unqualified success or lack of struggle. If life for many of them could be very hard, it could be even harder for women who had no trade, no family, or were old. It was because of hardship that Catalina Cestero petitioned the governor for a plot of land to build a small house in Puerta de Tierra, one of the extramural barrios.[41] Cestero, a free colored, was born in San Juan and lived in the nearby town of Cangrejos. She complained that because of her old age and poverty adolescents pelted her humble shack at night. She feared for her life. She decided to try to move into Puerta de Tierra because she felt that the proximity to Spanish military garrisons would protect her from the nightly assaults. After the governor requested an investigation of Cestero's claim, an aide suggested that her request be granted because she was "a poor soul worthy of receiving any good one might do on her behalf."

Free Women of Color, Racial Tensions, Labor Shortages, and Abolition

Between 1835 and 1873 several important changes occurred: a steady decline in sugar prices and increased competition from other sugar-producing regions; increased difficulty in securing slaves for Puerto Rico plantations as a result of added British pressure to Spain to enforce treaties for ending the slave trade;

added experimentation with different forms of coerced nonslave labor; increased momentum in favor of abolition of slavery on the island as many Caribbean islands adopted "free" labor arrangements; and heightened racial tensions in the society of Puerto Rico due to fears of a slave revolt modeled after Haiti or encouraged by other Caribbean slave revolts during the 1840s. All of these developments, in conjunction with the financial crises that San Juan experienced at that time, shaped the attitude of the colonial elite and government to the freedom of free women of color in San Juan. Libertas in San Juan paid the price for the uncertainty sanjuaneros and sanjuaneras faced in regard to the configuration of race, labor, and gender hierarchies once slavery dissolved in Puerto Rico.

No matter how free people of color in Puerto Rico responded to slavery—either by buying slaves themselves or by treating slaves without any sense of racial solidarity, for example—most of San Juan's white population feared the role that free coloreds could play should there be racial rebellion. The fact that free people of color had some black ancestry convinced whites that all nonwhites would join forces in the case of a slave rebellion—Haiti being the most prominent example. The predominance of people of color in San Juan's population until the middle of the nineteenth century exacerbated tensions in Puerto Rico, a colony perpetually in fear of a slave or mulatto uprising. Spanish officials and elite members of society also expressed concern about the potential demographic and cultural "Africanization" of Puerto Rico.[42] As a result, both Spanish law and colonial social custom always carried a suspicious bias against the activities of all free people of color in San Juan. Spanish colonial officials also regarded free people of color as untrustworthy because they perceived that antislavery and pro-independence (anti-Spanish) sentiment necessarily went hand-in-hand. The officials were convinced that one of the lessons to be learned from Haitian and South American independence struggles was that those who advocated severing colonial ties were also abolitionist agitators. In Puerto Rico, free people of color were regarded with fear and suspicion, not only because of their potential alliance with slave rebels but also because of their possible anti-Spanish and anticolonial sentiments.[43]

The business activities and places that people of color, free or slave, favored in San Juan were always under the careful scrutiny of colonial police officials. Night dances, cockfights, small parties, and even gatherings in makeshift food establishments were all under surveillance if those in attendance were people of color, free or slave. Dominga Muriel and Justa Santana, for example, were identified as "suspicious women" in a police report because both of these free colored women hosted parties on Saturday nights.[44] Although the police agent could find no evidence that illegal activities took place at those parties, the fact that people of color gathered was enough to attract official attention.

The same police agent who reported on Muriel and Santana also brought the activities of another free black woman, María Concepción, to the attention of his superiors. Concepción, a mondonguera, operated a small roadside shack where peons, workers, and other "characters of dubious reputation" would buy food.[45] Quite often they would engage in unruly behavior that finally drove the police agent to order Concepción to close her shop at 8 P.M. If Concepción did not obey the order she would be placed as a domestic in the house of a respectable family in San Juan. That the police agent considered such a form of punishment appropriate is indicative of the hardship and loss of personal freedom that domestic work imposed on women of color, serving as a good mechanism of social control to "domesticate" and train riotous and uneducated plebeian women.

The presence of laundresses in important public spaces such as plazas or water fountains placed them at odds with city authorities in San Juan. Laundresses, the majority of whom were women of color, made colonial officials uneasy because their gatherings were suspected to be perfect breeding grounds for seditious activity. The colonial elite also resented the boisterousness of these public spaces, where laundresses washed, rinsed, dried, and folded clothes. As they worked they were often accompanied by children and other relatives, so the work was combined with much loud conversation and active child supervision. Male colonial officials, most certainly, must have been uneasy about interacting within such a "feminine" environment in public plazas and fountains. Both church and crown officials complained about the lack of decorum and order they felt characterized the city's public wells and fountains. As San Juan's inhabitants grew more conscious of the latest European trends in the use of public spaces and plazas, the spectacle of laundresses in the plazas became objectionable. Late in the nineteenth century, city officials drafted plans for the construction of a huge fountain and washing place outside the city's walls.[46] It would have been located in the Puerta de Tierra barrio, where unruly behavior would be less of a nuisance. Disguised behind a facade of urban development, hygiene, and ideas about progress, the attempt to remove poor and colored women from public spaces was a defensive strategy and reflected official apprehension of the dislocations the eventual emancipation of slaves might cause.

Laundresses posed a real threat to the colonial establishment. On several occasions they organized themselves to demand proper working conditions or defend their rights.[47] In 1842, for example, laundresses from the Hospital de la Caridad complained and went on strike because they could not get enough water from that hospital's cistern to supply their needs.[48] They wanted the town council to allow them access to cisterns in Ballajá; no water translated into no work and no pay. In 1856 laundresses were also able to secure an increase of 1 real per dozen from the chief of the Military Hospital, Don Pablo Canto.[49] When he became chief, Canto had wanted to improve the quality of the laundry service but was able to accomplish that only after negotiating the salary increase with the laundresses.

The racism inherent in Puerto Rico's slave-based society and economy undoubtedly stigmatized free women of color. Some racial classifications usually employed to describe them in official documents, such as "mulatta," were often fighting words if uttered publicly in San Juan. In 1860 two free women of color, Margarita Sola and Salustiana González, appeared in court to request public apologies from each other.[50] Sola argued that González called her "witch, drunk, and shameless." Gonzalez responded that it was true that she insulted Sola, but that was only after Sola called her "whore, *mulata,* and bitch." Furthermore, González said that Sola struck her with a brick. In the end the judge dismissed the case for lack of witnesses. In another case, two married women, López and Salcedo, who resided at the Casa de Beneficencia, also exchanged racial epithets and went to court seeking a public apology.[51] López accused Salcedo of insulting her by calling her a "woman of the street, a mulata, and a *lame plato* [plate-licker]."[52] Salcedo agreed that she insulted Lopez, but she did so only after being first branded a mulatta. The initial hearing of this case was suspended until eyewitnesses from the Casa de Beneficencia could be summoned to testify. They affirmed that they had no knowledge of the incident, but Salcedo was a known troublemaker and often insulted others by calling them mulatto or mulatta. Salcedo finally pleaded guilty, apologized to López, and agreed to leave the Casa de Beneficencia within a month. It is obvious that the apparently descriptive racial categories used by census takers and other officials in nineteenth-century San Juan carried a very different meaning when used in everyday life. For many women, white or colored, being called a mulatta was the same as being called a prostitute and/or a lower-class woman without honor.

Officials in San Juan were also concerned about the stability of families in the city. The example of the mulatta Balbina Alonso indicates the attention that church and colonial officials gave to affairs concerning adultery, particularly if women of color were involved. Such concerns, particularly acute among members of the Catholic clergy, were not guided exclusively by moral and religious principles but more importantly by concerns about the quality of the city's labor pool. For colonial officials and San Juan's elite, concubinage was also a problem that often led to vagrancy. In 1849 Governor Juan de la Pezuela argued that concubinage "destroys the inner peace of families, diminishes the population and the number of laborers, and sets a pernicious example for the unwary."[53]

Because officials were concerned about securing an abundant supply of household workers in the second half of the nineteenth century, concubinage became an important issue in religious and political circles. The emergence during the mid-nineteenth century of an anticoncubinage campaign affected free women of color directly and not only because of the racial attitudes that associated sexual promiscuity with mulattas and other free colored women. It was also because of the high number of female-headed households among free women of color in San Juan. The large demographic imbalance between male and female free coloreds in the city has been identified as one of the causes of this high incidence of female-headed households.[54]

Free colored women as heads of households worried city authorities for three reasons. First, the unmarried status of these women meant that they tended not to bear children regularly and thus did not adequately replenish the labor pool. Second, the women were perceived as an "easy" temptation or prey for men, particularly white men. Third, the existence of such women who were not under the clear control of a male head of household provided a destabilizing model in a society deeply rooted in patriarchy, authority, and colonialism. For a variety of reasons, therefore, all of them related to the character of colonial slave society in Puerto Rico, free women of color were collectively subjected to official surveillance and control.

As the debate about the emancipation of slaves in Puerto Rico advanced during the 1850s, urban authorities worried about replacing the urban domestic slaves. Indeed, San Juan residents were also much concerned about the example that free people of color, particularly women, would set for newly liberated slaves in a postabolition society.[55] The abolition of slavery clearly presented problems of labor supply and of alterations to the racial and social hierarchies that had ruled city life since the turn of the nineteenth century. San Juan experienced a shortage of workers in the second half of the nineteenth century, but it was not that there were not enough women available to work as domestics. It was because demographic and economic changes in the city made women less willing to accept the elite's terms of employment. The supply of domestic workers in San Juan was affected by demographic changes (fewer women and fewer people of color), a cholera epidemic in 1855, an increase in the price of slaves as a result of the end of the slave trade, and fears arising from the impending abolition of slavery in Puerto Rico.

Beginning in the second half of the nineteenth century, urban slavery in San Juan entered an economic crisis. Rising inflation, ever-increasing prices of basic goods, a shortage of domestic slaves, and the difficulty of providing for those slaves directly affected the viability of slavery in the city. The crisis, similar to those in several other Caribbean and Latin American cities and combined with the changing demographic patterns of San Juan, marked not only the limits of attempts to regulate domestic work but also terms of supply and demand for domestic work.[56] The crisis also complicated the lives of many of San Juan's free women of color.

With urban slavery in economic and ideological jeopardy, colonial authorities and the sanjuanero elite tried to find new methods for securing a reliable urban domestic labor force. The difficulty of obtaining domestics forced Spanish authorities to initiate a campaign to identify and control workers early in the second half of the nineteenth century. In 1858 the central government of Puerto Rico prepared lists of domestics and unemployed people in each of the island's towns.[57] By 1864 the town council of San Juan went further and collected a list of women and men older than fourteen who would "rent themselves for permanent domestic work in someone else's home, cooking, washing, cleaning and taking care of a home or family or analogous occupations."[58] The municipal compilation, created from an islandwide one, included information regarding all work contracts issued to domestics. The 1864 regulations required that domestics show "obedience, fidelity and respect" to employers, whose reciprocal obligations were not stated. Violations applied to domestic workers, and penalties included a fine of 4 reales or a day in jail. For employers, there were no specific penalties.

These regulations were part of an islandwide effort during the 1860s to reinstate and reinforce some of the coercive labor policies designed during the 1830s and 1840s.[59] In 1871, just two years before the abolition of slavery and a year after the Moret Law freed older slaves, the government of Puerto Rico enacted another set of regulations pertaining to domestic work.[60] It was evident that the colonial elite was preparing to secure the numbers of domestic workers that would be needed once slavery disappeared. Most of these domestic workers were free women of color.

Conclusion

Throughout the nineteenth century, free women of color were a fundamental part of San Juan's urban culture. They walked the city's streets and occupied the city's plazas, selling goods or services to sanjuanero residents. By providing these services, free women of color catered not only to the racially diverse civilian population but also to the military, ecclesiastical, and colonial bureaucracies that made San Juan their home. Free women of color also owned more sedentary businesses such as food and recreation establishments, small stores, and real estate, particularly in the city's northeasternmost barrio of Santa Bárbara. Although difficult, the lives of many of them provided some independence and flexibility not readily available to white or slave women.

But the fragile independence and mobility of free colored sanjuaneras carried a price in the relentless supervision and control imposed on them by Spanish colonial officials and members of San Juan's elite. The upper-class fear of increased demographic and cultural "Africanization" of Puerto Rico made free women of color a target of suspicion and scorn. Still, San Juan's reliance on the domestic work they performed meant that colonial officials were forced to tolerate some of their urban mobility and freedoms. As the political struggle about the emancipation of slaves in Puerto Rico began to favor the abolitionists, the colonial authorities and elite of San Juan became concerned about the potential example for independence and autonomy that free women of color, particularly domestics, could set for urban slaves. Whites in San Juan were evidently concerned not only about being able to retain reliable and cheap domestic workers after emancipation but also with maintaining the racial, gender, and class hierarchies that slavery had guaranteed.[61]

Toward the end of the 1860s the impact of the growing economic crisis in the sugar export economy and the threatened or anticipated collapse of the slave-based labor system greatly complicated relations between white sanjuaneros and sanjuaneras and free women of color. Instead of marking a point of rupture in San Juan, the abolition of slavery in Puerto Rico in 1873 continued the racial and gender-based tensions and hierarchies that free women of color of the city had experienced since the 1840s, particularly the large majority of them who earned their livings as domestic workers.

Notes

1. Alonso was born in the nearby Spanish colony of Santo Domingo. Her case is found in the Archivo General de Puerto Rico (hereafter AGPR), Fondo Gobernadores Españoles (hereafter FGEPR), Caja (hereafter C) 285, Ecclesiastical Affairs. She was classified as both a *parda* and a *mulatta* in several documents, a warning about employing nineteenth-century racial classifications rigidly.

2. For an example of how the state can intervene in public morality to solidify its power, see Teresita Martínez Vergne, *Discourses of Domination and Resistance in Nineteenth-Century San Juan, Puerto Rico* (Austin: University of Texas Press, 1999); Eileen Findlay, "Domination, Decency, and Desire: The Politics of Sexuality in Ponce, Puerto Rico (1870–1920)," Ph.D. diss., University of Wisconsin-Madison, 1995; Anne Staples, *"Policía y Buen Gobierno:* Municipal Efforts to Regulate Public Behavior, 1821–1857," in *Rituals of Rule, Rituals of Resistance: Public Celebrations and Popular Culture in Mexico,* ed. William H. Beezley, Cheryl E. Martin, and William E. French (Wilmington: Scholarly Resources Books, 1994), 115–26; and Elizabeth Dore, "Property, Households, and Public Regulation of Domestic Life: Diriomo, Nicaragua, 1840–1900," *Journal of Latin American Studies* 29 (Oct. 1977): 591–612.

3. For a review of the literature regarding women's history in Puerto Rico, see Félix V. Matos Rodríguez, "Puerto Rican Women's History: The Last Thirty Years," in *Puerto Rican Women's History: New Perspectives,* ed. Félix V. Matos Rodríguez and Linda Delgado (Armonk: M. E. Sharpe, 1998), 9–37. For reviews of the Caribbean literature on colored women, see, among others, Verene Shepherd, Bridget Brereton, and Barbara Bailey, eds., *Engendering History: Caribbean Women in Historical Perspective* (Kingston: Ian Randle, 1995); David Barry Gaspar and Darlene Clark Hine, eds., *More than Chattel: Black Women and Slavery in the Americas* (Bloomington: Indiana University Press, 1996); Barbara Bush, *Slave Women in Caribbean Society, 1650–1838* (Bloomington: Indiana University Press, 1990); Hilary Beckles, *Natural Rebels: A Social History of Enslaved Black Women in Barbados* (New Brunswick: Rutgers University Press, 1989); and Marietta Morrissey, *Slave Women in the New World: Gender Stratification in the Caribbean* (Lawrence: University of Kansas Press, 1989).

4. Félix V. Matos Rodríguez, "Spatial and Demographic Change in Nineteenth-Century San Juan, Puerto Rico, (1800–1820)," *Journal of Urban History* 24 (May 1999): 478–81.

5. For a detailed discussion of demographic change in nineteenth-century San Juan, see Matos Rodríguez, "Spatial and Demographic Change."

6. With these figures it is surprising that many scholars interested in the fate of free colored populations in the Americas have often disregarded nineteenth-century Puerto Rico. For population comparisons, see Jay Kinsbruner, *Not of Pure Blood: The Free People of Color and Racial Prejudice in Nineteenth-Century Puerto Rico* (Durham: Duke University Press, 1996), 29–31.

7. The data come from Matos Rodríguez, "Spatial and Demographic Change," 486.

8. Jay Kinsbruner, "Caste and Capitalism in the Caribbean: Residential Patterns and Household Ownership among the Free People of Color of San Juan, Puerto Rico, 1823–1846," *Hispanic American Historical Review* 70 (Aug. 1990): 438. For additional information on these gradations in the context of other Latin American and Caribbean societies, see Thomas M. Stephens, *Dictionary of*

Latin American Racial and Ethnic Terminology (Gainesville: University of Florida Press, 1989), 160–62, 167, 178–79, 197–98, 246–50.

9. For a more comprehensive review of the rights and limits of free coloreds in Puerto Rican society in the mid-nineteenth century, see Kinsbruner, *Not of Pure Blood,* 19–27; and Jorge L. Chinea, "Race, Colonial Exploitation and West Indian Immigration in Nineteenth Century Puerto Rico, 1800–1850," *The Americas* 52 (1996): 506–17.

10. Anibal Sepúlveda Rivera, *San Juan: Historia ilustrada de su desarollo urbano, 1508–1898* (San Juan: Carimar, 1989), 192–225, 251–69; Matos Rodríguez, "Spatial and Demographic Change."

11. Kinsbruner, *Not of Pure Blood,* 79–80, 138–41; Mariano Negrón Portillo and Raúl Mayo Santana, *La esclavitud urbana en San Juan: Estudio del Registro de Jornaleros de Esclavos de 1872* (Rio Piedras: Ediciones Huracán, 1992), 71–78; Félix V. Matos Rodríguez, "Economy, Society and Urban Life: Women in Nineteenth Century San Juan, Puerto Rico (1820–1870)," Ph.D. diss., Columbia University, 1994, 235–42.

12. AGPR, Censos San Juan, Barrio Santa Bárbara, 1846, 14v (Tanco) and fol. 34 (De los Santos).

13. The slaughterhouse was east of the La Perla garrison. Sepúlveda Rivera, *San Juan: Historia ilustrada,* 292.

14. AGPR, Fondo Municipal de San Juan, Actas del Cabildo, Nov. 15, 1843, fol. 231 and June 15, 1846, fol. 160.

15. AGPR, Censos San Juan, Santa Bárbara barrio, 1823, House no. 62.

16. Alejandro Tapia y Rivera, *Mis memorias o Puerto Rico como lo encontré y como lo dejo,* 3d ed. (Rio Piedras: Editorial Edil, 1979), 51.

17. AGPR, Censos San Juan, Barrio Santa Bárbara, 1846, 45v.

18. Ibid., 57 (González) and 63v (Mosquera).

19. José E. Flores Ramos, "Eugenesia, higiene pública y alconfor para las pasiones: La prostitución en San Juan de Puerto Rico, 1876–1919," master's thesis, University of Puerto Rico–Rio Piedras, 1995, 104–10, 203–4. Like Susan Socolow in her research on Cap Françaid in Haiti, I was unable to locate direct references to prostitutuion in my research. Susan Socolow, "Economic Roles of the Free Women of Color of Cap Français," in *More Than Chattel: Black Women and Slavery in the Americas,* ed. David Barry Gaspar and Darlene Clark Hine (Bloomington: Indiana University Press, 1996), 281.

20. Sheena Boa, "Urban Free Black and Coloured Women: Jamaica, 1760–1834," *Jamaican Historical Review* 18 (1993): 4.

21. See, among others, Levi Marrero, *Cuba: Economía y Sociedad* (Madrid: Editorial Playor, 1986), 13: 152–53; Bernard Moitt, "Women, Work, and Resistance in the French Caribbean during Slavery, 1700–1848," in *Engendering History: Caribbean Women in Historical Perspective,* ed. Verene Shepherd, Bridget Brereton, and Barbara Bailey (Kingston: Ian Randle, 1995), 70; and Rosemary Brana-Shute, "Negotiating Freedom in Urban Suriname, 1770–1830," in *From Chattel Slaves to Wage Slaves: The Dynamics of Labour Bargaining in the Americas,* ed. Mary Turner (Bloomington: Indiana University Press, 1995), 148–64.

22. AGPR, Censos San Juan, Barrio Santa Bárbara, 1846, fol. 39 (Gabiel) and fol. 40 (Dorado).

23. The data from Guzmán and the other street vendors come from AGPR, Censos San Juan, Barrio Santo Domingo, 1846, fol. 27.

24. For a general discussion of the number and characteristics of domestic workers in mid-nineteenth-century San Juan, see Félix V. Matos Rodríguez, "Street Vendors, Pedlars, Shop-Owners, and Domestics: Some Aspects of Women's Economic Roles in Nineteenth-Century San Juan, Puerto Rico (1820–1870)," in *Engendering History: Caribbean Women in Historical Perspective,* ed. Verene Shepherd, Bridget Brereton, and Barbara Bailey (Kingston: Ian Randle, 1995), 184–90.

25. AGPR, Censos San Juan, San Francisco barrio, 1846, 4–4v.

26. Ibid., 9v-10.

27. AGPR, Censos San Juan, Santo Domingo barrio, 1846, 2.

28. AGPR, FGEPR, C-563, "Padrón de Almas de Santa Bárbara, 1823," House no. 7.

29. Ibid., House nos. 9–10.

30. AGPR, FGEPR, C-563, "Padrón de Almas de Santa Bárbara, 1823," House no. 113.

31. AGPR, Censos San Juan, San Francisco barrio, 1846, 113.

32. Félix V. Matos Rodríguez, *Women and Urban Change in Nineteenth Century San Juan, Puerto Rico (1820–1868)* (Gainesville: University of Florida Press, 1999), 66–70. Kinsbruner has also explored San Juan's housing market (*Not of Pure Blood*, 68–79).

33. There is not much information about real estate owned by women of color in other colonies of the Caribbean. Socolow, "Economic Roles of Free Women"; David P. Geggus, "Slave and Free Colored Women in Saint Domingue," in *More Than Chattel: Black Women and Slavery in the Americas*, ed. David Barry Gaspar and Darlene Clark Hine (Bloomington: Indiana University Press, 1996), 269–73.

34. Kinsbruner, *Not of Pure Blood*, 70. The city was segmented into four quarters by using Luna (north/south boundary) and Cruz (east/west) streets as dividing lines. Between 1800 and 1859 the city's four intramural barrios were (1) Santo Domingo on the northwestern side, surrounding the Dominican convent and the small plaza by the convent's side; (2) Foraleza on the southwestern side, including the cathedral, the Carmelite convent, the Plaza de Armas, and the captain general–governor's quarters; (3) Santa Bárbara (named after the hermitage located there), which included the northeastern side and the new market and a gunpowder arsenal; and (4) San Francisco in the southeastern part of the city, named after the Franciscan church and convent located at the barrio's center. For a history of the development of these barrios, see María de los Angeles Castro, *Arquitectura en San Juan de Puerto Rico (siglo XIX)* (Rio Piedras: Editorial Universitaria, 1980), 134–36; and Sepúlveda Rivera, *San Juan: Historia ilustrada*, 248–51.

35. Kinsbruner, *Not of Pure Blood*, 71.

36. AGPR, FPNSJ, Juan B. Nuñez, C-502, July 19, 1844, 202–2v. This property is listed in Torres's will. She also owned a female slave valued at 300 pesos and numerous pieces of furniture. Torres did not know her parents.

37. AGPR, FPNSJ, Juan B. Nuñez, C-502, Aug. 14, 1844, 231v-34.

38. AGPR, FPNSJ, Juan B. Nuñez, C-478, Feb. 18, 1829, 124v-25.

39. AGPR, FPNSJ, Manuel Camuñas, C-29, Nov. 29, 1861, 574v-75.

40. AGPR, Censos San Juan, Santa Bárbara barrio, 47v. Baez was the source of scandal in 1846 when church officials allowed her to be the cathedral's bell-ringer in place of her incapacitated, later deceased, husband. Matos Rodríguez, *Women and Urban Change*, 1–2.

41. AGPR, FGEPR, C-566, Oct. 30, 1826.

42. For an account of the fear of a racial uprising and of the "Africanization" of Puerto Rico, see Chinea, "Race, Colonial Exploitation," 510–17.

43. Ibid., 509–18.

44. AGPR, FGEPR, C-163, April 23, 1840.

45. Ibid.

46. The 1878 proposal for the public *lavadero* is found in AGPR, Fondo Obras Publicas (hereafter FOP), Obras Municipales, L-62LL, E-15, C-326.

47. See, for example, the account of the struggle between Cangrejo's alcalde and the laundress who used the San Antonio fountain. AGPR, FOP, Obras Municipales, L-62LL, E-13, C-236, July 14, 1857.

48. The incident is mentioned in various documents. AGPR, FMSJ, Actas del Cabildo, May 4, 1842, 88v and June 30, 1842, fol. 122; another reference is found in AGPR, FOP, Edificios Públicos, San Juan, L-119, C-693.

49. Archivo Historico Nacional, S-Ultramar, Se-Gobierno de Puerto Rico, L-5087, E-10, July 4, 1862.

50. AGPR, FMSJ, L-73E, P-4, E-68, Feb. 24, 1860.

51. On the role and objectives of the Casa de Beneficencia, see Teresita Martínez Vergne, "The Allocation of Liberated African Labour through the Casa de Beneficencia—San Juan, Puerto Rico,

1859–1864," *Slavery and Abolition* 12 (1991): 200–216; Teresita Martínez Vergne, "The Liberal Concept of Charity: Beneficencia Applied to Puerto Rico, 1821–1868," in *The Middle Period in Latin America: Values and Attitudes in the Seventeenth-Nineteenth Centuries,* ed. Mark D. Szuchman (Boulder: Lynne Rienner, 1989), 167–84; Vergne, *Discourses of Domination;* and Matos Rodríguez, *Women and Urban Change,* 105–14.

52. AGPR, FMSJ, L-73E, P-4, E-67, July 5 and 10, 1860.

53. This is my translation from Pezuela's 1849 antivagrancy and anticoncubinage *bando* (edict). The bando is quoted in the *Boletin Eclesiástico,* Sept. 15, 1861, 217.

54. Kinsbruner, *Not of Pure Blood,* 107–9. Kinsbruner has also argued that racial groups in San Juan tended to marry within their own group.

55. Pedro L. Welch, "Notes from the Bridgetown Underground: Control and Protest in Post-Emancipation Barbados," presented at the annual meeting of the Society of Caribbean Historians, Bridgetown, Barbados, April 17, 1996.

56. María Odila Silva Dias, *Power and Everyday Life: The Lives of Working Women in Nineteenth-Century Brazil* (New Brunswick: Rutgers University Press, 1995).

57. The list also included agricultural workers. AGPR, FGEPR, Censo y Riqueza, 1858, C-16.

58. "Reglamento que ha de observarse en la locación del trabajo personal para el servicio doméstico," ch. 5, art. 6, in AGPR, FGEPR, S-Nunicipios, C-480, June 8, 1864.

59. Labor Gomez Acevedo, *Organización y reglamentación del trabajo en el Puerto Rico del siglo XIX: Propietarios y jornaleros,* (San Juan: Instituto de Cultura Puertorriqueña, 1970), 117–23.

60. AGPR, FMSJ, L-24G, E-941, April 3, 1876.

61. See Francisco Scarano's remarks about the "four hierarchies of difference" connected with slavery in "Liberal Pacts and Hierarchies of Rule: Approaching the Imperial Transition in Cuba and Puerto Rico," *Hispanic American Historical Review* 78 (Nov. 1998): 595–96.

CHAPTER 11

Landlords, Shopkeepers, Farmers, and Slave-Owners: Free Black Female Property-Holders in Colonial New Orleans

Kimberly S. Hanger

During the era of effective Spanish rule (1769–1803) free *libre* (black) women—whether single, married, or widowed—came to control a substantial portion of the economic resources of New Orleans. There emerged what might be considered a free black elite, although not on the scale of the *gens de couleur* (people of color) of Saint-Domingue in the same period or of the large free black property-holders that made Louisiana distinctive in the antebellum U.S. South.[1] Nevertheless, it was during the Spanish period that free black women in New Orleans made their greatest advances in regard to demographics, privileges, responsibilities, and social standing.[2] As the number of libre women of colonial New Orleans increased, they inherited or purchased with their earnings many of the city's residential and rental properties, retail outlets, taverns, and surrounding farmlands as well as the slaves to operate them.

Most free black women struggled to survive, and they worked hard. Few were able to lead a life of idle luxury. Even those fortunate enough to acquire estates through inheritance had to work to preserve them intact and pass them on to the next generation. A careful survey of free black economic activities discounts the contemporary view of travelers and residents, popular throughout the Americas, that libres were by nature "idle, debauched, drunken, liars, ridiculously vain, insolent, and cowardly."[3] On the contrary, free blacks astutely availed themselves of legal, demographic, economic, and political conditions in Spanish New Orleans to attain economic stability—even prosperity—and advance their own and future generations' social standing. Occasionally, their actions incited the envy and resentment of their white neighbors, tenants, and customers and led to legal and even physical contests over scarce resources.

Under the French (1699–1769) and Spanish regimes libres ideally had legal rights and privileges equal to those of white citizens. Local regulations and customs occasionally curtailed their efficacy, but in general free blacks "were guaranteed equal property rights and full rights to make contracts and engage in all business transactions."[4] Unlike the French *Code noir,* Spanish law also permitted Louisiana's libres and slaves to accept donations of realty and personalty, including slaves as property, from whites and other free blacks. During the Spanish period "the free colored class was economically active and enjoyed full freedom to arrange contracts, own and transfer property, and bring suit, even if it involved civil litigation against whites."[5] Free black women in particular exercised these rights to assert their independence and provide for their own welfare and that of their families.

Landlords

Libre women participated actively in the burgeoning economy of New Orleans. They bought, sold and leased land and houses in the city. A census of the Third District of New Orleans for 1796 listed the proprietors and tenants of each house. Although including only about one in seven of all residents (200 of 1,408) and one in five free inhabitants (200 of 1,043), free black women owned more than a fourth of the houses in the district (64 of 231). Comparable figures for white women were fewer than one in ten total residents (130 of 1,408), one in eight free residents (130 of 1,043), and about one-eighth of homeowners (31 of 231, or fewer than half that of libre women).[6]

A list of losses incurred earlier in the first great fire that swept through colonial New Orleans in March 1788 is another useful source for estimating the real and personal property holdings of the city's free black women, and for comparing these holdings with those of libre men and white men and women. In September 1788, city officials submitted to the Spanish crown a compendium of 496 claims for damage to buildings and interior furnishings (plus ten claims to government and church property) that totaled more than 2.5 million pesos (the peso being equivalent to the dollar at the time). Fifty-one claimants were free black women, whose average estimated loss of real and personal property was 1,814 pesos. Free black men made up only twenty-one of the claimants, with an average loss of 1,700 pesos. Another sixty-seven claimants were white women (average loss of 2,880 pesos), almost half of them widows; the remaining 357 claims were made by white men. The average claim of white males, 6,090 pesos, was more than double that of white females and about three and a half times greater than that of free black women or men.[7] Clearly, white men possessed the vast majority of material wealth in late-eighteenth-century New Orleans.

Nevertheless, more free black women held property than did free black men, and that property was also more valuable.

The rents libre landladies could claim in the tight housing market of New Orleans occasionally earned them the ire of white tenants who found themselves helpless. One recourse was to appeal to the Spanish judicial system's sense of order, hierarchy, and fairness according to status. This is exactly what Andrés Barba did when the free *mulata* (an offspring of a white and a black or *negro*) Mariana Brion raised his rent twice in a two-year period. Barba had agreed to lease two houses and a room from Brion at 19 pesos per month for one year, when Brion, without warning, increased the rate to 24 pesos. Because it was too inconvenient to move and the houses were full, Barba reluctantly agreed to pay what he considered an unfair rate. He continued to pay the rent punctually each month. At the end of another year Brion again raised the rent, this time to 40 pesos per month. Barba could stand no more and looked to the court for redress against an "abuse so prejudicial to public tranquility" (un abuso tan perjudicial a la tranquilidad pública). In particular, Barba asked authorities to assess a just rent that he would be more than happy to pay. Apparently justice was not swift enough to satisfy Barba. He submitted a second petition two and a half weeks later, claiming that nothing had been done about his initial complaint. The case ended without judicial resolution.[8]

Shopkeepers

Entrepreneurial libre women also sometimes angered the white and libre men with whom they competed as small business owners. Free black women dominated local retail activity. They ran small commercial establishments such as shops and stalls or peddled goods, which they either made themselves or purchased wholesale from another merchant or producer, through the streets of the city and along roads leading into it. Ethnohistorian Daniel H. Usner, Jr., emphasizes the important contribution of women to food marketing and the frontier exchange economy: "Women in general played a prominent role in town markets, but African-American women became perhaps the most influential buyers and sellers of food in New Orleans."[9] City Treasurer Pedro Pizanie collected 81 pesos from the slave women and other individuals who sold in the Congo marketplace (las negras y otros individuos que venden en la Conga del mercado), Congo Square of later fame, in 1787.[10] Early in the nineteenth century, Thomas Ashe, a traveler, remarked that "people of color, and free negroes, [along with Spaniards] also keep inferior shops, and sell goods and fruits."[11] According to the 1795 census of New Orleans, seventeen free black female household heads were *revendeuses* (secondhand dealers), and eleven were *marchandes* (shopkeepers).[12] One retail dealer, the *morena* (dark-skinned) libra Margarita Trudeau, saved enough money to purchase the freedom of her forty-year-old son for 800 pesos from the Widow Trudeau, who was also Margarita's former owner.[13]

In response to increases in the number of retailers and to complaints that street vendors posed unfair competition, the *cabildo* (municipal council) resolved to construct a central and permanent market near the levee in 1784. Cabildo members in part created the marketplace to tax and regulate the city's burgeoning commerce. Such an arrangement benefited several interested parties. The cabildo would receive rents for the use of the stalls. Shopkeepers could reduce prices, costs, and competition because their overhead expenses would now more closely match those of stall renters. And the general public could purchase officially regulated products at a central location. When the fire of 1788 consumed the marketplace the cabildo authorized its replacement in the mid-1790s.[14]

Few libre women rented stalls directly from the city council; whether they chose not to do so or were pressured into it is unknown. Of the thirty-three persons licensed to vend goods from stalls on the levee in 1795, only two were free blacks, both of them males.[15] Apparently, however, license-holders rarely actually sold items from these stalls but rather sublet them to free black and slave women. In 1797 Manuel de Guerra conferred a power of attorney upon Perina Armesto, a free morena, to sell goods from his *tienda* (shop) on the levee at prices that would bring him the greatest advantage.[16] Describing the market that "adjoins the levée at the lower end of the Town," the New York merchant John Pintard wrote in 1801:

> Market hours commense at 6 & are mostly over by 8. . . . Very few people go to the market in person. . . . All is brought by domestics . . . especially the females . . . who seem to be the chief buyers & sellers of the place. . . . One meets with wenches with large flat baskets containing all kinds of goods with a measure in her hand traversing the streets & country in all directions . . . they are experts in selling . . . wait upon the ladies with their wares and are very honest & faithful to their employers.[17]

From this account it appears that hawkers, most of whom were women, continued to roam city streets long after the marketplace was established. In 1797 Don Fernando Alsar and Co. together with fifty other *mercaderes* (shopkeepers or retail merchants) petitioned the town council to prohibit the activities of increasing numbers of women—slave as well as free black—who daily sold merchandise on the streets and other parts of New Orleans and even on plantations in the countryside. Lamenting that such practices hurt their livelihood, petitioners asked the cabildo's mercy in the matter.[18]

Not all relations between white and free black retailers were antagonistic; a few formed partnerships and ran shops together. Pedro Viejo jointly owned a small dry goods store with a *morena libra*, Juana. A native of Guinea, Juana was a former slave of Luis Poirson and the legitimate daughter of slaves. Half of the enterprise belonged to her, and she designated Viejo as her only heir.[19] Antonio Sánchez and María Juana Ester, a free *cuarterona* (quadroon), were partners in another retail business. Born in New Orleans to a *parda* (light-skinned) libre and an unknown father, María Juana had one natural daughter, also a free cuarterona. In her will, María authorized Sánchez to sell her share of the partnership's goods and place the proceeds in her daughter's possession.[20]

Several libra women operated taverns and boardinghouses, most of which were located on streets along the levee, providing ready access for sailors, soldiers, and travelers who disembarked from boats or left their barracks. Like other port cities in the Americas, New Orleans catered to the needs of a large transient population that kept numerous tavernkeepers, innkeepers, and billiard hall owners in business. New Orleans probably had more publicans per capita than any other city in North America during the late eighteenth century. There was one tavernkeeper for every 694 residents in Boston, and one for every 429 in Philadelphia, whereas New Orleans could boast one tavernkeeper for every 71 inhabitants.[21]

Colonial governments taxed and regulated establishments where travelers and residents alike quenched their thirst. Local authorities tried to protect the public from adulterated or sour alcohol, keep spirits out of the hands of Indians and Africans, and, at the same time, raise revenues from licensing fees.[22] Only six of the seventy-three persons in 1787, and six or seven of the sixty-six persons in 1800, whom the cabildo licensed to operate a cabaret were libre women. As in the case of free black retailers, however, additional women probably ran taverns, the licenses for which were in another person's name, or had partnerships with men. When he was imprisoned for debt, for example, the free *moreno* (dark-skinned person) Francisco Barba begged the court for leniency. He and his wife ran a tavern and boarded soldiers of the Mexican fixed regiment. Without him, his wife would have a difficult time managing the service by herself.[23]

The morena libre Carlota Derneville was among those who paid a 30-peso licensing fee to operate a tavern for the year 1787 and a 40-peso fee in 1799 and 1800. According to the 1795 census, she also owned several rental houses despite losing 2,000 pesos' worth of property in the 1788 fire. Both as a slave and as a free person Carlota had labored diligently and saved her earnings. At thirty-seven she purchased her freedom from Don Pedro Henrique Derneville, her father, for 400 pesos. Two years later, in 1775, she agreed to serve Santiago Landreau—without running away and for as long as the court ordered—if he would free her twenty-one-year-old son, Carlos. When she wrote her will in 1801 Carlota possessed a house and one slave, whom she manumitted. She had outlived her son and named as her heir a niece, Carlota Wiltz, the free parda consort of Don Pedro Cázelar.[24]

Rents also helped sustain the free morena seamstress Prudencia Cheval and her family. Cheval, *de nación Pular* (a native of the African Pular nation), was given her freedom, along with that of her two *pardo* children, at age seventeen by Don Francisco Cheval. In his will dated three years later, Don Francisco designated Prudencia and her children as his only and universal heirs. The inheritance included a two-story house. Prudencia soon leased the top floor to a prominent white Spaniard at a monthly rent of 6 pesos for the first eighteen months and 8 pesos for the second eighteen months. Boarders and renters often provided libres like Cheval and Derneville with supplemental income, as they did in the case of Mariana Brion.[25]

Farmers

In addition to holding urban properties, free black women who considered themselves to be *vecinas* (citizens) of New Orleans owned and managed some of the farms that surrounded the city. They raised livestock, poultry, vegetables, fruit, and staple crops that they sold in town. When Francisca Montreuil, a morena libre and baker by trade, died in 1803 at the age of seventy, she possessed an estate valued at 10,459 pesos, to be divided among her three living children and her deceased daughter's three surviving children. Included in this substantial legacy were five slaves worth 2,650 pesos; a house and lot in New Orleans worth 2,825 pesos; two farms along the Bayou Road that ran between the city and Lake Pontchartrain worth 1,735 pesos; and livestock, furniture, and household goods.[26] María Juana Ester, who maintained the partnership with merchant Antonio Sánchez, also owned two farms. Although her primary residence was on the German Coast just upriver from New Orleans, Ester was born and raised in New Orleans and filed her will there. Included in her estate inventory were agricultural and carpentry implements, wagons, oxen, cows, horses, lumber, a canoe, and one male slave. She gave names to all seven ox teams but not to the other animals.[27]

A 1796 census of Metairie (literally "the country" but now a suburb of New Orleans) enumerated the families, employees, slaves, and blocks of land (measured in arpents, about 190 feet to the arpent, with variable amounts of arpents in front and a customary depth of forty arpents) of two white male, five libre male, and two libre female heads of household. As was true with calculations of urban property holding, white men were the most prosperous persons. It is somewhat surprising that libre men and women owned about equal average amounts of land and slaves even though agriculture was gender-prescribed as "men's work" (no white females headed households in Metairie). The two white male heads of household possessed a combined fifty slaves and twenty-four arpents of land. The two households headed by free black women included ten slaves and eleven arpents of land; their five male counterparts owned twenty-four slaves and farmland totaling thirty-one arpents.[28] That free blacks had fewer slaves per arpent than the whites did probably meant that they worked in the fields alongside their male and female slaves.

Slave Owners

Free black and slave women used resources they gained as landlords, shopkeepers, and farmers to free themselves or purchase and either manumit or retain enslaved relatives and friends. They also owned slaves for service and speculation; compared to whites, a smaller proportion of libres owned slaves and in smaller numbers. The holding of slave property by libres was customary throughout the Americas, and most colonial governments guaranteed the property rights of free black citizens. Ownership of black slaves fostered free black identification with white society and thus dissipated white fears of racial collusion. The pattern of free black ownership of slaves in Spanish Louisiana closely resembled that of other Spanish, Portuguese, and French American colonial regions where there were few legal restrictions on manumission. In these areas free blacks employed slaves in both rural and urban labor. As long as slave prices remained low, free people of color who could afford bondpersons used them. In addition, free blacks often could afford to purchase their slave relatives and free them with few constraints, and thus they did not need to hold them as slaves.[29]

In Spanish New Orleans, libres purchased increasing numbers of slave laborers into the 1790s, but there was a slight dip during the 1800s as prices rose. Free blacks purchased more non-kin slaves. Analysis of a sample of notarial records also indicates that almost two-thirds of the slaves whom free blacks acquired were females. Initially, a disproportionately large percentage of slave buyers were free morenas and pardas, but with each decade the percentage of female purchasers declined while that of males increased. By the early 1800s, the percentage of purchasers by sex almost mirrored sex ratios among free blacks. Census and purchasing data show that in 1777 females included 67.9 percent of the free black population in New Orleans, but they purchased 77.8 percent of the slaves bought by libres from 1771 through 1773. Respective proportions for the 1780s were 71.6 and 75.8 percent; for the 1790s, the proportions were 62.4 and 64.8 percent; and, for the 1800s, 60.2 and 60.4 percent. During the first years of the nineteenth century the percentage of males among the free black population rose from 32.1 percent (in 1777) to 39.8 percent; the percentage of free black buyers rose from 22.2 percent (between 1771 and 1773) to 39.6 percent.[30] Why female purchasers were so prevalent during the early years of Spanish rule is not clear. Perhaps they had greater access than males to cash or credit resources.[31]

Libre women purchased greater numbers of female than male slaves, whereas libre men preferred to buy male slaves. Intended use of the slave based on gendered occupational roles, along with higher prices for male slaves, probably influenced that pattern. Free black women used slaves to perform domestic chores, peddle their trade goods, and serve customers in their boardinghouses and taverns; free black men were more likely to buy slaves who could assist them in their trades and care for their houses. Both free men and women augmented their incomes by hiring out skilled slaves, and they bought and sold slaves for speculative purposes. María Teresa Cheval, a free parda tavernkeeper, purchased a *morena bozal* (slave newly arrived from Africa) from a man for 90 pesos and sold her the next day to another man for 300 pesos.[32] Another libre woman repurchased a slave from a white man who could not satisfy his debt to her and promptly sold the slave to a free black man at a price 50 pesos higher (a 10 percent increase over the 500-peso original price of the slave). For unknown reasons he then sold the slave two days later at a 25-peso loss.[33]

In addition to procuring bondpersons through purchase, libres acquired slave and other types of property by way of testamentary and inter vivos acts. Heirs rarely contested these generous bequests to free blacks, and Spanish colonial courts usually upheld the wishes of the deceased as long as a written and witnessed last will and testament existed. According to the December 1779 will of Henrique Mentzinger, who was a sergeant in the white militia, the two-year-old free *pardito* Juan Baptista was to receive Mentzinger's twenty-six-year-old morena slave named Fatima. In addition, Mentzinger left to the parda libre Luison, eight, his eight-year-old moreno slave named Manuel. Both Juan Baptista and Luison were the children of the free morena Gabriela, Mentzinger's former slave and probable common-law mate, to whom he willed 200 pesos.[34]

Doña Magdalena Brazilier's will stipulated that María Luisa, a free parda about seven or eight, was to receive two slaves—Batista (twenty) and Luisa (eighteen)—along with Brazilier's residence in New Orleans and all her clothes, jewelry, household goods, kitchen utensils, and furniture. María Luisa was the daughter of Brazilier's mulatta slave, Maneta. In the will, Brazilier freed seven of her slaves, several of them being other children of Maneta, but not Maneta. The transition of Maneta's children to free status was probably made smoother with this gift of property and the assistance of their brother Poiquon, a free pardo whom Brazilier had manumitted before making her will.[35]

When he died in 1791, Don Marcos de Olivares, a native of Coruña in Spain, left his natural daughter, the free parda María Josepha de los Dolores, ownership of a morena slave and her two children along with another morena slave. Olivares also willed her 2,000 pesos, two houses, furniture, clothing, silver, and various household effects. Thirteen years earlier Olivares had given his daughter, then four, perhaps the most precious gift: her freedom. In his will, Don Marcos left María Josepha's mother (the free morena Mariana Voisín), a morena slave, a small house and land and 1,000 pesos, and he instructed her to administer their daughter's inheritance until she reached full legal age. Other free blacks, including María Josepha's grandmother, also benefited from Olivares's generosity.[36]

Although not as common as testamentary bequests, inter vivos donations of slaves to libres occasionally appear in notarial registers. In 1782 Don Francisco Raquet gave two young morena slaves and two pieces of land to Adelaida, a free cuarterona and daughter of the free parda Francisca Lecler, alias "Raquet." In his will dated twenty years later Don Francisco recognized the twenty-four-year-old Adelaida as his natural daughter. He left 3,000 pesos to her, 400 pesos to her mother, Francisca, and 1,000 pesos to each of Adelaida's two sons. He also named Adelaida's daughter, Adelaida Dupry, as heir to his plantation and twelve slaves.[37] Apparently, Don Francisco preferred his grand-daughter to his grandsons. His generosity improved the material well-being of three generations of free black women.

Some of the most valuable information about ownership of slaves by free blacks can be found in wills and marriage contracts made by libres themselves (transactions in which they used their slave property as collateral) and also in tax lists. Sometime during the late 1790s or early 1800s Spanish administrators compiled a list of persons who owned land along the levee near New Orleans, a list that recorded the amount of land and the number of slaves each individual possessed, most likely for purposes of taxation.[38] Whites on these properties held more than four times as many slaves as did libre landowners. In all, fifty-two landowners held 562 slaves, an average of 10.8 slaves per proprietor. Of the fifty-two owners, forty-six were white, and they held 540 slaves for an average of 11.7. The six remaining free black owners possessed twenty-two slaves, or an average of 3.7. Pedro Demouy and Antonio Conway, both free pardos, owned eight slaves each, but the morena libre Agnes (Inéz) Mathieu and the parda libre Felicita Forneret each owned only two slaves. The *pardo libre* Joseph and the morena libre Fanchon Carrière (also known as Francisca Montreuil) owned only one slave apiece. Carrière also owned land and slaves within the city. White slaveholdings ranged from a low of one to a high of forty.

An inventory of slaves belonging to residents of the Second District of New Orleans taken at about the same time in 1796 reflected similar patterns. Libre females owned slaves, as did libre males (and in this case in greater numbers), but white men possessed an overwhelming percentage of slave property. In June 1796 the *comisario del barrio* (ward commissioner) compiled two lists. One list was of slave-owners (and also a couple of residents who did not own slaves) who made a voluntary contribution of 6 reales (8 reales to 1 peso) per slave to a fund established to compensate planters in Pointe Coupée, a settlement upriver from New Orleans where slaves were killed as a result of a conspiracy the year before. The other list was of those slave-owners who refused to contribute. Not one free black slave-owner contributed to the fund. Taking those who contributed and those who did not together, free black women made up 3.7 percent of all slaveholders in the Second District, owning 3 percent of all slaves. Respective figures for free black men were 1.5 percent of slaveholders, owning 0.6 percent of total slaves; for white women, 15.7 percent of slaveholders, owning 12.9 percent of the slaves; and for white men, 79.1 percent of slaveholders, owning 83.5 percent of the slaves (where the total number of slave-owners was 134 and the total number of slaves was 503).[39]

During the Spanish period, thirty-one of the sixty-nine libres who recorded wills listed slaves as part of their estates.[40] These thirty-one individuals possessed a total of 102.3 slaves (one testator owned a slave jointly with his two brothers) for an average of 3.3 slaves per testator. The number of slaves belonging to any one person ranged from one to thirteen, with half owning only one or two slaves. Three-fifths of the slaves owned were females. Slightly fewer than two-thirds of the owners were female, and they owned slightly more than two-thirds of the slaves. These percentages generally agree with data about slave purchases. Free black women owned more slaves than did free black males, and libres owned more female than male slaves, as did the slave-owning population as a whole. When he wrote his will in 1802, Pedro Demouy claimed ownership of only four of the eight slaves declared on the levee landowners' tax list; the other four— along with half the remainder of his property—belonged to his common-law wife Juana, with whom he had *trabajado en comunidad* (worked jointly or as a partnership) since 1779. He named as heirs to his half of their communal property their five natural children. By marrying Juana that same day and legitimating their children, Demouy made their claims as his heirs even stronger, stabilized their position in society, and, in his own words, lifted them from *la vida viciosa* (depraved way of life) they had led up to that point.[41]

Between 1771 and 1803, notaries recorded ten marriage contracts in which both partners were libres. Of these twenty persons, nine made known the slave property they were bringing into the marriage. In the remaining eleven cases, it was not clear whether the parties did not own slaves or grouped them with other property in a declaration of their general worth. The nine who explicitly listed slave property owned a total of eighteen and one-third slaves (one bride had a one-third interest in a slave), an average of about two slaves per owner. The number of slaves owned by any one party ranged from one to five. These numbers were lower than those for testators but represented an earlier stage in the life-cycle, a point at which persons generally had not accumulated as much property. The free pardos Joseph Cabaret and María Juana Prudhome, for example, entered into a prenuptial contract. Cabaret brought to the marriage land, three cabins, a garden, a canal, eight cows, and four slaves, all located on the Camino del Bayou San Juan (Bayou St. John Road) between New Orleans and Lake Pontchartrain. A forty-year-old militia officer and recent widower, Cabaret also brought two children from his previous marriage, one of whom died a few months after the wedding. Three of his other children had already died. Prudhome contributed to the union two houses in New Orleans, one slave, and three children from previous connections (another had died shortly after birth). She also possessed 325 pesos that her former white consort, Don Juan Antonio Lugar, had given her. When she died the money was to go to the couple's two natural daughters, Rita and Petrona.[42]

Property Accumulation

Although most libres exhausted their incomes on daily necessities, some were able to save a portion of what they earned and accumulate property holdings, occasionally large estates. They invested in jewelry and other personal goods, real estate, and slaves. A few libres were also the beneficiaries of donations of these types of goods, either inter vivos or by will. These free blacks then passed on their goods to friends and lineal and lateral kin, thereby contributing to the well-being of succeeding generations. Both the Spanish and French practiced partible inheritance whereby children received at least somewhat equitable portions of their parents' estates. Even illegitimate children could inherit up to one-third, and consorts up to one-fifth, of an estate, although parties often left larger shares without having their wills contested by other heirs.[43] Second- or third-generation free blacks usually inherited the accumulated riches, no matter how meager, of past generations, and slaves who had well-established free black friends or relatives stood a better chance of being "rescued" from slavery than those who had no ties to the libre population.

At the age of forty-one Naneta Cadis died, three years before her mother, Francisca Montreuil; like her mother, she left a large estate that she acquired during the quarter-century she had been free. Naneta's father was a white man, Don Pedro Cadis. She had married Pedro Bailly, also a recently freed pardo, in 1778 and brought to the marriage a dowry of 350 pesos in silver and cows worth 40 pesos. Naneta gave birth to five legitimate children, two of whom died before they reached the age of ten; all had leading white citizens and officials as godparents. Naneta was left to care for her family, properties, and slaves while her husband spent more than two years in prison in Cuba, convicted of espousing radical French ideals and conspiring to overthrow the Spanish government in 1794. Pleading for the welfare of her children, Naneta successfully petitioned the Spanish crown to release her husband in 1796. The children, second-generation free blacks, benefited greatly from the business acumen of their mother and grandmother when they inherited their estates in the early 1800s.[44]

Testaments and estate inventories like those for Montreuil and Cadis reveal the extent of property libre women could accumulate during their lifetimes and bequeath to relatives and friends when they died. They also reveal intricate kinship and patronage ties among free blacks, whites, and slaves as well as the economic activities in which libre women engaged. The childless parda libre María Francisca Riche distributed her estate among her closest kin and long-time friends as well as among the poor. A natural daughter of the free morena Carlota Riche, native of Pointe Coupée and resident of New Orleans, Riche donated 10 pesos to indigent patients at Charity Hospital and 100 pesos and a harness decorated with silver to Doña Julia Bauvais of Pointe Coupée (Riche had served as Bauvais's nurse when she was a child). She ordered her executor to sell her household goods and a morena slave and use the proceeds to liberate her brother and sister, Pedro and María Luisa. In turn, the siblings were to use the remaining funds to purchase the freedom of María Luisa's two daughters, and those nieces were to inherit Riche's estate.[45]

Unlike Riche, the free morenas Janeton Laliberté and María Belair had living children, and their estates can be traced down through at least two generations during the Spanish period. A native of Senegal in West Africa, Laliberté wrote her will in 1771 and noted that thirty years earlier she had been married to a moreno named Gran Jacot (also known as Luis) and that they had had a daughter named María Juana. She later married another free moreno, but the union produced no children. A farmer, Laliberté willed to her daughter her half-lot in New Orleans, a plantation downriver from the city at English Turn and located adjacent to lands of her son-in-law Pedro Tomás, and four cows with their calves. Thirty years later the daughter, María Juana Tomás, wrote her will. Her marriage to Pedro Tomás had produced eight children, six of whom were still living, the eldest forty-four and the youngest twenty-five. María Juana Tomás owned only the half-lot and house inherited from her mother, which she left to her children and the son of one of her dead children.[46]

Before her marriage to the pardo libre Luis Daunoy, María Belair had two natural daughters, Carlota and Martona, and she willed one-fifth of her estate to each of them when she died in 1794. The rest of her estate was left to her and Daunoy's legitimate son, also named Luis. María's property consisted of her dowry (500 pesos) and half of the goods communally owned with her husband, which included a half-lot and cabin in New Orleans. Martona Belair followed her mother to the grave one year later and left her one-fifth share of María's estate to her six natural children who ranged in age from thirteen years to twenty months. Martona made her living as a dry-goods retailer, and during her lifetime she acquired much more property than her mother. Appraisers valued her estate—furniture, household goods, personal clothing, a half-lot and house in New Orleans, a promissory note, and dry goods for her business—at 1,572.5 pesos. Martona owed one white woman and eight white men (most of them wholesale merchants) 553 pesos, thus leaving 1,019.5 pesos for her six children. In addition, Martona held as guardian one female slave (valued at 400 pesos) for two of her minor children and another female slave (valued at 350 pesos) for one of her other minor children. Two white men, probably the respective fathers, had donated the slaves to the children.[47]

Conclusion

Evidence from wills and estate inventories, court cases, censuses, tax lists, and such notarized transactions as sales, purchases, and donations of property make abundantly clear the active participation of libre women in the growing economy that characterized the vibrant port of New Orleans at the turn of the nineteenth century. Free women of African descent in colonial New Orleans acquired slave, real, and personal property by working for wages, operating successful business enterprises, and receiving inheritances or donations from whites, slaves, and other libres. Within their own lifetimes or over generations some free black women amassed sizable estates which, although they were generally much smaller than those recorded for wealthy white New Orleanians, were nevertheless larger on average than those of libre men. No matter how much or what they owned, however, most libre women actively endeavored to protect and increase their resources in order to improve their own material conditions and social standing and that of their kin and friends.[48] Their struggles to protect their rights within a society that exploited them as nonwhites and as women, but also gave them some advantages over slaves and even white women, are apparent from the records.

Notes

Research for this essay was made possible through the generous assistance of the Program for Cultural Cooperation Between Spain's Ministry of Culture and United States Universities, the Alfred G. Beveridge Grant for Research in the History of the Western Hemisphere, the American Philosophical Society, the Oklahoma Humanities Council (formerly the Oklahoma Foundation for the Humanities), the University of Tulsa Faculty Development Summer Fellowship Program, and the University of Tulsa Faculty Research Grant Program

1. John Garrigus, "Blue and Brown: Contraband Indigo and the Rise of a Free Colored Planter Class in French Saint-Domingue," *The Americas* 50 (Oct. 1993): 233–63; John Garrigus, "A Struggle for Respect: The Free Coloreds of Pre-Revolutionary Saint Domingue, 1760–1769," Ph.D. diss., Johns Hopkins University, 1988; David P. Geggus, "Slave and Free Colored Women in Saint Domingue," and Susan M. Socolow, "Economic Roles of the Free Women of Color of Cap Français," both in *More Than Chattel: Black Women and Slavery in the Americas,* ed. David Barry Gaspar and Darlene Clark Hine (Bloomington: Indiana University Press, 1996), 259–78, 279–97; David P. Geggus, *Slavery, War, and Revolution: The British Occupation of St. Domingue 1793–1798* (New York: Oxford University Press, 1982); Paul F. Lachance, "The Formation of a Three-Caste Society: Evidence from Wills in Antebellum New Orleans," *Social Science History* 18 (Summer 1994): 211–42; and Loren Schweninger, *Black Property Owners in the South, 1790–1915* (Urbana: University of Illinois Press, 1991). For more on the economic activities of slave women in antebellum New Orleans, see Virginia Meacham Gould, "'If I Can't Have My Rights, I Can Have My Pleasures, and If They Won't Give Me Wages, I Can Take Them': Gender and Slave Labor in Antebellum New Orleans," in *Discovering the Women in Slavery: Emancipating Perspectives on the American Past,* ed. Patricia Morton (Athens: University of Georgia Press, 1996), 179–201. The only nucleus to boast the title of *ciudad* in all of northern New Spain, New Orleans had a resident population that grew from about three thousand to more than eight thousand between the 1770s and the early 1800s, with a large transient population adding to that number. The proportion of free blacks rose from 10 to 20 percent of New Orleanians over the same period; two-thirds were female. The rest of the population was about evenly divided between whites and slaves, with varying numbers of *indios* and *mestizos* residing in and around the city. Kimberly S. Hanger, *Bounded Lives, Bounded Places: Free Black Society in Colonial New Orleans, 1769–1803* (Durham: Duke University Press, 1997), 22.

2. This is the primary argument I make in *Bounded Lives, Bounded Places.* When a version of this chapter was first presented as a paper at the Fourth Southern Conference on Women in Charleston, South Carolina, in June 1997, Gwendolyn Midlo Hall provided a more francophone perspective in her commentary. She argues that 152 slaves were manumitted under French colo-

nial jurisdiction between 1723 and 1769—or slightly more than three per year—and that many blacks lived as free persons in informal arrangements. As a rejoinder, I would offer that this number pales in comparison with the more than fifty-five slaves on average who were manumitted per year during the thirty-five years of Spanish rule (1769–1803) and that blacks who could prove their freedom with a piece of paper experienced more secure, productive, and fulfilling lives than those whose informal arrangements kept them on edge at all times. Gwendolyn Midlo Hall, *Africans in Colonial Louisiana: The Development of Afro-Creole Culture in the Eighteenth Century* (Baton Rouge: Louisiana State University Press, 1992).

Many documents reveal that racial identity in New Orleans's hierarchical, patriarchal society was very malleable and subjective. A person's racial designation depended on who recorded it, what purpose it served, when it was recorded, and what physical characteristics were considered most relevant. For example, censuses taken during the era of French rule grouped New Orleanians into whites, blacks, and Indians, with no differentiation as to free or slave. When the Spanish took over residents were now white, free pardo or moreno, and slave pardo or moreno. Where did all the Louisiana Indians go? They still lived in or around New Orleans (Daniel H. Usner, Jr., "American Indians in Colonial New Orleans," in *Powhatan's Mantle: Indians in the Colonial Southeast*, ed. Peter H. Wood, Gregory A. Waselkov, and M. Thomas Hatley [Lincoln: University of Nebraska Press, 1989], 104–27), but because Spanish officials outlawed Indian slavery, Native Americans most likely "became" (were reclassified as) persons of African descent. That way, they could still be slaves and would have to sue for their freedom based on native ancestry in later decades. In addition, the terms used to designate phenotype were many and varied, as they were throughout the Spanish empire. People were not black or white based on biological factors, but rather they fit into the racial hierarchy according to a complex formula that combined physical features, clothing style, language, religion, family reputation, occupation, and other factors, and that differed depending on locality and period. This is what Patricia Seed best defines as "social race" in "Social Dimensions of Race: Mexico City, 1753," *Hispanic American Historical Review* 62 (Nov. 1982): 569–606.

3. The quotation is from Pierre-Louis Berquin-Duvallon, *Vue de la colonie espagnole du Mississipi, ou des provinces de Louisiane et Floride occidentale* (Paris: l'Imprimerie Expédite, 1804), 252. See also Claude C. Robin, *Voyages dans l'interieur de la Louisiane, de la Floride Occidentale, et dans les Isles de la Martinique et de Saint-Domingue, pendant les années 1802, 1803, 1804, 1805 et 1806*, 3 vols. (Paris: F. Buisson, 1807), 2: 75. French physician Paul Alliot ("Historical and Political Reflections," in *Louisiana under the Rule of Spain, France, and the United States, 1785–1807*, trans. and ed. James Alexander Robertson, 2 vols. [Cleveland: Arthur H. Clark, 1911], 1: 85) wrote in 1804 that libre women in New Orleans "inspire such lust through their bearing, their gestures, and their dress, that many quite well-to-do persons are ruined in pleasing them."

4. Laura Foner, "The Free People of Color in Louisiana and St. Domingue: A Comparative Portrait of Two Three-Caste Slave Societies," *Journal of Social History* 3 (Summer 1970): 416–17.

5. The quotation is from Thomas Marc Fiehrer, "The African Presence in Colonial Louisiana: An Essay on the Continuity of Caribbean Culture," in *Louisiana's Black Heritage*, ed. Robert R. Macdonald, John R. Kemp, and Edward F. Haas (New Orleans: Louisiana State Museum, 1979), 21. See also Hans W. Baade, "The Law of Slavery in Spanish Luisiana, 1769–1803," in *Louisiana's Legal Heritage*, ed. Edward F. Haas (Pensacola: Perdido Bay Press for the Louisiana State Museum, 1983), 49.

6. "Resumen del Tercer Barrio de la Nueva Orleans echo el día 18 de Febrero del ano 1796," Papeles Procedentes de Cuba, Archivo General de Indias, Seville, Spain (hereafter AGI PC), legajo 212–A, fols. 33–40. Urban property-holding among libre women in New Orleans reflects patterns also found in Saint-Domingue and other regions with large free black populations. About one-fifth of private homes in Cap Français in 1776 belonged to nonwhites (Geggus, "Slave and Free Colored Women in Saint Domingue," 270).

7. "Relación de la perdida que cada Individuo ha padecido en el Incendio de esta Ciudad . . . ," Archivo General de Indias, Audiencia de Santo Domingo (hereafter AGI SD), legajo 2576, fol. 532, Sept. 30, 1788. The document gives phenotype and status for libres but not for whites, yet other

documents indicate that some individuals who were not identified as free blacks were such. For example, in a separate petition for damage remuneration, María Methode is identified as a *parda libre*, whereas in the "Relación" she is not. Thus, the "Relación" might include more free blacks and fewer whites than those who appear.

8. Acts of Carlos Ximénez, no. 16, fol. 146, July 24, 1799 (hereafter all notarial "Acts" and "Court Proceedings" will be cited by notary's name, volume number, folio number[s], and date). The notarial records are located in the Orleans Parish Notarial Archives, New Orleans.

9. Daniel H. Usner, Jr., *Indians, Settlers, and Slaves in a Frontier Exchange Economy: The Lower Mississippi Valley before 1783* (Chapel Hill: University of North Carolina Press, 1992), 202.

10. City Treasury Accounts for 1787, Cabildo Records, box 1 folder 4, Lower Louisiana and Mississippi Valley Collection, Louisiana State University (hereafter LLMVC). In New Orleans as well as in Rio de Janeiro, "one of the most important peddling operations was the vending of all types of foodstuffs, fresh and prepared." Mary C. Karasch, *Slave Life in Rio de Janeiro, 1808–1850* (Princeton: Princeton University Press, 1987), 207.

11. Thomas Ashe, *Travels in America Performed in 1806*, 3 vols. (London: Richard Phillips, 1808), 3: 260. In addition to poor libres and whites, other marginal economic groups—"primarily city slaves engaged in selling the surplus of their gardens and loot from nocturnal activities, or Indians peddling vegetables, fish, blankets, and trinkets"—participated in the city's retail industry. John G. Clark, *New Orleans, 1718–1812: An Economic History* (Baton Rouge: Louisiana State University Press, 1970), 256.

12. "Recensement du 1er, 2me, et 3me quartiers," AGI PC, legajo 211 (hereafter 1795 Census).

13. Acts of Andrés Almonester y Roxas, fol. 97, Feb. 15, 1782; 1795 Census.

14. Records and Deliberations of the Cabildo (hereafter RDC), vol. 3, no. 1, Sept. 10, 1784; Petitions, Decrees, and Letters of the Cabildo (hereafter PDLC), book 4079, doc. 234, Sept. 2, 1794. Both French and Spanish local officials actively involved themselves in ordering daily living, their most vital task being regulation of colonial food supplies. Authorities attempted to provide adequate, edible foodstuffs to the population at fair prices for both producer and consumer. During the Spanish period, government supervision of the New Orleans market intensified as the cabildo began exercising "a direct and increasing influence upon the daily economic life of the town." In this capacity town council members "set prices, inspect[ed] for quality, assure[d] the use of standard weights and measures, and prevent[ed] recurrent food shortages from benefiting monopolists and forestallers at the expense of the public welfare." Clark, *New Orleans*, 257.

15. Report from Juan de Castañedo, City Treasurer, 1795, Cabildo Records, box 2, folder 6, LLMVC.

16. Acts of Pedro Pedesclaux, no. 29, fol. 262, April 25, 1797.

17. John Pintard, "New Orleans, 1801: An Account by John Pintard," *Louisiana Historical Quarterly* 34 (July 1951): 232. U.S. officials increased restrictions on license holding with similar results: "In the month of January, 1823, thirty-two vending licenses were issued by authorities. Only free males could procure the licenses, but the license-holders seldom did the actual selling. That task was generally reserved for black slaves: many plantation owners regularly sent their slaves into town to hawk surplus produce in the street. Most of these hawkers were women." Lilian Crété, *Daily Life in Louisiana, 1815–1830*, trans. Patrick Gregory (Baton Rouge: Louisiana State University Press, 1981), 64. Travelers to Rio conveyed the general impression that city market stalls were the domain of African women. These women, however, actually owned the stalls. Karasch surmises that "since so many stall owners were freedpersons, perhaps they had acquired a stall and freedom." Karasch, *Slave Life in Rio*, 207.

18. PDLC, book 4079, doc. 287, Oct. 6, 1797. The merchants referred to the "crecido número de Mulatas y Negras tanto libres" (increased number of female mulattas and blacks that were free). The New York merchant John Pintard wrote that "one finds however but very little interchange of courtesy among the merchants . . . too great jealousy of each other prevails." Pintard, "New Orleans in 1801," 232.

19. Acts of Andrés Almonester y Roxas, fol. 389, Sept. 1, 1775.

20. Court Proceedings of Narciso Broutin, no. 53, fol. 225–98, June 11, 1802.

21. Comparative data on Boston and Philadelphia obtained from Jacob Price, "Economic Func-
tion and the Growth of American Port Towns in the Eighteenth Century," *Perspectives in American History* 8 (1974): 123–86; Census of the City of New Orleans, Nov. 6, 1791, Louisiana Division,
New Orleans Public Library (hereafter 1791 Census).

22. "Proclamación por Governador Unzaga y Amezaga para regular las casas de Trujos, Posadas,
y Tabernas," AGI PC, legajo 110, Aug. 26, 1770; Jack D. L. Holmes, "Spanish Regulation of Taverns
and the Liquor Trade in the Mississippi Valley," in *The Spanish in the Mississippi Valley,* ed. John
Frances McDermott (Urbana: University of Illinois Press, 1974), 149–82. In 1791 New Orleans boast-
ed more tavernkeepers than any other occupation; a full seventy heads of household (1791 Census).

23. RDC, vol. 3, no. 2, 1787; Court Proceedings of Carlos Ximénez, fols. 243–45, Nov. 30, 1804;
"Carpeta y resumen del importe de las quatro reaciones trimestres del derecho de tabernas," Dec.
31, 1800, Spanish Judicial Records, Louisiana State Museum Historical Center (hereafter SJR).

24. Acts of Andrés Almonester y Roxas, fol. 268, Oct. 27, 1773, and fol. 85, Feb. 16, 1775; City Trea-
sury Accounts for 1787, Cabildo Records, box 1, folder 4, LLMVC; "Relación de la perdida . . . ,"
AGI SD, legajo 2576, fol. 532, Sept. 30, 1788; 1795 Census; City Treasury Accounts for 1799, Cabildo
Records, box 2a, folder 8, LLMVC; List of Duties of Tavernkeepers, Dec. 31, 1800, SJR; Acts of Pedro
Pedesclaux, no. 39, fol. 513, Sept. 9, 1801.

25. Acts of Francisco Broutin, no. 7, fol. 89, Dec. 23, 1790; Court Proceedings of Francisco Broutin, no. 23, fols. 277–88, Aug. 20, 1793; Acts of Carlos Ximénez, no. 6, fol. 162, April 25, 1794. Don
Francisco also donated a house and land to the free pardo carpenter Pablo Cheval and Pablo's sister Luison Cheval, the mother of seven cuarterones by Don Carlos Vivant. Acts of Francisco Broutin, no. 25, fol. 169, June 9, 1793, and no. 40, fol. 177, May 31, 1796.

26. Court Proceedings of Narcisco Broutin, no. 59, fols. 1028–76, June 28, 1803; Court Proceedings of Carlos Ximénez, fols. 246–63, May 28, 1804.

27. Court Proceedings of Narciso Broutin, no. 53, fols. 225–98, June 11, 1802.

28. "Tableau des habitationes et Individus, composant Le Quartier de La Metairie . . . à L'Epoque
du 12 Mars 1796," AGI PC, legajo 211, fol. 185.

29. Although the following is not all inclusive, some studies that discuss slaveholding by free
blacks are: Ira Berlin, *Slaves without Masters: The Free Negro in the Antebellum South* (New York:
Pantheon Books, 1974); Frederick P. Bowser, *The African Slave in Colonial Peru, 1524–1650* (Stanford: Stanford University Press, 1974); James R. Brewer, "Negro Property Owners in Seventeenth-
Century Virginia," in *The Making of Black America: Essays in Negro Life and History,* ed. August
Meier and Elliott Rudwick (New York: Atheneum, 1969), 201–5; Léo Elisabeth, "The French Antil-
les," Eugene D. Genovese, "The Slave States in North America," and Jerome S. Handler and Ar-
nold A. Sio, "Barbados," all in *Neither Slave nor Free: The Freedmen of African Descent in the Slave
Societies of the New World,* ed. David W. Cohen and Jack P. Greene (Baltimore: Johns Hopkins
University Press, 1972), 134–71, 258–77, and 214–57; E. Horace Fitchett, "The Traditions of the Free
Negro in Charleston, South Carolina," *Journal of Negro History* 25 (April 1940): 139–52; John Hope
Franklin, *The Free Negro in North Carolina, 1790–1860* (Chapel Hill: University of North Carolina
Press, 1943); Michael P. Johnson and James L. Roark, *Black Masters: A Free Family of Color in the
Old South* (New York: W. W. Norton, 1974); Karasch, *Slave Life in Rio;* Franklin W. Knight, *Slave
Society in Cuba during the Nineteenth Century* (Madison: University of Wisconsin Press, 1970); Larry
Koger, *Black Slaveowners: Free Black Slave Masters in South Carolina, 1790–1860* (Columbia: Uni-
versity of South Carolina Press, 1985); John H. Russell, "Colored Freemen as Slave Owners in Vir-
ginia," *Journal of Negro History* 1 (July 1916): 233–42; William F. Sharp, *Slavery on the Spanish Frontier*
(Norman: University of Oklahoma Press, 1976); and Carter G. Woodson, ed., *Free Negro Owners
of Slaves in the United States in 1830* (New York: Negro Universities Press, 1924).

A few scholars have addressed the topic of free black slaveholders in Louisiana, but they con-
centrate on the antebellum period: Alice Dunbar-Nelson, "People of Color in Louisiana," *Journal*

of Negro History 1 (Oct. 1916): 361–76; Foner, "Free People of Color in Louisiana and St. Domingue," 406–30; Joseph Karl Menn, *The Large Slaveholders of Louisiana—1860* (New Orleans: Pelican Publishing, 1964); Schweninger, *Black Property Owners in the South*; and Loren Schweninger, "Prosperous Blacks in the South, 1790–1880," *American Historical Review* 95 (Feb. 1990): 31–56; H. E. Sterkx, *The Free Negro in Ante-Bellum Louisiana* (Rutherford: Fairleigh Dickenson University Press, 1972); and Joe Gray Taylor, *Negro Slavery in Louisiana* (Baton Rouge: Louisiana Historical Association, 1963). For the British Caribbean, Arnold A. Sio notes that "most recent research indicates that the free coloured owned relatively few slaves, were no more than 20 per cent of the owners in 1832, and owned a much smaller proportion of the slave population than did the whites." Sio, "Marginality and Free Coloured Identity in Caribbean Slave Society," in *Caribbean Slave Society and Economy*, ed. Hilary Beckles and Verene Shepherd (Kingston: Ian Randle Publishers, 1991), 156.

30. Hanger, *Bounded Lives, Bounded Places*, 71–72.

31. Again, Sio finds, for the British Caribbean, that "more free coloured females than males owned slaves. They were most likely to have owned slaves in units of rarely more than ten, many of whom would have been domestics" ("Marginality and Free Coloured Identity," 156). The sample years referred to were the first three years in each decade of Spanish rule: 1771–73, 1781–83, 1791–93, and 1801–3.

32. Acts of Pedro Pedesclaux, no. 17, fol. 295, April 18, 1793, and fol. 297, April 19, 1793; Kimberly S. Hanger, "*Personas de varias clases y colores:* Free People of Color in Spanish New Orleans, 1769–1803," Ph.D. diss., University of Florida, 1991, 203–7.

33. Acts of Pedro Pedesclaux, no. 4, fols. 981 and 982, Aug. 21, 1788, and fol. 986, Aug. 23, 1788.

34. Acts of Andrés Almonester y Roxas, fol. 683, Dec. 22, 1779, and fol. 684, Dec. 23, 1779.

35. Acts of Francisco Broutin, no. 15, fol. 344, Nov. 14, 1792.

36. Acts of Juan Bautista Garic, no. 9, fol. 91, Feb. 27, 1778; Acts of Pedro Pedesclaux, no. 13, fol. 764, Dec. 18, 1791. Olivares was buried on December 20, 1791. "White Funerals," book 2, Archives of the Archdiocese of New Orleans.

37. Acts of Leonardo Mazange, no. 5, fol. 283, March 18, 1782.

38. "Lists of Slave Ownership" [1790s], AGI PC, legajo 205. From the first years of the Spanish regime, administrators established a tax on all slaves (commonly 4 reales per slave), the proceeds from which the government used to compensate slave-owners for any losses incurred when officials killed runaways or slave rebels or when slaves were lawfully executed for crimes committed. Periodic censuses recorded the number of slaves each subject possessed. During the 1790s, local authorities also taxed land frontage, chimneys, market stalls, and taverns, inns, and dancehalls to fund upkeep of the city's police force, hospital, theater, and street lighting system. For examples see PDLC, book 4083, doc. 33, Aug. 6, 1773; RDC, book 1, Oct. 27, Nov. 17, 1775, and April 9, 1779; RDC, book 3, vol. 3, June 27, 1794; RDC, book 4, vol. 1, May 22, 1795, and vol. 3, Feb. 21, 1800. Gilbert C. Din and John E. Harkins provide an in-depth appraisal of local New Orleans governmental activities in *The New Orleans Cabildo: Colonial Louisiana's First City Government, 1769–1803* (Baton Rouge: Louisiana State University Press, 1996).

39. AGI PC, legajo 212–A, fols. 54–56, May 31, June 8, 9, 1796.

40. Testaments taken from the notarial records.

41. Acts of Pedro Pedesclaux, no. 41, fol. 578, Aug. 20, 1802; "Nonwhite Marriages," book 1, no. 75b, Aug. 20, 1802, Archives of the Archdiocese of New Orleans.

42. Acts of Narciso Broutin, no. 3, fol. 78, March 5, 1801; "Nonwhite Baptisms," books 4a, 5a, and 6a, 1789–99, and "Nonwhite Funerals," book 2, 1790–96, Archives of the Archdiocese of New Orleans.

43. Henry Plauche Dart, "Courts and Law in Colonial Louisiana," *Louisiana Historical Quarterly* 4 (July 1921): 255–89; Henry Plauche Dart, "The Place of the Civil Law in Louisiana," *Tulane Law Review* 4 (Feb. 1930): 163–77; Judith K. Schafer, "'Open and Notorious Concubinage': The Emancipation of Slave Mistresses by Will and the Supreme Court in Antebellum Louisiana," *Louisiana History* 28 (Spring 1987): 165–82.

44. Acts of Narcisco Broutin, no. 2, fol. 13, Jan. 29, 1800, fol. 13; Acts of Andrés Almonester y Roxas, fol. 25, April 25, 1778; "Nonwhite Baptisms," book 2, July 17, 1782, book 3, May 31, 1784, and book 4, April 15, 1791, all in Archives of the Archdiocese of New Orleans; AGI PC, legajo 211–A, fol. 160, 1796.

45. Acts of Pedro Pedesclaux, no. 12, fol. 47, Jan. 21, 1791. Riche's household goods included (in addition to the silver harness): a walnut armoire, a bedstead with two feather mattresses and two Spanish moss mattresses, two feather pillows, four pairs of sheets, one linen mosquito net, two woolen blankets, one cotton blanket, four chairs, eight pots, one frying pan, and her personal clothing.

46. Acts of Juan Bautista Garic, no. 2, fol. 181, June 1, 1771; Acts of Narcisco Broutin, no. 3, fol. 367, Nov. 24, 1801.

47. Acts of Pedro Pedesclaux, no. 21, fol. 728, Aug. 1, 1794; "Autos fechos por fallecimiento de Martona Belair," Aug. 15, 1795, SJR.

48. Schweninger has observed similar endeavors among free blacks for a later period in Louisiana and the rest of the antebellum southern United States. Schweninger, *Black Property Owners in the South.*

CHAPTER 12

Free Women of Color in
Central Brazil, 1779–1832

Mary C. Karasch

The most invisible group in colonial Brazilian history must be free women of color. They rarely appeared in official correspondence except when their role in *batuques* (social dances) was denounced or when they were accused of prostitution. Not even the many surviving censuses of the colonial period record their presence in Brazil. Slaves and former slaves have received more scholarly attention than free women of color.[1] This chapter is, therefore, an initial attempt to explore the lives of free women of color during the late colonial period between 1779 and 1832 in a frontier society in Central Brazil, in what was then called the Captaincy of Goiás (before 1822) and Province of Goiás (after 1822).[2]

Afro-Brazilians were not just slaves during the eighteenth and nineteenth centuries but also free people of color who often rivaled many whites in wealth and slave-ownership. The single largest population group in the Province of Goiás in 1832 was composed of free females of color. To explain how and why they emerged as a larger group than whites or slaves requires exploration of the themes of identity, numbers and age structures contained in census records, occupations and slave-ownership, marital status and families, and roles in the black lay brotherhoods of mining towns. Men alone did not live in and forge the society and economy of the mining towns of Central Brazil during the late colonial period.

During the early nineteenth century, Portuguese authorities based in the capital city, Vila Boa de Goiás, complained about the decadence and ruin of the region and the decline of its population. One observer described Goiás as "a poor naked man."[3] The discourse of colonial rulers on decadence and population does not, however, reveal what actually happened in Central Brazil. The censuses do show that the population continued to increase between 1779 and independence in 1822, a trend that persisted in the early provincial censuses of 1825 and 1832. The modest population expansion of the late eighteenth and early nineteenth centuries was not of individuals defined as white but of free people of color. Hence the Portuguese concern with the collapse of population was clearly related to the white Portuguese population in the region. The retreat of Portuguese authority and presence permitted other populations to flourish, including people of color who migrated into Central Brazil from the neighboring provinces of Maranhão, Piauí, Bahia, Pernambuco, Minas Gerais, São Paulo, Mato Grosso, and Pará. Central Brazil was land rich and sparsely populated. Its rugged terrain offered refuge to many who fled the plantation societies of the coast. The region was dotted with numerous settlements of fugitive slaves (*quilombos*), including the largest continuously occupied quilombo, now called Kalunga, located near Cavalcante, Goiás, in Brazil.[4]

The *gente de cor* (people of color) who migrated into the region, where gold mining had once flourished, no longer labored in rich mines but turned instead to agro-pastoral occupations to support their families. North of Goiás, cowboys migrated with their families from Maranhão and Piauí to occupy the east banks of the Tocantins River. Others herded cattle near the eastern banks of the Araguaia River or to the west of it in Mato Grosso. The majority of migrants from São Paulo and Minas Gerais took up subsistence farming on small plots of land (*roças* and *sítios*) in the region of the South. Free women of color were essential to the survival and success of small farmers in the new economy, and they performed much of the agricultural labor.[5]

Not all people of color in the region were recent migrants, however. They were also descendants of persons manumitted during the eighteenth century, some of whom had achieved status and slave-ownership and were related to the powerful white families of the region. Undoubtedly, some descendants of enslaved Africans came to be defined as white because of their wealth and family connections. The ancestors of Goiano-born free people of color achieved manumission during the eighteenth century because they had access to gold. African men who mined for gold were able to keep a portion of their find as their daily wage, but in exchange they had to use gold dust to purchase food and drink from the African women who worked as cooks and market women. Both men and women, therefore, could save toward the price of their own freedom or that of a family member.[6]

Slave women and children were also frequently manumitted in the eighteenth century through purchase by their free or enslaved "husbands" and fathers. Because few white women went to the gold fields in those years, most women who lived in mining towns were nonwhites, including many West African slave women usually defined as Mina or Guiné. Concubinage between white men and black slave women was the norm rather than the exception in early-eighteenth-century Goiás. Their mulatto descendants, known as *pardos*, were either freed through manumission and became *forros* (freedmen and women), or they were born free after a mother's manumission.

Not all free people of color were pardos, however. The census records reveal that African men and women also had descendants who were defined as free *crioulos* (blacks born in Brazil). Free blacks (*prêtos livres*) were numerous enough to be a census category. The size of the free black population of African or Brazilian birth developed out of the special circumstances created by the open lands where black men could work as miners and farmers and provide militia services in black regiments, the Henriques.[7] Entire villages and towns were settled by free blacks and their families and slaves.

How and why whites tolerated free people of color in the midst of a slave society can best be explained by their dependence on slaves and clients on a violent frontier. In the early eighteenth century, miners and their slaves were commonly attacked by the Amerindian nation, the Kayapó, in the South. To protect their mines and families, mine owners armed slaves and permitted freedmen and free men of color to join militia forces to defend towns and villages. Frontier warfare continued throughout the eighteenth century as additional Amerindian nations challenged the Portuguese, almost driving them from the North by the time of independence in 1822. Pardo regiments and black troops in the Henriques fought in the wars to defend their families and communities against attacks on mines, farms, and ranches. Without the armed help of black and pardo troops, the Portuguese could not have held the frontier and extracted the gold of Goiás.[8]

Not all relationships between Amerindians and blacks were violent, however. Household records report that blacks, including free women of color, lived in *aldeias* (Indian mission villages). Enslaved African men and Amerindian female captives (acquired by right of conquest in the frontier wars) or mission Indians also formed consensual unions and created families.[9] Thus, free people of color also included many *cafuzos,* whose ancestry was mixed African and Indian. The censuses, however, apparently subsumed this group among persons defined as pardos. It is uncertain how significant they were in number. Another common term, *cabra,* was used in all but census records to define a person of indeterminate racial mixture but at least of some African ancestry. African women were also listed as the mothers of cabra children.[10] Free people of color, therefore, had diverse identities imposed by the regional society. They were black (prêto or crioulo), cafuzo or cabra, pardo or *mulato.* For the Brazilian-born, one or both parents could be African or Amerindian. Many *mestizos,* people of mixed Portuguese-Amerindian ancestry, also lived in Central Brazil, but the censuses did not use this term as a category of identification. Free women of color obviously shared all of these identities.

To establish the presence of free women of color, it is necessary to turn to the census records for the Captaincy of Goiás, which begin in 1779. Earlier population data tended to trace the male slave population involved in mining. Census data compiled by parish priests at the command of Portuguese governors reflected late colonial values and constructions of identity. Thus, *brancos* (whites) were placed first without attention to gender in the 1779 count. Second, according to Portuguese status values, were the pardos, and third were the prêtos. Amerindians were not included until 1825. In 1780 the governor sent aggregate data to Lisbon about the inhabitants of the Captaincy of Goiás for 1779. After listing the total number of whites, pardos, and prêtos in each town and its surrounding *julgado* (judicial district) without distinction by sex, he reported the number of women in the captaincy as 3,470 *brancas* (whites), 5,233 *pardas,* and 8,698 *pretas* (blacks), with 578 newborns—a total of 17,979 (33 percent of whom were female). The legal status (free, freed, or enslaved) of the women was not reported, although it must be assumed that some pardas and pretas were free women of color. Overall, 34,882 blacks composed almost two-thirds (64 percent) of the total population of 54,489.[11]

The first significant recording of free women of color occurred in the incomplete census of 1783, which grouped them in extended families of dependents and slaves as well as heads of households of children, slaves, *agregados* (household dependents), and "obligated persons" (*pessoas de obrigação*).[12] Unfortunately, the census is frustratingly incomplete. It lacks data from many julgados, including two of the largest, Meia Ponte (now Pirenópolis) and Natividade. For judicial districts reported in detail, however, the census has some household lists that include free women of color. The data by household record information on gender, legal status (free or enslaved), number of family members, and dependents such as agregados and pessoas de obrigação, as well as slaves attached to each male or female head of household, here identified as *chefe* (a head of household), including free women of color.

Among the districts with the best data on free women of color was the capital of the captaincy, Vila Boa de Goiás. The *vila* (city) in 1783 had 554 *fogos* (households); an additional 630 were located in the countryside, where people lived on *sítios* (small plots of land suitable for food crops) and *fazendas* (large estates, often ranches in Goiás). The total population for both urban and rural portions of the julgado numbered 8,159, of whom 4,689 (57.5 percent) were enslaved persons. The free female population was 1,770, including 591 whites, 644 free pardas, and 535 freed blacks. Thus, free females of color composed two-thirds (66.6 percent) of the female population of the District of Vila Boa; only a third (33.4 percent) of the district's female population was defined as white.

The first fairly complete surviving census by color, civil status, and age was done for 1789, the first in a series of censuses completed between 1789 and 1792. The census of 1789 recorded a total population of 58,504, slightly lower than the total for 1783. The captaincy's 37,309 slaves (63.8 percent of the population) indicate the continued significance of slavery. The census is particularly valuable, however, in that it is the first to include females by color (whites, pardas, and pretas) and legal status (*livres* [free] and captives), as well as their births and deaths (table 12.1). In census records of eighteenth- and nineteenth-century Brazil, the livre category could include both liberated slaves and freeborn people of color and sometimes whites. This chapter, however, will employ the term *livre de cor* to mean people of color who were not of the slave status. The term *captive* is more problematic because it was used for both black and Amerindian slaves in Goiás. That census takers employed the term *captive* rather than *slave* may indicate they were including Amerindians. Unfortunately, the census and correspondence about it do not clarify the ethnic identities of those persons listed as livre or captive.

Although census takers did not compile data for free females of color in 1789, the size of the female population of color (i.e., pardas and pretas) can be estimated by subtracting white females (3,740), presumed to be all freeborn, from

Table 12.1. Number of Females by Color and Legal Status in Goiás, 1779–1832

| Year | People of Color[a] | | | | Slaves | Livres de Cor[b] | Other[c] | Total |
	Whites	Pardas	Pretas	Total				
1779	3,470	5,233	8,698	13,931	—	—	578	17,979
1789	3,740	5,629	8,599	14,228	12,019	2,209	689	18,657
1791	3,736	5,658	8,623	14,281	—	—	—	18,017
1792	3,570	4,871	8,882	13,753	10,105	3,648	673	17,996
1804	3,442	8,084	4,728	12,812	7,933	—	—	24,187
1825	5,144	18,439[d]	1,441[e]	19,880	6,046	—	319	31,389
1832	5,575	16,290[f]	4,982[f]	21,272	6,041	—	535	33,423

Sources: Instituto Histórico e Geográphico Brasiliero, Rio de Janeiro (hereafter IHGB), arq. 1.2.7, Relação em que o Governador, e Capitão General da Capitania de Goyaz Luiz da Cunha Menezes apresenta o numero existente dos habitantes da mesma Capitania, e dos que morrerão divididos pelos Arrayaes, e seus respectivos julgados . . . até o prezente anno de 1780, July 8, 1780, fols. 246–47; Arquivo Histórico Ultramarino, Lisbon (hereafter AHU), caixa 35, Goiás, 1790–98, Mappa em que Tristão da Cunha Menezes . . . apresenta ao Real Ministerio . . . até o prezente anno d'1789, Oct. 19, 1790; Rio de Janeiro, IHGB, arq. 1.2.8., vol. 37, Relação em que Tristão da Cunha Menezes Governador e Capitão General d'esta Capitania de Goyaz apresenta ao Real Ministerio pela extração das relações dos Parochos dos seus respectivos julgados . . . até . . . 1791, fols. 7–8; AHU, caixa 35, Goiás, 1790–1798, Mappa em que o Governador, e Capitão General da Capitania de Goyaz Tristão da Cunha Menezes apresenta ao Real Ministerio . . . , July 29, 1792; AHU, cod. 2109, Reflexoens Economicas Sobre As Tabellas Statisticas da Capitania de Goyaz Pertencentes ao anno de 1804 e feitas no de 1806; Biblioteca Nacional, Rio de Janeiro, Manuscript Section, 11,4,2, Estatistica da Provincia de Goyáz remettida á Secretaria de Estado dos Negocios do Imperio . . . , 1825; and Rio de Janeiro, Arquivo Nacional, cod. 808, vol. 1, Goiás, Censo da População da Provincia de Goyaz, fol. 96.

a. Includes livres and slaves in 1779 and from 1789 to 1792. The census categories were pardas and pretas in 1779 and from 1789 to 1792. In 1804 the census used "mulattas" rather than pardas.

b. My calculation of the number of free people of color based on the subtraction of the number of slaves from the total for the people of color (both slave and free) in 1789 and 1792.

c. Newborns in 1779, 1789, and 1792; *Indias* (Indians) in 1825 and 1832.

d. *Ingênuas de Cor* (freeborn women of color).

e. *Libertas de Cor* (freedwomen of color).

f. Livres, including free and freedwomen of color.

the free female total of 5,949. The estimated free female population of color was, therefore, 2,209, or 11.8 percent of the female population. In contrast, the captive female population was 12,019. Three-fourths (76.3 percent) of the female population was composed of women of color; 20.1 percent were white, and 3.7 percent were newborn, the color and civil status of whom were unrecorded. The census of 1789 can provide, therefore, the basis from which to establish the relatively rapid expansion of the free female of color population and the decline in the numbers of enslaved females in the region.

Two years later, in 1791, the governor of Goiás reported only aggregate totals of 3,736 white females, 5,658 pardas, and 8,623 pretas (18,017 females); he did not make distinctions by legal status.[13] Far more useful is the census of 1792 (table 12.1), which followed the same form as the 1789 census but documented an important social transformation in the captaincy. The white female population remained at almost 20 percent, but the number of white females dropped from 3,740 (in 1789) to 3,570, a loss of 170 white females. More important, the number of enslaved females fell by 1,914 to 10,105. In 1789 an estimated 2,209 females were livres de cor; in only three years their numbers increased to 3,648, or 20.3 percent of the total female population. Female births decreased slightly to 673 (3.7 percent). Although the census cannot reveal why these population changes occurred, the data suggest that more women of color moved into the livre status, which apparently included freedmen and women between 1789 and 1792.

The next census year was 1798. Although Portuguese bureaucrats collected data on the population of their empire for that year, only fragments of that census have been located for the Captaincy of Goiás. This is indeed unfortunate because five of the reporting parish priests recorded totals by sex, age, color, and legal status. The sixth parish, São José de Tocantins located to the northeast of Vila Boa de Goiás, reveals a typical mining town profile, with few children under fifteen in the population (table 12.2). More important for my purposes, however, the parish priest also recorded the free black female population, although he did not identify the pardas as livres. Thus, free black females numbered 264, or 19.5 percent; another 441 (32.6 percent) were defined as captives. Parda women totaled 581, while only sixty-six white females, fewer than 5 percent, lived in São José. In other words, 95 percent of the female population was composed of females of color, and only a third endured slave status.

Of course, it would be useful to know how comparable São José's female population was to that of other mining towns, but the other five parishes did not report legal status. The seventh, the city of Vila Boa and its rural district, recorded three thousand forros and livres out of a total of eight thousand without distinguishing by sex. Thus, in the capital of the captaincy, 37.5 percent of the population was composed of freed and free people of color. It is possible that nine hundred to a thousand free and freed females of color lived in the capital city.[14]

The census of 1804 is one of the most accurate for the Captaincy of Goiás dur-

Table 12.2. Female Population of the Parish of São José de Tocantins in 1798

Age (Years)	Whites		Pardas		Pretas Livres		Captives		Total[a]
	Number	Percent	Number	Percent	Number	Percent	Number	Percent	
1–7	15	22.7	64	11.0	15	5.7	43	9.8	137
7–15	4	6.1	62	10.7	11	4.2	23	5.2	100
15–60	44	66.7	430	74.0	209	79.2	375	85.0	1,058
60 and older	3	4.6	25	4.3	29	11.0	—	—	57
	66		581		264		441		1,352[b]
	(4.9%)		(43.0%)		(19.5%)		(32.6%)		

Source: Arquivo do Museu das Bandeiras, City of Goiás, no. 342, Mappa das Pessoas que contem a Freguezia de São José de Tocantins no anno de 1798.

a. Excludes forty-two female newborns. There were twenty female deaths.

b. Of the 1,909 males for which there is age data, there were 116 whites, 647 pardos, 229 prêtos livres, and 917 captives, including 867 captive males between the ages of fifteen and sixty. There were also fifty male newborns and twenty-seven deaths.

ing the colonial period (table 12.1). Conducted during the period of the decline of mining, it reflected official concern to determine the size of the population able to revitalize the economy and recover more gold for export to Portugal. Because of the greater care taken and the improved ability to collect data, this census may be one of the most accurate concerning the number of free females in the late colonial period. In 1804 pardas (here termed *mulatas*) continued to outnumber other females at 8,084, with 4,728 pretas and 3,442 whites. Furthermore, the census of 1804 recorded married couples. Overall, there were 16,254 free females in the captaincy, more than double their number since 1792. White women composed only 21.2 percent of the free female population. In other words, 78.8 percent of the free female population was made up of women of color, and the enslaved female population added another 7,933 pretas and mulatas. Together, enslaved and free females of color outnumbered white females by 20,745 (85.8 percent) to 3,442 (14.2 percent). These statistics reveal why Portuguese bureaucrats complained about population decline in the captaincy. There were more free mulatas (8,084) than white men and women combined (6,950).

The first census taken after independence in 1822 abandoned some Portuguese census categories but kept a similar format to the 1804 census. Thus, some population change can be traced over the twenty-year period from 1804 to 1825. In the 1825 census (table 12.1), officials divided the population by sex, color, and marital status, but instead of the category of pardo they used "*homens de cor livres*" (free men of color) and "*mulheres de cor livres*" (free women of color). Furthermore, they subdivided each of these by "*Ingênuos*" and "*Libertos*" (freed).[15] Apparently, the term *Ingênuo* identified a freeborn person of color; thus, the census recognized the separate legal status of the freed population from the freeborn population of color. It also included the Amerindians living in mission villages, which added yet another category of free people of color to the census. Because of these census categories, the further growth of the free population of color can be documented, although it is uncertain whether this expansion occurred through in-migration, natural reproduction, or a combination of the two.

In 1825 free females of color numbered 19,880, 92.8 percent of whom (18,439) were Ingênuos; *libertas* (freedwomen) numbered only 1,441 (7.3 percent). The number of white females had increased from 3,442 in 1804 to 5,144 but made up only 16.4 percent of the total female population. The number of enslaved females had decreased to 6,046 (19.3 percent). Only 319 Amerindian females (1 percent) lived in three mission villages. Obviously, the vast majority of Amerindian females did not live in Christian missions in 1825. The nonwhite female population of color continued to outnumber that of white females; 84 percent of females in the province were women of color in 1825.

The last census to be discussed recorded an increase in the female population in 1832 (table 12.1). This census is especially useful because of what it reveals about the new categories of crioulo and African. For the first time, a census identified Africans as a social group worth counting. Thus, females who were white, parda, *crioula*, African, enslaved, or free can be distinguished. The census also included Amerindians. The single largest female group was composed of pardas (17,169), almost all of whom (94.9 percent) were free. Only 879 pardas (5 percent) were still enslaved. Second in number at 9,307 were the crioulas, 4,771 of whom were free and 4,536 (48.7 percent) enslaved. Although a slight majority of crioula females were free blacks, three-fourths (74.8 percent) of the 837 African females were still enslaved. Only 211 African females in the entire province enjoyed the livre status. The census showed, therefore, that enslaved African females were a definite minority by 1832, far outnumbered by both free and enslaved crioulas. Overall, 21,272 free women of color (63.6 percent of the total female population) lived in the Province of Goiás, with fewer than one-fifth (18.1 percent), or 6,041, still enslaved. Only 5,575 white females (16.7 percent of the total female population) dominated the provincial social structure, and 535 Amerindians (1.6 percent) lived in the mission villages. In other words, more than four-fifths (83.3 percent) of the province's total female population of 33,423 was composed of women of color in 1832.

Some censuses also provide insight into the age profile of the female population of Goiás. Age data were included for the censuses of 1786, 1789, 1792, 1798 (São José de Tocantins only), and 1825. These censuses help document the transition from a mining economy with a large proportion of adult males and a minority of children before the 1780s to the agro-pastoral economy of the early nineteenth century, which had a more balanced population profile and a significant percentage of female children under age twelve for whites, livres de cor, and slaves. Only the female Amerindian percentile was lower.

The first age data on the female population of the captaincy, but without distinction by color, survives in a report on the ages of men and women in 1786.[16] Of a total population of 56,303, there were 21,399 females (38 percent of the population); female children and teenagers to age fourteen formed 34.2 percent of those females. Most females (12,389, or 57.9 percent) were in the productive age group of interest to the Portuguese, between fourteen and sixty. At 1,697 (7.9 percent of the population), the elderly, those sixty and above, composed the smallest age group. In contrast, almost twice as many males (24,417) were in the productive ages between fifteen and sixty (table 12.3).

Three years later, the first detailed census by sex, color, and age, that of 1789 (table 12.4), provided a more comprehensive age profile of the captaincy's population. It reveals a general increase in the population to 58,499 but a drop of 2,742 in the female population to 18,657. Why such a decline occurred in only three

Table 12.3. Age Structure by Sex in the Captaincy of Goiás in 1786

| Age (Years)[a] | Males | | Females | | |
	Number	Percent	Number	Percent	Total
Newborns	725	2.1	696	3.3	1,421[b]
1–7	3,685	10.6	3,191	14.9	6,876
7–15	3,469	9.9	3,426	16.0	6,895
15–60	24,417	70.0	12,389	57.9	36,806
60 and older	2,550	7.3	1,673	7.8	4,223
90 and older	58	0.2	24	0.1	82
	34,904		21,399		56,303
	(62.0%)		(38.0%)		

Source: Instituto Histórico e Geográphico Brasileiro, Rio de Janeiro, arq. 1.2.8., vol. 37, Estatistica, Relação da população . . . da Capitania de Goiaz tirada das Freguesias, que tem a mesma Capitania no anno de 1786, fol. 4.
a. The ages of the females were seven to fourteen and fourteen to sixty years; the males were seven to fifteen and fifteen to sixty years.
b. In contrast to the births, there were 817 male deaths and 435 female deaths.

Table 12.4. Female Age Structure by Color in the Captaincy of Goiás in 1789

| Age (Years) | Whites | | Pardas | | Blacks | | Undeclared Color and Civil Status |
	Number	Percent	Number	Percent	Number	Percent	
Newborns							689[a]
1–7	802	21.4	1,388	24.7	1,560	18.1	
7–15	863	23.1	1,406	25.0	1,495	17.4	
15–60	1,792	47.9	2,625	46.6	4,621	53.7	
60–80	269	7.2	197	3.5	751	8.7	
90 and older	14	0.4	13	0.2	172	2.0	
	3,740		5,629		8,599		689
	(20.1%)[b]		(30.2%)[b]		(46.1%)[b]		(3.7%)[b]

Source: Arquivo Histórico Ultramarino, Lisbon, caixa 35, Goiás, 1790–1798, Mappa em que Tristao da Cunha Menezes . . . apresenta ao Real Ministério . . . até o prezente anno d'1789, Oct. 19, 1790.
a. There were 598 female deaths.
b. Percentage of total female population of 18,657. Males numbered 39,842 (scribe's total was 39,847), of which, there were 26,645 black males with 20,654 between the ages of fifteen and sixty (77.5 percent).

years is uncertain; the 1789 census recorded only 598 deaths. More important, however, the census listed whites, pardas, and black females by age, as well as 689 newborns. The distinction by color reveals different age profiles, with the largest percentage of females being children and teenagers to age fifteen among the pardas. The fact that 50 percent of pardas were under the age of fifteen is similar to recent Brazilian population profiles in which half of the total population is under fifteen. The white proportion of the population was 44.5 percent. Black females, however, had the lowest proportion (35.5 percent) of children and teenagers under age fifteen, which was undoubtedly due to the significant proportion of adults among the slave population.

For ages fifteen to sixty, black females had the highest percentage of the population, 53.7, followed by whites at 47.9 and pardas at 46.6. Not too surprisingly, more than three-fourths (77.5 percent) of black males were in the productive ages of fifteen to sixty years. The elderly population above sixty was also most numerous among blacks, with female blacks having the highest percentage above the age of sixty (10.7 percent) as opposed to white women (7.6 percent) and parda women (3.7 percent). The number and proportion of elderly black women undoubtedly reflected the aging of enslaved African women introduced into the captaincy as teenagers and young women during the eighteenth century, whereas the lower percentile for pardas may only be due to their having a more normal age structure (i.e., a higher proportion of children and teenagers), which was to be expected in a native-born population.

The census of 1792 (table 12.5) recorded similar patterns of age structure. Black males, at 28,963, had the highest proportion of their group (77.6 percent, or 22,483) in the productive ages, nearly the same percentage as in 1789. Once again, the overall population increased from 56,904 in 1791 to 60,428 in 1792, whereas

Table 12.5. Female Age Structure by Color in the Captaincy of Goiás in 1792

Age (Years)	Whites		Pardas		Blacks		Undeclared Color and Civil Status
	Number	Percent	Number	Percent	Number	Percent	
Newborns							673[a]
1–7	797	22.3	1,079	22.2	1,527	17.2	
7–15	816	22.9	1,158	23.8	1,500	16.9	
15–60	1,818	50.9	2,485	51.0	5,029	56.6	
60–80	130	3.6	140	2.9	704	7.9	
90 and older	9	0.3	9	0.2	122	1.4	
	3,570		4,871		8,882		673
	(19.8%)[b]		(27.1%)[b]		(49.4%)[b]		(3.7%)[b]

Source: Arquivo Histórico Ultramarino, Lisbon, caixa 35, Goiás, 1790–1798, Mappa em que o Governador, e Capitão General da Capitania de Goyaz Tristão da Cunha Menezes apresenta ao Real Ministerio . . . , July 29, 1792.

a. There were 651 deaths.

b. Percentage of total female population of 17,996. Males were 42,432, of which there were 28,963 black males, with 22,483 between the ages of fifteen and sixty.

the number of females declined from 18,017 (1791) to 17,996—a loss of twenty-one females. Black women made up the largest number and proportion of females between fifteen and sixty, as well as among the elderly age sixty and above. In fact, 122 black women were ninety and above, as opposed to only nine whites and nine pardas. In contrast, the largest percentage of those under age fifteen were pardas (45.9 percent) and whites (45.2 percent). In other words, there was still a smaller proportion of children among black females as well as a higher proportion of elderly, patterns consistent with a slave-based economy that had imported enslaved Africans.

The age data for 1789 and 1792 by color and sex reveal a more normal age profile for pardas, which helps explain the natural growth of the free parda population during the early nineteenth century. Unfortunately, however, those censuses did not isolate livres de cor as a census category and distinguish them from slaves. In 1798, however, the parish priest of São José de Tocantins (now Niquelândia) sent his report on the people of his *freguesia* (parish), with 3,261 differentiated as whites, pardos, prêtos livres, and captives. In 1798 São José was a mining town with a total captive population of 1,358; 94.6 percent of its male slaves were between the ages of fifteen and sixty, and free black males made up 164 (71.6 percent) of the same age group, suggesting that they, too, worked in the mining economy. The female population of 1,352 was composed of 66 whites (5 percent), 581 pardas (43 percent), and 264 pretas livres, or 19.5 percent, who outnumbered the 229 free black males. Fifty-four percent of free blacks were female, and almost one-third of the female population (441) was enslaved. There were also forty-two female newborns who were not distinguished by color or legal status. In other words, this mining community had almost one-fifth of its female population in the category of "free black," with pardas adding another 43 percent. Including the 32.6 percent enslaved, females of color composed 95 percent of the female population (table 12.2).

Analysis of age structure reveals a number of significant patterns for the town of São José. First, the proportion of women between fifteen and sixty varied by color and legal status. White females were 66.7 percent, pardas 74 percent, pretas livres 79.2 percent, and captives 85 percent. São José was, therefore, a typical mining town with a large proportion of working adults; it had a small percentage of children under seven (10 percent), with even fewer between seven and fifteen (7.4 percent). There were even fewer elderly women (fifty-seven), most of whom were pardas and pretas livres. The priest reported that the parish had no individuals above age ninety, and there were no elderly black slave women above the age of sixty. Twenty-nine pretas livres, however, were older than sixty.

In contrast to the unique data from São José, the census of 1804 reported no age-related data, but that of 1825 did so (table 12.6). Although the later census was somewhat different from the colonial censuses, it nonetheless clarified some age patterns across color categories, including slaves. First, the census documented a higher proportion of children under twelve for all groups except for

Table 12.6. Female Age Structure by Color and Legal Status in the Province of Goiás in 1825

Age (Years)	Whites		Livres de Cor[a]		Indians		Slaves	
	Number	Percent	Number	Percent	Number	Percent	Number	Percent
0–12	1,282	24.9	4,745	23.9	52	16.3	1,426	23.6
12–25	1,238	24.1	4,887	24.6	70	21.9	1,361	22.5
25–50	1,452	28.2	4,967	25.0	98	30.7	1,851	30.6
50–60	852	16.6	3,526	17.7	63	19.8	901	14.9
60–80	270	5.3	1,364	6.9	34	10.7	350	5.8
80–90	46	0.9	360	1.8	2	0.6	154	2.6
90–100	4	0.1	31	0.2	—	—	3	0.1
	5,144		19,880		319		6,046	
	(16.4%)[b]		(63.3%)[b]		(1.02%)[b]		(19.3%)[b]	

Source: Biblioteca Nacional, Rio de Janeiro, Manuscript Section, 11,4,2, Estatistica da Provincia de Goyáz remettida á Secretaria de Estado dos Negocios do Imperio . . . , 1825.
a. Free women of color.
b. Percentage of sum total of 31,389.

Amerindians. Whites had 25 percent; livres, 24 percent; slaves, 24 percent; and Amerindians, 16 percent. Another 22 to 25 percent of females were between twelve and twenty-five, and 25 to 31 percent were between the ages of twenty-five and fifty. Between 15 and 20 percent were fifty to sixty. The largest number of elderly women between the ages of sixty and one hundred were livres de cor, although their percentile (8.8) was similar to that of slave women (8.4). Only 6.2 percent of white women were sixty or older, whereas 11.3 percent of the Amerindian women were elderly.

Overall, the census of 1825 revealed that free females of color were dominant numerically—that is, 63.3 percent of the female population. Another 19.3 percent were enslaved, and free Amerindians represented 1.02 percent. White females were clearly outnumbered by free females of color, who had grown in numbers from the 2,209 in 1789 to 19,880 in 1825. Their numbers rose even higher in 1832, to 21,272 livres de cor (table 12.1). At the same time, the number of female slaves had declined from a high of 12,019 recorded in 1789 to only 6,046 in 1825 and 6,041 in 1832 (table 12.1).[17] The census data draw attention to the social transformation that occurred in Goiás at the end of the colonial period and the beginning of the national era: the decline of female and African slavery and expansion of the free population of color. In 1789 slave females formed 64.4 percent of the total female population of the captaincy, but free females of color composed 63.6 percent of the female population by 1832. To explain why these transformations occurred, other sources about the status and roles of free women of color must be consulted.

During the early nineteenth century two foreign travelers captured two distinct realities of life for free women of color in Goiás. The first observer focused on their wealth and the second on their hard work. After noting that whites believed in their superiority to other races, Johann Emanuel Pohl criticized them for inactivity and laziness. The majority of whites were so poor, he reported, that they lacked proper clothing to attend Sunday Mass. Expressly created for them was an early-morning Mass at 5, the *"missa da madrugada"* (emphasis in the original). Poor white women, dressed in mantles of inferior quality, went to that Mass in order to avoid "the disdainful eyes of the black women" who wore gold chains and lace when they attended a later Mass.[18] In a few words Pohl captured a world turned upside down for poor white women in which black women had more wealth than they did.

In contrast to Pohl's image of well-dressed black women, the traveler James W. Wells provided one that described the hard work behind the gold chains and lace. In the 1880s Wells visited a fazenda from which dried beef and hides were transported to the town of Pedro Affonso on the Tocantins River, and there he met with the workers on a *roça* (small plot of land) where foodstuffs were raised on a cattle ranch. After observing "some dozen men on the farm, sons, or slaves, of the Capitao," he complained that he "did not see any one man do a fair day's work." Instead, those who "appear to do the most work" were "the whity-brown, and black, women." Unlike most travelers, he then described their work. They cleaned by hand and spun cotton, weaving it into "a rough cloth." When necessary, they also worked in the fields. Furthermore, Wells also noted their labor-intensive activities of "pounding maize or castor beans" as well as "making *farinha* [manioc meal] or *rapadouro* [bricks of unrefined sugar]."[19] Although his description was brief, Wells identified the key role of free women of color in food and cloth production on a cattle ranch.

How typical were such women for the entire region? Had they pursued similar activities a century earlier? Fragmentary data from the 1783 census recorded data about free women of color as chefes who lived on small plots of land (roças and sítios). Even if what they did there cannot be documented, at least they can be placed in the countryside. In the mining town of Aguaquente during the 1820s, two free women of color were miners, although they probably owned the mine and did not work it themselves.[20] More important, the partial census of 1783 revealed much about the role of free women of color as owners of slaves and supervisors of household dependents. Many ruled slaves and servants because of the fact they were married, yet single and widowed free women of color, identified as chefes, also appeared in the censuses for both mining towns and rural districts.

Although ownership of slaves and gold jewelry might suggest that free women of color could challenge the Portuguese elite for high social status, the census of 1783 illuminated their actual social status with reference to whites, especially white men, who controlled the wealth of the captaincy through ownership of slaves, mines, ranches, sugar plantations, and businesses. Where slave owner-ship is indicated on the census, it is obvious that free black women owned the fewest slaves of any social group in the captaincy. Free pardas, either as married women or widows, controlled more slaves than free blacks did, thus reflecting the captaincy's social hierarchy at that time. White men and women, either married or widowed, owned the greatest numbers of slaves, often in the hundreds, especially if they owned mines and sugar plantations. Where slave ownership can be documented, free black females owned only one to three slaves; many did not possess even one. Single pardas, unless married or widowed, also had only a few slaves, in which case the pardas ranked among the moderately wealthy of the province.

That white men owned the most slaves, and free black women the least, is hardly surprising for the Brazilian slave system. It is significant, however, that the census of 1783 recorded another system of labor control that free women of color as well as other social groups used—their role in dominating household dependents and obligated persons. The agregado is a well-documented colonial social group, especially common in the Captaincy of São Paulo. Less well known is the pessoa de obrigação, also documented in the eighteenth-century mining town of Sabará in Minas Gerais, where a free woman exchanged a year of servitude for gold.[21]

Although it is uncertain how an obligated person came to be under the control of free women of color in Goiás, it is likely that some may have exchanged their services for a loan of gold, and others may have been captured in the Indian wars. Amerindian captives, however, were usually counted as agregados, as they were by Raymundo da Cunha Mattos in the households of the mining town of Pontal and the river port of Porto Real (now Porto Nacional) on the Tocantins River in the 1820s.[22] If African women loaned gold in exchange for services, and if the obligated persons appear in the households of pardas and blacks, as recorded in the census of 1783, then we may be able to document a labor system similar to pawnship in West Africa.[23] The pessoa de obrigação as a census category, however, appeared only in the partial census of 1783.

The supervisory role of free women of color over their own families, slaves, and dependents is abundantly clear, but it is not possible to describe the types of work they did in their homes. Their female slaves and servants may have done the cooking, one of the occupations most associated with slave women in Goiás. In the few household lists that recorded the occupations of free women of color, not one identified such a woman as a cook. This is in sharp contrast to the occupational lists for slave women in the nineteenth century.[24] Free women of color were also not recorded as laundry women, another common occupation for slave women.

In the mining regions of Brazil, black women were often involved in the processing and selling of *aguardente* (strong sugar cane liquor). Slave women appear as *alambiqueiros* (aguardente distillers), but free women of color owned some of the taverns where such drinks were sold and *vendas* (market stalls). Others undoubtedly worked in the town markets as *quitandeiras* (market women), a common occupation of enslaved and freedwomen elsewhere in Brazil, but the household lists consulted did not identify free women of color as quitandeiras.[25]

The reason for a lack of statistical data on the occupations of free women of color who cooked or entered the marketplace may be a bureaucratic preoccupation with the economic revival of the region, in particular its developments in cotton production and mining. Thus, the census of 1825 not only recorded the small number of gold mines still in production (forty-one) but also the number of looms (1,581). At first, it may appear that 1,581 women were weavers, but household lists from the mining town of Pontal identify two free men of color as weavers. If men in West Africa have long worked as weavers, it is hardly surprising that men were weavers in a part of the captaincy that received so many enslaved West Africans during the eighteenth century. The household lists for both the village and rural district of Pontal, however, recorded few women as weavers—there were only two in the village, presumed to be white or nearly white. In the rural district where there were large fazendas, only five free pardas and one free black woman were identified as weavers. Only a few women were weavers in the neighboring river port of Porto Real on the Tocantins River.

The presence of these few weavers, who were usually of lighter color, suggests that weaving was an occupation associated with women of higher social status. In contrast, the single largest occupation recorded for free women of color was *fiandeira* (spinner). These women dominated the household "cottage industry" of spinning cotton into threads in Pontal and its rural district. In the village of Pontal, fourteen pardas and fifteen black females formed 83 percent of the fiandeiras; only six (17 percent) were identified as "A" (for *alvo,* another word for "white," with the connotation of purity). The lower social status linked with spinning as an occupation in rural districts was reflected in the absence of white women, none of whom was recorded as a fiandeira in seventy-four households, in contrast to eighteen free pardas, fourteen free black women, and one Amerindian woman. These free women of color lived on roças and fazendas where cotton was cultivated, so they were probably involved in its cultivation and harvesting—if, that is, there were no slave women to do the work. Why so many women were spinners was partially explained by Auguste de Saint-Hilaire. When he visited the town of Corumbá near Meia Ponte (now the city of Pirenópolis), he observed that the women there received merchandise as their salary in exchange for the string they produced. Thus, spinning provided essential goods for their households. During the nineteenth century, women of all colors in Goiás were involved in the production of string and cloth for export or use of their own households.[26]

Another occupation followed by free women of color was that of seamstress (*costureira*). In Pontal, two whites, three pardas, and one crioula woman worked as seamstresses. In the neighboring rural district no whites did so and only one parda. Obviously, free women of color as well as slave women sewed the cotton clothing spun and woven by other women of color. Only a small minority of white women were documented as engaged in these occupations. They did, how-ever, enter household lists as *lavradoras* (agriculturalists), or they were married to lavradoras or owners of fazendas and sugar plantations with many slaves, which is to be expected in a typical Brazilian rural social structure. It is perhaps surprising that women of color were also lavradoras. A free parda, for example, an *agregada* of a wealthy priest and plantation owner, owned five slaves herself and also had an Indian agregada. Three other free pardas were also lavradoras, and two crioulas (aged sixty and forty-six) enjoyed the same status.[27] Unfortu-nately, household lists did not clarify how the black women obtained small farms. It is important to note, however, that free women of color had access to land and could work it with the assistance of family members, slaves, and agregados.

In the status hierarchy established by the whites of the Captaincy of Goiás, free black women were limited to the ownership of a few mines, small farms, cloth production, taverns and market stalls, and a few slaves. They did not ap-proach the great wealth and high social and economic position of the richest white women of Goiás, nor did they enjoy the "middle-class" status of many pardas who owned more slaves than black women did and had more choice of marriage partners. Yet free black women had superior social status to the en-slaved women of the region. They could travel where they wished. They could marry if they chose to do so and keep their children with them. They could also work at home as spinners and barter their string for household goods to benefit their families. After their deaths, they could pass on their houses, slaves, and plots of land to their children or, if they were childless, to religious brotherhoods. Single, elderly women without protectors, however, often ended their lives sup-porting themselves through the charity of others. The death registries from Natividade, a mining town in the north of the captaincy, recorded the number of elderly black women who died on the steps of churches after prolonged ill-nesses and lives as beggars.[28]

In contrast to the sketchy information about the work lives of free women of color of Goiás, much more has survived about marriage patterns and fam-ily, starting with the household lists of the 1783 census. There are also many images of the sexual mores of the region, which scandalized visiting foreigners and Portuguese priests. Their descriptions of the *"libertinagem"* of white men with women of color informs the historical stereotypes of colonial Goiás.[29] Because other studies of African women in slave societies have corrected racist stereotypes, historians have learned to be cautious with outsider reports about the sexuality, marriage, and family life of black women. Such caution is also warranted here because household lists and marriage records also identify stable, multigenerational black families, and free black women appear as the mothers of many children (more than six) and the grandmothers of still others. Further-more, freedmen and freedwomen had one of the highest marriage rates in 1825.

Typical of the outsider comments about the licentiousness of the region were those of Auguste de Saint-Hilaire, who noted the lack of marriage in late colonial Goiás (ca. 1819) and ascribed it to customs of the early days of settlement when white miners traveled to the region with black women. Their pride did not permit them to marry the women. "White men," he reported, "maintain an unregulated life in the company of black women or Indians." Saint-Hilaire seems to refer to racially mixed marriages when he wrote that marriages were rare and "always ridiculed." Because of the opposition by other whites in the region, white men often lived in consensual unions with women of color. Even white men of high social standing, including Portuguese bureaucrats and priests, lived openly in their houses with lovers, women of color, as if they were spouses. Saint-Hilaire was scandalized to observe that the priest's mistress accompanied him to church when he went to say Mass.[30]

The most notable example of this social custom involved the Portuguese governor of Goiás, Fernando Delgado Freire de Castilho, who lived in Vila Boa at the time of Saint-Hilaire's visit. When Saint-Hilaire met him, the governor introduced him to his two natural children, who were seven and eight. On the occasion of a dinner with the governor in which they discussed "the strange customs of the place," the governor pointed to the two children and asked, "Do you think . . . that I could marry the mother of these children . . . the daughter of a carpenter?" When the governor was recalled to Portugal in 1820, he took his mistress and their children with him as far as Rio de Janeiro. While waiting to embark for Lisbon, the mistress declared that she wanted to go to Europe as his "legitimate wife." Faced with the dilemma of either marrying the daughter of a carpenter or leaving her in Brazil, the governor committed suicide. Saint-Hilaire did not identify the carpenter's daughter by name or color, but most carpenters in Goiás were men of color. It is probable that the governor's dilemma involved not only marriage to a woman from a lower class but also one who was a free woman of color.[31]

From the woman's perspective, the request was not unusual in terms of the marriage customs of the only place she knew, the Captaincy of Goiás, where some white men married women of color after long-term consensual unions that involved children. Such marriages raised the social status of the women and their children. Otherwise the women were likely to face the more usual situation of a transitory relationship with a white man that left them as impoverished single mothers raising one or two pardo children with the meager earnings of a spinner. The household lists, however, also record black women with a single parda child, their eldest, followed by much younger black children, suggesting that they could later establish a stable relationship with the father of their black children.[32]

White men, however, did not have only one partner. Free women of color who entered relationships with white men were often only one of a number of women associated with the male head of household. In household lists subordinate women appear as agregadas, often with one or two children. Conversely, one woman of color often had many male sexual partners. In the north of the captaincy, captive women, often Indians, were shared by the male head of household and his male *camaradas* (workers). That was also the fate of other free women of color who lived alone with a gang of miners, river boatmen, or cowboys on remote ranches.[33]

As a result of the shortage of women and the rarity of marriage to solidify Catholic families in many parts of Goiás, prostitution, usually involving enslaved and free women of color, was endemic to the region. During the late colonial period it is almost impossible to document the prevalence of prostitution except for general references in official correspondence, reports of travelers such as Pohl and Saint-Hilaire, and military hospital records of the early nineteenth century that showed a high incidence of syphilis among troops. Raymundo da Cunha Mattos was well aware of the deleterious impact of prostitution on the health of his troops, who often suffered from venereal diseases.[34]

The unprotected women of all colors commonly experienced sexual exploitation and rape. Slave women were especially vulnerable to the sexual demands of their masters, but such vulnerabilities also extended to other subordinate young women, especially those of lighter skin color than African women. In addition, they faced kidnapping, mutilation, and murder in frontier warfare because the Canoeiro and other Amerindian nations massacred women of all colors to avenge the atrocities committed against their own women and children. In one region where black and pardo troops were heavily involved in frontier warfare, often fighting on the side of the Portuguese in enslaving *bandeiras* (expeditions), the Indians singled out a black woman for vengeance and burned her body because of their "hatred for persons of black color." The others they killed with arrows and war clubs.[35]

The sexual exploitation of young women was so common that fathers of "good families" of all colors tried to prevent contact between their daughters and strange men. They cloistered them in their households and did not permit them to talk to visiting foreigners. Thus, foreign travelers usually remarked upon their lack of social interaction with women whose husbands or fathers hid them from view. They could not even meet women during the day on the streets of the capital, the City of Goiás. Women only went out at night and in groups. They would be draped in wool capes, their heads covered with scarves or hats. To Saint-Hilaire, these women of all races seemed to be shadows passing in the silence of the night "in search of amorous adventures."[36]

The descriptions of sexual promiscuity, prostitution, rape, and concubinage might lead to the conclusion that free women of color never married or formed families. That was not the case, however, as marriage records reveal (table 12.7). Although Saint-Hilaire used the word *rare* when discussing marriage in 1819, the censuses, based on reports of parish priests who kept marriage records during the colonial period, show that men and women of all colors married, some across color lines. White women had the highest marriage rate (table 12.8), followed by pardas and free blacks in 1804. By 1825, however, freedwomen and Amerindian women had the highest rates (table 12.9).

Table 12.7. Married Couples in the North of the Captaincy of Goiás in 1783

Town or District	Whites			Pardos			Blacks		
	Number	Percent	Total[a]	Number	Percent	Total[a]	Number	Percent	Total
Conceição de Traíras	18	25.0	72	27	40.3	67	13	14.4	90
Aguaquente	14	29.2	48	12	40.0	30	14	15.2	92
Cocal	15	19.7	76	36	38.3	94	23	18.1	127
Cavalcante	14	33.3	42	22	56.4	39	4–6[c]	—	—
	16[b]	—	16	—	—	—	—	—	—
São José de Tocantins	40	38.1	105	38	46.3	82	23	14.9	154
Cachoeira	1	20.0	5	5	55.6	9	4	26.7	15
Santa Rita	3	60.0	5	5	29.4	17	7	15.9	44
Moquem	7	77.8	9	8	50.0	16	4	23.5	17
Amaro Leite	12	44.4	27	25	67.6	37	5	17.9	28
São Félix	56	—	—	14	—	—	21	—	—
Arraias	32	100.0	32	49	—	—	16	—	—

Source: Biblioteca Nacional, Rio de Janeiro, cod. 16,3,2, Notícia Geral da Capitania de Goiás, 1783.
a. The rest of the total were identified as *solteiro* (single).
b. White men who were married to parda women.
c. Four or six freed blacks. There were also four or six houses of single freed blacks.

Table 12.8. Married Individuals by Color and Sex in the Captaincy of Goiás in 1804

Sex	Whites		Mulattos		Blacks	
	Number	Percent	Number	Percent	Number	Percent
Male	901	25.7	1,518	20.6	546	17.0
Females	809	23.5	1,605	19.9	576	12.2
	1,710	24.6[a]	3,123	20.2[b]	1,122	14.1[c]

Source: Arquivo Histórico Ultramarino, Lisbon, cod. 2109, Reflexoens Economicas Sobre As Tabellas Statisticas da Capitania de Goyaz Pertencentes ao anno de 1804 e feitas no de 1806.
a. Of total number of whites, 6,950 (3,508 males and 3,442 females).
b. Of total number of mulattos, 15,452 (7,368 males and 8,084 females).
c. Of total number of free blacks, 7,936 (3,208 males and 4,728 females).

Table 12.9. Married Individuals by Color, Sex, and Legal Status in the Province of Goiás in 1825

Sex	Whites		Indians[a]		Ingênuos[b]		Libertos[c]	
	Number	Percent	Number	Percent	Number	Percent	Number	Percent
Males	1,745	32.6	108	35.5	4,242	25.6	550	35.7
Females	1,519	29.5	111	34.8	4,486	24.3	544	37.8
	3,264[d]	31.1	219[e]	35.2	8,728[f]	24.9	1,094[g]	36.7

Source: Biblioteca Nacional, Rio de Janeiro, Manuscript Section, 11,4,2, Estatistica da Provincia de Goyáz remettida á Secretaria de Estado dos Negocios do Imperio . . . , 1825.
a. Mission Indians from São José, Carretão, and Duro.
b. Free people of color.
c. Freed persons.
d. Of a total number of 10,495 whites (5,351 males and 5,144 females).
e. Of a total of 623 Indians (304 males and 319 females).
f. Of a total of 35,005 ingênuos (16,566 males and 18,439 females).
g. Of a total of 2,980 libertos (1,539 males and 1,441 females).

The first census to provide insights into marriage patterns by color was the partial census of 1783. Although it did not distinguish marriages by legal status as did later censuses, the partial census confirms that single men (*solteiros*) outnumbered married men in almost all parishes in 1783, thus confirming general observations about the prevalence of single males in the mining towns. Vila Boa and São Félix, bureaucratic centers as well as mining towns where gold foundries were located, had the largest number of married white men and women in each of their respective *comarcas* (the administrative unit of a captaincy): Vila Boa had 559 couples, and São Félix had 56. Vila Boa also had 330 married pardos forros and 295 prêtos forros.[37] Otherwise, data on marriages of pardos and blacks were largely tabulated for the northern comarca. In these official counts, men and women of color outnumbered white couples in all parishes except for São Félix in the north of the captaincy. Only sixteen racially mixed marriages were reported between white men and parda women in the mining town of Cavalcante (table 12.7). Pardo men had higher marriage rates than white men in seven parishes, and black men had the lowest rates of marriage, presumably because of the large numbers of black men who were single and enslaved.

The next census to identify married couples was that of 1804 (table 12.8). The census documented the trend suggested in 1783 that more people of color married than whites, but it is also possible to calculate marriage rates by color and sex because of the greater accuracy of the census data. Thus, about one-fourth of white males were married in 1804, with a similar proportion for white females. As for free mulattos, about 20 percent of the males and females were married. Finally, the lowest marriage rates were for free blacks. Seventeen percent of black males were married but only 12 percent of free black females, and they had the highest percentile of single persons in the captaincy (88 percent), possibly reflecting pervasive racial prejudices against marrying black women. In the free population, blacks were the least likely to marry in 1804, as was the case in 1783. Pardo marriage rates had fallen behind white rates by 1804, although more mulattos than whites married.

The census of 1825 also included data about marriages (table 12.9). It permits insight into the marriage patterns of whites, ingênuos de cor, and libertos. In 1825 freedmen and freedwomen had the highest marriage rates (35.7 and 37.8, respectively), followed by Indian men (35.5 percent) and Indian women (34.8 percent). Free people of color had the lowest rates—25.6 percent for men and 24.3 percent for women. Clearly, by 1825 free people of color, excluding libertos, were least likely to marry.

In addition to the general marriage statistics for 1825, a more detailed report of 1828 exists for the mining town of Cavalcante (table 12.10). The parish priest's accounting of the marital status of 2,282 persons is illuminating because he also distinguished among Amerindians, free blacks, and pardos and also between free blacks who were African and those who were Brazilian-born (crioulos). The

Table 12.10. Marital Status by Color in the Town of Cavalcante in 1828

Color	Married		Widowed		Single		Total
	Number	Percent	Number	Percent	Number	Percent	
Whites	81	31.3	12	4.6	166	64.1	259
Indians	5	20.8	—	—	19	79.2	24
Pardos	338	26.7	57	4.5	870	68.8	1,265
Blacks							
Crioulos	105	15.5	20	3.0	553	81.6	678
Africans	16	28.6	3	5.4	37	66.1	56
	545		92		1,645		2,282[a]
	(23.9%)		(4.0%)		(72.1%)		

Source: Arquivo Histórico de Goiás, Goiânia, Seçao de Municípios, Cavalcante, Informação circunstanciada, que se remette do Julgado de Cavalcante, sua Estatistica,...satisfazendo-se a todos os quizitos expecificados na Ordem de 14 Abril 1828.

    a. Included in this number were 416 *cativos* (captives), 21 libertos (freed persons), 48 *moços de servir* (servant boys), and 19 *mendigos* (beggars). In the previous year ten had married.

Cavalcante statistics revealed that the highest percentage of married persons was among whites. It is notable, however, that the records show that the next-highest percentage was for free Africans, followed by pardos, Amerindians, and crioulos. That was similar to the marriage experience of freed blacks in the capital of Vila Boa de Goiás in 1783, and it undoubtedly reflected the custom of freed persons marrying after their manumission.

    The official marriage records demonstrate that some free parda and black women did marry and begin families. It is far more difficult, however, to describe the family life of free women of color. On household lists of 1783 and the 1820s these individuals appear as *mulheres* (women) after the names of male heads of household, with their children recorded after the woman's name. Widows who were heads of households were also listed along with their children, grandchildren, dependents, and slaves. Single women of color, often with children, were also common, but none of the household lists identified the children of slave women. The household lists of free people of color for 1783 indicate that the mining town and its district of Barra, located near Vila Boa, had a high proportion of single men and women and few children.[38] Among free blacks who lived in the rural district of Barra, there were eighteen households. Only six had listed children: a widow with three children, a married couple with seven children, a woman alone of unknown marital status with four children, a freedwoman who was the mother of five pardo children by a white man, a married couple with two children, and another widow with one son. The other black women were either single or childless. The only woman identified as African was Izabel Angola, a childless widow.

    The family data of São Félix for free pardas and blacks reveal that only five of eighteen pardo households included children.[39] Five couples were married, and one had six children; that same couple also owned nine slaves. One of the single mothers had four children, and another had nine children; a widow had six children, and one man had a child living with him. Overall, twenty-six free children lived in the eighteen households of pardos. There were fewer households of free black married couples (ten), of which only four had families. Two couples had three children each, another had four children, and the last had ten children. The other black couples were childless. Two single women had children—one had three and the other had only one child. Twenty-two black women and four black men were single.

Only one pardo couple and one black couple lived in the mining town of Carmo, and both couples were childless.[40] Two parda widows, however, had children—one had three and the other four. Three single black women, one of whom was the African Maria Benguela, had two children each. In the village of Chapada there was one pardo couple and thirteen black married couples. None of them, however, had children listed. The sparse data for these districts, taken together with the omission of children from other household lists for 1783, suggest that women of color, even when married, had few children or none at all. It might also suggest that the census takers failed to list children. The preoccupation of Portuguese authorities with determining the number of miners may have led them to ignore children of free women of color. One suspects, however, that child mortality was high, especially in areas where malaria was common.

By the 1820s, household lists from the north of the captaincy do record the number of women and their children by color. It is also obvious from the lists that family members were not always the children of married couples but included grandchildren, nephews or nieces, brothers or sisters, and even aunts. In the village of Aguaquente, 102 free black males and 154 free black females lived in a community where there were only thirty-five whites. Pardos numbered 306. The detailed lists for all inhabitants of Aguaquente permit a reconstruction of the variety of families blacks formed in that village in the 1820s.[41] Forty-eight children lived in households headed by nineteen couples (i.e., the male head of household and his mulher). In contrast, twenty-four children lived in households headed by twelve single mothers. Thirteen single women were childless. Only two children lived with a widow, and five of the widows were childless. In addition, three grandchildren lived in the households of single and married women. This small sample shows that fifteen black women lived in two-parent households that included children. These married women tended to have more children than single women. Thus, to be defined as a free black woman in this slave society did not exclude all such women from marriage or family life. The sources reveal that white women had the highest rates of marriage and numbers of children, followed by pardas, and that free black women were disadvantaged in their access to marriage and a stable family life.

Although censuses and household lists established the presence of free women of color in Central Brazil between 1779 and 1832 and identified how some could earn livings and form families, little is known about their associational and/or religious lives. That some Afro-Brazilian religious customs survived in the late colonial period can only be traced through arrests of black women as *feiticeiras* (witches or sorceresses) and fortune-tellers (i.e., diviners) or for dancing at night. Nineteenth-century sources occasionally identified them as *curandeiras* (healers) or described the use of charms and amulets in the region.[42]

The great majority of sources about free women of color and their religious and associational life come from the surviving manuscripts of the lay brotherhoods (*irmandades*). These were Catholic religious associations of laymen and women associates that raised money and built chapels or churches dedicated to their patron saints during the colonial period. Much useful information can be found in minutes of the meetings of the brotherhoods of Our Lady of the Rosary of the City of Goiás and of Natividade, including the lists of queens, female judges, and female procurators of brotherhoods, and the 1772 and 1788 charters of Our Lady of Mercies of the Brotherhood of São Joaquim in Cocal, one of the richest of the mining towns of the late eighteenth century.[43]

To be an officer in a brotherhood required donations in gold. Queens and judges were therefore women of property and status in the black community. Such women also entered the historical record when they donated houses and slaves to the Brotherhood of the Rosary. Membership in a brotherhood as a female associate was especially important for aging free black women who had no master, spouse, or child to care for them when they were sick or to arrange their funeral and burial and have prayers said for their souls after death.

Among the earliest descriptions of black women who took part in a Catholic religious ceremony in a role usually reserved for white men is one that came from an investigation into the forced expulsion of two Jesuit priests from the north of the captaincy. To the scandal of the Portuguese who were concerned with maintaining their prerogatives, the Jesuits permitted four crioulas to carry the (Blessed) "Sacrament" on a bier during a religious procession in Pontal.[44] The episode suggests that the Jesuits, as well as other Catholic priests, had laid the basis for an Afro-Brazilian Catholicism that flourished in the mining towns of the captaincy, particularly in Natividade.

According to one tradition, the slaves of Natividade were so devoted to Our Lady of the Rosary that they tried to erect in her honor the largest church in the entire captaincy. Pohl maintains that it was free blacks who tried to build the church, which was never finished.[45] The Brotherhood of Our Lady of the Rosary that undertook the construction of the church during the late eighteenth century was sizable. It included an enormous board of black men and women with many male and female officers, each of whom donated gold to join the brotherhood and still more gold to serve as an officer or board member (table 12.11).

Black women played an active role in lay brotherhoods, particularly in fundraising, in colonial Brazil. The prominent role of free women in the Brotherhood of the Rosary of Natividade is noteworthy. The irmandade elected kings, queens, judges, procurators, and other officers who seem to have been either

Table 12.11. Queens, Judges, and Sisters of the Brotherhoods of Cocal, Natividade, and the City of Goiás, 1772–1840

Year	Queen	Judge of the Vara	Judge	Sisters
Cocal				
1772	Francisca Fernandes Lima	Catharina Leite de Barros	—	—
Natividade				
1786–87	Roza Fernandes da Silva	Eugenia Barboza	Cezilia Furtado de Mendonça	14
1787–88	Marianna ____ [?][a] de Mello Gervazia	Gervazia [?] da Cunha Mendes	Romana Rodrigues Ferreira	16
1788–89	Ritta da Cunha [?] David	[?] Ribeiro Lustoza	Maria Fernandes ____ [?]	16
1789–90	Herculia Teixeyra da Costa	Roza Maria de Paulla	Mariana Francisca de Souza	20
1790–91	Anna Luiza Ferreira de Barros	Maria Luiza da Silva	Antonia ____ [?]	32
1791–92	Helena Barboza	Rosa Maria de Souza	Rosa Dias da Costa	25
1792–93	Cuztodia Gonçalvez Pereira	Quiteria de Souza Estrela	Rosa Barboza	26
1793–94	Qiteria da Costa Gomes	Maria do Rozario	Maria de Souza	10
City of Goias				
1827–28	Marta Antonia da Silva	Maria de Carvalho	Thereza Antonia da Costa, slave	8 slaves, 1 *forra*[a], 3 free
1828–29	Custodia Thomazia	Eva, spouse of Izidro Pinto	Luiza Barbara Rodrigues	6 slaves
1829–30	Barbara Maria da Silveira	Francisca Roz.e [Rosário?] De Morais	Quiteria Valenca [Valença]	2 *forras*, 4 free 5 slaves, 7 free

Table 12.11. Cont.

Year	Queen	Judge of the Vara	Judge	Sisters
1830–31	Ignacia Luduvica de Almeida	Maria Ferreria do do Espirito Santo	Euzebia Maria de Bada	9 slaves, 3 free
1831–32	Maria Rodrigues de Jezuz	Quintiliama Moreira de Carvalho	Emerenciameis [?] Soares de Bulhoens	9 slaves, 3 free
1832–33	Maria Joaquina Taveira	Maria Alves de Brito	Felippa da Costa Mattos	7 slaves, 5 free
1833–34	Maria Joaquina de Campos	Maria de Castro	Anna Xavier, slave	8 slaves, 4 free
1834–35	Rosa Ferreira dos Santos	Maria Barboza	Martha Ferreira Gomes	4 slaves, 5 free, 3 uncertain
1835–36	Luisa Barboza	Maria de Santa Anna	Anna Marques Fogaça	6 slaves, 6 free
1836–37	Lauriana Alvares dos Santos	Rosa Francisca Paxeca	Maria, slave	4 slaves, 8 free
1838–39	Emerenciana Maria de Jezus	Maria do Carmo de Passos	Maria Francisca Izidoria da Silva	8 slaves, 4 free
1839–40	Germana Fernandes, Maria Leite[b]	Jozefa de Belém	Gregoria *crioula*, slave	8 slaves, 4 free

Sources: Archive of the Curia, Goiânia, Compromisso da Irmandade de Nossa Senhora das Mercês dos Captivos do Arrayal de São Joaquim do Cocal, 1772; and BFEG, City of Goiás, Livro [or livros?] dos termos e assentos of Nossa Senhora do Rosário, Natividade, 1786–1801; and Livro dos Termos de Meza, Nossa Senhora do Rosário, City of Goiás, 1826–40.

Note: A line and/or a question mark indicates that a name was either missing or illegible.

a. Freedwoman.

b. Maria Leite was an agregada who replaced Germana as queen.

freed persons (usually indicated by a saint's name as their surname) or free persons of color (with typical Portuguese surnames). Some may also have been pardos and whites. Although white irmandades were racially exclusive, black brotherhoods were more tolerant. Unlike the Brotherhood of the Rosary in the City of Goiás, where a person's slave status was carefully noted, the scribes of Natividade recorded no woman as a slave in the brotherhood between 1786 and 1801. Presumably, all members were free blacks or freedwomen. Up to thirty-two women were board members between 1786 and 1794. This wealthy brotherhood must have received a substantial sum in gold from its many officers and board members. The brotherhood also had a "perpetual queen" named Joanna Maria de Assumpção who reigned every year between 1787 and 1794. Because many enslaved Africans then worked in Natividade, one wonders if she had been a queen in Africa or whether she made such a substantial donation in gold that the brotherhood honored her with the title of perpetual queen. The fact that she bore a saint's name strongly suggests that she was a former slave.[46]

Also on the Natividade brotherhood lists are the black women who appeared over and over in high-ranking positions or served on the board, which means that they had accumulated enough gold to serve more than once and had sufficient authority and prestige to be elected more than once. Thus the lists point to a continuity of individuals in power. Members of the board of Natividade also served for several years. Most officers on the more egalitarian boards of the City of Goiás, however, served only once. The queens in both irmandades of the Rosary of Natividade and the City of Goiás were elected and served only once, apparently because of the large donation in gold required to assume the office. Another brotherhood dedicated to the black saint Efigênia, the Princess of Nubia, had no queen, possibly because members were subjects of the queen of the Brotherhood of the Rosary.[47]

In the coastal cities of Salvador da Bahia and Rio de Janeiro, membership in the brotherhoods of the Rosary or Saint Efigênia was often linked to African ethnicity.[48] The registries of brotherhood officials from Central Brazil, however, did not limit membership in a specific brotherhood to one ethnic group. Brotherhoods included both crioulo and African-born individuals, usually listed as "Angolan" or "Mina." Not all brotherhood records identified the members by legal status. Only the Brotherhood of the Rosary of the City of Goiás distinguished among free persons, the freed, and the enslaved.[49] The top positions in this brotherhood—judge of the *vara* (staff of office), which was placed before that of queen, and queen—were apparently monopolized by free or freed black women. Not one of them was identified as a slave, undoubtedly because of the financial resources needed to be judge and queen. The brotherhood also had another female judge, the *Juiza de Ramalhete*. Her responsibilities remain unclear. Did she care for the brotherhood's valuables? What is of interest is the fact that a few slave women served in the office, presumably because it was a position of lower status. Judges were always listed after judges of the vara and queens. The board consistently had twelve elected sisters (*irmās*) who were particularly important in fund-raising, collecting donations needed for the support of the brotherhood and its activities. Free black women seated on the board varied from a high of seven in 1829 and 1830 to a low of three freeborn black women in 1827 and 1828 and 1830 and 1832. In many years the majority of sisters on the board were still enslaved. Their slave status was officially recorded because they could only serve with their owner's permission. Only three such freedwomen were identified in all of the years examined.[50]

Although brotherhood lists permit recovering the names of black women who were the elected queens, judges, and (in the case of Natividade) female procurators, we know little about the responsibilities of each officer. There is, however, a more detailed brotherhood charter that reveals how a black brotherhood functioned on the frontier and the role of black women within its administrative structure: the founding charter of the black brotherhood dedicated to Our Lady of Mercies in Cocal, a mining town of 4,002 inhabitants in 1789.[51] The charter of 1772 is richly ornamented with large red capitals ornamented in gold leaf. It was obviously done with great care and expense. Who mastered the elegant form of an illuminated manuscript is unknown. The charter opens with a deferential statement in which the brothers identify themselves as "the miserable, and most humble natives of Ethiopia, slaves of your Magesty." These Africans sought royal protection, in particular from a local priest who demanded high fees in gold for his services. After their appeal to the monarch, they made certain that the reader knew that they were the ones who built the "spacious chapel" dedicated to Our Lady of Mercies in Cocal. Historically, the Brotherhood of Our Lady of Mercies was linked to the liberation of Christian captives in Muslim North Africa. The brothers' choice of this patroness suggests that they sought her protection and assistance in obtaining freedom. Our Lady of Mercies was also a popular brotherhood in the Province of Minas Gerais, where it was mainly associated with crioulo slaves.[52]

To belong to this brotherhood, each member, whether male or female, paid an entrance fee of 2 oitavas of gold in 1772; the fee was reduced to 1 oitava in 1788.[53] Afterward, each member had to make an annual donation of 1 oitava of gold as was set in 1772, but that was reduced to .5 oitava until the member reached age twenty-five in 1788. In other words, each brother and sister was obligated to continue to donate gold every year. The same requirement to donate an oitava of gold occurred in the charter of the Brotherhood of the Rosary in the City of Goiás. The Brotherhood of Our Lady of Mercies of Cocal was to be governed by a board that included an elected queen, a female judge, and twelve sisters. In order to be queen, a woman had to donate 25 oitavas of gold in 1772 (20 oitavas in 1788), the same amount as the king. In that period, 25 oitavas of gold could buy an infant's freedom. The two judges, however, paid less—16 oitavas in 1772 and 12 oitavas in 1788. Each person who sat on the board paid 2 oitavas of gold in 1772 and 1788. In all, the black women who served on the board in 1772 were required to donate a total of 65 oitavas of gold, an amount about equal to the price of a child's freedom.[54] The charter of the Brotherhood of Our Lady of Mercies also reveals how queens were chosen. The reigning queen nominated four candidates, two of whom were freedwomen, and the other two were captives (slaves). Thus, slave women were eligible to be queen if they could make the donation in gold. The members of the board then voted on who would be queen for the following year. Female judges and sisters on the board also nominated their successors.

One of the principal obligations of the brotherhood was to celebrate the feast day of Our Lady of Mercies each year during the eight days of the Christmas holidays. The king and queen presided over the festivities with the insignias of their majesty, presumably capes and crowns as in the captaincy of Minas Gerais, while the male judge, dressed in the brotherhood's *opa* (confraternity cape), carried his vara and was accompanied by the female judge of the vara. The obligation of each of the twelve sisters of the board was to ask for alms for the brotherhood in the month assigned to her. Apparently, each sister walked about the town begging for contributions to support the brotherhood, its church, and its charities. Sisters were, therefore, most important in the fund-raising activities of the brotherhood. All brothers (and sisters?) were obligated to assist at the feast day celebrations, wearing a white opa inscribed with a red cross, and to attend board meetings.

Why so many women were willing to pay so much gold and undertake the heavy responsibilities of brotherhood membership can in part be explained by religious beliefs that are difficult to recover from eighteenth-century documentation. More pragmatic explanations can be related to ideas about death, including the preoccupation of people on the frontier with dying a good death, that is, receiving the last sacraments and a proper burial within a church. Our Lady of the Good Death, whose brotherhoods were supported by pardos, and Our Lord of the Good Death, whose image was found in many private chapels, were very popular in Central Brazil.[55]

Similar preoccupations with death and burial, as well as with prayers for the souls in purgatory, are reflected in the charter of Cocal. The brotherhood carefully enumerated the rights of members to a funeral and burial in the church. It is of particular interest that queens were buried in the same place as kings, close to the central altar. Male and female judges were buried from the arch to the railings of the church, and the members of the board from the railings to the principal door.[56] Thus, the hierarchy in life was maintained in death.

The charter also explained the duties of the black procurator. There was only one procurator in Cocal, but in Natividade the brotherhood had two men and two women who presumably carried out similar duties as in Cocal. Perhaps the responsibilities defined as feminine, such as washing and starching altar cloths, fell to the female procurators of Natividade. In Cocal, however, the one male procurator sent altar cloths out to be washed and starched, undoubtedly by black women. He also cared for the church's ornaments and lamps, made hosts, rang the church bells, marked burials, and helped any sick brother who was in danger of death. Did the female procurators of Natividade cook for and otherwise care for the sick? Or perhaps they were restricted to cleaning, washing up, and decorating the statues of saints and the altar dedicated to Our Lady of the Rosary.

Because of the focus of many brotherhoods on care for the sick and the dying, even pardos and whites were affiliated with black brotherhoods and held office in them, mainly as scribes, treasurers, or procurators. Men of high social status belonged to as many brotherhoods as they could, and a man's social position in local society was reflected in the number of brotherhoods represented in his funeral procession. In Cocal, the charter welcomed whites and pardos, but they were excluded from voting unless they were a scribe, treasurer, or procurator. The brotherhood also bound itself to provide burial to whites who had served it, unless they chose to be buried elsewhere. In such cases, the black brothers participated in the funeral procession. The charter language suggested, therefore, that white men were more involved with the black brotherhoods than white women. Free men with military titles were among those most associated with the Brotherhood of the Rosary of the City of Goiás, perhaps because the black women to whom they were attached were actively involved on the board. The most famous man associated with that brotherhood was an artist, José Joaquim da Veiga Valle, who enjoys an international reputation for the quality of his sculptures.[57]

Through the fragmentary brotherhood records it is quite possible to identify black women who were free, freed, and enslaved, and who established status and rank within their own communities. They exercised leadership roles as queens, judges, procurators, and board members and invited whites to associate with them. They made donations in gold equal to those made by men, and they were rewarded for their contributions and services with burial in equal places within the Church. To be judges or queens meant that black women had amassed some material wealth. The emphasis of brotherhoods on service to the sick and dying, followed by burial in the church they had built, reflected not only Christian charitable concerns but also those of African-style burial associations.[58]

That free black women valued the Luso-Brazilian institution of a Catholic lay brotherhood can be traced through their yearly donations in gold registered in some of the brotherhood records. The sizable donations of gold year after year in Natividade indicate that black women had continued access to gold, either through their own market activities or the mine labor of spouses and family members. The emphasis brotherhoods placed on legitimate marriages may also explain why so many freed blacks married in the Church. Catholic marriage ensured the rights to burial of one's spouse and legitimate children up to the age of twelve.

Most African women imported as slaves died as slaves in Central Brazil during the eighteenth century. As long as the gold economy prospered, their crioulo descendants also died as slaves. But when gold mines no longer yielded their treasures so easily, fewer and fewer new Africans were imported, and African slavery began its decline in the region. Enslaved women were increasingly crioulo in identity, or they escaped slave status through manumission. At the same time, the free population of color, particularly that of free women of color, grew in size and importance. People who were racially mixed (pardos) gained the upper hand in numbers and improved their social position and property ownership as wealthy Portuguese miners returned to Portugal, a process solidified by independence in 1822.

Although the Portuguese complained of declining population in the region, it was their ethnic group, in particular Portuguese women, who lost in population size. Increasingly, the frontier belonged to free and enslaved people of color. North American images of a white-Indian dichotomy forged in the crucible of North American frontier conflicts must therefore be abandoned for central Brazil and should be replaced by a Luso-Brazilian model of the *sertão* (backlands), in which Portuguese, African, and Amerindian men and women intermixed. What resulted was a new people of the back lands who settled and then held the land between the Tocantins and Araguaia rivers, first for Portugal and then for Imperial Brazil.[59] Critical to these interconnected processes of settlement were free women of color, who governed brotherhoods, formed families, and performed the difficult household and agricultural labor of a violent frontier. Their hard labor and constructive cultural contributions merit further historical study.

Notes

1. Among the studies of slavery that devote only a few pages to free blacks is Mary C. Karasch, *Slave Life in Rio de Janeiro, 1808–1850* (Princeton: Princeton University Press, 1987).

2. During the colonial period, the Captaincy of Goiás was divided into two *comarcas* (administrative units of a captaincy): The comarca of the North, roughly equivalent to the modern state of Tocantins, and the comarca of the South, now the modern state of Goiás. This enormous region in the interior of Brazil was governed from the capital of Vila Boa de Goiás, later named the City of Goiás. With independence in 1822 the captaincy became known as the Province of Goiás. During the eighteenth century, the governor based in Vila Boa supervised an area of nine hundred thousand square kilometers that I have chosen to call Central Brazil based on nineteenth-century concepts of the region as the "heart" or center of Brazil. Modern geographers usually group the state of Goiás with the region of West Central Brazil and Tocantins with the Amazon region. Horieste Gomes and Antônio Teixeira Neto, *Geografia Goiás-Tocantins* (Goiânia: Editora Universidade Federal de Goiás, 1993), 59.

3. Arquivo Histórico Ultramarino, Lisbon, caixa 43, Goiás, 1800–1825, unsigned, undated letter in folder 1804.

4. Mary Karasch, "Os quilombos do ouro na capitania de Goiás," in *Liberdade por um fio: história dos quilombos no Brasil,* ed. João José Reis and Flávio dos Santos Gomes (São Paulo: Companhia das Letras, 1996), 240–62.

5. Mary Karasch, "Interethnic Conflict and Resistance on the Brazilian Frontier of Goiás, 1750–1890," in *Contested Ground,* ed. Donna J. Guy and Thomas E. Sheridan (Tucson: University of Arizona Press, 1998), 115–34.

6. Payments in gold for manumissions were registered in the Cartório do Primeiro Ofício, Cartas de Liberdade, 1792[93]–99, which are archived in the City of Goiás at the Biblioteca de Fundação Educacional da Cidade de Goiás (hereafter BFEG).

7. The occupations of black men enrolled in the Henriques regiment of São José de Tocantins were recorded, along with their ethnicity (crioulo, Mina, Guiné), literacy, and slave-ownership. They were largely small farmers, miners, and craftsmen. This rare document is in Goiânia and was located, attached to a Boa Morte document dated 1799, at the archive of the Curia.

8. Pardo officers detailed their services in the frontier wars in a petition they sent to Lisbon, part of which is reprinted in *História de Goiás em Documentos: I Colônia*, ed. Luis Palacín, Ledonias Franco Garcia, and Janaína Amado (Goiânia: Editora da UFG, 1995), 188–89.

9. In 1837, in the church of Nossa Senhora do Monte do Carmo, Manoel de Nação Angola, a slave, married the Amerindian Luiza Ayres da Silva of the Caraô [Krahô] nation. Casamentos, Nossa Senhora do Monte do Carmo, BFEG.

10. The same marriage registers from Carmo recorded the marriage of Antonio Pereira da Fonseca and Anna Maria de Conceição, both cabras livres, in 1836. On cabra, see Karasch, *Slave Life*, 6.

11. The total of 54,489 is my calculation. The governor's total was 55,514. A copy of the census is in the Instituto Histórico e Geográphico Brasileiro, Rio de Janeiro (hereafter IHGB), arq. 1.2.7, vol. 36, Estatística, Ofício de Luiz da Cunha Menezes á Martinho de Mello e Castro, remetendo o Mapa da população da Capitania de Goiáz, com distinção de classes, Vila Boa, July 8, 1780, fols. 245–47

12. Biblioteca Nacional, Rio de Janeiro (hereafter BN), Manuscript Section, cod. 16,3,2, Notícia Geral da Capitania de Goiás, 1783. A copy of this census was published as *Notícia Geral da Capitania de Goiás em 1783*, 2 vols., ed. Paulo Bertran (Goiânia: Editora da Universidade Católica de Goiás, 1997). I have compiled my tables based on the manuscript copy rather than the published version which has many errors. The governor's report on the total population of the captaincy in 1783 is in arq. 1.2.7, vol. 36, Ofício de Luiz da Cunha Menezes á Martinho de Mello e Castro, Feb. 15, 1783, fols. 273–78, IHGB. Because so many julgados are missing, it is uncertain how the governor calculated the total population. In other cases, the parish priests forwarded unanalyzed household lists or aggregate totals on marital status. In such cases, free females were not tallied except in São Félix to be discussed below.

13. Arq. 1.2.8., vol. 37, "Relação em que Tristão da Cunha Menezes Governador e Capitão General d'esta Capitania de Goyaz apresenta ao Real Ministerio pela extração das relações dos Parrochos dos seus respectivos julgados abaixo declarados até o prezente anno de 1791," fols. 7–8, IHGB.

14. City of Goiás, Arquivo do Museu das Bandeiras, Vários Assuntos, vol. 353, no. 15, Freguesias, letter of the Vigario Joao Pereira Pinto Bravo to Tristão da Cunha Menezes, Vila Boa, May 22, 1799. The priest reported that the *freguezia* in 1798 had eight thousand "souls," of which six thousand were of "Confição" and of these three thousand were *"forros, e livres,"* and of these, no more than three hundred were married or couples. Furthermore, he noted that *forro* births numbered 131; deaths 112. In contrast, there were only eighty-two captive births and seventy-five captive deaths.

15. B. J. Barickman also found *ingênuos* in Bahia in 1835. "Crossing Color Lines: Afro-Brazilian Slave-Owners and Their Slaves in Rural Bahia in the Early Nineteenth Century," presented at the conference on "Rethinking the African Diaspora," Atlanta, Ga., April 17–18, 1998, 6.

16. Arq. 1.2.8, vol. 37, Estatistica, Relação atual da Capitania de Goiáz no ano de 1786, Aug. 28, 1787, fol. 4, IHGB.

17. The male population in 1832 was composed of 6,186 whites, 21,209 livres de cor, 7,220 slaves, and 459 Amerindians, or a total of 35,074. The sum total for the province was 68,497. Arquivo Nacional, Rio de Janeiro, cod. 808, vol. 1, Goiás, Censo da População da Provincia de Goyaz, fol. 96.

18. Johann Emanuel Pohl, *Viagem no Interior do Brasil*, trans. Milton Amado and Eugênio Amado (Belo Horizonte: Editora Itatiaia, 1976), 141–42.

19. James W. Wells, *Exploring and Travelling Three Thousand Miles through Brazil* . . . (Philadelphia: J. B. Lippincott Company, 1886), 187.

20. Arquivo Histórico de Goiás, Goiânia, Doc. Diversa, no. 68, Correspondência do Comandante da Armas—Raymundo José da Cunha Mattos, fols. 112–21 (Aguaquente), AHG.

21. Alida C. Metcalf defines "agregados" as "dependents," who "might be kin, orphans, or poor people who worked in the fields, in the preparation of food, and as domestic servants in exchange for food and lodging." *Family and Frontier in Colonial Brazil* (Berkeley: University of California Press, 1992), 126–27. On the pessoa de obrigação in Sabará, see Kathleen J. Higgins, *Slavery and "Licentious Liberty" in Brazil's Gold Mines* (University Park: Pennsylvania State University Press, 1999).

22. Doc. Div., no. 68, Correspondência, Cunha Mattos, 1824, fols. 175–85 (Pontal) and 186–93 (Porto Real), AHG.

23. On pawnship in which persons were held for security for debts in Africa, see Paul E. Lovejoy, *Transformations in Slavery* (New York: Cambridge University Press, 1983), 13–14.

24. Mary C. Karasch, "Slave Women on the Brazilian Frontier in the Nineteenth Century," in *More Than Chattel: Black Women and Slavery in the Americas*, ed. David Barry Gaspar and Darlene Clark Hine (Bloomington: Indiana University Press, 1996), 87.

25. Karasch, "Slave Women on the Brazilian Frontier." Free women of color who ran taverns appear on the household lists for Pontal and Porto Real. In Pontal, the parda Maria Ferreira dos Santos was sixty-one and the single mother of a twenty-one-year-old son. The other tavern keeper was a widow, Jozefa Carneira, who was identified as a crioula, aged sixty-one.

26. Auguste de Saint-Hilaire, *Viagem à Provincia de Goiás*, trans. Regina Regis Junqueira (Belo Horizonte: Editora Itatiaia, 1975), 33; Karasch, "Slave Women," 88–89. The continuation of the textile tradition to the present is richly documented in Norma Simão Adad Mirandola, *As tecedeiras de Goiás: Estudo lingüístico, etnográfico e folclórico* (Goiânia: CEGRAF/UFG), 1993.

27. For pardas as lavradoras, see Doc. Div., no. 68, Correspondência, Cunha Mattos, 1824, fols. 175–85 (Pontal) and 186–93 (Porto Real), AHG.

28. [Uncataloged manuscripts], Natividade, Livro de óbitos, 1809–59, BFEG.

29. In Sabará, Higgins (*Slavery and "Licentious Liberty"*) found similar patterns of "libertinagem."

30. Saint-Hilaire, *Viagem*, 53, 56, 125.

31. Ibid., 56. The editor notes that Fernando Delgado's son died in Paris at a young age when he was serving with the Brazilian legation.

32. An example of a black woman with one parda child is that of Ponsiana Rodrigues, fifty-nine, whose eldest child was a parda, twenty-three, and her two black children, who were fourteen and sixteen. She lived in Aguaquente. Doc. Div., no. 68, Correspondência, Cunha Mattos, 1824, fols. 175–85 (Pontal) and 186–93 (Porto Real), AHG.

33. One of the best descriptions of this custom is in the historical novel *O Tronco* (Rio de Janeiro: José Olympio, 1979), 25, by Bernardo Élis, who based his novels on the oral traditions of the region. After describing the multiple tasks of a *coronel*'s servants, the descendants of slaves still maintained in slavery (1917–18), he reported that the young girls of that household "prostituted themselves with the patrons, with the relatives of the patrons, with the camaradas." In other words, young servant women were "shared" by the coronel and all those in his immediate circle of male relatives and workers. All of this happened in a household ruled by the coronel's wife as if she were a "queen."

34. On venereal disease, see Doc. Diversa, no. 70, Registro de Correspondências Militares ao Governo Civil da Província, 1823–1826, fol. 56, and no. 69, Origenais dos Comandantaes do Registros e Présidios da Provincia, 1823–1825, fol. 164–66 (sick soldiers), both AHG.

35. Seção de Municípios, Porto Nacional, Goiânia, caixa 1, Joaquim Ayres da Silva para o Chefe da Polícia, Porto Imperial, July 13, 1870, AHG.

36. Saint-Hilaire, *Viagem*, 42, 54. Some of these women may have been prostitutes, because he also noted that they walked through the streets of Goiás at night in single file. An illustration of black "Venuses" being led through the streets of Rio de Janeiro in single-file is in Karasch, *Slave Life in Rio*, 208.

37. Table 12.7. The use of the term *casal* (couple) makes it difficult to determine if the couples

had actually been married by a priest. Household lists commonly described the female partner as *mulher* (woman), which could indicate a woman living in a consensual union. When priests used the term *cazado* (married) for parishioners, we have greater certainty that the couples had married in their churches and were known to them.

38. For Barra in 1783, see note 12.

39. For São Félix in 1783, see note 12.

40. For Carmo in 1783, see note 12.

41. Doc. Div., no. 68, Correspondência, Cunha Mattos, fols. 112–21 (Aguaquente), AHG.

42. On African healing traditions, see Luis R. B. Mott, *Escravidão, Homossexualidade e Demonologia* (São Paulo: Ícone, 1988), 88–89 (for *feiticeiros* and herbs in Paracatú on the road to Goiás); Pohl, *Viagem,* 124–25; and Wells, *Exploring and Travelling,* 78 (on charms).

43. The brotherhood records of Our Lady of the Rosary for the City of Goiás and Natividade are at the BFEG. Used here were the Livro dos Termos de Meza, 1826–40, the Compromisso of Nossa Senhora do Rosário of the City of Goiás, and fragments of a *livro* (*livros?*) dos termos and asentos of Nossa Senhora do Rosário from Natividade, 1786–1801. The two *compromissos* (charters) for the Irmandade de Nossa Senhora das Mercês dos Captivos in São Joaquim do Cocal (1772 and 1788) were found in the archive of the Curia in Goiânia. None of the brotherhood records were cataloged as of 1996.

44. Arquivo Nacional da Torre do Tombo, Lisbon, maço 598, Ministerio do Reino, Negocios do Ultramar, Letra B, 1753–63, letter to the Vigario Geral Pedro Barboza Cannaes from José dos Santos Pereira in São Félix, Oct. 5, 1761.

45. Pohl, *Viagem,* 271. The ruins of the uncompleted church without a roof were still there when I visited and photographed the church of Rosário in Natividade in 1994. According to the Termo de Asento, the brotherhood was building the church in 1786. Uncataloged papers of Nossa Senhora do Rosário, Natividade, 1786, fol. 77, BFEG. The high costs of constructing such a large church may explain why this brotherhood had a large board and numerous officials.

46. Joanna Maria de Assumpção is listed on brotherhood records between 1787 and 1794. Ibid.

47. Santa Efigênia's fragmentary records are also at the BFEG. The brotherhood was located in the church of Nossa Senhora do Rosário of Natividade in 1786 (Termo de Asento). In Rio de Janeiro, the brotherhood dedicated to Efigênia was composed of Mina slaves. Karasch, *Slave Life in Rio,* 84. The poor condition of the few documents from the brotherhood in Natividade makes it difficult to identify its members by ethnicity.

48. Mieko Nishida, "From Ethnicity to Race and Gender: Transformations of Black Lay Sodalities in Salvador, Brazil," *Journal of Social History* 32 (Winter 1998): 329–48; Karasch, *Slave Life in Rio,* 82–86.

49. Nossa Senhora do Rosário, City of Goiás, Livro dos Termos, 1826–40, BFEG.

50. Ibid. Freedwomen served on the board in 1827 and 1828 and 1828 and 1829.

51. The 1789 population of Cocal is in the Biblioteca da Ajuda, Lisbon, 54–V-12, no. 5, Noticia de todos os Governadores e população das provincias do Brasil, 1782, fols. 33–34.

52. Julita Scarano, *Devoção e Escravidão,* (São Paulo: Companhia Editora Nacional, 1976), 39.

53. The first year, 1772, refers to the compromisso of that year, the second year of 1788 is from the revised charter that lowered the required amount due to the decline of mining in Cocal.

54. For example, 64 oitavas of gold was paid for the freedom of Adão, a mulato child, in 1780.

55. The Irmandade da Senhora da Boa Morte dos homens pardos (brotherhood of Our Lady of the Good Death of the pardo men) was installed in 1779 in a chapel of the same name in Vila Boa de Goiás. Manuscript Section, 9, 2, 10, "Momoria sobre o Descobrimento, Governo, População e cousas mais notaveis da Capitania de Goyaz," Vila Boa, Aug. 13[?], 1786, fol. 35, BN.

56. Damián Bayón and Murillo Marx, *History of South American Colonial Art and Architecture: Spanish South America and Brazil,* Jennifer A. Blankley, Angela P. Hall, and Richard L. Rees (New York: Rizzoli, 1992), 357 (picture of a church in Minas Gerais that shows the railings that separate the main and side altars from the congregation).

57. Bayón and Marx, *History of South American Colonial Art and Architecture,* 389–90.

58. On the importance of burials and the role of brotherhoods in providing church burials, see João José Reis, *A Morte e Uma Festa: Ritos fúnebres e revolta popular no Brasil do século XIX* (São Paulo: Companhia das Letras, 1993), 171–202.

59. A. J. R. Russell-Wood, "Frontiers in Colonial Brazil: Reality, Myth, and Metaphor," in *Society and Government in Colonial Brazil, 1500–1822,* ed. A. J. R. Russell-Wood (Brookfield: Variorum, 1992): 2: 26–61. My thanks to the author for a copy of this essay.

CHAPTER 13

Henriette Delille, Free Women of Color, and Catholicism in Antebellum New Orleans, 1727–1852

Virginia Meacham Gould

In the early morning hours of April 1, 1838, Henriette Delille, a twenty-six-year-old free Creole woman of color, left her family home on Burgundy Street in New Orleans and walked eight blocks to the nearby chapel of the St. Claude Street Convent. It was the second Sunday before Easter, the Paschal period during which the Catholic church traditionally baptized its adults. Delille arrived early at the chapel on this chilly Lenten morning, shivering perhaps from the cold but also from anticipation. She came to the chapel well before mass in order to take part in a short ceremony during which she pledged to serve as godmother to the fourteen-year-old, free black catacumen Marie Therese Dagon.[1]

Delille's pledge to this young free woman of color was telling. It is likely that Delille evangelized Dagon. Delille belonged to a pious Catholic women's organization whose members were dedicated to evangelizing and catechizing slave women and free women of color. It was a tradition for women to serve as godmothers to those they had evangelized. But Delille's commitment to women and children through godparentage had begun years before. She was only seventeen the first time she stood as godmother. That had been nine years earlier. On this particular occasion the French immigrant priest who officiated, Etienne Rousselon, stood beside Delille as the young woman's godfather. Delille's shared role of godparent with Rousselon bound them together in a commitment to their godchild and signified nothing less than their spiritual equality.

The baptism of Marie Therese Dagon—the symbolic conjoining of a French priest and a free woman of color—provides a window into the historical dynamic that shaped slavery and the church in New Orleans. In order to explain how it was possible for Delille to stand side by side with Rousselon in spiritual mutuality it is necessary to explore how, in the eighteenth century, Ursulines first transplanted an aggressive program of evangelization and catechesis from France to Louisiana.

This chapter will examine the Ursuline tradition in which women evangelized and catechized enslaved women and free women of color; it will then tie Delille to that tradition. It is also necessary to discuss what happened to this tradition after Louisiana was ceded to the United States in 1803. At the same time, the traditions and beliefs that nineteenth-century female French missionaries brought to New Orleans are important, particularly in regard to how Delille adapted the French model of social activism to fit the needs of her community. That model ultimately offered free women of color in New Orleans some autonomy and even power they would not have enjoyed otherwise.[2]

Born in 1812, Delille grew into womanhood in New Orleans, a city that has been noted historically for its vibrancy, exoticism, and racial diversity. By the time Delille reached maturity, New Orleans's economy was booming. The city's location near the mouth of the Mississippi River made it the South's busiest port. By the 1830s and 1840s New Orleans was only second to the port of New York as a commercial center. Unlike New York, however, New Orleans lay at the juncture of two worlds. It was there, as in other southern commercial centers, that the social system of slavery met capitalism. And it was there that commercial capitalism redefined opportunity and thus social relations. Its commercial economy, household arrangements, and social relations made New Orleans a city with slaves rather than a slave city. Although it depended on plantation slavery to support its commercial economy, the city did not depend upon the labor of its slaves. Nineteenth-century New Orleanians knew that slavery, at least in urban environs, was a domestic institution and dependent almost entirely upon women.[3]

The political economies of all the South's cities of the early nineteenth century provided opportunities for robust communities, numerically dominated by women, of free people of color. Yet even as the inhabitants of these cities relied on the domestic labor of free women of color they sexualized and racialized their identities. Frances Trollop, a visitor, noticed that no matter their skin color, wealth, education, degree of acculturation, or visibility, free women of color were deemed by racist ideology to be tainted by their African heritage. Free women of color in New Orleans were always socially juxtaposed with white women. According to the predominant theory, they were nothing less than impure, immoral women not worth protecting. Yet this taint of impurity transmuted in New Orleans where the descendants of the *ancienne population*—those women descended from the original French, Spanish, and African inhabitants who thought of themselves as *les femmes de couleur libre* (free Creole women of color)—were deemed to be models of seductive beauty. They were inevitably romanticized or described as "desirables." However, that did nothing to protect them from exploitation by white men, and, indeed, enhanced it.[4]

These free Creole women of color were often racially mixed and thus shared in the identity of the city's other Creoles, both unmixed Europeans and Africans. The term *Creole* in the eighteenth century was originally a Portuguese label, soon adopted by the French and the Spanish, that designated anyone born in the Americas. "Creole," in that sense, was a term that separated persons born in the Colonies from those born in Europe or Africa. In eighteenth-century Louisiana the term was used interchangeably with "native of the colony." The term changed, however, after Americans began pouring into the region after the Louisiana Purchase treaty of 1803. The ancienne population began to identify themselves as Creoles in a cultural sense. Black, white, and racially mixed Creoles of New Orleans, whether slave or free, were bound together by webs of kinship (both real and fictive), language, tradition, and Catholicism. Creoles in nineteenth-century New Orleans, whether of French ancestry or not, took great pride in their French cultural connections, which they believed were far superior to the culture the detested "Americans" brought with them.[5]

During the first decades of the nineteenth century most New Orleanians were Creoles, and a surprisingly large number of them were free Creoles of color. Free people of color were attracted to ports and commercial centers throughout the South. There they found economic opportunity and community. In that regard New Orleans outstripped the rest of the region, with its large, prosperous, and influential community of free Creoles of color. A breakdown of the population in 1805 demonstrates that approximately 20 percent of the population were free Creoles of color. Women dominated the free colored population numerically, and they owned more property than did either free men of color or white women. The pattern did not change until mid-century, when Americans overwhelmed the Creole population and began passing restrictive laws against them. It was only then that free Creole women of color began to lose ground. Yet even then, as the women faced increasingly difficult times they worked diligently to protect and even extend their gains.[6]

Henriette Delille inherited this tradition of ambition, success, and influence from the generations of Creole women who preceded her. Her first matrilineal ancestor in Louisiana was an African woman given the name Marie Ann at her baptism but fondly called Nanette by those who knew her. Marie Ann arrived in Louisiana aboard the slaver *Le Ruby* in 1720, one of 127 Africans (of an original 130) who survived the voyage from Senegambia, West Africa. Marie Ann's children included four daughters, Cecile, Marianne, Fanchonette, and Tonica, and a son, Etienne. Marie Ann's daughter, Cecile, was Henriette Delille's great-grandmother, and Cecile's daughter, Henriette, was Henriette Delille's grandmother. All of these women and their children remained in slavery until the 1760s and 1770s, when they began attaining freedom. Henriette Delille's mother, named Maria Josepha at baptism, was the first of Delille's maternal ancestors to be born into freedom.[7]

Delille's female ancestors freed themselves or were freed by white relatives or godmothers. Her white ancestors were some of the most notable persons in

Louisiana. Marie Ann's owner, Claude Joseph Dubreuil, was one of Louisiana's most prosperous colonists. He was the wealthiest planter in the New Orleans area. He was also a contractor, engineer, and slave trader. He and his partner Etienne Dalcourt commissioned the ship *Le St. Ursin* that in 1743 carried the last shipment of enslaved Africans to Louisiana during the French colonial period. By his death in the 1750s, Dubreuil owned more than five hundred slaves, one of whom was Marie Ann. Out of all of his enslaved Africans, Marie Ann was Dubreuil's domestique. She and her children lived in the Debreuil household.

But Dubreuil was more to Marie Ann than her master. He was also the father of her children. Yet despite his wealth and prestige, or because of it, Dubreuil failed to free Marie Ann or their children. It appears instead that he donated his slave kin to his son, Claude Joseph Dubreuil *fils,* who in a later document identified himself as a half-brother to Marie Ann's children. Young Dubreuil allowed Marie Ann to purchase her freedom on October 16, 1763. He sold her daughter, Marianne, to Marianne Piquery in 1767. She, in turn, freed Marianne and her four children about ten years later, in 1777. Dubreuil fils sold Cecile and her children to Marie Ann for 2,800 livres. The official act, dated October 1, 1770, stated that Cecile and her children were freed under private act in 1769. Neither Marie Ann nor her children or grandchildren obtained their freedom easily, but they obtained it nonetheless. By the 1790s, just two decades after they had escaped bondage, Cecile and Marianne, Marie Ann's daughters and Henriette Delille's great-grandmother and great-aunt, could be counted among the most well-to-do property-holders in New Orleans.[8]

The women who preceded Delille achieved remarkable success. They sought and won freedom when such a goal was rarely attainable. They accumulated property. They also acquired education for themselves and their daughters. The legacy they left Delille, and from which she shaped her identity, included self-dependence, hard work, and dedication. It is obvious that Delille drew upon the example of her female ancestors, but it is also evident that she rejected some of their choices. Each of the women who preceded Delille cohabited with white men. Delille chose otherwise. She did not live in concubinage, nor did she marry. She thus did not follow either of the slim choices available to free women of color. Instead, Delille created a new opportunity for free women of color in New Orleans by building upon the Catholic tradition of her ancestors.

The church began to evangelize enslaved African women as they began to arrive in Louisiana during the first decades of the eighteenth century, as was explicitly stated in the *Code noir* (Black Code) of 1724, France's most comprehensive colonial legislation on slavery. In many ways it embodied the interwoven nature of France's political culture and religion. Originally implemented for the French Antilles in 1685, it was made more restrictive and then enacted in Louisiana in 1724. The intentions of the church and the crown were implicit in the second article of the *Code,* which required slaveholders to baptize all slaves and instruct them in the Catholic faith. It was believed that only in this way would the "true faith" be brought to all Africans in the New World. At its heart, the *Code noir* was based upon the Christian justification of slavery that held that enslaved Africans were more fortunate than the heathens they left behind in Africa.[9]

French missionaries who occupied the lower Mississippi Valley after settlement administered the sacrament of baptism to newly arrived Africans, but these first missionaries were Capuchin friars who were far more comfortable standing behind their pulpits saying mass to the faithful than evangelizing and catechizing the unfaithful. It was not until the Ursulines, bringing a concept of female universalism with them, arrived in New Orleans in 1727 that an aggressive policy of catechesis was pursued. The Ursulines had no experience evangelizing slaves when they arrived, but they had a long and aggressive tradition of missionizing women. They believed it was through the education of women, regardless of social standing, that they could plant in every home at least one defender of Christ and Christ's doctrine and thus reform Catholic society.[10]

Within weeks of their arrival the Ursuline women opened a school for girls. Their primary ministry was to educate white girls, but, true to tradition, they also turned their attention to nonwhite women and girls. The Ursulines instructed Native Americans and Africans, preparing them for baptism and first communion, although they were far more successful with African women. One of their reports of the early eighteenth century stated that they were achieving great success with the "negresses" in the settlement. They did not mention the Native Americans, who rarely appear in sacramental records. Ursuline nuns also educated the daughters of free women of color. They wrote in their minutes for the spring of 1728 that there were "seven slave boarders to instruct for baptism and first communion and a large number of day students and Negresses and Indian girls who come two hours each day for instruction."[11]

The Ursulines' goal to ensure the piety of the colony's women, and hence the future of the church was advanced in 1730 when eight laywomen requested that the nuns help them organize a confraternity of women and girls in honor of the Very Blessed Virgin Mary. The nuns readily agreed to sponsor the organization, giving it the name Ladies Congregation of the Children of Mary. Members of the Children of Mary defined specific duties for themselves. The first was assurance of their own piety, but they also committed themselves to extending their piety to other women. They were also obligated to "have a special zeal for . . . the instruction of their children and their slaves."[12]

The ministry of the Children of Mary is evident in the baptism of the slaves of Claude Joseph Dubreuil. Madame Marie Payen Dubreuil, Sieur Claude Joseph Dubreuil's wife, was a member of the Children of Mary. She was responsible for the evangelization and baptism of her family's slaves, and there is abundant evidence that she and her family members took their responsibilities seriously. Madame Dubreuil, her husband, her two sons, and her daughter-in-law, Felicité de la Chaise, who was one of the founding members of the Chil-

dren of Mary, had their slaves baptized. The Dubreuil slaves appear frequently
in the baptismal records. Nearly all were baptized. The Africans introduced into
the faith by the Dubreuils also baptized their infants. Marie Ann and her children are representative of the process. When Marie Ann arrived in New Orleans
in 1720, she was evangelized and baptized. Nanette bore four daughters who survived infancy to be baptized at the St. Louis Cathedral in New Orleans: Marianne
in 1735, Fanchonette in 1737, Tonica in 1742, and Cecile in 1744.[13]

It is true that Marie Ann's baptism and those of her children and the other
Dubreuil slaves might signify nothing more than the effectiveness of the instruction of Madame Dubreuil and her daughter-in-law, Felicité de la Chaise, although the pattern was repeated often enough in New Orleans. There is evidence
that some enslaved Africans rejected evangelization, but most African women
in early-eighteenth-century New Orleans welcomed it. In general, the first generation of African women was evangelized, baptized, and then had their infants
baptized. The second generation of enslaved infants, baptized soon after birth,
assumed a greater and more assertive role in the church after they reached adulthood. They inducted others into the faith and served as godmothers. People of
African descent, both slave and free, represented the majority of persons baptized throughout the eighteenth century.[14]

Godparenting patterns demonstrate the increasing commitments of slave
women and free women of color to the church, and they also indicate the degree to which people of African descent appropriated religion and were, in turn,
viewed by priests as possessing the qualifications necessary to meet requirements
of Catholic canon law. During the eighteenth and nineteenth centuries, canon
law required that a godparent should be a baptized, confirmed Catholic who
led a virtuous life in harmony with the faith. A godparent was also obligated to
take personal interest in the baptized person and ensure that he or she would
lead a Christian life. Whereas most godparents of slaves in the early decades of
the eighteenth century were white, by the closing decades they were slaves and
free people of color. In 1731, when 162 slaves were baptized, only 2 percent had a
godparent of African descent. By 1765, 68 percent of the 197 slaves baptized had
at least one godparent of African descent. By 1804, when 385 slaves were baptized, 76 percent had at least one godparent of African descent. Throughout the
eighteenth and early nineteenth centuries, women of African descent numerically dominated men of African descent as godparents. John Watson, a journalist
who visited New Orleans in 1805, captured the appropriation of the Catholic
belief system by women of African descent. As he entered the Cathedral during
Holy Week, Watson was struck by a scene dominated by black women at wor-
ship. "Visit the Churches when you will," he noted, "and the chief audience is
formed of mulatresses and negresses."[15]

The church in New Orleans during the early nineteenth century was more
black than white and more feminine than masculine. Yet as slave women and free
women of color continued to numerically dominate the church, the missionary

fervor directed at them began to wane. That is not to suggest that the Ursulines were less interested in ensuring the salvation and piety of the city's slave women and free women of color. Instead, it was a response to changes that occurred in the church after Louisiana was ceded to the United States in 1803. When first Spain and then France withdrew from Louisiana, the church found itself, for the first time, without state support. The few priests and nuns who remained were left virtually powerless and penniless, at the mercy of parishioners who chose to remain loyal to them. And even the most loyal were overwhelmed by newcomers who poured into the city. Between 1805 and 1810 the population of New Orleans more than doubled. In 1805 there were 8,475 people living in the city, 57 percent of whom were people of African descent. In 1810 the inhabitants of New Orleans numbered 17,242, and 63 percent were people of African descent. The growth in the number of slaves and free people of color outstripped that of whites. The population increase began to occur as the number of nuns and priests declined. By 1810 only a handful of Ursulines were available to minister to the expanding number of slave women and free women of color in New Orleans.[16]

The inability of the church to meet the needs of the growing population of slaves and free people of color was finally addressed in 1812 when Louis William DuBourg was appointed administrator apostolic of the Diocese of Louisiana and the two Floridas. DuBourg did not seek the appointment. He doubted, indeed, that he possessed the ability to administer the vast diocese. By 1815 he became so disheartened by conditions in New Orleans that he withdrew to Rome, hoping to be officially relieved of his duties. Instead, he was assigned to return to Louisiana as its bishop. Although DuBourg dreaded his duties, he did not, in reality, flinch or turn away. It appears that his appointment was pivotal, because he not only began the long process of restoring the vitality of Louisiana's Catholic church but also looked to France to do so. That he did so is not difficult to understand. He was tied to France and the French Antilles through kinship and commerce, and his familiarity with the New World and its racially diverse slave societies made him especially suited to resurrect the church in Louisiana.[17]

French scholars who have written about the revival of the missionary effort in France during the nineteenth century all point out that DuBourg's visit to France—particularly to Lyon—between 1815 and 1817 could not have occurred at a more auspicious moment. Pauline Jaricot, a *devoté* (secular religious woman), and her brother, Philias, who was a Sulpicien priest, had just begun a movement in Lyon that led to the founding of the Propogation de la Foi (Propogation of the Faith) and eventually also to La Rosaire Vivante (Living Rosary), two organizations devoted to missionary work. At the same time, the Missionaires Étrangères (Foreign Missionaries) began to be reorganized in Paris after being devastated during the French Revolution. The three organizations responded to DuBourg's appeal and sent missionaries and financial aid to Louisiana. When DuBourg returned to Louisiana from Lyon, he had succeeded in reconnecting Louisiana's church directly to that of France.[18]

The missionary fervor that DuBourg secured for Louisiana was representative of the revival of Catholic spirit that increasingly gripped France after 1815. The French church struggled to redefine itself after the devastation of the revolution, and even though many French men and women continued to reject the church or were only nominally Catholic, others were joining the revivalist spirit sweeping through the French countryside. As revolutionary promises remained unfulfilled, well-known Catholic thinkers and founders of religious orders soundly rejected liberalism and rationalism. They proposed, instead, that France return to an organic, coherent, Catholic system. They had a vision of a global world order responsive to all the problems of humanity. The organic system proposed by the church was not entirely new; it reflected in many ways the older ideals of the seventeenth century. Only this time the church sought a larger constituency that would actively seek to remold society.[19]

The battle to restore Catholic order in postrevolutionary France was waged mostly by women. By 1815 some of the older French orders, having existed in clandestine havens during and after the revolution, were sweeping off their stoops and opening their windows. As nuns in these older orders began to put renewed vigor into their work, other smaller groups of pious women began to gather in houses, doing manual labor in order to support their charitable works. All of these women, in one way or another, attempted to build their communities on familiar models. Yet as they tried to reestablish themselves in communities, as if the revolutionary period had only disorganized them, they did so in a new age. Some women's religious orders of the eighteenth century had supported themselves, but those of postrevolutionary France were no longer associated with or supported by the state. Women living in community had no choice. They were forced to be financially independent. As Yvonne Turin has argued, after their experiences of the revolution many purposefully sought and cherished their newfound autonomy, and they used it to address the social ills they saw all around them.[20]

Congregation after congregation of religious women in nineteenth-century France used their autonomy to work directly with the poor, elderly, sick, and orphaned. It was from these communities, formed during the first half of the nineteenth century for the purpose of ameliorating the human condition, that female missionaries emerged, committed to transmitting their universalist consciousness far and wide. The female missionaries from France who traveled to New Orleans after DuBourg's visit were determined to establish active apostolates. They came as teachers and nurses. They came to work with the sick, needy, and elderly as well as with the uneducated and uninstructed. They came to evangelize and catechize. They came in small groups and with few assets, but they established a massive complex of inclusive charitable organizations meant to address the social needs of all the city's inhabitants.

The French missionary women who transplanted their apostolate to New Orleans found themselves ministering a Creole Catholic slave society. There is no evidence that any of them objected to slavery. Many of them even purchased slaves when they arrived. French missionary thought accommodated slavery. New Orleans offered them the organic society they envisioned in which the church would address the suffering of the needy. French women stepped into the breach, evangelizing and catechizing slaves and teaching them the virtues of orderliness and obedience. The first missionary who dedicated herself solely to the city's people of African descent was Sister Ste. Marthe Fontiere, who was a Dames d'Hospitaliere when she left Belley, France. Arriving in New Orleans in 1817, she stayed with the Ursalines and took over their ministry to the city's women of African descent. The scope of her ministry is hinted at in a report. According to the account, the Ursulines were instructing more than three hundred "pauvres negresses" in 1822. Besides instructing slaves, Sister Ste. Marthe took over the education of free girls of color. In 1823 when the Ursulines moved their convent several miles downriver, she remained in the city, where she established a school for girls. In that school on St. Claude Street, Henriette Delille received her education. Years later, she stood beside Etienne Rousselon in the same convent chapel and pledged herself to Marie Therese Dagon's baptism.[21]

The success of the school under the leadership of Sister Ste. Marthe can be surmised from a letter Bishop DuBourg wrote to Father Antoine Blanc in June 1824. DuBourg asked Blanc, who was in Lyon, to try to recruit "two good Sisters of St. Charles to cooperate with good Sister St. Marthe," whose "school is doing much good. She has some eighty pupils," DuBourg added, "and the number would increase quickly if she had helpers."[22]

About the same time Sister Ste. Marthe was establishing the St. Claude Street convent and school, Michael Portier, another French missionary, formed, as a part of his ministry, a confraternity of young free people of color. In describing the confraternity in 1820, Portier said that he met with a group of sixty of these young people every night. A dozen of them were "fervent, like angels." Generally, after reading the gospel to the young people, he would explain it. The members of this congregation were Portier's consolation. "They wear a red ribbon and a cross and they promise to fight daily like valiant soldiers of Jesus Christ," he said. Portier went on to explain that he had the congregation assemble each Sunday and that he usually presided at their assembly. Further, he regulated their practice of religion and was happy to see them as faithful as the seminarians in Lyon. Seminarians in Lyon, however, lived in a seminary, whereas free people of color in New Orleans lived in Babylon, in the midst of scandals. These young people of color, he explained, were "like angels; they teach the Blacks to pray, they catechize, they instruct, and they communicate." Portier was training the young free people of color to reach out to slaves and prepare them for baptism and their first communion.[23]

By the 1830s, free women of color made a determined move into the church's apostolate. They recognized how important they were to the church and pressed for a more formalized, activist role. The transition they experienced, from a sta-

tus of powerlessness to one of empowerment, occurred in stages. During or before the early 1830s the women began to act collectively to more fully meet the
needs of their community. They appropriated the form of lay religious groups
that previously were reserved for white women. Their organization, known as
the Sisters of the Congregation of Presentation of the Blessed Virgin Mary, was
a significant move forward for free women of color who had theoretically been
denied virtue, as women descended from slaves. The mission of the women can
be seen in the rules and regulations of their constitution, written in French and
placed in the center of a leather-bound account book. According to the carefully
worded document, the women elected a large ruling council of more than twenty
officers. They referred to themselves as sisters, and they recognized three primary
obligations: to themselves, to each other, and to their people.[24]

Their first obligation was to be pious women, beyond reproach. Their rules
stated that each woman should "seek to bring back the Glory of God and the
salvation of the neighbor by a charitable and edifying behavior." The women's
second goal recognized that as individuals they could do little for themselves
or for others. It was only through collective strength that they could address the
needs of the population to which they ministered. Their third goal, and the one
for which they existed, was commitment to their community. The women wrote
in their constitution that "the sick, the infirm, and the poor" were the "first and
the dearest objects of the solicitude of the Congregation." The lay sisters visited the sick at home and assisted the dying. They brought food to the hungry
and fuel to warm cold homes. They obligated themselves to instruct the uninstructed about "the principal mysteries of religion and the most important
points of Christian morality." These women recast their identities and thus their
influence and power within their community. If they did not have many choices
and little if any power as women of color some years earlier, now they were able
to redefine themselves as pious women and collectively combat the social problems they saw around them. In 1836 Henriette Delille wrote down her intentions
as a simple prayer in the front of one of her prayer books: "I believe in God. I
hope in God. I love. I wish to live and die for God."[25] In 1842 she and two women
who shared her fervor, Juilette Gaudin and Josephine Charles, moved into a
house on St. Bernard Street near the St. Claude Street Convent and School. With
that move they began a life of conventual living and, under the direction of
Delille, founded the Sisters of the Holy Family.

In 1847, Henriette Delille established an asylum for the care of elderly, sick
women. In 1848, after a wounded man was brought to the asylum, she incorporated it under the name of the Asylum of the Holy Family and ceded control to
a group of laypeople. She moved away from that endeavor because her ministry was solely to women and children. Delille was also positioning herself to take
the next step. By 1851 she prized open the door of feminine religious life previously available only to white women. In that year she vowed to abide by the
ancient Catholic tradition that demanded her to live a life circumscribed by

poverty, chastity, and obedience. In order to visibly mark her transition from pious woman to religious sister, she changed her blue percale dress to black and began wearing a rosary around her neck.

She followed her more formal entrance into religious life by beginning an aggressive program of expansion. From 1851 to 1853 she served as mistress of novices, instructing Juilette Gaudin and Josephine Charles in the duties of religious life. Under her tutelage, between 1851 and 1862 the Sisters of the Holy Family grew to include twelve women who lived in a house Delille purchased and transformed into a convent.[26]

Delille's original ministry, the catechesis of enslaved and free women and children of African descent and provision for the poor, did not fade as she pushed her apostolate forward. Under her direction, the Sisters of the Holy Family extended their mission to include another asylum for elderly, sick, and abandoned women and a school for free girls of African descent. She continued to instruct the uninstructed and provide food and clothing for the poor.

Henriette Delille died in the fall of 1862, just six months after Union troops captured New Orleans. Death claimed her a mere quarter century after she stood at the baptismal font in the chapel of the St. Claude Street Convent and pledged herself to the spiritual care of Marie Therese Dagon. Delille's step from spiritual guardian to nun during that quarter century flew in the face of slaveholders in New Orleans, who deemed women of African descent to be impure and impious. The imprint of nineteenth-century universal Catholicism on the city's populace allowed Delille to challenge that paradigm, when she responded to the needs of those she called "her people." Henriette Delille and her religious sisters only succeeded because they provided religious energy necessary to respond to the needs of their own. The institutions they founded under the authority of the church might have been inspired by their religious zeal, but they also offered them opportunities for organizational activities, public service, and leadership unknown elsewhere in the antebellum Deep South. They conferred power and respect on the women where none had existed before.

Delille was long dead by 1876 when her sisterhood attained official approval. The constitution and "rule of life" of the Sisters of the Holy Family were sanctioned at the same time. That was also when the women changed their black dresses to religious habits. By the end of the nineteenth century the women had spread their apostolate to cities and towns scattered throughout the United States. They also ran a school in Belize in Central America. The institutions they established continued to challenge assumptions held by whites and eventually challenged their dominance of the Catholic church in the United States.

Notes

This essay was first presented at a nineteenth-century French studies colloquium at the University of Georgia, Athens, in 1997. I would like to thank Jean Friedman, who commented on that paper, for her encouragement and insight. The essay was rewritten, with Emily Clark, in 1999, and presented at the Association of Caribbean Historians. That presentation, which expands on the Africanization and feminization of the Catholic church in New Orleans, was published as "The Feminine Face of Afro-Catholicism in New Orleans, 1727–1852," in the *William and Mary Quarterly*, 3d ser., 54 (Oct. 1997): 769–94.

1. "Ursuline Convent Chapel Baptismal Register, 1837–1845," April 1, 1838, Ursuline Convent of New Orleans Archives, New Orleans. The entry, translated from French, reads: "On this first of April of eighteen hundred and thirty-eight, I baptized, in the Convent Chapel of St. Claude Marie Therese Dagon daughter of Charles Dagon and of Charlotte Diggs born the twenty-fifth of December of eighteen hundred and twenty-three. The godfather being the undersigned and the godmother being Henriette Delile. [signed] E. Rousselon, Chaplain of the Ursulines." The records of the St. Claude Street Convent are in the Ursuline Convent Archives.

2. Henriette Delille served for the first time as a godmother when she was seventeen. For the baptisms in which she was godmother, see the baptismal registers of the St. Louis Cathedral, the St. Claude Street Convent, St. Augustine's Church, and St. Mary's Church, Annunciation, and Immaculate Conception; St. Louis Cathedral Baptismal Register (1826–27), vols. 20–32; and St. Mary's Baptismal Register (1805–44) and (1844–67). Henriette, without a last name, is described as a godmother on numerous occasions. Not all of those records, however, would point to Henriette Delille, but many do; still others include her first and last name. Dorenda Dupont of the Archdiocesan Archives of New Orleans (hereafter AANO) has conducted a thorough study of all baptisms in New Orleans's Catholic churches from 1812 to 1862.

3. Delille's baptismal record has not been identified. Many baptisms for slave women and free women of color list the baptisand as Marie, daughter of Marie. Henriette Delille was probably named Marie Henriette at her baptism and thus listed by the priest as Marie. Her mother was Marie Josephe. Several records state that Marie daughter of Marie was baptized in 1812 (Baptismal Records of the St. Louis Cathedral, AANO). The records of her siblings have been identified and are all located in the baptismal records of the St. Louis Cathedral, AANO. Records found in the Sisters of the Holy Family Archives state that Delille was born and baptized in 1812 (see, for instance, the Matricula of the Sisters of the Holy Family, Motherhouse, New Orleans). For a discussion of the political economy of the city, see Virginia Meacham Gould, "The House That Was Never a Home: Slave Family and Household in New Orleans, 1820–1850," *Slavery and Abolition* 18 (Aug. 1997): 90–103. Ira Berlin describes colonial Louisiana as a society with slaves rather than a slave society, and New Orleans can be explained in much the same way, in *Many Thousands Gone: The First Two Centuries of Slavery in North America* (Cambridge: Harvard University Press, 1998), 77. Leonard Curry also discusses the demographics of urban slavery in *The Free Black in Urban America, 1800–1850* (Chicago: University of Chicago Press, 1981); also see Richard Wade, *Slavery in the Cities: The South, 1820–1860* (New York: Oxford University Press, 1964).

4. Ira Berlin, *Slaves without Masters: The Free Negro in the Antebellum South* (New York: Oxford University Press, 1974), 182–216. Kimberly Hanger has described the evolution of this middle strata of free people of color in New Orleans in *Bounded Lives, Bounded Places: Free Black Society in Colonial New Orleans, 1769–1803* (Durham: Duke University Press, 1997). Also see Frances Trollop, *Domestic Manners of the Americans*, ed. Donald Smalley (New York: Alfred Knopf, 1949), 10.

5. Gwendolyn Midlo Hall, *Africans in Colonial Louisiana: The Development of Afro-Creole Culture in the Eighteenth Century* (Baton Rouge: Louisiana State University Press, 1992), 157–59; Joseph Tregle, "Creoles and Americans," in *Creole New Orleans: Race and Americanization*, ed. Arnold R. Hirsch and Joseph Logsden (Baton Rouge: Louisiana State University Press, 1992), 131–85; 1805 Census of New Orleans, Louisiana Division, New Orleans Public Library.

6. Donald Everette, "The Free Persons of Color in New Orleans, 1803–1865," Ph.D. diss., Tulane University, 1952; Lois Virginia Meacham Gould, "'In Full Enjoyment of Their Liberty': The Free Women of Color of the Gulf Ports of New Orleans, Mobile, and Pensacola, 1769–1860," Ph.D. diss., Emory University, 1991.

7. Marie Ann appears in Debreuil's household in the 1721 Census of New Orleans, Archives Coloniale, Aix en Provence, France. Her baptism record was lost in the fire of 1788. Salmon to the Ministry of the Colonies (extract), Sept. 3, 1739, series C13A 24, fols. 158–60, Archives Coloniale; Vaudreuil and Michel to the Ministry of the Colonies, May 10, 1751, series C13A 35, fols. 10–11, Archives National, Section Coloniale; Henry P. Dart, "The Career of Dubreuil in French Louisiana," *Louisiana Historical Quarterly* 18 (1935): 267–331; Hall, *Africans in Colonial Louisiana*, 137–39.

8. Dubreuil, *fils* was the son of Dubreuil, *sieur*. The document that ties Claude Joseph Dubreuil to Henriette Delille is the emancipation record of Cecile and her daughters (Acts of Fernando Rodriquez, 1772, Notarial Archives, Civil Court Building, New Orleans). Marie Ann was freed on October 16, 1763, by Claude Joseph Dubreuil fils, with authority of the governor, Luis de Kerelec, and the indendent, Juan Santiago D'Abbadie. Her freedom was recorded in Acts of Almonester y Roxas, Jan. 10, 1770. Marie Ann was first freed privately before the French colonial governor Louis de Kerelec and was later publicly emancipated by notarial act under the Spanish regime. Cecile was freed two years later (Acts of Fernando Rodriquez, 1772). The emancipation of Marianne and her children can be found in Acts of Juan Garic, Sept. 23, Feb. 11, 1772, Notarial Archives, Civil Court Building, New Orleans. One place to see the pattern of property-holding by free women of color, especially by Delille's ancestors, is the 1795 Spanish Census of New Orleans: "Recensement de 1er, 2eme, et 3eme quartiers, July 1795," Archivo General de Indias, Papeles Procedentes de la Isla de Cuba, Seville, Spain, legajo 211, microfilm copy, Historic New Orleans Collection.

9. France formally instituted civil government in Louisiana in 1712. The law in Louisiana was based on the Custom of Paris. That code, with sixteen titles and 362 articles, was in the Roman tradition. The codes and ordinances of the Custom of Paris were augmented by the *Code noir* implemented in March 1724, that is, Louis XV's "Edit concernant les nègres esclaves à la Louisiane." "Le code noir ou édit du roi: Servant de réglement pour le government & l'administration de la justice, police, discipline & le commerce des esclaves négres, dans la Province ou Colonie de la Louisiane. Donné à Versailles au mois de Mars 1724," in *Le code noir ou recueil des reglemens rendus jusqu'à present, concernant le gouvernement, l'administration de la justice, la police, la discipline & le commerce des negres dans les Colonies Françaises* (Paris, 1742).

10. The Ursulines were the first order of noncloistered nuns, but after moving into France during the seventeenth century they were ordered into the cloister by the church. Ursuline Convent Archives, New Orleans; Jane Frances Heaney, *A Century of Pioneering: A History of the Ursuline Nuns in New Orleans, 1727–1827* (New Orleans: Ursuline Sisters, 1993); Glen Conrad, ed., *Cross, Crozier, and Crucible: A Volume Celebrating the Bicentennial of a Catholic Diocese in Louisiana* (New Orleans: Archdiocese of New Orleans in cooperation with the Center for Louisiana Studies, 1993), 203–18; Emily Clark, "A New World Community: The New Orleans Ursulines and Colonial Society, 1727–1803," Ph.D. diss., Tulane University, 1998.

11. The difference between instruction and education is an important one. The women "instructed" females, slave and free, in religion. They educated, or taught, the daughters of free women of color the basics of reading and writing. It was against law and tradition to educate slaves, although some slaves in eighteenth-century New Orleans were educated, and it appears from their handwriting that the Ursulines educated them. Scattered manumission and property records are in the New Orleans Notarial Archives.

12. *Premier registre de la congrégation des dames enfant de Marie, 1730–1744,* Ursuline Convent Archives, Ursuline Academy, New Orleans. The records of the Ladies Congregation of the Children of Mary are also in the Ursuline Convent Archives. Emily Clark, "'By All the Conduct of their Lives': A Laywomen's Confraternity in New Orleans, 1730–1744," *William and Mary Quarterly*, 3d ser., 54 (Oct. 1997): 769–94.

13. Nanette and her children are enumerated in the inventory of Claude Joseph Dubreuil's estate. They are identified as a family of domestics living in the household and are protected by codicil to the will. (Inventory of the Estate of Claude Joseph Dubreuil). The fire of 1788 destroyed the

baptismal records of Nanette and her children, Marianne, Fanchonette, Tuyanne, and Tonica. The baptisms of Nanette and Marianne are inferred from the women's appearance in sacramental records as godmothers. See, for example, "St. Louis Cathedral Baptisms and Marriages, 1753–59," May 13, 1775, ANNO; "St. Louis Cathedral Baptisms and Marriages, 1759–62," March 23, May 25, and Sept. 7, 1760, ANNO; "St. Louis Cathedral Baptisms and Marriages, 1763–66," Oct. 27, 1765, ANNO; and "Libro donde se asientan las partidas de baptismos de negros esclavos y mulatos que se han celeb[a]do en esta Iglesia parroquial de Sr. San Luis de la ciudad de la Nueva Orleans desde el día 1 enero de 1777 que empezó hasta el año de 1781 que es el corrente," March 4, July 23, 1775. Cecile was baptised on Dec. 31, 1744 (Baptismal Record, St. Louis Cathedral, vol. 2, 1744).

14. Clark, "'By All the Conduct of Their Lives'"; Emily Clark and Virginia Meacham Gould, "The Feminine Face of Afro-Catholicism in New Orleans, 1727–1852," *William and Mary Quarterly*, 3d ser., 59 (April 2002): 409–48.

15. For the best broad discussion of the void left in the church after the Louisiana Purchase, see Roger Baudier, *The Catholic Church in Louisiana* (1939, repr. New Orleans: Louisiana Library Association Public Library Section, 1972). Also see the voluminous correspondence that addresses the matter in the Louisiana Collection, Archives of Notre Dame University, and John F. Watson, "Notia of Incidents of New Orleans in 1804 and 1805," *American Pioneer* 2 (May 1843): 230–34.

16. The Census of the City of New Orleans, 1805, Louisiana Division, New Orleans Public Library; Third Manuscript Census of the United States, 1810. The U.S. Census of 1810 shows that slaves composed the largest percentage of that segment of the population, 5,961. Free people of color numbered 4,950.

17. Baudier, *The Catholic Church in Louisiana*. DuBourg's correspondence can be found in the records of the Propagation de la Foi, Les Oeuvres Pontificale Missionaire, Lyon, France. The records of the Rosaire Vivante are housed at La Maison Domincain, also in Lyon. Elisabeth Dufourcq, *Les aventurières du Dieu: Trois siècles d'historie missionnaire française* (Paris: J. C. Lattès, 1993); Annabelle M. Melville, *Louis William DuBourg: Bishop of Louisiana and the Florida, Bishop of Montauban, and Archbishop of Besancon, 1766–1833*, vols. 1 and 2 (Chicago: Loyola University Press, 1986).

18. There is much valuable testimony and documentation in the *pozitio* (position papers) of Pauline Marie Jaricot, Congregation of Saints, Rome. They are a part of the documentation for her case for canonization.

19. Yvonne Turin, *Femmes et religieuses au XIXeme siecle: Le feminism "en religion"* (Paris: Nouvelle Cite, 1989); Dufourcq, *Les aventurieres de Dieu;* Claude Langlois, *Le catholicisme au feminin: Les congregations francaises a superieure generale au XIX siecle* (Paris: Éditions du Cerf, 1984); Melville, *Louis William DuBourg;* also see the diary of Father Jean-Marie Tessier, Archives of the Sulpiciens of Baltimore, RGI BX9A, now housed in the Archives of the Archdiocese of Baltimore, St. Mary's Seminary, Md. A group of letters from DuBourg to John Carroll is in the archives of the Archdiocese of Baltimore; see also DuBourg to Carroll, Archives of the Daughters of Charity, Emmitsburg, Pa.

20. Turin, *Femmes et religieuses*, 26.

21. One group of nine women left France to spread their devotion in response to a call for aid issued from the Ursulines through Bishop DuBourg and arrived in New Orleans in 1817. Baudier, *The Catholic Church in Louisiana*. For information on Dubreuil, see Dart, "The Career of Dubreuil," 291–331. Most records concerning Dubreuil are located in the records of the Superior Council, Louisiana History Center, Louisiana State Museum, New Orleans. Data from the census from U.S. Census, City of New Orleans, State of Louisiana, 1810; see also *Nouvelles Recues Des Missions*, no. 2 (Lyon: Chez Perisse Freres, Libraires, 1823), 17, 27.

Sister Ste. Marthe tried to establish a community of women religious at the school between 1826 and 1828. The school in those years was referred to as a "convent." The Ursulines asked DuBourg to find someone to aid them in teaching young free women of color ("List of the Ursuline Sisters," vol. 4, Ursuline Convent Archives, Ursuline Academy, New Orleans). Sister Ste. Marthe returned to France in 1831 in order to recruit women for her school. The trip is described in a letter from Antoine Blanc to an unnamed priest, his cousin, who lived at or near Lyon, probably in 1831. Mother Joanna Miles, Sisters of Loretto, to Bishop Rosati, Feb. 6, 1828, Archdiocesan Archives of St. Louis, St. Louis, Mo.; see also Joan Campbell, *Loretto in Louisiana; The Legacy of La Fourche* (Nerina, Ky.: Sisters of Loretto, 1987), 28–29.

No records of the St. Claude Street School are left for those years, but that is where Henriette DeLille was educated according to the oral tradition of the Sisters of the Holy Family and the "Deggs Journal," a document written by Sister Mary Bernard Deggs between 1894 and 1896. The journal has been edited and translated by Virginia Meacham Gould and Charles Nolan in *No Cross on Earth, No Crown in Heaven* (Bloomington: University of Indiana Press, 2000). The Sisters of Mount Carmel eventually took over the school on St. Claude Street. The definitive work on the Sisters of Mount Carmel, also founded in France, remains Charles E. Nolan, "Carmelite Dreams, Creole Perspectives: The Sisters of Mount Carmel of Louisiana (1833–1903)," Ph.D. diss., Pontificale Gregorian University, Rome, 1970. The description of Fontiere is included in a report at the Ursuline Convent in Bordeaux.

22. Bishop Louis Guaillaume DuBourg to Father Antoine Blanc, France, June 27, 1824, La Congregation pour le Propagation de la Foi, Ouvres Pontificle Missionaire, Lyon.

23. Portier was one of the missionaries who accompanied DuBourg from Lyon to New Orleans in 1817. Michael Portier to the Directors of le Propogation de la Foi, Sept. 1820, Oeuvres Pontificale Missionaire, Lyon

24. The Constitution of the Congregation of the Sisters of the Presentation of the Blessed Virgin Mary is recorded by hand in French in the account book and located in the Sisters of the Holy Family Archives, Motherhouse, New Orleans.

25. The prayer, written in French and signed by Delille, was inscribed in a French book of spirituality. Madame La Comtese de Carcado, *L'ami unie a Jésus-Christ dans le trés Saint Sacrement de l'autel . . .* (1830), Sisters of the Holy Family Archives, Motherhouse, New Orleans.

26. The records of Delille's activities and the formation of her community are found in the Sisters of the Holy Family Archives, Motherhouse, New Orleans. In particular, see the matricula and the pages of a memoir written by Mary Bernard Deggs between 1894 and 1896 (*No Cross, No Crown*, ed. Gould and Nolan, 8–18). Deggs was a pupil at the school for free girls of color founded by Henriette Delille before the Civil War. She knew Delille personally, although as a pupil knows a teacher. The school, still in operation, is St. Mary's Academy, which is located just behind the motherhouse. Following Catholic tradition, the school educates young girls and women to be successful and good Catholics, mothers, and wives.

CHAPTER 14

Religious Women of Color in Seventeenth-Century Lima: Estefania de San Ioseph and Ursula de Jesu Christo

Alice L. Wood

Seventeenth-century Franciscan narratives from Spanish Peru contain two valuable portraits of religious women of color. The first, the "Vida de Estefania de San Ioseph" written by the Franciscan chronicler Diego de Cordova Salinas, was published in his *Coronica de la Religiosissima Provincia de los Doze Apostoles del Perú* in 1651. The second, the story of Ursula de Christo, is found in an unpublished manuscript entitled "Espejo de Religiosas" (1698), which is preserved in the Convent of San Francisco in Lima.[1]

The stories of Estefania de San Ioseph and Ursula de Christo demonstrate that even under restrictive conditions women of color could find creative—indeed, inspirational—expressions of religious faith. Both women stand out in these narratives as remarkable and admirable individuals. The narratives also show that at a time when the lives of few women—let alone women of color—were recorded, the women were considered so exemplary and such a credit to the Franciscan order that their stories were preserved with care and detail. Moreover, the lives of the religious women Ursula and Estefania illustrate that the history of the Catholic church in the Americas is incomplete without consideration of the contributions of women of color.

The city of Lima and its environs was undoubtedly the largest population center in colonial Peru. Called the "City of Kings," Lima was the seat of both vice-regal and ecclesiastical authority for most of South America.[2] Frederick Bowser has estimated that by the mid-seventeenth century, approximately thirty thousand persons of color lived in Peru, two-thirds of them (twenty thousand) most likely concentrated in the metropolitan area around Lima, the total population of which was fewer than thirty-five thousand.[3] Bowser also estimates that probably 10 percent of the population of color in Peru was free (or about two thousand in Lima) by the mid-seventeenth century. Population estimates for the period are uncertain, however, because most censuses did not distinguish between free blacks (*negros*) and slaves. Tax laws encouraged free persons of color to avoid enumeration in order to escape paying tribute, and most persons who had lighter skin found it to their advantage to be categorized as Spanish if possible.[4]

Estefania and Ursula were natives of Peru, and both were born into slavery. It appears also that both were of mixed African and European ancestry. Although an elaborate caste and color nomenclature existed in the Spanish colonial world, neither text gives much information about the women's skin color. Estefania's mother was a slave described as a *morena* from Portugal. "Morena" was a term used in Spain to identify someone of "Moorish" or North African ancestry or of a dark complexion. In the Americas, the term generally meant "dark," but often it was applied to a woman of mixed African and European parentage, as did the words *parda* and *mulata*.[5]

There are no indications in the text about Estefania's complexion; she is only referred to by name or as "this woman" (*esta mujer*). Ursula, however, who was referred to as *"morena, negra criolla,"* was probably fairly dark-skinned. Her father is named in the text but not described at all. Her mother, also named, is described as "a black Creole slave" ([*una*] *negra Criolla esclava*). Most Spaniards in colonial Peru would have used the term *negro* or "black" to refer to anyone of African descent, slave or free. In the text of the "Espejo," Ursula was referred to as *negra,* and she is quoted as referring to herself as *una negra*. When translating the original texts, I will use the term *black* for "negro" or "negra" even though in actual usage the term referred in general to people of color, not just to those with very dark skin. "Creole" (*criollo/criolla*) was a term used in the colonial period as an adjective to indicate that a person—not an Indian—had been born in the New World. Scholars reserve the term, however, to refer specifically to the American-born colonists of Spanish descent and custom, thus distinguishing them not only from European Spaniards but also from other colonial populations of Africans, Indians, and those of "mestizo," or mixed parentage. I shall use the term *Creole* in this latter sense.

Although the majority of African slaves in Peru worked in agriculture, most urban slavery involved household service.[6] Slave labor was also vital to the operation of religious institutions such as monasteries, convents, and hospitals. Patrons endowed religious houses with slaves, and many religious from wealthy families brought slaves to convents as their personal servants. Free persons of color were considered subjects of the Spanish crown, on the one hand, with the accompanying obligation to pay taxes and provide military service. On the other hand, blacks who were not slaves were regarded as "unproductive," and their liberties and opportunities were severely restricted by law. Colonial administrators attempted to control free persons of color through curfews and ordinances mandating that all persons of color, slave or free, had to live with a master or owner of a business and had to claim some occupation and known residence.[7]

Such measures improved the collection of taxes and increased social control over free blacks, who, like unattached women of the period, were seen as threats to a well-ordered society.[8] Strict regulations were deemed necessary to reduce prostitution, vagrancy, and thievery associated with indigent blacks. The same laws also put pressure on free persons of color to take menial jobs such as street-cleaning for little or no recompense.[9] In that context it is understandable that the religious life might have been appealing to some.

The narratives presented here illustrate two types of religious life that were open to women of color in the seventeenth century. One involved existence as an independent religious living "in the world," and the other was that of a nun within a cloister. Although Estefania and Ursula may have been exceptional, their religious vocations and general circumstances were not. During the sixteenth and seventeenth centuries, devout women could don habits and pursue private religious lives without living in convents. Estefania made that choice, and it was while she lived in a priest's household that she attracted the attention of clerics who wrote down her story. A different kind of life is depicted for Ursula in the "Espejo," which portrays the situation of both slaves and free women in the cloister. Ursula came to the convent as a slave, but after obtaining her freedom she adopted the religious life.

In the discussion that follows I intend to direct attention to the life histories of Estefania and Ursula and to the ways in which their stories are narratively framed. Strictly speaking, these texts are a form of hagiography, a term that means literally "writing about saints." Although neither woman was officially canonized, both were recognized as saintly by their communities and esteemed as saintly by their biographers.[10] Accordingly, their lives were presented in what would have been considered a suitable literary form with particular narrative conventions. The story of a saintly person was expected to contain, for example, some mention of childhood pieties; an enumeration of saintly virtues (themselves relatively conventionalized); a description of the subject's last days, death, and funeral; and discussion of displays in public. Despite these conventions, the narratives are not merely formulaic as is often assumed. Authors had to adapt and edit available biographical and anecdotal material in order to present the subject as both unique and recognizably saintly. Equally important, each narrative deliberately presented its subject as a member of a real, historical community whose members all shared by association their exceptional grace and holiness.

Hagiography underwent a transformation in the early modern period. The Catholic church, sensitive to reformers' accusations that many saints were mere inventions and not historical figures, instituted changes in canonization procedures at the end of the sixteenth century.[11] One forbade the writing of hagiography in which someone was referred to as a "saint" before that title had been conferred upon them by the pope. "Official" lives of saints were to be approved from Rome. Hagiography was further refined by a group of Jesuit scholars, the Bollandists, who began to reevaluate the catalog of saints based on historical sources.[12]

Other changes also affected hagiography. The literature of seventeenth-century Spain brought a new sense of power and importance to individual lives, as can be seen in the emergence of autobiography as a literary form. Indeed, the writing of the great St. Teresa of Avila drew attention to the power of spiritual autobiography. The texts to be examined in this study are not remarkable for literary innovation, but they provide vivid portraits of two women whose freedom, although limited, nevertheless allowed them to find creative and independent forms of religious expression. These texts also provide a window into seventeenth-century attitudes about gender and race. Comparison of the accounts of Estefania and Ursula with other examples of colonial hagiography shows that saintliness was defined differently for people of color. Saintly virtue was generally presented as the overcoming of vices associated with a subject's race and gender. Careful reading of the arguments in support of these women's holiness reveals the vices commonly attributed to a person of their "kind." In other words, the narrative strategies used in the descriptions of Estefania and Ursula contribute much to a general picture of contemporary social prejudice in colonial Peru as a background to the individual portraits of the women.

The life of Estefania de San Ioseph (1561–1645) is found in the fifth book of the 1651 chronicle of Cordova Salinas in a section devoted to the lives of Franciscan tertiaries, or lay members of the order, who had earned saintly reputations.[13] Estefania chose to follow a religious life not as a nun but as a *beata* (a woman who lived out religious vows of poverty, chastity, and obedience to God either alone or with a small group of other beatas rather than in convents). Beatas prayed, conducted private devotions, performed acts of public charity, and often attended daily mass. They wore the habit of the religious order with which they were formally or informally connected. Beatas were usually supervised and instructed in personal and religious matters by a confessor or spiritual advisor—often a priest from the local church or religious order.[14] They might live alone in a hermitage or in a house donated by a benefactor, but often they lived with relatives or in the households of wealthy sponsors who chose to demonstrate their own piety by supporting these saintly figures.[15]

Estefania must have taken the Franciscan habit as her own sometime in the early 1580s. She is described as "professed," that is, having made formal vows, and said to have been conscientious in discharging her duties to the order. Cordova Salinas notes that she was one of the first in Lima to take the habit of a Franciscan tertiary and that he knew her to have been diligent in the observation of the Franciscan rule.[16] He stated that he had personally known Estefania and had administered the Eucharist to her from time to time over a period of almost forty-five years. In an effort to write a truly authoritative biography of this saintly woman, Cordova Salinas turned to Don Francisco Davila, canon of the cathedral in Lima, with whom Estefania had lived for many years.[17] Most of the narrative that follows here is based on Cordova Salinas's version of the account of Estefania's life given to him by Davila.

Estefania was born about 1561 in the city of Cuzco, Peru, to a slave woman named Isabel and a Spanish father. A native of Portugal, Isabel was brought to the New World by her wealthy owner, a Captain Maldonado ("el Rico"). Upon the death of Captain Maldonado, Isabel was freed.[18] She then entered the Convent of Santa Clara in Cuzco as a *donada* (donation).[19] Donadas, the lowest caste in a convent community, were obligated to work as servants in return for their room and board. They were considered members of the order, however, and as such they were given care in their old age and assured a Christian burial. Davila confirmed that he had known Isabel and that he had spoken with her before her death in the early 1580s. That was surely how he first became acquainted with her daughter, Estefania.

In his will, Captain Maldonado freed Estefania and her mother, but the heirs to his estate were unwilling to acknowledge the manumission of the younger woman. Estefania was therefore forced to travel from Cuzco to Lima to pursue her cause at the *Real Audiencia* (Spanish court of law).[20] Neither the problem described here, nor its resolution in court in favor of the plaintiff, appears to have been unusual in colonial Peru.[21] Davila gave no details of the event but only noted that "the Lord disposed the case in her favor for the sake of her salvation, freeing her soul as he had her body."[22] Davila added that Estefania promptly "adopted the habit of a beata of the penitential order of St. Francis and endeavored to live a holy life." This abrupt statement stood by itself. Davila said nothing about why Estefania chose a Franciscan habit nor about where or how she lived. He wrote only that she went to confession and received the Eucharist.[23] One can imagine that Estefania's choice of a religious habit, even without formal connection to a religious house, might have provided the best way for her to move about in the city as a free woman without the protection of a husband or family. In addition, it afforded her compliance with the colonial mandate that free persons of color have a known occupation and ties to some place of employment or institution.

Fifteen or more years elapsed between Estafania's choice of life as a beata and the renewal of acquaintance with her biographer, but we have no account of this period. Davila next encountered Estefania after he left Cuzco for Lima to be ordained. He related that one morning after Easter in 1596, Estefania came to the Franciscan church for confession. He recognized her and invited her to become his housekeeper. Estefania agreed and performed her duties to Davila's great satisfaction, "providing a good example to everyone."[24]

Her life during these years was little different from that of many other free women of color who were housekeepers in wealthy homes. It must have been somewhat easier for her to combine household duties with a religious vocation because her employer was a priest. According to Davila, she diligently arose during the night for prayers and joined clerical members of the household to observe the night offices, just as she would have done in a convent.[25] She also, apparently, had a good deal of free time to pursue her chosen charitable works. Over the years Estefania raised four orphans, two boys and two girls. The placement of orphans in suitable households was common, and most women raised several children besides, or instead of, their own.[26] All of Estefania's four "children" eventually adopted the religious life. One of them became a Jesuit priest, another joined the regular clergy, and the two girls became nuns, one an Augustinian and the other a Dominican.[27] Estefania's ability to raise four children with such success convinced Davila that she possessed true Christian devotion and virtue.

Estefania apparently lived for many years in Davila's household before she left his service. He implied that he continued to have contact with her but provided no details about whether she lived alone or with other beatas in the city. He said she supported herself sewing pillows, which she sold for 4 reales. She kept only a little of that money for herself, donating the rest as alms for the poor.[28] Davila held Estefania in high esteem for her charity. He wrote that she was very compassionate toward the sick in the convent infirmary and visited them late into the night. She did not shirk difficult or unpleasant tasks such as applying medicine and poultices. She collected rags for bandages, washed them very clean, and took them to hospitals, where she also visited patients.[29] Cordova Salinas, in summarizing Estefania's virtues, characterizes her as having lived a "celestial" life of humility and charity to others.

In her personal ministry to the sick, Estefania was very much like her contemporary St. Martin de Porres (1579–1639), who lived only a short distance from the Franciscan convent at the nearby Dominican convent of the Rosary.[30] Biographers of both individuals hasten to point out that such ministry to the sick was indicative not only of charitable caring for others but also of Christian humility and self-sacrifice, because nursing duties required many disgusting and menial chores. It is not surprising, of course, to find the virtue of charity extolled in any saint. The predominance of this virtue in descriptions of Estefania and Martin de Porres, however, exceeds references found in the hagiography of most Creole saints.[31] The difference is notable but hard to interpret. One possible explanation is that free blacks were often conscripted to do this type of menial work, and hagiographers of saints of color were most comfortable describing a type of charitable work that seemed to locate their subjects appropriately. If that were the case, the narratives might reassure readers that Estefania was suitably humble not only for a saint but also for a woman of color. Another explanation may be that Spaniards generally considered that free blacks lacked a sense of civic responsibility and performed no useful social functions.[32] That saints of color would be presented as especially generous, selfless, and sacrificing on behalf of others would then take on significance. If saintly virtues were signs of God's grace, what would better illustrate that grace than overcoming the vices associated with their race?

Davila also drew special attention to Estefania's trustworthiness in financial matters. He wrote that Estefania assisted the abbesses of the convent with whatever they needed, including service as treasurer of alms that she performed with great care.[33] In a convent as large as that of Lima's San Francisco, this position would have involved responsibility for large sums of money. Davila singled out this particular volunteer activity for comment because it was unusual to mention responsible money-handling in the life of a saint. It was far more common to encounter saintly disregard for money. The few other contemporary references to saintly skill in handling money—and the accompanying implications of scrupulous honesty—are to be found in the *Lives of Martin de Porres.*[34] Evidently, Spanish hagiographers emphasized the virtues of charity, honesty, and stewardship in saintly individuals of color to refute cultural assumptions that blacks were dishonest and untrustworthy.

More differences of emphasis can be found when some of the details about Estefania's life are compared to those of Creole women saints. Davila mentioned that Estefania disciplined her body with scourges and hair shirts, but he did not elaborate. She fasted on Monday, Wednesday, Friday, and Saturday weekly, and she was "even more abstinent during Advent and Lent." Through it all Estefania never showed displeasure or anger. She always appeared peaceful and patient.[35] As descriptions of saintly mortifications go, Estafania's were very mild, but Davila intentionally mentioned them as evidence of her piety and devotion and also stressed the sweetness of disposition that made her "saintly." Was sweetness of temper more remarkable than self-denial?

The spiritual discipline associated with enduring bodily pain was not at all unusual in late-medieval and early-modern Catholic practice. There are many stories of saints who experienced severe mortification of the senses and brutal self-torture.[36] The simply stated facts in Estefania's case are in sharp contrast with the elaborate descriptions frequently given for other saints. In the same section of the *Coronica* that contains the account of the life of Estefania, Codoba Salinas extensively praises the physical austerities of the Creole saint Marianna de Jesus.[37] Likewise, in his description of the ecstatic nun Doña Isabel de Porras, laid out in the chapter immediately preceding the story of Estefania, Cordoba Salinas draws special attention to Isabel's physical sufferings and mystical wounds.[38]

The most famous Creole saint, Rose of Lima, was widely acclaimed for her physical mortifications. Seventeenth-century biographies of Rose included whole chapters that described her penances in excruciating detail. Spanish Creole women, whose lives were generally perceived as easy and whose bodies were perceived as weak, were driven to prove their "heroic" virtue through physical suffering and disfigurement.[39] That was not necessary to the same degree for an account of the life of Estefania, a woman of color and former slave.[40]

Neither did Davila emphasize Estefania's lack of what many contemporaries considered to be the most prevalent female vice: vanity. He wrote that she usually wore a rough habit and veil, both "mended in a thousand places," but on major feast days she put on slightly better clothing, particulary when she assisted with the Sacrament.[41] Creole saints like Rose of Lima or Marianna de Jesus never dressed up, especially not for public occasions. Davila presented Estefania's concern for the clothes she wore to church as a positive reflection of her piety and decorum. She was never suspected of vanity or immodesty.

Estefania earned the admiration of everyone who knew her. She listened to the sermons in church "with such attentiveness that she edified all who saw her." Davila praised her ability to move freely and comfortably among people of all social classes. "She was happy, affable, humble, and gracious and with these qualities she was welcomed by the richest and most distinguished ladies of the city, by rich men, students, and clergymen."[42] It is significant that Davila made much of Estefania's social grace, because although the "classless" nature of saints was a very old paradigm that had existed in Christian hagiography for centuries it was not a common theme in Spanish hagiography of the era. It was far more common for saintly individuals to be praised for their simplicity and acceptance of humble circumstances or, in the case of those born to privilege, for their indifference to the benefits of class and wealth.[43] Estefania, in any case, enjoyed a wide social world by virtue of her position as housekeeper for a well-to-do churchman. What is remarkable—and saintly—is her use of that mobility to minister and "preach" to those who might have ordinarily dismissed a woman of color.

During the seventeenth century, women of any station were not allowed to preach or give religious instruction. Nuns were not even allowed to carry on missionary work among the Indians. Estefania, however, developed her own creative form of missionary work among her neighbors in Lima. Davila gave an example. Leaving home for church one day, Estefania stopped at the house of an acquaintance. In the long sleeve of her habit she carried one of her many devotional books, one she knew quite well and had chosen specifically for the edification of this particular woman. Estefania expected that she and her friend would read the book together if time and opportunity permitted. After an exchange of pleasantries, Estefania removed the book from her sleeve and gave it to her friend. "Please, read a little of this to me, señora," she said. After a while she asked her friend to read "just a little more, please." In this way Estefania succeeded in exposing her friend to the uplifting contents of the book.[44]

According to Davila, by selecting texts and having people read them aloud to her Estefania in essence "preached" between four and six times a day "to the benefit of many." Davila acknowledged that she "preached" to him many times, and, "knowing her zeal and concern for his soul," he always read to her when she asked, and "each time it was to his own benefit."[45] It is not clear from the story whether Estefania was able to read. In any case she capitalized on the prevalent assumption of those times that she could not do so in order to compel people to read to her.

Estefania also developed a unique method of encouraging devotion to the rosary. She carried, tucked in the sleeves of her habit, small laced-paper packets of raisins. Passing a group of children, she would stop one and ask, "Do you have a rosary with you?" If the child could show her a rosary, she would hand out a packet of raisins as reward. No rosary, no raisins. This, said Davila, had the effect of sending many neighborhood children running to their parents, begging for a rosary. Estefania did such things with such obvious pleasure and grace, we are told, that "one could see God at work in her."[46]

In his account of Estefania's death, Davila made it clear that he believed she was a saint. At the end of her life Estefania was gravely ill, and she suffered with great patience. She was by then living "in her own poor house" somewhere in Lima. Eventually, she asked to be taken to the Hospital de la Caridad, which cared for women. She went there having already received the Sacrament at home, but she took it again "for the virtue it inspired and the heavenly solace it gave her soul." From time to time she would sing a few verses of a hymn to the Virgin and Child, asking to merit meeting them in heaven.[47] Estefania died on May 9, 1645. She was eighty-four.

Most Catholics of the period considered a quiet and peaceful death, arriving after the administration of the Sacraments and pious contemplation of heaven, to be a sign of utmost faith and trust in the Lord as well as an appropriate reward for a life well-lived.[48] Davila's report of Estefania's funeral bore testimony to her popularity and saintly reputation. She was given a solemn burial at the Convent of San Francisco in Lima. Her funeral was attended not only by the Franciscan community but also by many secular priests and staff from the cathedral and "a great multitude of people" from the city of Lima. The mourners accompanied her body "with great veneration as was due a saintly woman." The padre guardian, director of the convent, himself sang the mass, and she was given a special casket and crypt. Cordova Salinas reports being present for the eulogies, when the body was exposed in the main chapel of the convent. Many men and women came to view the body, "to venerate it and kiss the hands with tender devotion."[49] More indicative of sanctity than even this acclaim, however, was the condition of Estefania's body after death. Cordova Salinas claims that her face was bathed in a special beauty, "revealing the joy of her soul." He took hold of her hands, he added, "and even thirty hours after her death they felt soft and flexible and the fingers moved readily. I raised her arms and moved them around easily as if she were still alive."[50]

Such fascination with the body of the deceased was a usual part of an assessment of sanctity. For centuries the Catholic church has interpreted incorruptibility of a dead body as a powerful indication of sainthood. Flexible limbs, soft flesh, and the absence of foul odors were all considered signs that the deceased continued to live on in heaven. At the time of Estefania's burial, Cordova Salinas points out, many priests and even the reverend padre provincial, head of the Franciscan Order in Peru, moved her limbs and "with great care and attentiveness" placed their noses near her body and mouth. But they could detect no odor of death.[51] On the basis of these signs the Reverend Father Juan de Durana, commissary general of the Province of Peru, pronounced Estefania a "saintly woman."[52]

Cordova Salinas specifies the titles of several dignitaries, including the provincial, who attended the funeral in order to make the point that Estefania's reputation for sanctity was so great that important administrators of the religious order wished to be counted in attendance. He mentions their assessment of the body in order to add authority and credence to references about its condition. "So highly esteemed and so meritorious was this humble woman," Cordova Salinas concludes, "that even among so many illustrious Franciscans she shone miraculously like a morning star in the heavens of the Seraphic Order."[53]

Although the Franciscans never promoted the beata Estefania de San Ioseph for canonization, the official recognition of sainthood by the Vatican, "Madre" Estefania, as she was called, had clearly touched the lives of those among whom she lived. For them, she was a saint whose gentle presence proclaimed God's own.

Estefania provides an example of a woman of color who found in the religious life a means to relative independence and freedom. Free to move about the city and interact with a wide variety of people, she enjoyed considerably more liberty and self-direction than she would have had in a convent. Her life was, nevertheless, very hard in many ways, and she did not enjoy the security that her mother found by becoming a donada.

But if the conventual life was hard, it could also be hard to leave, as the account of Ursulade Jesu Christó will show. It should be remembered that the texts of these women's life stories were shaped by male clerics in positions of power. The story of Estefania was written by her former employer, a prominent churchman and canon of the cathedral, Doctor Davila. The text was then edited and incorporated into a larger work by another prominent and educated man in a volume aimed at a male readership. It is therefore difficult for scholars to know what aspects of Estefania's life might have been omitted or given different emphasis, given her biographers' male perspectives and official positions. It is a little easier to discern some of the male perspective that permeates the "Espejo" and descriptions of Ursula.

* * *

Ursula de Jesu Christo (1604–?) was a visionary. Under the direction of her male confessor, she recorded her mystical experiences and conversations with God. Only about ten of the forty-five manuscript pages of the "Espejo" are devoted to the story of Ursula herself. Most of the manuscript describes visions for which biographical details about Ursula provide a frame. While the anonymous author narrates the events of her life, the accounts of the visions themselves are,

ostensibly, those recorded by Ursula herself. She received so many of these favors from God that she could not store them easily in her memory. Her confessor, a priest, advised her to write down those she could recall.[54] It is not known
whether Ursula was able to write or if she dictated the account of her visions to
someone else. In any case, her convent preserved an account of her visions, and
a narrative of her life was later added to it.

Because Ursula was a visionary it was absolutely essential in the eyes of the
Catholic church that she be under the direction of a male spiritual advisor who
could evaluate and validate her experiences. This need for external authority—
specifically, male authority—was particularly critical in the case of women visionaries because women, deemed gullible by their very nature, were not to be
trusted in the discernment of spirits and visions.[55] Only men were believed to
have the rationality and judgment to determine whether supernatural events
were sent from God or from the devil. The spiritual director, often a visionary's
confessor, served both the visionary and the religious community by assessing
the nature, content, and authenticity of the visions according to established
criteria called the *discretio spirituum*.[56] Among the primary functions of that
assessment were protection of the faithful from demonic influences disguised
as visions and the ensuring of orthodoxy. And because women, more so than
men, were suspected of feigning visions in order to gain attention and power, a
spiritual director was entrusted with establishing a visionary's veracity and good
character.[57] Ursula's confessor most probably ordered the first recording of her
visions to enable him to review and judge them.

Ursula was a free woman of color who, as a slave, came to live in a Franciscan
convent. Years later, she chose the religious life as her own. The account of her
life, unlike that for Estefania, was not written for readers outside the convent,
and the document was never published. It exists as a manuscript in the Convent of San Francisco in Lima, entitled "Espejo de Religiosas" (the Nuns' Mirror). The introduction to the work introduces it as a copy of earlier, "original"
documents.[58] The record of Ursula's visions, reportedly written down by Ursula
herself at the request of her confessor, was subsequently edited, and all individual
names were removed.[59] Its intended audience was the nuns at the convent, and
its date suggests that some of the nuns would surely have had firsthand knowledge of the events described in the stories and could evaluate the authenticity
of the text.

The "Espejo" is anecdotal in style, often stringing a series of stories and visions together with little chronological information to connect them. It includes
many details and even a few unflattering stories that might well have been
omitted in any formal published work. Although the biography of Ursula tells
a story about the transformative power of the religious life, her visions were often
critical of the clergy and her fellow religious. In her prophesies about God's
justice in the world to come, Ursula revealed the injustice and hypocrisy of the
community around her. The omissions of the names of nuns at the convent who

befriended Ursula and the name of the nun who purchased her freedom suggest that the "Espejo" was intended as a devotional book for the convent and not primarily as hagiography.[60]

The life of Ursula offers a view of seventeenth-century convent life as experienced by women of color. The Franciscan convent of Lima reflected the stratifications of colonial Spanish society as a whole, and Ursula's place was at the very lowest level because she first came to the convent as a slave. Franciscan nuns were (and are) members of the Order of Saint Clare, the "second" order of St. Francis. Almost all Claretian nuns in Lima came from well-to-do Creole families.[61] They were sometimes called "choir" nuns because only they were allowed to sing the canonical hours in the choir of the chapel. They were the voting members of the chapter, and they held all administrative positions. These women brought substantial dowries with them, lived in spacious apartments at the convent, and retained the marks and titles of their social status.[62] Women from less wealthy Spanish and mestizo families served in less prestigious posts. At the bottom of the hierarchy were tertiaries, or members of the "third order" of Franciscans.

Tertiaries came from families that could not provide substantial dowries for their daughters. They worked in menial positions at the convent and were not allowed to vote at chapter meetings. They were, nevertheless, considered vowed members of the order and wore nuns' habits with a white veil (instead of a brown one). The lowest strata within the company of tertiaries were donadas. They were very poor women, often former slaves, who gave themselves, or were given by their owners, to the convent. That was the case for Estefania's mother, Isabel. Donadas were indentured servants who were obligated to work in exchange for support, and they usually ate and went to chapel separately from the other nuns at the convent.

A large number of servants and slaves lived and worked at the convent, but they were not members of the Franciscan order. Most of the women were personal maids who had accompanied their mistresses to the convent and who waited upon them in the same way they would have done in any other household. Their lives were little different from those of servants elsewhere. Although they would have been expected to observe public forms of religious expression like any layperson, they were not bound by convent rule, nor were they accountable to anyone but their mistresses. Ursula first came to the Convent of San Francisco as a personal maid.

Ursula's biographer wrote that she was a native of Lima and the legitimate daughter of Juan de Castillo and Isabel de los Rios, a slave of Doña Geronima de los Rios.[63] Born to a slave, Ursula was also a slave. When she was seven her owner, Geronima de los Rios, died, and the young Ursula went to live with another mistress, Doña Luisa de Soto Melgareso. As a child she received some instruction in the Catholic faith, and she developed a special devotion to the Virgin of Carmel. At the age of twelve, Ursula was sent off to the Convent of San

Francisco to be the slave of a religious female cousin of Geronima de los Rios. Every day, "without fail and despite many diversions," she retired alone to a quiet place and recited the rosary upon her knees. She fasted on Wednesdays and prepared for and received the sacraments of confession and holy communion, and all this, her biographer noted, began even before her "conversion" to the religious life.[64] Ursula was not, however, without fault. According to one anecdote of her early life at the convent, friends who saw her withdrawn in prayer after communion commented, "That fibber ought to seek confession because she goes around telling lies."[65] It would seem logical that the fault of dishonesty was acknowledged in order to imply that Ursula's later conversion erased this vice and to improve her credibility.

The event that prompted Ursula's first turn toward the spiritual life was a frightening accident that took place when she was thirty (ca. 1635). One day, as she was trying to wash and dry a piece of cloth at a well, she fell in and was held, suspended over the water, by a nail. Holding onto the nail with one hand and clenching a scapular of Our Lady of Carmel in the other, Ursula prayed fervently, "Lady, ask your Son not to condemn me!" A large crowd from the monastery gathered to watch with horror. No one could reach Ursula to help her because the mouth of the well was too deep. The helpless crowd encouraged her to "die well": to repent of her sins, ask for God's mercy, and calmly prepare for death.[66] Miraculously, "through the mercy of God and the power and intercession of His Mother," Ursula was saved. No details of the rescue are given in the "Espejo," but the circumstances elicited "great admiration from the crowd who praised God and gave thanks for this remarkable sign."[67]

Ursula was so grateful to God and to his Holy Mother for the great blessing of her rescue that she sold all her dresses and finery and swore service to God. She gave herself completely to prayer and the interior life. She spent long nights and any other time during the day asking God to instruct her and be her master. Predictably, Ursula's mistress became quite displeased that her maid neglected her work and was so frequently away at her prayers. Another nun, whose name is not given in the "Espejo," realized Ursula's distress; she was on the verge of leaving the convent. The nun offered to give Ursula's mistress whatever she wanted for Ursula's liberty, "more for the love of God than out of friendship or any worldly concern."[68]

The negotiations for the transaction, however, took some time. Meanwhile, Ursula became increasingly miserable. She was prepared to leave the convent and even become the slave of another person. Passing an image of Christ carrying the cross, Ursula reportedly said, "I'm leaving, Lord, because you must wish it, since you have not wanted to help me."[69] Before she had gone much further along the cloister, however, she encountered the nun who was arranging to buy her liberty. She told Ursula to hurry and gather her things because she would soon be free. Suddenly, with a *carta de libertâd* in hand, Ursula was finally free to enter the Lord's service.[70]

But Ursula balked. Her friends and the nuns advised her to take the habit of a donada, but she was reluctant. The life of a donada was still that of a menial servant, and although a donada would not be sold nor cast out in old age, as a slave might be, she would not be free to leave nor to choose another life. Therefore, the author of the "Espejo" noted, as much as Ursula did not wish to leave the convent, she also did not want to place herself into yet another form of servitude without ever having been in full possession of liberty.[71]

Ursula finally chose to continue to live at the convent for almost another decade without taking formal vows. A number of other young women would have been there as well, sent by families to be educated and for "safe keeping" rather than the religious life. A legally free person who worked as a servant at the convent must have been unusual. Ursula's decision not to join and adopt the habit must have been regarded as rebellious, even by her friends. Once, when one of her younger cell mates was about to take vows, she asked, "Ursula, why don't you take the habit?" Ursula replied that she would have to be strongly motivated to do that. Her friend pressed her further, and Ursula responded that such a step would require a great sign from God.[72] Ursula would not "go through the motions" without the certainty of a true vocation. The occasion of her conversion and calling was therefore given additional importance and credibility in the "Espejo."

Another life-threatening accident precipitated Ursula's final conversion to the religious life. She and a friend occupied cells near a chapel where there was a particularly beautiful image of Christ. Among the many works of art that depicted Christ and the Virgin in that chapel were symbols of the Passion used in the Good Friday procession. On the night of October 20, 1645, a major fire broke out in the convent and destroyed the chapel and all of its beautiful treasures, but the two cells on either side of the chapel were not touched. Ursula grieved and wept inconsolably. Lying on the floor "in a sea of tears," she cried out "Lord, wouldn't it have been better for me to have burned and not your holy images?" But God surprised her by replying, "You refuse me such a little thing and yet you wish to burn?" Ursula later understood that this cryptic reply referred to her reluctance to accept the habit. Soon after, she asked to be allowed to take the habit of a donada. She prepared for the occasion with great sincerity, through prayer, fasting, and penance. According to the "Espejo," Ursula took these events as the great sign from God, which she needed.[73]

Ursula took the Franciscan habit on December 18, 1645, less than two months after the fire. In her year of probation, between taking the habit and making her final vows, she became an exemplary religious. Her biographer wrote that "from the time she took the habit, Ursula was modest, devoted, and humble; that she never lifted her eyes from the floor, and that whenever a nun passed her, she made a 'reverence' so deep that it appeared that she kissed the floor. She was *obedientissima* not only to prelates but to all ranks of nuns."[74] The author stressed that during this time Ursula made singular progress in her spiritual development through continual mortifications, penance, and repeated fasts. She used *cilicios* (hair shirts) and wore a crown of thorns hidden by her hair. On her back she carried a cross of splinters held in place by a bodice made from animal hide, its bristles turned to the inside.[75] She "disciplined" herself, that is to say, she flagellated herself, twice a day, once before bedtime and again at four in the morning. She prepared herself for her final vows by continual prayer, spending much of the night and other moments during the day on her knees in the choir.[76]

These physical mortifications proved Ursula's piety and zeal. The seriousness with which she prepared to take her vows eradicated all doubt about her new vocation and spirituality. She gained membership in the religious community by embracing a form of initiation that the nuns greatly admired. She was spiritually cleansed by physical suffering. Early modern hagiography generally presented the mortification of the flesh as the simultaneous eradication of desire. In a narrative concerned with the rapid transformation of a somewhat willful middle-aged woman into a spiritual visionary, beloved of Christ, almost nothing else would have sufficed. The author of the "Espejo" understood that it was essential to demonstrate membership in the community and a transformed nature if Ursula's visions were to be believed.

As in the case of Estefania, the accounts of Ursula's penitential practices can be compared to the hagiography of other female saints of the period. The practices of this woman of color were again much more moderate than those described for other saints. Many female saints, following a long ascetic tradition, employed pain in their devotions in order to destroy all pretense of control over their lives—an illusion of power a former slave would never have acquired. Unlike St. Rose of Lima, who frequently experienced raptures and visions during intense physical pain, Ursula experienced her visions while absorbed in prayer. Pain and mortification in Ursula's story were not pathways to God or to sanctity. They only served to establish credibility in the human community.

For all her prayers and disciplines Ursula gained great mercies in the form of visions and frequent conversations with God. In particular, God helped Ursula remember all her sins, the punishments she would merit, and then showed merciful release of her from them. This "mercy" should be understood as another essential feature of Ursula's complete conversion. According to the Catholic church, a complete confession, in which all one's past sins are recalled and confessed, is necessary in order for the sacrament of penance to be wholly transforming. Ursula believed that God conducted her through purgatory and through hell and showed her not only the torments there but also the sins that brought them about.[77]

Ursula doubted these visions at first, fearing they were illusions of the devil. When they first began to appear to her, she spoke of them aloud in the convent, asking "Do you know from whence these lies come?" Her biographer explained that although she was neither simple nor ignorant, such things had not come to her attention before; nor did she understand the obligation to prudent silence that one should have concerning revelations. Another nun finally told Ursula, "Do not go about talking openly of these things . . . it is better that you discuss them only with someone who understands such matters."[78]

One story revealed Ursula's hesitancy to accept her calling as a visionary and her concern that she was merely deluded. One day, when she was working in the infirmary and changing linens, she looked up and saw that Mary, Queen of Heaven was also there, making the bed. The sight so upset and confused Ursula that she left the infirmary and did not return to her work there for several days. Finally, Christ addressed her directly and asked, "Why have you abandoned your service?" "Because I am afraid," Ursula responded. "Do not ensnare me with such deception. Señor mio, padre mio, I do not want to see anything—I want only to love you and serve you and do your will." To this Christ replied, "If you wish to do my will, how can you say 'I don't want to see anything'? I never said 'I don't want' to my eternal Father, I only obeyed Him unto death. If He desired that I be born in a manger, I said, 'Thy will be done'; if He wanted that I should die an ignoble death on the cross, I said, 'Thy will be done' and this is what you also have to do. And do not be afraid of any demon for it will have no power over you."[79]

That reassurance was a turning point in Ursula's acceptance of her calling as a visionary. Her new confidence is revealed in yet another story. One morning at four o'clock, while on her way to the choir, Ursula passed the place where black women (*las negras*) did the washing. There she saw a fierce dragon that threatened her. She confronted it: "You cannot hinder me because I am on my way to pray to my Lord God." She made the sign of the cross, and the dragon, although furious, left her alone.[80]

The appearance of a dragon where black women gathered is no coincidence. Ursula herself had spent many hours there with the other servants. By rebuking the dragon, she evidently conquered or rejected something in her past. The story also supported Ursula's authenticity as a visionary. In it she proved her ability to refuse deception by evil apparitions. Maureen Flynn has pointed out that the credibility of a female visionary in particular depended upon the continual demonstration of the ability to distinguish good spirits from demonic ones and her obedience and submissive manner.[81] In the light of these expectations of any woman visionary, not just a woman of color, the description of Ursula's submissive manner and self-deprecation, as well as accounts of her continual fears of being deceived by the devil, can be seen as part of the defense of her holiness in the "Espejo."

Most of Ursula's visions were of the afterlife, of the departed souls that either languished in purgatory or endured torment in hell. The visions contained revelations about persons who may have been considered righteous in life but were fated to suffer after death for the sins they concealed on earth. Many of these individuals were known to Ursula and the convent community, but the author of the "Espejo" did not mention names. The visions were not dated by year and cannot be ordered chronologically. When a vision occurred on a saint's feast or other holy day, the occasion was mentioned, perhaps because the saint or virgin being celebrated, and to whom Ursula would have been saying special prayers that day, was considered to be especially receptive and helpful on their feast day. Sundays, considered special, were therefore sometimes specified for the connection with the Eucharist and the Sabbath.

Many pages of the "Espejo" were devoted to visions in which deceased nuns and priests appeared to Ursula and requested assistance. Once, in the early hours of the day of the feast of St. Francis (October 4), Ursula was meditating in the choir when God granted her a great favor and brought to mind a cleric who had been buried in the church for more than a year. Her memory thus divinely awakened, Ursula was surprised to hear a loud sound coming from the tomb. It interrupted her meditation. She returned to her devotions and began to meditate again upon St. Francis. Then, her eyes still closed, she saw that same cleric appear "in his familiar form"—that is to say, she could not have mistaken who she saw. The cleric implored her to pray for him and to thank God for not condemning him outright. "From the interior of her spirit," she questioned him about how he came to her from purgatory. He answered that he came to her just as he existed there—as a spirit, no longer alive. The next day, as she prepared to take communion, the spirit appeared to her again, asking Ursula to commend him to Christ. This she did, offering up the Holy Sacrament for the good of his soul and dedicating all of her good works for that day in praise of God. These efforts evidently succeeded because the apparition troubled her no more.

One Sunday while in meditation Ursula saw the apparition of a deceased nun, a long veil over her face. Moments later two other apparitions, similarly veiled, joined her. Ursula, filled with dread, asked herself, "What procession is this? Well, if God has brought it, may his will be done." The first nun approached Ursula and revealed her name and the names of her cousin and her aunt who accompanied her. Ursula expressed surprise that they had been in purgatory for such a long time, but the nun responded, "Don't be surprised Ursula; twice I was the abbess of this convent and now I am paying for the faults that I permitted those in my care."[82] Entreating Ursula for prayers on their behalf, the apparitions returned to their crypt, and Ursula saw them enduring terrible flames and unspeakable punishment.[83]

The point emphasized in these stories is that Ursula helped departed souls through her prayers and sacrifices. This is extremely interesting in that it inverts the usual relationship between saints and the living. In accounts about most saints there are stories in which the living receives assistance from the departed saint. By contrast, in story after story of the "Espejo," it was the dead who sought the help of the living Ursula. The "Espejo" thus became a strong apology for the religious life, demonstrating that the nuns' prayers were not just about personal spiritual advancement but also about charity to those in spiritual need. Ursula worked and prayed on behalf of all the departed souls whose salvation would otherwise have been far from assured. According to the "Espejo," Ursula's prayers were effective. In one case, she experienced a vision of four souls beautifully clothed in white. One of them was someone who had appeared in an earlier vision and asked for her help. Giving her thanks, they told Ursula, "May God reward you for what you have done and may Our Redeemer be with you in everything you undertake."[84] Redeemed through Ursula's prayers, the souls were able to go to heaven.

Some of Ursula's visions are critical of false piety or some practices within the convent. In one vision, she saw a nun from her order who had been dead more than fifteen years. The nun appeared seated at one side of the choir, near a doorway and holding a little light. Ursula could clearly see the nun's face and her skeletal hands; she wore her funeral garb to which bits of earth still clung.[85] When Ursula spoke to the nun about the length of time she had done penance, the nun replied, "The penances I did here on earth were very short, and most of them were no more than the pastimes of this age. In order to go to heaven, souls have to be purified by fire, like gold; until they are as pure and flawless as crystal they cannot go to glory."[86] The nun also said that added to every soul's account with God were all the faults they committed while in the convent—the little regard given to the rules, to obedience, and to the constitutions of the order. "In the end," the apparition said, "all the lashes, nails, [rough] garments, [hard] beds, and other such 'pasttimes' [*entretinimientos*] were useless."[87] The nun stayed with Ursula for more than half an hour. When Ursula asked her guardian angel why this apparition was shown to her, the angel replied that it was "in order that you might commend her to God." Ursula then prayed for the nun, and the vision disappeared.[88]

This vision's criticism of the then-current practices of extreme penance, here referred to as "relaxations" (*relaxiones*) and "pasttimes" might seem surprising considering the earlier description in the "Espejo" of Ursula's own mortifications. But if, as I have suggested, the community considered these mortifications as signs of membership and devotion, this critique of Spanish and Creole spirituality could only come from someone who belonged to that community but at the same time stood at its margins—a woman of color like Ursula who was capable of performing these feats and also clearly beyond need of them.

The "Espejo" made it clear that the transforming power of the religious life was neither automatic nor inevitable and that many wicked souls wore righteous vestments. The reverse was also true: Those despised in this life would be exalted in the next. One story describes Ursula's vision of a soul's assurance of heaven. While she was prostrate in prayer before the figure of Christ in the chapel some black women of the convent came in, crying over the death of one of their companions. Ursula, in a flash of insight, realized that "all was vanity" in the face of death. Moved by charity, she asked God about the fate of the deceased woman. God revealed to her a vision of St. Francis and St. Clare on their knees in heaven, praying for the departed, and thus reassured Ursula of the woman's salvation.[89]

Such a story is rare in its portrayal through a vision of someone's happy fate. It is the only vision that includes an appearance of the Franciscan order's founding saints, who intervene on behalf of someone from the convent. The deceased woman was, in all probability, not a tertiary but a servant, and the story makes clear the Gospel's message that "those who are last shall be first." That the saints in heaven were moved to intercede with God for a black servant was a striking contrast to the case of the souls of the departed religious—Spanish or affluent Creoles—who were left to knock on their tombs for Ursula's prayers. The remarkable story ended, however, on a somber note. Ursula warned the mourners that just as God made heaven for the good, hell was for the bad, and those who summoned the prince of darkness would get what they deserved.[90] It was the only such direct warning Ursula gave to any members of the convent, and one of the very few references to the devil in the entire "Espejo" manuscript. Like the story about the dragon, this one with Ursula's warning marked her separation from her previous life and affirmed the exalted status of a black servant in the eyes of heaven.

Toward the end of the "Espejo" it was recorded that Ursula once asked Christ to be allowed to read a book by St. Teresa of Avila, the famous Spanish Carmelite mystic.[91] Christ replied that it was better that she should learn directly at his feet than from a book. Again, when she wanted to hear the fifteenth-century spiritual classic *The Imitation of Christ* read aloud, Jesus told her that she had "no need to search further than his own crucified feet."[92] "Should you ever doubt something," Jesus said, "you have only to ask your Guardian Angel about it." He told Ursula that her imitation of him should consist "in being humble, and poor, and in having nothing more than [your] habit, bare feet and bare head." He instructed her further that "prompt obedience to God is the truest Imitation of Christ." The story is significant on several levels. Scholars can interpret the disparagement of the spiritual value of reading as yet another example of widespread resistance to educating women and blacks and to allowing nuns to read. Ecclesiastical prejudices against women in general, especially women visionaries, support such an interpretation. Allowing a black woman to read might have been scandalous enough, but allowing a female visionary to read mystical literature might have discredited her completely, raising the suspicion that she was feigning visions based on knowledge gained from books. Within the larger context of the overall narrative, however, the story provides one more case of Jesus telling Ursula that she knew more than her "betters" and that education, like wealth, white skin, or social standing, was no indication of spirituality or grace. Jesus' words in the story carry a critical judgment against Spanish and Creole nuns and priests—those who would have been reading books. These were the same people who appeared repeatedly in Ursula's visions as sinful and in need of her prayers. The hierarchy of the convent was overturned. Here the educated elite were represented as further from true knowledge than a simple donada.

The information that Ursula either did not or was not allowed to read increases her credibility as a visionary. At a time when women's religious visions were suspect, charges of fraud and heresy were always real possibilities. This may have been, in fact, at least part of Ursula's initial rejection of this spiritual gift. The "Espejo" repeatedly affirmed the doctrinal orthodoxy of Ursula's visions, and Christ often reassured her that she should not be afraid because all was in accordance with the faith. By removing the possible suspicion that Ursula could have read theological treatises in books, the "Espejo" ensured that she would not be suspected of having merely imagined these "visions" or that she had forgotten her "place" both as a woman and a servant.

Several visions that occurred immediately after Ursula took her vows as a nun illustrate the emphasis on both orthodoxy and social reversal in the "Espejo." While Ursula was at prayer in the church, she saw the tabernacle where the consecrated host was kept on the main altar open. Christ appeared with a shining countenance and garbed in a purple tunic. Parting his tunic with his right hand, Christ showed Ursula his heart, and in his heart she saw an image of herself. "What is this, my Lord?" Ursula cried. "A black woman and a great sinner! Are there not plenty of queens and fine ladies?" Christ replied, "It is far better to be in my grace than to be a queen." He then took Ursula on a tour of purgatory, where there were innumerable people who told her about their noble rank and high office and about the sins for which they were suffering."[93] Later that same night, Ursula had a vision of the Annunciation: a beautiful angel kneeled before the Virgin, telling her she was to bear the son of God. A resplendent dove appeared and placed its beak in the Virgin's mouth. Then there appeared within the Virgin a tiny child holding a radiant globe in his right hand. Along with these mysteries of the faith, God showed Ursula a vision of his final judgment. She asked Christ what would become of those still living. He replied, "I will send great burdens and trials to purify those who are to be saved."[94]

The manuscript of the "Espejo" ends abruptly. There must have been additional pages that described the end of Ursula's life, because the subtitle of the account promises her "Life, Virtues, and Death" (*Vida, Virtudes, y Muerte*). We do not know if Ursula was widely praised as a saintly individual as Estefania. In all probability, her reputation remained within the closed convent community. Clearly, however, the life and visions of this remarkable woman of color were valued sufficiently within that community for them to have been carefully copied and preserved for the nuns themselves to read.

Ursula's portrait at the beginning of the "Espejo" emphasized the human over the saintly. That made Ursula's character more believable and more compelling—a woman transformed in midlife by religious conversion. It was not, however, Ursula's life that was held up in the text as an example for others to follow. Instead, it was presented as an espejo, or mirror, into which her sister nuns were invited to gaze. In Ursula's visions, not in her life story, readers were expected to find their reflections and glimpse what lay in store for them after death. In her visions Ursula revealed the fate of all those who only pretended to be religious and deluded themselves that their parentage or wealth made them superior to her.

Perhaps because her life as a slave had taught Ursula how to be deferential, or perhaps because of the assumption that black women were subservient by nature, her confessor was willing to direct her instead of trying to discourage her. It would appear from the text that her confessor and superiors did not regard Ursula as suspiciously as many other visionary women would have been viewed. It was, in fact, dangerous for any woman in the seventeenth century to claim to have had religious visions. Many visionaries were forced to endure "examinations" by priests and even inquisitors of the Holy Office who attempted to discredit them. There is no mention in the life story of Ursula of any such suspicion of her or her visions. The cultural assumptions about the nature of black women probably worked in her favor insofar as she was deemed less vulnerable to the "typical" feminine vices of vanity, pride, and love of physical comfort. Because she had no formal education, she was not suspected of being able to deliberately deceive her learned confessor about the orthodoxy of her visions. Because she was forced by her lack of social status into the lowest level of the convent community, she was not suspected of using her visions to seek attention or authority over her religious sisters.

* * *

The "Vida de Estefania de San Ioseph" and the "Espejo de Religiosas" are extraordinarily rich texts, and the discussion in this chapter has by no means exhausted their significance. Three areas of particular interest to scholars of free women of color in the Spanish colonies have been explored. First, the narratives have illustrated some paradoxes about social marginalization. To some extent all religious lives are lived "at the margin" of society. "In" the world but not "of" it, Christians have long felt themselves to have a special perspective from which to comment upon society and morals. In the case of both Estefania de San Joseph and Ursula de Christo, the multiple levels of marginalization that women of color experienced provided effective positions from which they could pursue innovative religious vocations. Both women were marginalized by virtue of their sex and their race and in addition by their roles within their communities.

As a free woman and housekeeper to a wealthy cleric, Estefania lived in a Spanish household but could not enjoy privilege. Confided in as a friend and welcomed as a visitor, she moved among the well-to-do of Spanish society without being a member of their circle. As a beata, she set herself apart from the world as a religious but also apart from the cloister. Her exemplary life was much more publically visible by virtue of these multiple marginalizations, and, as her biographers point out, she was beloved by a wide variety of people both secular and religious, rich and poor. Life at the margins is also the perfect "saintly" place. Estefania capitalized upon this boundary position. She made conscious use of her ambiguous status in order to instruct by example and "preach" effectively to those who considered themselves her betters.

Ursula, likewise, lived between worlds. As a tertiary and a donada, she was a member of the convent but restricted to a subordinate status. She lived half of her life as a slave and half as a religious, truly a member of two very distinct communities within the convent. Racial boundaries were at least partially obscured by the inclusion that came with vowed status, even that of a donada, if only by comparison to the dichotomy between insiders (religious) and outsiders (nonreligious). As a visionary, too, Ursula walked in the borderlands between here and the hereafter, between heaven and hell, between life and death. It was, in fact, by virtue of this multiple marginalization that she could criticize her contemporaries. Her biographer downplayed racial differences in the interest of preserving religious community. Although Ursula's visions were strongly critical of many religious individuals and practices within the convent, they nevertheless supported the idea of religious community.[95] Just as Ursula made the world of the spirit present within the convent through her visions, so, too, did the written record of her life and visions make her present and accessible to her Franciscan sisters. Both women of color, Estefania and Ursula, were able to turn marginality to their advantage by choosing the religious life.

These lives of women of color have also dealt with a second set of important issues related to the need for a revision of the traditional discourse about women in the colonial Spanish world. In traditional Christian hagiography, female saints are generally portrayed as having overcome the "usual" vices of their gender.[96] The hagiography of women of color makes it obvious that the "usual" vices that they must demonstrate to have overcome are not those of white, European women (such as vanity, frivolity, and love of comfort) but rather the vices that Spaniards considered to be "usual" for their race (such as dishonesty and lack of social concern).

The descriptions of Estefania and Ursula reveal that women of color were not suspected of, nor praised for resisting, the same temptations that Spanish Creole women faced. Although severe mortification has long been considered the hallmark of early modern Spanish devotions, we do not read at length about either Estefania's or Ursula's physical fortitude or their discipline of the body. Perhaps because physical labor and hardship shaped the lives of so many black women, these virtues were not required to demonstrate sanctity for a woman of color. Vanity, likewise, was not considered a "usual vice" among women of color, although it was frequently considered the most "feminine" of vices in Spanish hagiography. In the "Espejo," Ursula's biographer employed a familiar symbol of woman's vanity, the mirror, as a literary device for revealing the flaws and vanities of her superiors. In this hagiography, some virtues are clearly emphasized over others in order to counter negative cultural assumptions about race. Recognition of these differences in hagiography between women of color and other women is important because they make it clear that the discourse about gender in the colonial Spanish world was always about race as well.

The accounts of Estefania and Ursula have also demonstrated a third set of issues about women of color in shaping their own lives. Colonial Peru was characterized by appalling conditions of slavery and pervasive racial and class prejudice. Even within religious communities, slavery and sharp social stratification mirrored the injustices of Spanish society. Against this grim backdrop, the portraits of Estefania and Ursula stand out. These two women of color overcame the restrictions placed upon them and negotiated their own routes to freedom and respect. Estefania found significant physical and social freedom as a beata, living out her religious vocation independently of convent rules. She also found public recognition and acclaim for her devotion to God and her service to the community. Ursula did not enjoy the same latitude of freedom. Her slavery within the convent and her later hesitation to adopt the indentured servitude of a donada demonstrated that the well-ordered life of the convent offered security but few liberties. She did, however, find freedom of expression as a religious visionary. That freedom allowed Ursula to criticize the biases and inequalities within her convent and to speak with remarkable authority.

Notes

1. Diego de Cordova Salinas, "Vida, Y Muerte de la Humilde Madre Estefania de S. Ioseph: professa de la Tercera Orden de nuestro Padre S. Francisco," lib. 5, capitulo 25; Diego de Cordova Salinas, *Coronica de la Religiosissima Provincia de los Doze Apostoles del Peru, de la orden de N. P. S. Francisco de la regular observancia* (Lima: Iorge Lopez, 1651); "Espejo de las Religiosas, Vida, Virtudes, y Muerte de la Venerable Hermana Ursula de Christo, Morena, Criolla de Lima, Donada professa de N. M^e. S. Clara en su Religiosissimo Convento dela ciudad delos Reyes," Convent of San Francisco, Lima, Registro I-17, no. 1, 45 (hereafter "EDR"). When quoting whole passages from these documents I will retain the original nonstandard spelling and archaic accents in order to preserve something of the charm of the texts. Where characters are omitted I supply them in brackets—[ ]—for improved readability, and where portions of the manuscript are illegible I will denote that with a question mark in brackets: [?].

2. Cuzco was the first city "founded" by the Spaniards in the existing Inca capital high in the Andes. Although significant in its primacy and as the symbol of Spanish conquest over the Inca, its location was too remote and inaccessible for trade. The larger city of Lima, close to the seaport of Callao, rapidly became the cultural and administrative hub of the South American empire.

3. Frederick P. Bowser, *The African Slave in Colonial Peru, 1524–1650* (Stanford: Stanford University Press, 1974), 341.

4. Bowser, *The African Slave in Colonial Peru,* 300–301.

5. On Spanish color categorizations there are various sources. See, for example, Emilio Harth-Terre, *Presencia del negro en el Virreinato del Peru* (Gainesville: University of Florida Press, 1971), 12–13; and Rolando Mellafe, *Negro Slavery in Latin America,* trans. J. W. S. Judge (Berkeley: University of California Press, 1975), 112–16. On the use of the term *parda* as a synonym for *mulata* (in contradiction to the definition given by Mellafe), see Bowser, *The African Slave in Colonial Peru,* 274. Also see Nancy E. van Deusen, "Defining the Sacred and the Worldly: *Beatas* and Recogidas in Late-Seventeenth-Century Lima," *Colonial Latin American Historical Review* 6 (Fall 1997): 453.

6. Bowser, *The African Slave in Colonial Peru,* 300.

7. Mellafe, *Negro Slavery in Latin America,* 109–10.

8. Lyle N. McAlister, *Spain and Portugal in the New World, 1492–1700* (Minneapolis: University of Minnesota Press, 1984), 397.

9. Bowser, *The African Slave in Colonial Peru,* 308.

10. The Catholic church uses the term *saint* very specifically. It refers to a deceased person, officially canonized or approved by the pope, believed to be in heaven and able to intercede with God on behalf of the living. For that reason the church (at least since the sixteenth century) only bestows the title of saint on individuals after the Vatican has conducted an extensive investigation into their lives and after the confirmation of several posthumous miracles—these latter constitute the real "proof" of sanctity. The Catholic church acknowledges that there are many more saints in heaven than are officially recognized. Canonization of a saint is a costly and often political process that takes many years. As a result, only a few candidates, whose causes are well-financed by sponsors, are ever promoted for consideration. Individuals like Estefania and Ursula, whose reputations remained within smaller, local communities, were almost never promoted by their religious orders for official canonization. As a result, they cannot be referred to as "saints" despite their "saintly" reputations. The life stories of saints are referred to as "Lives." Hagiography is not the same as "biography" in its modern sense. Nevertheless, to avoid the confusion between lived "lives" and written "Lives," I have sometimes used the term *biographies* to refer to the life stories of saints and saintlike individuals.

11. On canonization history and reforms, see Eric Waldram Kemp, *Canonization and Authority in the Western Church* (New York: Oxford University Press, 1948).

12. On the changes in hagiography instituted by the Bollandists, see Hippolyte Delehaye, *The Work of the Bollandists through Three Centuries: 1615–1915* (Princeton: Princeton University Press, 1922).

13. Cordova Salinas, "Vida, Y Muerte de la Humilde Madre Estefania de S. Ioseph." The Franciscans have three "orders" or divisions. The Order of St. Francis is composed of vowed religious brothers, many of whom are also ordained as priests; the Order of St. Clare is made up of vowed nuns; and the Third Order is composed of men and women bound by the monastic rule but still considered "lay" and not "religious" members of the order.

14. The relationship between a beata and a religious order was often informal. The best-known example of this is provided by Rose of Lima, who followed an eclectic, highly personalized form of spirituality. Her earliest costume was self-styled and probably that of a Franciscan, but she later adopted a Dominican habit when she took formal vows as a tertiary of that order. Rose had numerous confessors and advisors, among whom were several Jesuits. For an excellent treatment of Rose and the religious climate in colonial Lima, see José Flores Araoz, Ramón Mujica Pinilla, Luis Eduardo Wuffarden, and Pedro Guibovich Pérez, *Santa Rosa de Lima y su tiempo* (Lima: Banco de Crédito del Perú, 1995).

15. Although beatas had existed for centuries in Western Europe, their acceptability declined markedly after the Catholic Reformation, when the church discouraged solitary religious vocations and began to insist on cloistering religious women. Beatas were placed under the authority of the local clergy and bishop, and most were severely restricted if not forced to join convents. The situation in Spanish America was different, however. Beatas appeared in Lima during the early sixteenth century before female convents were organized, but their numbers declined when the first convents were constructed in the 1560s. *Beaterios* (lay houses that provided a communal setting for beatas) became popular again at the end of the seventeenth century. For an excellent article on the late-seventeenth-century beatas in Lima, see Nancy E. van Deusen, "Defining the Sacred and the Worldly: *Beatas* and Recogidas in Late-Seventeenth-Century Lima," *Colonial Latin American Historical Review* 6 (Fall 1997): 441–77; see also James Lockhart, *Spanish Peru, 1532–1560: A Colonial Society,* (Madison: University of Wisconsin Press, 1968), 184.

16. By the "rule," Cordova Salinas means not only the vows of poverty, chastity, and obedience but also the more comprehensive rules of conduct and dress that governed the Franciscan order:

"paso en lo florido de su edad a esta ciudad de Lima con la ocasion que abaxo le dira, donde la conoci y comunique quarenta y cinco años en diferentes tiempos, hasta su muerte, y sie[m]pre vestida con el habito y manto de sayal de la Orden Tercera de penitencia de nuestro Padre San Francisco, porque fue de las primeras que en esta ciudad professaron su regla; lo qual hizo con maravillosa observancia de sus constituciones." Cordova Salinas, "Vida, Y Muerte de la Humilde Madre Estefania de S. Ioseph," 520.

17. "Y you para mas autorizar esta relacion pornè a la letra, la que a instencia mia escrivio desta sierva de Dios el Doctor Don Francisco Davila, . . . y al presente Canonigo desta de los Reyes, que tratò largos años à la referida hasta que murio. Dize pues assi." Ibid., 520.

18. It was common for a slave-owner to grant manumission upon his death to favored slaves, and it was common to free slaves considered too old or sick to work. On the manumission of slaves see Mellafe, *Negro Slavery in Latin America*, 119–20; and Bowser, *The African Slave in Colonial Peru*, 272–301.

19. "La madre Estefania de San Ioseph, fue natural de la ciudad del Cuzco, hija de una *morena* llamada Isabel la Portuguesa . . . esclava del Capitan Maldonado el rico. Muerto su amo, que la dexó libre, entró por *donada* Religiosa en el Convento de Santa Clara de la mesma ciudad, donde la conoci, y hablé muchas vezes. Professo y murio con opinion de santa por los años de 1580." Cordova Salinas, "Vida, Y Muerte de la Humilde Madre Estefania de S. Ioseph," 520.

20. "Quedo Estefania en la casa, y familia de su amo, moça de buena gracia, y el amo en su testamento la dexo libre si bien los herederos procuraron que no lo fuesse, con que la obligaron à salir del Cuzco huyendo a esta ciudad de Lima a seguir su causa de libertad y fue Dios servido la consiguiesse enteramente en la Real Audiencia." Ibid., 520–21.

21. Although their focus is on the nineteenth century, the long-standing phenomenon of slaves who took their case for manumission to the Spanish courts has been treated in depth by Christine Hünefeldt, *Paying the Price of Freedom: Family and Labor among Lima's Slaves 1800–1854* (Berkeley: University of California Press, 1994), and by Carlos Aguirre, *Agentes de su propia libertad: Los esclavos de Lima y la desintegracion de la esclavitud, 1821–1854* (Lima: Pontifica Universidad Catolica del Peru Fondo Editorial, 1993).

22. "Con esto la fue nuestro Señor disponiendo para que obrase su salvacion, y pusiesse en libertad el alma, como lo avia hecho con el cuerpo." Cordova Salinas, "Vida, Y Muerte de la Humilde Madre Estefania de S. Ioseph," 521.

23. "Pusose habito de *Beata* de nuestro Padre San Francisco. Tratava de confessarse a menudo, y de recebir al Señor." Ibid., 521.

24. "Vineyo del Cuzco a esta ciudad a estudiar el año de 1590 ordeneme de Sacerdote el de noventa y seis; y estando una mañana de Pascua en la Catedral oyendo de confession, se llegò a mi sin conocerme, y me pidio la confessasse; hizelo, y de aqui resulto saber quien era, y todo lo referido, y tambien irse a vivir a mi casa, donde cuydava della a mucha satisfacion, y con su buen exemplo edificava a todos." Ibid.

25. "Iuntava de noche a rezar el servicio, y les tratava de Dios con particular cuydado." Ibid.

26. For more on the practice of taking in orphans, see Lockhart, *Spanish Peru*, 185.

27. "Era muy compasiva en este tiempo, y de pura caridad crio dos niños, y dos niñas Españoles pobres con grande amor; los quales con su buena criança, dotrina, y exemplo vinieron a ser el uno Sacerdote, Religioso de la Compania de IESVS, y el otro Clerigo y las muchachas se encorraron a servir a Dios Religiosas, la una en el Monesterio de la Encarnacion de Monjas Agustinas, y la otra en el de Santa Catalina, Dominicas." Cordova Salinas, "Vida, Y Muerte de la Humilde Madre Estefania de S. Ioseph," 521.

28. "Sustenavase del trabajo de sus manos en hacer colchones . . . y con los quatro *reales* q[ue] la davan pas[?] su pobreza, y lo que le quedava dava de limosna." Ibid.

29. "A los enfermos, principalmente deste Orden, visitava con gran caridad; y si era necessario les curava, y aplicava los remedios de que necessitavan. Iuntava trapos de lienço que pedia de li-

mosna, y haziendolos lavar muy limpios . . . Estas llevava a los Hospitales para curar los enfermos, que continuo visitava con grandissima caridad." Ibid.

30. An account of St. Martin's life that is contemporary with Estefania's is Bernardo de Medina, *Vida Prodigiosa del Venerable Siervo de Dios Fr. Martin de Porras, Natural de Lima* (Madrid: Domingo Garcia Morràs, 1675). See also an earlier edition of Medina's work, reprinted in Juan Melendez, *Tesoros Verdaderos de las Yndias En la Historia dela gran Provincia de San Juan Bautista del Peru*, vol. 3 (Rome: Nicolas Angel Tinassio, 1681). St. Martin was assisted in his ministry to the sick by his sister, Juana, a free woman of color about whom we know very little. Her portrait is eclipsed by the attention given to her famous brother, but she nevertheless appears in his stories as a patient and generous woman who opened her home as a hospital to those for whom the Dominican infirmary had no room. Juana is only a minor figure in early accounts of St. Martin, but she receives somewhat more attention in biographies of the nineteenth and twentieth centuries.

31. Although St. Rose of Lima was said to have been very charitable, it was not her charity that received emphasis in seventeenth-century accounts of her life. See, for example, Andres Ferrer de Valdecebro, *Vida Maravillosa y Admirable De La Esclaricida y Bienaventurada Virgen Rosa de Santa Maria* (Madrid: Maria Rey, 1669); and Antonio Gonzales Acuña, *Rosa mistica vida y muerte de Santa Rosa de S. Maria Virgen* (Rome: Nicholas Angel Tinas, 1671).

32. McAlister, *Spain and Portugal in the New World*, 397.

33. "Ayudava alas Abadesas todo lo que era menester a su ministerio; era cobreadora de las limosnas para las Missas; y fiestas de los Santos de su Orden, que juntava con puntualidad." Cordova Salinas, "Vida, Y Muerte de la Humilde Madre Estefania de S. Ioseph," 521.

34. Melendez, *Tesoros Verdaderos de las Yndias*, 237.

35. "Ayunaba los Lunes, Miercoles, Viernes, y Sabados en cada semana con rigor de abstinencia, y en especial los Advientos, y Quaresmas. Por disgustos que le diessen, nunca mostro enojo, siempre se mostrava pacifica, y muy paciente." Cordova Salinas, "Vida, Y Muerte de la Humilde Madre Estefania de S. Ioseph," 521.

36. Maureen Flynn, "The Spiritual Uses of Pain in Spanish Mysticism," *Journal of the American Academy of Religion* 64 (Summer 1996): 257–78.

37. Cordova Salinas, *Coronica*, book 5, ch. 27, 528–34. Marianna de Jesus is known also as Marianna de Quito, a city which is now in Ecuador but was then a part of Peru.

38. Ibid., book, 5, ch. 23, 511–19. Documents in the Lima's Archivo Arzobispal reveal that an investigation into the sanctity of Isabel de Porras was begun in the early eighteenth century, but it never led to her beatification or canonization.

39. For comparison with contemporary lives of Rose, see de Valdecebro, *Vida Maravillosa;* and Gonzales Acuña, *Rosa mistica.*

40. Flynn, "The Spiritual Uses of Pain in Spanish Mysticism," 268.

41. "Andava comunmente con un habito y manto viejo de sayal, con mil remiendos, pero en las fiestas principales se ponia otro para assistir a ellas . . . y en particular quando assistia a las fiestas del Santissimo Sacramento, en que era continua." Cordova Salinas, "Vida, Y Muerte de la Humilde Madre Estefania de S. Ioseph," 521.

42. "Era alegre, afable, humilde, graciosa, y co[n] estas pa[?]s tenia entrada con las señoras mas ricas y principales de la ciudad, y con hombres ricos, Estudiantes, y Clerigos." Ibid.

43. Among the seventeenth-century lives of Peru's second archbishop, St. Toribio de Mogrovejo, is Antonio de Léon Pinelo, *Vida del Ilustrissimo i Reverendissimo D. Toribio Alfonso Mogrovejo Arcobispo de la Ciudad de los Reyes Lima* (Madrid: Iulian de Paredes, 1679). Another Spanish saint in seventeenth-century Lima, Francisco Solano, is described as being completely indifferent to money management—so much so that he begged to be relieved of the responsibility of serving in administrative positions. Padre Fray Diego de Cordova, *Vida, Virtudes, y Milagros del Apostol del Peru el Venerable P[adre]e Fray Francisco Solano dela Serafica Orden de los Menores de la Regular Observancia* (Madrid: Emprenta Real, 1643).

44. "Salie[n]do de ôyr Missa ivase a la casa dela señora que le parecia, llevava en la manga uno de los muchos libros, y libritos que tenia de devocion, y espiritu, y muchas vezes señalado, lo que ya ella sabia, seria a proposito para aquella señora, y su casa. Entrava diziendo: loado sea Jesu Christo; . . . Pues estava en lo interior atenta a su intento, que era hazer que le leyesen en el libro que llevava; y si era tiempo oportuno, demanera que no causase molestia, ni enfado, sacava su librito, y dezia con mucha gracia a la señora, leame aqui señora mia un poquito, y luego passavan otra parte diziendo: aqui otro poquito; con que dava en lo que era necessario para quien leia, o escuchava. Pero esto con mucho dissimulacion sin dar sospechas de que lo hazia con cuydadado, y luego con mucha gracia se despedia, obligando a que la dixessen, buelvase por acà madre." Cordova Salinas, "Vida, Y Muerte de la Humilde Madre Estefania de S. Ioseph," 521–22.

45. "A mi me predico muchas con aprecio de su zelo, yternura de mi alma, y assi quando me pedia le leyese, lo hazia de buena gana." Ibid., 522.

46. "Solia traer a vezes in las mangas muchos papelitos atados, en cada uno algunas pasas, y en viendo a los niños del estudio, o de la escuela, se llegava a uno delante de otros, y le dezia, traes rosario niño, y en mostrandoselo le dava un papelito de pasas, y faltava otro diziendo, madre, yo tambien lo traygo, y davale otro papelito, y en no trayendo, no se lo queria dar, con que los muchachos pedian rosarios a sus padres, y como despues la encontravan, se llegavan a ella, y mostravan sus rosarios, y ella les dava sus papelitos de pasas, y todo esto co[n] ta[n]ta gracia, y agrado, que se echava de ver estava Dios en ella." Ibid.

47. "Pidio la llevasen al hospital de la Caridad, que es de mugeres, muy bien servido, y que el nobre le quadra con propriedad: aqui fue a veynte de Abril, donde aviendo ya en su pobre casa recibido al Señor lo bolvio a recebir, y se fue disponie[n]do para morir con el exercicio de muchas virtudes que exercitava, y celestiales afectos que passavan por su alma, resignada toda en la voluntad divina, y siempre alegre prorrumpia a vezes cantando coplas a la Virgen nuestra Señora, y al Niño Iesus, pidiendoles mereciese su vista en el cielo." Ibid.

48. For a study of Spanish ideas about death, see Carlos M. Eire, *From Madrid to Purgatory: The Art and Craft of Dying in Sixteenth-Century Spain* (New York: Cambridge University Press, 1995).

49. "Yo me halle presente a las obsequias desta sierva de Dios, ocupara la capilla mayor de nuestro Convento el cuerpo, y el ayre sus alabanças: atropellavanse hombres y mugeres de todos estados por venerarle, y besarle las manos, que hazian con ternura y devocion. Bañava el rostro especial hermosura, pronostico de la felicidad del alma." Cordova Salinas, "Vida, Y Muerte de la Humilde Madre Estefania de S. Ioseph," 523.

50. "Yo lleguè, y le tomè las manos con las mias, y con aver mas de treinta horas que avia muerto, las senti suaves, y muy tractables, y que jugava los dedos dellas con facilidad. Levantele los braços, y los traxe a todas partes sin ningun apremio, antes con tanta facilidad, y mas que si estuviera viva." Ibid.

51. The religious orders designated geographical territories for administrative purposes. In the seventeenth century, the city of Lima was, for example, within the archdiocese of Peru. Its churches and secular clergy were the responsibility of the archbishop of Peru. Roughly the same geographical area, however, was administered separately by each religious order that staffed convents and missions in Peru. Lima, for example, fell within the Franciscan Province of the Twelve Apostles (los Doze Apostoles) and within the Dominican Province of Saint John the Baptist (San Juan Bautista). Although each convent would have had its own guardian or abbot, supervision of all the orders' monastics, clergy, and staff would have been organized by the province within their respective orders. The administrative head of the Franciscan province was called the provincial, and he wielded the highest authority in the colony.

52. "Llegò a la cabeza el muy Reverendo Padre Fr. Iuan de Durana, comissario general de todas estas Provincias del Perù, y viendo su agilidad, y la hermosura de su rostro, la llamò muger santa." Cordova Salinas, "Vida, Y Muerte de la Humilde Madre Estefania de S. Ioseph," 523.

53. "Tal era el concepto que aun en vida se tuvo de los meritos desta bendita muger, pues entre tantas, y tan calificadas personas de todos estados, que ilustran esta insigne orden, y professan su

regla, sobresalio, y lucio maravillosamente, como un refulgente luzero de la mañana entre los demas claros astros del espiritual firmamento y cielo de virtudes de nuestra Serafica Orden, la hu-
milidad de la madre Estefania de San Ioseph, fiel emuladora de su Serafico Patriarca, hija de la
caridad Christiana, querida de Dios, y obra de su gracia." Ibid.

54. "Y fueron tantas las mercedes que recibiô de Dios, y continuas, que dixo la Religiosa que
por orden del Señor . . . y licencia del Confessor, para que las escribiesse, que era imposible reten-
erlas en la memoria todas con las circunst[anz]as que contenian." "EDR," 7.

55. Rosalynn Voaden, *God's Words, Women's Voices: The Discernment of Spirits in the Writing of
Late-Medieval Women Visionaries* (York: York Medieval Press, 1999), esp. 57–71.

56. Voaden, *God's Words, Women's Voices,* 46ff.

57. Ibid., 67.

58. The "EDR" has two differing sets of page numbers (579–602 and 585–608), counting the recto
of the leaves but not the verso. Because both sets of numbers become illegible in many places, I
have chosen to simplify things by conventionally renumbering the pages here (1–45). At the bottom of the second page is an annotation: "Dispône la vida, segun loque hallar âs copiado de buenos originales en el trasumpto siguiente." In quoting the text, I have retained the underlining, which
connotes spoken dialog.

59. The removal of the names from Ursula's own manuscript is indicated in at least two ways.
First, one would have expected her to tell her confessor the names of individuals whom she saw
in visions as part of the complete disclosure of the visions. Second, the specific identifications
substituted in the place of names, such as "a nun who had died ten years before" or "a priest who
had died in September," implies named individuals.

60. The inclusion of the names of a saint's associates is characteristic of narratives written as
hagiography by the saint's community—both in the interest of authenticating the stories and in
order to allow others to share "supporting roles" in the saint's narrative. For an excellent discussion of how the first documents of a saint's life are constructed within a community, see Aviad
Kleinberg, *Prophets in Their Own Country* (Chicago: University of Chicago Press, 1991), 21–26.

61. Augustinians and Dominicans were considered more élite than Franciscan nuns, but choir
nuns in all religious houses came from prominent families that had contributed substantial sums
of money to the convents. For a study of convent life in colonial Peru, see Kathryn Burns, *Colonial Habits: Convents and the Spiritual Economy of Cuzco, Peru* (Durham: Duke University Press,
1999).

62. Mark A. Burkholder and Lyman L. Johnson, *Colonial Latin America,* 3d ed. (New York: Oxford
University Press, 1998), 101ff.

63. "Fue la sierva de Dios Ursula de [Chris]to, Criolla de esta ciudad de Lima, hija de Isabel delos
Rios, negra Criolla esclava de D[on]a Geronima de los Rios." "EDR," 3. On the previous page,
however, in an introduction inserted before the beginning of the "Vida," it reads: "Nació por dicha
nuestra, Ursula, por el mês de Noviembre, hija legitima de Juan de Castilla, y de Isabel de los Ri[os]."

64. "Desde muy niña fur devotissima dela Virgen Ssma del Carmen: ayunabalos Miercoles, rez-
aba el Rosario entero [a + points to note in margin which says + de rodillas] todos los dias, y para
resarlo con mas devocion se retiraba de sus compañeras, y se iba al lugar mâs quieto, y solitario; y
aunque como muchas tenia sus galas, y amistades de monjas, y algunas niñas por ellas, nunca
dexaba de resâr su Rosario, y devociones." Ibid., 3.

65. "Apartandose estos dias de sus amigas, desuerte que, en viendola retirada decian: Ya se debê
dequerer confesiâr la embustera, que anda haciendo embustes." Ibid.

66. "Y siendo yâ demas de 30 años, le maneharon una saya nueva, que avia prestado, y con enfado la lavô, y fue â tender en el pozo del convento, que es el mâs hondo, que ay en la ciudad; y
subiendo sobre una cubieta de tablas que tenia, para tender la saya, y echarla sobre un palo que
atravesaba en medio, al pararse sobre ellas, se le hundieron las tablas, y quedô Ursula colgada en
medio del pozo, con una mano azida al palo, y con otra del s[an]to escapulario de N[uestr]a
S[enor]a del Carmen, que siempre traya puesto. En tan horrendo susto, y conseida riesgo, la es-

forzô el S[eñ]or para que invocasse el soberano auxilio de su M[adr]e, y asi la dixo con todo el afecto que pudo: <u>Señora pide â tu Hijo que no me condene.</u> Acudiô al suceso lo gran parte del Monasterio, y por ser la boca del pozo muy ancha, nadie la podia socorrer, conque todas las ayudaban â bien morir, no teniendo esperanza alguna de su Vida." Ibid.

67. "O misericordia de Dios! [?]ô efficacia del Poder ê intercesion de M[adre]! sin saber como, se viô milagrosam[en]te fuera del pozo, libre de tan grava trabajo con mucha admiracion delasque estaban presentes que nô cesaban de dâr al S[eño]r gracia por tan singular portento. Ovedô con esto Ursula tân grande agradecia â Dios, y â su Madre Sacratissima por este señalado beneficio, que al punto vendiô todas sus galas, y vestidos, ê hizo gran proposito de servir muy deveras al Altissimo, y dedarse mucho al oracion, y trato interior con su Magestad. Y para tenerle, hacia sus preguntas â las siervas de Dios, y se iba al coro las noches enterar, y las horas que podía del dia, a pedir a Dios la enseñaste, y fueste su Maestro." Ibid., 4.

68. "Y como hacia alguna falta a su ama por estos ratos que se iba a Dios, tenía algunos disgustos, y sinsabores con ella. Y una Religiosa víendola asi afligída, y que estaba âpique de salirse del convento, tratô de libertarla, mas por Dios que por amistad, u otro interez mundano, y asi prometiô dar a su ama loque le pidieste por su libertad." Ibid.

69. "Dilatose no obstante la execucion de este negocio, y viendose Ursula cada dia mas desconsolada, determino (permitiendolo asi Dios, para que luciessen mas su misericordias) de huirse del convento, ô deirse fuera con licencia del ama (que se lo mas veridico) â servir alquilada a otro Senor y pasando por un claustro, donde estaba retratado el Senor con la cruz a cuestas, alçô Ursula los ojos, y le dixo <u>Ya me voy, S[en]or, porque vos lo quereis, pues no me aveis querido ayudar.</u>" Mas no se vio bien apartado de aquel lugar ni acabado de dar sus quexas al soberano de amor, quando encontrô alli a la Monja que avia tratado de libertarla, la qual le dixo: Ursula, junta lo que tienes, que quiero concluir con tu ahorrío. Con esta palabra cesô atras de su proposito, y [?] la escritura y carta de libertâd quedo Ursula sin impedimiento para entregarse toda al servicio de N[uestro] Señor." Ibid.

70. "Encontrô alli a la Monja que avia tratado de libertala, la qual le dixo: Ursula, junta lo que tienes, que quiero concluir con tu ahorrío. Con esta palabra cesô atras de su proposito, y [?] la escritura y carta de libertâd quedo Ursula sin impedimiento para entregarse toda al servicio de N. Señor." Ibid.

71. "Luego que las monjas, y compañeras la vieron horra, la decian que tomasse el habito de *donada*, pero ella no tenia por entonces desto de esto; porque aunque no queria dejar el convento, no queria sujetarse en el al voluntad agena, sino hacer por si loque pudiesse, y passar a si su vida, dueño de su libertad." Ibid.

72. "Ultimamente tomô el s[an]to habito una niña de su celda, y bolviendose â Ursula, la dixo: <u>Ursula, porque no toma tu el habito?</u> Aque ella respondiô, como dando â entender un [?]: <u>â de aver una grân cosa, quando yo le tome.</u> Y dixole la Niña: <u>Señal â de aver, paraque tu le tomes?</u> Y respondio ursula: <u>si, una gran señal â de aver.</u>" Ibid., 5.

73. "Y postrada en el suelo echa un mâr de llantro y amarguras, le dixo al Señor con grande affecto: <u>S[eñ]or mis, no fuera mejor que yo me quemara, y no sus santas imagenes?</u> Aque respondio el Señor <u>no haces por me una cosa tan corta, y quieres quemarte?</u> Entendio luego Ursula que era, porque no tomaba el habito, y trato luego de pedirle, solicitando con muchas veras, elque se lo diessen, y preparandose, para recibirle, con grandes ayunos, cilicios, y penitencias: conque se vio cumplidala señal, grande, que dixo avia de aver par su habito." Ibid., 5.

74. "Quedo desde este dia tan modesta, devota, y humilde, que nunca levanto los ojos del suelo, y donde quiera que via alguna Religiosa hacia una Reverencia tan profunda, que parece, queria poner la boca en el suelo; obedientissima, no solo â las Preladas, sino a todas qualquier Monjas, por amor de aquel Señor que se hizo obediente has la muerte por otro remedio y exemplo." Ibid., 5–6.

75. "Prosiguiô su año de aprobacion con singulâr adelantam[ien]to de su espiritu, continua mortificacion se sus sentidos, y rara exemplaridad de peitencias, ayunos repetidos, cilicios, y una

corona de espinas en la cabeza oculta debaxo del cabello, y en la cintura, y brazos apretadores con puntas de serro, y en las Espaldas una cruz de puas, apretada con un corpino de cuero de animal de cerda, las cerdas para dentro." Ibid., 6.

76. "Dabase crueles Disciplinas, una denoche antes de acostarse, y otra â las quatro dela mañana, preparandose para la Profession con continua oracion, pasando las noches de rodillas, y enel coro los mâs ratos que podia del dia, donde Dios le hacia grandes mercedes." Ibid.

77. "Hablola Dios muchos veces en la oracion, trayale a la memoria todos sus pecados, y las penas que por ellos merecia, deque le avia librado por su infinita misericordia, y todos los beneficios que le avia hecho sus inefable liberalidad. Mostrabale el Purgatorio, y los que alli padecian, y porque culpas. Y asimesmo le mostraba el Infierno, y los terribles tormentos, que alli se padecen, y los pecados porque se padecen." Ibid.

78. "Todo lo qual â los principios tenia por ilusiones del enemigo, y con mucha sinceridad, y maneza los contaba diciendo: nosabes, conque me vino aquel embustero? Conesto y esto. Y contabalo todo en la celda donde vivia; que aunque no era simple ni ignorante, para esto lo era mucho; que tales cosas no avian llegado â su noticia, ni la obligacion del sigilo, que se debe tener en punto de revelaciones; hastaque una Religiosa ledixo, no andes diciendo estas cosas, mira que entran en hondo, y es menester tratarlas solo conquien las entienda." Ibid.

79. "Y una vez estando haciendo las camas de las enfermas, viô que la Reina del Cielo tambien las hacia; y quedô tan asombrada, y confusa, que en muchos dias no oso bolver â hacerlas, hastaque la verrebendiô N[uest]ro S[eñ]or la dixo porque avia dexado aquel exercicio? Respondiô Ursula: Porque temo no me engane aquel embustero, que yo, señor mio, y padre mio, no quiero ver nada, sino amarte, y servirte, y hacer tu voluntad. Aqui dixo [Chris]to S[eñ]or N[uest]ro: si quieres hacer mi voluntad, como dices, no quiero vêr nada? Yo nunca dixe, no quiero, sino obedêci hasta la muerte â mi eterno P[adr]e. Si quiso que nasciesse en un pesebre, dixe: hagase tu voluntad; si quiso que muriesse en una cruz una muerte tan afrentosa, dixe: hagase tu voluntad. Asi lo ai de hacer, y no temer â aquella bestia fiera, que no tiene poder para nada." Ibid., 7.

80. "Siendo una mañana â las quatro, para el coro, pasó un lugar que llaman de Ballanos, donde lavan las *negras*, y viô un dragon muy feroz, que la amenazaba, y dixole: no puedes tu impedirme, loque voy â hacer que es alabar â mi Dios y Señor. Y diciendo esto, hizola señal de la cruz conq[ue] el dragon se fue rabioso, y la dexô." Ibid.

81. For discussion of the fact that these two qualities—obedience and submissiveness—are primary among those that establish a woman's holiness, see Voaden, *God's Words, Women's Voices,* 69–70.

82. "Otro Domingo . . . viô venir para ella una Monja difunta con un velo muy largo delante del rostro, y luego dos otras con sus velos echados como la primera; y cubierta de un terrible pavor decia entre si: que procesion erâ esta? Mâs si el S[eñ]or la trae, hagase su voluntad. Y llegandose junto â Ursula la primera la dixo su nombre y el de las otras dos, que eran una tia y una sobrina. Y admirandose mucho la Sierva de Dios, de que estuviesse tanto tiempo en Purgatorio, la respondiô: no te admires, Ursula, que fuí dos veces Prelada, y aora estoy pagando las faltas que permitia en mis subditas." "EDR," 12.

83. "Y entrandose en la boveda, las viô padecer rigorosos incendios, inexplicables penas." Ibid.

84. "En otra ocasion estando â la hora de siesta recogida en el coro, se le representaron quatro almas vestidas hermosam[en]te de blanco; y dice, que una de ellas â hecho yâ mencion antecedem[en]te y dandole muy rendidas gracias, y affectuosos agradecim[ien]tos la decian: Dios te pague, loque con nosotros as echo. Bendita seas del S[eñ]or Nuestro R[edent]or sea contigo in todas las cosas enque pusieres la mano." Ibid., 10.

85. "A una religiosa de su orden, que avia mâs de quinze años que avia muerto, la viô sentada en un escaño âun lado del coro, junto â la puerta; y con una lucecita que tenia delante, la vio con mucha distincion, su proprio rostro y faiciones, el torado baxo segun las entierran, los ojos al sucio, las manos como de un esqueleto, solo quesos, el habito como desenterrado." Ibid.

86. "No se admirase que eran muy cortas las penitencias que hizo en esta vida, y los mâs fueron

entretinimientos deeste siglo; que par ir al cielo se purificaban las almas con fuego como el oro, y que avian de estâr como un cristal purissimo y sin pelo alguno para entrâr en la gloria." Ibid.

87. "Aque añidieron Entre otras cosas todos los defectos que se cometian en el monasterio, y el poco caso que se hacia de las leyes, obediencias, y consti[tu]ciones de la Religion. Enfin noquedaron tocados, puntas, [?], trajes, camas ni otras relaxaciones, que no se las dixessen un por pena y por ultimo que con los seglares no avia tanto que hacer." Ibid.

88. "Y diciendole entonces al S[an]to Angel de su Guarda, que para que la traya â ver esto, la respondiô que paraque la encomendava â Dios, y la hiciera encomendâr: y conesto desparaciô la vision." Ibid., 11.

89. "Estando en el coro postrada delante del S[eño]r, entraron unas *negras* del conv[en]to llorando por otra que se avia muerto; pareciendole que todo aquello era vanidad, y que lo que importaba era deprender â morir. Con todo movida de charidad pidiô al Soberano Padre de amor por la difunta. Y el S[eño]r la revelô que Francisco y Clara se avían hineado de rodillas, y rogado por ella. Quedô con esto muy esperanzada de su salvacion." Ibid., 9–10.

90. "Que asi como avia criado el cielo para los buenos, avia criado el infierno para los malos; y que aquellos que requian aloque llaman Principe delas tinieblas, tendrian del [?] merecido." Ibid., 10.

91. St. Teresa of Jesus, also known as Teresa of Avila, was canonized in 1622, and her mystical works received great attention. The text does not specify which of Teresa's books Ursula might have wanted to read, but perhaps it was *The Interior Castle,* the most famous of her autobiographical works. Several similarities exist between the visions of Ursula and those of Teresa, including the vision of a place in hell to which the mystic would have gone had she not responded to God's grace.

92. *The Imitation of Christ,* first published in 1418 by Thomas à Kempis, was one of the most widely read spiritual books in the Catholic world. It would have surely been available in most convents and used regularly for devotional reading. Its purpose was to instruct the soul in Christian perfection by using Christ as the model. Ursula's christocentric spirituality is very similar.

93. "Y estando en esta oracion, viô se abria el sagrario de l'Altar Mayor, y que se apartaba el Viril, y con una vista muy clara divisô al Señor con una tunica morada, y que desviando la tunica con la mano derecha, le mostraba el corazon y en el se via Ursula. Y hallandose indigna de tan gran merced, le dixo: que es esto, S[eño]r Mio! Una *negra* tan gran pecadora! No ay muchas Reynas, y Senoras? Y le respondiô el S[eño]r: mâs es estâr en Gracia Mia, que ser Reynas. Y consecutivam[en]te le fue mostrado el Purgatorio, donde vio innumerable gente; y le decian los grandes puestos, ye avian tenido, y las culpas porque estaban en aquellas penas." "EDR," 8.

94. "La misma noche que profesô, estando en oracio in viô venir un hermosissimo Angel, â arrodillarse â la Virgen N[uestra] S[eño]ra, y consecutivam[en]te â una candidissima, y muy resplandesciente Paloma, que puso su pico en la boca dela Virgen, y al punto viô dentro de sus entrañas un niño pequeño con el mundo en la mano derecha, despidiendo de si mucha lûz, y resplandor. Participô entonces de su Mag[esta]d singulares enseñanzas de algunos Mist[eri]os de la fê, y en especial del Juicio postrimero. Y preguntando Ursula â su Mag[esta]d D[ivin]a, que quê seria delos que entonces vivian, le respondiô el S[eño]r deesta suerte: Yo les embiare tales trabajos, que con ellos se purificarân los que se an de salvâr." Ibid.

95. The ideal of community underlies all hagiographic writing. On the importance of saints and hagiography for religious communities, see Kleinberg, *Prophets in Their Own Country.* Also see Kenneth Woodward, *Making Saints: How the Catholic Church Determines Who Becomes a Saint, Who Doesn't, and Why* (New York: Simon and Schuster, 1990).

96. For the prevalence of this trope in Christian literature, see Grace L. Jantzen, *Power, Gender and Christian Mysticism* (New York: Cambridge University Press, 1995).

Index

Contributors

B. J. Barickman is associate professor of history at the University of Arizona. He has published articles on slavery and the social and economic history of nineteenth-century Brazil and is the author of *A Bahian Counterpoint: Sugar, Tobacco, Cassava, and Slavery in the Recôncavo, 1780–1860* (1998). Another book project is "'We're Going to Invade Your Beach': A Social History of Beach-Going in Brazil."

Trevor Burnard is Reader in Early American History at Brunel University, West London, England. His research is concerned with plantation societies in eighteenth-century British America. He is the author of *Creole Gentlemen: The Maryland Elite 1691–1776* (2002) and several articles on Caribbean social and economic history. He is completing books on the life and diaries of Thomas Thistlewood, an Anglo-Jamaican owner of slaves, and about free society in Jamaica between 1655 and 1780.

María Elena Díaz is associate professor of history at the University of California at Santa Cruz. She is the author of *The Virgin, the King, and the Royal Slaves of El Cobre: Negotiating Freedom in Colonial Cuba, 1680–1780* (2000) and of other publications on royal slavery, copper mining, Our Lady of Charity and Marian shrines in Latin America, and popular culture and the satiric press in early-twentieth-century Mexico. She is at work on two additional colonial histories that will complete a trilogy of El Cobre, Cuba. Her research interests include comparative slavery and discourses of freedom, colonialism, popular culture and religion, gender, and ethnohistory in the Spanish and wider Atlantic world.

Martha Few is associate professor of history at the University of Miami, Florida. Her published work is concerned with colonial Latin America, and her research interests include gender, race and class, religion, medicine, popular culture, colonialism, and the Atlantic world. She is the author of *Women Who Live Evil Lives: Gender, Religion, and Politics of Power in Colonial Guatemala* (2002). Her new book project is "Monsters and Marvels: Colonial Medicine, Cultures of Healing, and the Body in New Spain, 1550–1850."

David Barry Gaspar is professor of history at Duke University, Durham, North Carolina. He has published widely on slavery, slave society, the Atlantic slave trade, and related fields, with particular reference to colonial British America, including the Caribbean, and to the history and cultures of the Atlantic basin between 1600 and 1800. He is the author of *Bondmen and Rebels: A Study of Master-Slave Relations in Antigua* (1985) and coeditor of *More Than Chattel: Black Women and Slavery in the Americas* (1996) and *A Turbulent Time: The French Revolution and the Greater Caribbean* (1997). He is working on a book about slavery and slave laws of the Anglo-Caribbean sugar islands and South Carolina during the seventeenth century.

Virginia Meacham Gould teaches the history of race relations, religion, and women at Tulane University, New Orleans. She is the coeditor, with Charles E. Nolan, of *No Cross, No Crown: Black Nuns in Nineteenth-Century New Orleans* by Mary Bernard Deggs (2001) and "The Feminine Face of Afro-Creole Catholicism, 1727–1852" (2002). She is completing a biography of Henriette Delille, the foundress of the Sisters of the Holy Family in New Orleans.

Kimberly S. Hanger was assistant professor of history at the University of Tulsa, Tulsa, Oklahoma. A specialist in colonial Latin American history and culture, she published several articles and chapters in anthologies about the free people of color of Louisiana and of colonial Latin America more generally. A relentless researcher and careful scholar, she was the author of *Bounded Lives, Bounded Places: Free Black Society in Colonial New Orleans, 1769–1803* (1997).

Darlene Clark Hine is Board of Trustees Professor of African American studies at Northwestern University. She is the author of *Black Women in White: Racial Conflict and Cooperation in the Nursing Profession, 1890–1950* and *Black Victory: The Rise and Fall of the Texas White Primary* and coauthor of *A Shining Thread of Hope: The History of Black Women in America*. She is also past president of the Organization of American Historians, Southern Historical Association, and Association of Southern Women Historians.

Rosemarijn Hoefte is head of the Department of Caribbean Studies of the Koninklijk Institut voor Taal, Land en Volkenkunde/Royal Institute of Linguistics and Anthropology in Leiden, the Netherlands, and managing editor of the *New West Indies Guide*. She has published extensively on the Dutch Caribbean and is editor, with Peter Meel, of *Twentieth-Century Suriname: Continuities and Discontinuities in a New World Society* (2001).

Mary C. Karasch is professor of history at Oakland University, Rochester, Michigan. She is the author of *Slave Life in Rio de Janeiro, 1808–1850* (1987), translated as *A vida dos Escravos no Rio de Janeiro, 1808–1850* by Pedro Maia Soares and published with a new preface in 2000. She served as associate editor for Brazil for the five-volume *Encyclopedia of Latin American History and Culture* (1996). Her current work focuses on Central Brazil in the late colonial period. Among her publications is "Central Africans in Central Brazil" in *Central Africans and Cultural Transformations in the American Diaspora,* edited by Linda M. Heywood (2002).

Wilma King is Strickland Professor of African-American History and Culture at the University of Missouri, Columbia. She is the author of *Stolen Childhood: Slave Youth in Nineteenth-Century America* (1995) and at work on two projects: "Africa's Progeny in America: Essays on African-American Children in Historical Perspective, 1600–2000" and "The Essence of Liberty: Free African-American Women before 1865."

Jane Landers is associate dean of the College of Arts and Science, associate professor of history, and director of the Center for Latin American and Iberian Studies at Vanderbilt University, Nashville, Tennessee. She is the author of *Black Society in Spanish Florida* (1999), editor of *Colonial Plantations and the Economy of Florida* (1996), and coeditor of *The African American Heritage of Florida* (1995). She has also published several articles and chapters on the African history of the Hispanic Southeast and on the circum-Carribean in a variety of journals and anthologies.

Bernard Moitt is associate professor of history at Virginia Commonwealth University in Richmond. He has published several articles and chapters in anthologies on francophone African and Caribbean history, with particular emphasis on gender and slavery. The author of *Women and Slavery in the French Antilles, 1635–1848* (2001), he is also editor of a work in progress that deals with sugar, slavery, and society from India to the Caribbean.

Félix V. Matos Rodríguez is director of the Center of Puerto Rican Studies at Hunter College (CUNY), New York. He is the author of *Women and Urban Change in San Juan, Puerto Rico* (1999) and coeditor of *Puerto Rican Women's History: New Perspectives* (1998). His research interests include Latino and Caribbean history.

Loren Schweninger is a professor of history and director of the Race and Slavery Petitions Project at the University of North Carolina at Greensboro. He is the author or editor of five books, including *The Southern Debate over Slavery: Petitions to Southern Legislatures, 1778–1864* (2001).

Jean Jacques Vrij, a Dutch freelance historian, has published several articles about free people of African descent in Suriname during the era of slavery. His research interests also include urban slavery and early modern migration of Surinamese of African descent to the Netherlands. He is at work on a book about free men of African descent in the civic militia of Paramaribo.

Alice L. Wood is an assistant professor in the Department of Religion and Philosophy at Bethune-Cookman College, Daytona Beach, Florida. Her research interests in slavery and slave society in the New World, particularly in Spanish America, spring from her intellectual foundations in church history, her main area of research.

The University of Illinois Press
is a founding member of the
Association of American University Presses.

———————————————————————

Composed in 10.5/12.5 Adobe Minion
with Gill Sans display
by Jim Proefrock
at the University of Illinois Press
Manufactured by Edwards Brothers, Inc.

University of Illinois Press
1325 South Oak Street
Champaign, IL 61820-6903
www.press.uillinois.edu